THE
CATHOLIC
CONCISE
ENCYCLOPEDIA

THE CATHOLIC CONCISE ENCYCLOPEDIA

Compiled and Edited by

ROBERT C. BRODERICK, M.A.

Line drawings by ADE DE BETHUNE

CATECHETICAL GUILD EDUCATIONAL SOCIETY

ST. PAUL 2, MINNESOTA

General Trade Distribution by

SIMON AND SCHUSTER, INC. NEW YORK

Nihil obstat:
JOHN A. GOODWINE, J.C.D.
Censor Librorum

Imprimatur:
✠ FRANCIS CARDINAL SPELLMAN
Archbishop of New York

August 31, 1956

INTRODUCTION

THE OFFERING of *The Catholic Concise Encyclopedia* is intended to present as comprehensive and serviceable a source-book as the limitations and format of this economical edition permit.

Information of things Catholic extends beyond the possibilities of a single volume. The theology, history, liturgy, and law of the Church penetrate many areas of knowledge. Interpretation and clarification involve a synthesis of many related and diverse subjects. However, with knowledge of the utility of such a book, its selection of items carefully based upon the needs of the student and others who seek a handy reference, it is possible to prepare a highly informative and serviceable book. This possible objective has been ours.

An encyclopedia from this approach is the fruit of research. It is not an exhaustive source of all knowledge. It presents the essentials of study as an aid to resolving the immediate lack of information, and it serves to lead the student and scholar to further research to gain complete knowledge.

In preparing this book, a breakdown of subjects was made, allotting to each a percentage of the whole field of information of things Catholic in proportion to the frequency and use of the subjects. Thus, emphasis was placed upon history and Sacred Scripture, theology and liturgy, in greater proportion than archeology or architecture.

There have been conscious limits established, not to curtail the service of this book but rather to confine it within the one volume. Besides the percentage breakdown of subjects, and as a departure from the wider sense of an encyclopedia, we have limited drastically the entries of biography, omitting all except the members of the Holy Family. Likewise we have omitted all names of cities or geographical places, with the exception of the most pertinent, as Rome, Jerusalem, etc. Further limitation was placed upon the abbreviated names of religious orders where such names are not widely used or are more local than universal. Of course, terms of general information not particularly Catholic, which are correctly defined in common works of reference, are not included herein.

A distinct effort has been made to make *The Catholic Concise Encyclopedia* serviceable to the modern student, using the most recent definitions of movements and the recent declarations of the Holy Father and eminent teachers. Appreciation is expressed to the staff of the Catechetical Guild and especially to the Reverend Louis A. Gales who suggested the project. Further thanks is given to the censor whose task was an extension of our work and an even more exacting chore. Most eminently, our gratitude is given to our Blessed Mother for the grace she mediated to us for this work undertaken during the declared Marian Year of 1954, and our hope that the content may redound to her glory and the greater knowledge and love of her divine Son, our Lord, Jesus Christ.

The Author

Note of Information: In the use of this book it is well to note that the abbreviation N.T. refers to New Testament of the Bible, and O.T. to the Old Testament. The briefest abbreviations referring to the Gospels have been used, e.g., Jn. for John, Mt. for Matthew, Mk. for Mark, Lk. for Luke. Other abbreviations: c. refers to a particular canon of Canon Law; *cf.* means "confer" or compare with other entry; *q.v.* means "which see" and refers to entry under preceding or following word or words.

R.C.B.

THE

CATHOLIC

CONCISE

ENCYCLOPEDIA

THE ABBEY OF SUBIACO

A

A–Ω, the first (*alpha*) and the last (*omega*) letters of the Greek alphabet, used symbolically as the *beginning* and the *end* of all things in God. In Ex. 3:14 God calls Himself "the beginning and the end," meaning He is the Creator of all things. St. John (Apoc. 22:13) applies this title to Christ and, used thus, it implies His divinity. These two letters are found as symbols in works of art from the earliest representations in the catacombs and early coins to present-day decoration in frescoes and churches.

ABADDON, a Hebrew proper word, meaning "destruction," a synonym for "sheol" or "hell." Also used in the Bible (Apoc. 9) to mean the "devil," the "destroyer."

ABANDONMENT or SELF-ABANDONMENT, a term used in mystical theology referring to the first stage of the union of the soul with God, whereby futility is found in all else other than God. Abandonment is achieved by conforming to His will, attaining a proper understanding of the use of worldly goods; it involves a passive purification of the soul through undergoing trials and sufferings and leads to a surrender of natural consolations that results in a feeling of desolation. It also refers to the darkness of the soul in undergoing a state of purgation. (*Cf.* UNION, MYSTICAL.)

ABBA, an Aramaic word meaning "father." It is used in the Gospels (also Rom. 8:15) with the appended word of translation, to indicate that God as Father is intended. The word is used as a title applied to bishops of the Syriac, Coptic, and Abyssinian Churches. It also is a Hebrew title of honor and forms part of some Hebrew names.

ABBACOMITES, name given to soldier-abbots or noble-abbots, who were lay intruders on whom the courts conferred abbacies for profit to the person or to themselves. It led in early medieval days to other abuses of lay investiture.

ABBÉ, French title applied first to abbots, and later, corresponding to the English "Father," applied to all priests or clerics. Sometimes applied to clerics not in Holy Orders who are engaged in teaching.

ABBESS, the spiritual and temporal superior of a community of nuns in those religious orders in which monasteries of men of the same order are governed by abbots. The title is the feminine of abbot. Today it is a title of dignity and authority, limited by canon law. It is permissible for an abbess after election to wear a ring and use a staff or crosier as a mark of her rank and authority, but she does not have the jurisdiction of an abbot.

ABBEY, an independent and canonically erected monastery governed by an abbot; a convent which is governed by an abbess. An abbey must have a minimum of twelve religious, and it embraces all the principal parts of a monastery which are considered essential to the religious life carried on within it. As such the abbey is usually constructed around a quadrangle formed of those units.

ABBEYLUBBER, term of ridicule used after the Reformation, implying that the residents of abbeys were idle and given over to soft living.

ABBEY NULLIUS, territory belonging to no diocese, or an area separated from any of the surrounding dioceses. It is governed under the active jurisdiction of a prelate, subject in most cases directly to the Holy See. In the United States, Belmont Abbey, N. C., is an abbey nullius.

ABBOT, the superior of a religious community of men, elected by the professed members of the religious order, who serves for life. His duties are: (a) quasi-episcopal; (b) paternal, whereby he administers the property, maintains the rule and constitutions and enjoins discipline. The position of abbot arose in the 3rd century and continues to the present.

ABBOT OF UNREASON, mock title given to the leader of the Christmas revels in Scotland before the Reformation.

ABDICATION, in the ecclesiastical sense the act of resigning or renouncing a benefice or clerical dignity. In each instance the resignation must be made to the proper authority; it must be freely made and apart from any simony or other consideration that would profit the one resigning or those who accept the resignation.

ABDUCTION, literally "to lead away." In canon law and in moral theology the term applies broadly to rape and violence of a physical na-

ture. It means the forcible carrying off or detention of a woman against her will, and it renders a marriage with her invalid so long as she remains in the power of the abductor. Thus abduction is a diriment impediment to marriage. (*Cf.* IMPEDIMENTS OF MARRIAGE.)

ABERCIUS, INSCRIPTION OF, authentic Greek inscription of the second century composed by Abercius, Bishop of Hieropolis in Phrygia, wherein he tells of his visit to Rome and the importance of the Church of Rome at that early time.

ABJURATION OF HERESY, the denial under oath whereby one renounces heresy, apostasy, or schism. It is required as a preliminary to receiving the sacrament of baptism on the part of a convert before making his confession of faith. More positively it may be considered a profession of faith. It must be made voluntarily and publicly, and must be accompanied by some act of satisfaction or penance.

ABLEGATE, an envoy of the pope who serves as a special representative. He is sent to carry the scarlet biretta in the pope's name to one whom the Holy Father has elevated to the Sacred College of Cardinals but who could not receive it directly. The conferring is reserved to the Holy Father alone, and the ablegate serves only in name and not as a delegate.

ABLUTION, in the rubrics of the Mass, both the washing and the wine and water used in the washing. After the Communion of the Mass, the priest washes his thumbs and index fingers with wine and water, using the same to purify the chalice, and then consuming this water and wine. It is a ceremony whereby the Church shows the reverence held for the body

ABLUTION

and blood of Christ, permitting no least particle to remain after the celebration of Mass. When a priest celebrates more than one Mass, the ablution of the earlier Masses consists of water alone, enabling him to preserve his eucharistic fast. In the Greek Church the public washing of newly baptized persons is referred to as an ablution. In the O.T. the washings before Jewish worship are referred to frequently as ablutions.

ABOMINATION OF DESOLATION, term applied in the O.T. (1 Mac. 1:57) to false worship or idolatry. In speaking of the destruction of the Temple of Jerusalem (Mk. 13:14–18), Christ indicated a future profanation of the Temple.

ABORTION. In its direct, limited sense, abortion is the intentional expulsion or extraction of a nonviable fetus from the human womb. This would be before the expiration of the seventh month of pregnancy or before the embryo could live independently. This act resulting in the extinction of an unoffending life is never permitted directly or intentionally. This direct abortion is mortally sinful and may incur further penalty from the Church. "Those who procure abortion, the mother included, incur excommuni-cation (c. 2350); those also are included who order the abortion, and those who are effectual or necessary co-operators in it." Grave fear and, of course, ignorance of the penalty excuses from the penalty. It is to be observed that mere intention does not suffice for incurring the penalty; actual abortion must have taken place" (Davis).

ABRAHAM-MEN also **ABRAM-MEN,** name of contempt given to those poor who, after the dissolution of the monasteries in Reformation days, could no longer appeal to the monks for alms but were forced to beg elsewhere.

ABRAHAM'S BOSOM, term used in Lk. 16:22, 23, referring to the place where the dead were to abide before admission to the beatific vision after the death of Christ. In the early writings of the fathers of the Church the term often is used as an expression for the "kingdom" or heaven.

ABRAXAS, a Greek word which was a magical symbol among Gnostic heretics referring to their concept of 365 heavens. Early Church writers mention the word in refuting the false teaching.

ABROGATION, term in canon law used of a law which is completely repealed, canceled, or revoked.

ABSOLUTE, a philosophical term. It denotes: (a) pure actuality, i.e., existing without an efficient cause; (b) complete, perfect, unlimited; (c) that which exists by its own nature and therefore independent of everything else. In these three senses it may be referred to God. More broadly it denotes that which is related to no other being, or the sum total of all actual or possible being.

ABSOLUTION. There are four types of absolution in Church usage. **1.** *Ab-*

solution from sin which is the act whereby a priest, acting as a judge, passes on to the penitent from Christ the remission of sin. This follows from the power to forgive sin given to the apostles by Christ and through them to their successors (Jn. 20:23). This power is exercised by the priest in administering the sacrament of penance. Two conditions are necessary without exception: absolution can be given by none but priests and, since this is a judicial sentence, the priest must have authority or jurisdiction over the penitent. Authority is had first by the bishop and arises from his office, and secondly by being delegated to priests by one having jurisdiction. Since the bishop has the prerogative of conferring power to absolve, he may reserve such power or limit this power as exercised by others. All priests, however, have the power from the Church to absolve from reserved matter when the penitent is in danger of death. The expression of absolution is given in prescribed words: "I absolve you from your sins, in the name of the Father, and of the Son, and of the Holy Ghost." This form of absolution must also be spoken by the absolving priest in the presence of the person seeking absolution (*cf.* PENANCE, SACRAMENT OF). A further expression of the forgiveness of sins is the *general absolution* which is an exception granted for use where absolution is considered necessary and where, due to circumstances, confession is not possible, e.g., a group of soldiers about to go into battle. However, anyone so absolved is obliged to mention his sins when he makes his next private confession. *Conditional absolution* is sacramental absolving of sins given when the administering priest is doubtful of the disposition of the penitent. It may not be given without serious reason and great caution on the part of the priest. **2.** *Absolution from censures.* This differs from the absolution of sins in the sacramental form in that it removes the penalties imposed by the Church and reconciles the penitent with the Church. The absolution from censures may be given either in the confessional or outside, as in a Church court, and may be given by anyone with the necessary jurisdiction. **3.** *Absolution for the dead.* This is the short prayer, imploring eternal rest, said after a requiem Mass over the body of the deceased. **4.** *Absolutions of the breviary.* These are certain short prayers petitioning the forgiveness of sin which are recited before the lessons of Matins in praying the Divine Office.

ABSTINENCE. In its limited and special sense, abstinence is the depriving of oneself of certain kinds of food, in a reasonable manner, for the purpose of benefiting the soul. It differs from fasting in that a fast limits the quantity of food, whereas abstinence affects only the kind of food. The Church law regarding abstinence does not forbid foods because they are impure; it looks upon abstaining as a means of spiritual good; it is reasonable in demand and application. The law of abstinence is binding to all over seven years of age. It forbids the eating of meat and soups of meat stock, gravy and sauces of meat. On days of complete abstinence, all Fridays, Ash Wednesday, Holy Saturday, and the vigils of Assumption and Christmas, these foods may not be eaten at all. On days of partial abstinence, Ember Wednesdays and Saturdays and the vigils of Pentecost and All Saints, these foods may be eaten at the principal meal. Dispensation from the law extends to every member of the armed forces in active service, and to his wife, children, parents or servants if he resides with them habitually, whether on or off the post of his duty, except on Ash Wednesday, Good Friday, Holy Saturday and the vigil of Christmas. Dispensation from the law may be obtained from one's parish priest or confessor if reason for not following the law exists. When a day of abstinence falls on Sunday, or when a holyday falls on a Friday, the law does not apply. The act of abstaining, while it is voluntary because of the intended good of the soul, is obligatory by jurisdiction of the Church and binds under penalty of sin under conditions of willful, knowing transgression.

ABSTINENTS, name applied in derision to certain heretics who professed abstinence from lawful things such as wine, marriage, etc.

ABUSE OF POWER. The Code of Canon Law applies this term to an evil and unlawful use of ecclesiastical power, office, or jurisdiction. Title XIX of the fifth book of the Code treats in detail of such abuses.

ABYSSINIAN or ETHIOPIAN CHURCH, a group of Monophysite Christians in Abyssinia who trace their origin back to the fourth century when its founding city was Axum. In the fifth century they rejected the Council of Chalcedon and their heretical position continues down to the present time. Their leader is the Abuna, a vicar of the Coptic patriarchate of Alexandria. The language of their liturgy is Geez, a mixture of Greek and Arabic. Their heresy consists in the teaching that Christ has only a divine nature; they reject all ecumenical councils since Ephesus.

ACACIANISM, the schismatic teaching of the Acacian schism which had its rise in the Monophysite heresy. As a teaching it was given impetus through an attempt of the imperial factions to control the Church by gaining the interpretative power of theological issues. Under the rule of Zeno (474–491 A.D.) of the Eastern Empire at Constantinople, in co-operation with Acacius, the patriarch of Constantinople, an attempt was made to achieve doctrinal unity, and political support, between the Catholics and Monophysites. This was done by demanding acceptance of a formula called the *Henoticon* which in part maintained that the Son is "like to the Father," contrary to the doctrine of consubstantiality. Pope Felix III rejected the *Henoticon* and excommunicated Acacius. The East was separated from communion with Rome by this schism for forty years. Members are called Acacians and also "Homoeans" since the difference was over the Greek words "like" or "unlike" in substance. (*Cf.* MONOPHYSITISM.)

ACADEMIES, PONTIFICAL, societies founded at Rome under the auspices of the Holy See to encourage special studies in science, literature, art, archeology, diplomacy, and music. Some countries have also established like academies in Rome and support these independently of the Holy See.

ACATHISTUS, title of either a hymn or an office in the Greek liturgy which is said in honor of the Mother of God. When it is sung the people must stand. The day on which this hymn is used, the fifth Saturday of Lent, is also so named.

ACCESS. 1. Name of the preparatory prayers which are recommended to be said by a priest before celebrating Mass. **2.** In canon law, a reserved benefice to which one may accede when certain conditions have been fulfilled.

ACCIDENT, a philosophical term meaning any reality which does not possess the power of subsisting alone but must have another reality to hold it in existence. It is thus that the taste of bread is an accident since it does not exist apart from the reality of bread.

ACCLAMATION, the elevation of one to an ecclesiastical dignity by the unanimous voice vote of the electors. As such it is one of the three modes by which a pope may be elected by the College of Cardinals. The term is also applied to the "voice" responses, called *laudes*, which were shouted by the people following the coronation of a king. These responses are still recited in the Mass of coronation of a pope, after the Collects, when the senior cardinal-deacon chants the words, "Hear, O Christ" to which all present respond, "Long life to our lord, N . . . , who has been appointed Supreme Pontiff and universal Pope." This is repeated three times and after each is added the invocation, "Do Thou help him!" Other meanings denote prayers and pious wishes found on tombs; short liturgical prayers or exclamations, as "Thanks be to God!"

ACCOLADE, the act whereby knighthood is conferred either by a kiss or a light blow upon the upper shoulder. The term is also applied to a form of salutation, as the "kiss of peace" given during a solemn Mass, and sometimes to a greeting or farewell used in some foreign countries by members of the clergy.

ACCOLADE—The kiss of peace.

ACCOMMODATION OF SCRIPTURE, BIBLICAL. In quoting Scripture to prove a point of doctrine, it is necessary to seek the precise meaning of the sacred writer and proceed to argue from the exact sense of the words. However, we may take the words of a text and make an application over and above that intended by the writer, thus "accommodating" the sense to our own words on some subject. This application is not intended by God and as such is not a sense of Scripture proper. Accommodation may be made in several ways: by *extension*, as when the words of a description in the Bible are applied to a saint (e.g., using the phrase in quotes: he is "a man sent by God"— referring to someone other than St. John the Baptist), or to some current affair; by *allusion*, as when the words are suitable to the purpose of argument, but are not alike in their idea, e.g., referring to one as a "mustard seed" in Catholic work. There are certain cautions to be followed in making an accommodation of Scripture: (a) An accommodation should not be held as a genuine sense of Scripture. (b) There should be some likeness to or analogy with the original text, for the application or adaptation should never contradict the literal sense. (c) An accommodation should not be held as a proof of doctrine. (d) The texts of Scripture should not be applied loosely to secular or vain subjects. This latter does not limit the use of texts in teaching, but merely says they should be properly applied rather than as vain illustrations of a point. (*Cf.* LITERAL SENSE OF SCRIPTURE.)

ACEPHALI, literally the "headless." A term of derision applied in the fifth century to those heretics who did not go along with all the terms set forth by their leaders, notably the Acacians.

ACHIROPOETA, literally "not made by hand." A plural term given to pictures or works of art which are alleged to have a miraculous origin. Examples are the painting of Christ in the *Sancta Sanctorum* of the Lateran which is claimed to have been outlined by St. Luke and completed by angels; also the painting of Our Lady of Guadalupe in Mexico.

ACOEMETI, literally "sleepless ones." A plural term applied to Eastern monks of the fifth and sixth centuries who constantly prayed in relays, day and night. In each monastery there were three choirs of monks who succeeded each other in their rounds of prayer. They fell into the Nestorian heresy and were condemned by the Fifth General Council.

ACOLOUTHIA, arrangement of the prayers in the Divine Office in the Greek Church. The sequence begins with Little Vespers, before sunset, and Greater Vespers, after it; the

ACHIROPOETA—The picture of Our Lady of Guadalupe, miraculously imprinted on the mantle of Juan Diego.

Orthros, in two parts, recited at midnight, which corresponds to the Matins and Lauds of the hours of the Roman Breviary; little Hours are recited during the day and the office closes with the *Apodeipnon.*

ACOLYTE, highest of the four minor orders conferred on aspirants to the

priesthood by a bishop before ordination. The duties imposed by this order are: to supply wine and water during the celebration of Mass and to carry candles during a solemn Mass. With a prayer, the ordaining bishop places cruets and a candle into the hands of the recipient. At the present time the ministrations of an acolyte are performed by laymen in serving Mass, and as a result Mass-servers are sometimes mistakenly called acolytes.

ACTA APOSTOLICAE SEDIS, official monthly publication which was begun in Sept., 1908, as a journal of the Holy See. CANON LAW (*q.v.*) names it as authoritative and official. Hence all decrees and decisions of the Roman Rota printed therein are officially promulgated and become effective after three months from the date of their promulgation.

ACTA SANCTAE SEDIS, monthly publication issued in Rome, but not by the Holy See, which presented important pronouncements of the Holy Father and Roman Congregations. For four years, 1904 to 1908, it enjoyed official status but was superseded by the *Acta Apostolicae Sedis*.

ACTION FRANÇAISE, title of a monthly publication founded in France in 1897 by an avowed atheist, Charles Maurras. In 1908 Maurras and Leon Daudet founded a movement bearing the name of the publication which became a daily newspaper. The movement grew into a political party, nationalistic, which sought the support of Catholic royalists. It was an attempt to use the Church for political and social purposes and won many Catholic followers. Its teaching led to an exalting of politics above religion and an identifying of the Church with a political movement opposed to established government, and a moral philosophy advocating hate and violence. As such it was condemned by Pope Pius XI in 1926. The pope insisted that Catholic Action or organized lay action for religious activities must be under the direction of the hierarchy. Pius XII lifted the ban on *Action Française* in 1939 when its directors expressed regret over past misconduct and promised to respect the wishes of the Holy See.

ACT OF GOD, legal term for an accident which occurs without the cause or foreknowledge of man. It is so attributed to God who is the author of the laws of nature.

ACT OF SETTLEMENT. 1. *English:* the law passed in 1701, and still in force, which requires that all future rulers of England be members of the Established Church of England. **2.** *Irish:* the law passed by the Irish Parliament in 1662 whereby the confiscated lands of Leinster, Munster, and Connaught were to be restored, first to the Protestants and, second, to Catholics who could establish their innocence. It resulted in the Anglican Church regaining its estates and the re-establishment of its hierarchy in Ireland.

ACT OF TOLERATION, law passed in England during the reign of William and Mary (1689) which granted freedom of religious worship to all except Catholics and persons who deny the Trinity.

ACTS, CANONICAL, actions which have a legal effect in ecclesiastical law, being either allowed or forbidden (c. 2256, n. 2). They include acts of official administrators of ecclesiastical property; the actions of personnel of ecclesiastical courts; those of sponsors at baptism and confirmation; the voting at ecclesiastical elections; and the actual exercise of advowson.

ACTS, HUMAN, the acts of human beings, performed under control of the will and done knowingly and willingly. As such they are imputable to the one acting to the degree that he knows what is being done and the import or consequence of his act. There arises from this the moral responsibility of the human act since it is freely performed with knowledge of its conformity or non-conformity to the law of rational nature or the moral law of man.

ACTS OF THE APOSTLES, the book of the N.T. which follows in sequence the four Gospels of the evangelists. The name "Acts" is derived from the Latin word *acta* and may be translated as the "proceedings" or "record" of happenings; the book in turn narrates the record of the early Church and the functions of the apostles. Evidence from early canons of Scripture and writings of the fathers of the Church of the second and third centuries indicates that St. Luke is the author of the Acts. From internal evidence in the writings themselves and from early tradition, it appears that the book was written during or at the end of St. Paul's first imprisonment, i.e., in 63 or 64 A.D. The Acts were quite certainly set down in Rome in the years just prior to the persecution by Nero. The sources of these accounts were the eyewitness details of the author, the direct testimony of eyewitnesses, notably SS. Paul and Mark, and written documents such as the writings on the early Church at Antioch. Besides recent archeological findings, the book's historical value is further attested by a comparison of the writings with other historical data such as the political functions of Roman authorities, governance of provinces at the time, etc. The work narrates the activities of SS. Peter and Paul, and to lesser extent those of SS. John, James the Less, James the Greater, and Barnabas. While being historical, this work presents such basic theological truths as early conversions, the working of God the Father through the Holy Spirit, that Christ was the Messias (2:16–36), the indwelling of the Holy Spirit, the sacraments and the early liturgy and prayer of the early Church. Recorded within these writings are also some eighteen speeches of apostles and early Chrisitians.

ACTS OF THE MARTYRS, the official and written accounts of a martyr's trial, sentence and death. Originally these documents, of great edification to early Christians, were gathered to be used in the public testimony of the Church. While many of these writings have been lost, there remain a considerable number which are outstanding sources of Church history. In the Western Church the most famous collection is the Golden Legend of Jacobus de Voragine (d. 1298). More recently the term "Acts of the Martyrs" has been broadly applied to writings of the lives and deaths of the saints without particular advertence to their historical position in the early record of the Church.

ACTS OF THE SAINTS ("ACTA SANCTORUM"), famous collection of the lives of the Saints gathered by the Bollandists. Also called "Legend of the Saints" or "The Golden Legend."

ACTUAL GRACE, the grace or supernatural gift from God, both operative and co-operative, which acts upon the human will or intellect, perfecting both the will and intellect, and making it possible for them to place acts directed toward eternal salvation. To clarify the twofold, operative and co-operative, divisions of actual grace, it may be pointed out that when the will is first appealed to by this gift of God, and before it responds, the grace is termed operative. When, however, the will accepts and responds to the gift, and we find both God and the soul operating to perform the act, the grace is said to be co-operative. Thus man through his intellect (*gift*) being moved by God in the natural order, might be said to have the first desire of happiness (*operative motion*) which then, through recognition and performance of the good necessary to attain such happiness (*co-operative motion*), ascends to the supernatural order where the supernatural end is sought (*operative gift*) and the virtues exercised to accomplish this end (*co-operative gift*). This sequence of desire, recognition and action demonstrates in some manner the reception of the supernatural gift of actual grace.

ACTUAL SIN, a personal act which is morally bad, or the omission of some obliged good, or an act against right reason or the law of God. It is a voluntary transgression of a moral law or a law obliging the will resulting in either sins of commission or omission. According to the manner of their commission such sins may be interior or exterior; committed against God, one's neighbor, or one's self, according to their object; in gravity, either mortal or venial; from their cause, either committed in ig-norance, weakness or malice; and capital or non-capital as to whether they do or do not give rise to other sins.

ACUS, a small pin of gold or silver used to fasten the pallium to the chasuble.

ADAMITES. 1. An obscure sect of the Gnostic heresy said to have been founded in the second century by Prodicus. They observed pagan practices, met together without clothing and were horribly immoral. **2.** A group of fanatics of the Middle Ages supposedly founded by one Picard, a Frenchman, who called himself Adam. They practiced sensuality and like their early predecessors went naked at their gatherings. They had their chief headquarters in Bohemia and were spread through France, Germany and Holland. They were destroyed with great losses by the Hussite general, Jan Ziska, in 1421.

ADJURATION, an appeal or command to act, given in God's name or in the name of a saint or holy thing (Mt. 26:63). Such a command is not to be given lightly and should be given only when there is serious cause, when the request is not unjust and when the person truly seeks a right answer or action. It is either solemn or private: the first is that used in the Church in an exorcism and by a set rite; the latter may be used by anyone.

AD LIMINA, abbreviated form of the Latin phrase *ad limina Apostolorum* which is translated "to the thresholds of the apostles." The word *limina* (thresholds) is not used in a restricted sense but refers broadly or inclusively to the "places" or "houses" themselves. It is a term descriptive of the quinquennial reports which all bishops are required to make to the Holy See. While in Rome, the bishop is expected to visit the tombs of SS. Peter and Paul and he receives a document attesting this fact. The cycle of visits of the bishops is a five-year span with bishops from various parts of the world assigned to a particular year. The report made by the bishop is a most detailed account of affairs concerning his diocese and other ecclesiastical jurisdictions, and is made to the Sacred Consistorial Congregation of which the pope is prefect. When unable to go in person, the bishop may send a delegate. (*Cf.* SACRED CONGREGATION.)

ADMINISTRATION APOSTOLIC, form of a diocesan organization established by the Holy See where a new national boundary cuts off a portion of an existing diocese. This portion, made remote from the diocesan seat by the new boundary or for other reasons, is constituted an *administration apostolic*, and usually placed under a titular bishop.

ADMINISTRATION OF THE SACRAMENTS, act of the authorized minister in conferring the sacraments on one of the faithful. Since all the sacraments are from Christ and take efficacy from Him, the minister acts in Christ's name and by His authority. As the sacraments are for the faithful, as means of sanctification, they are to be administered frequently, and, on their part, the recipients are to be properly disposed to receive them. (*Cf.* SACRAMENTS.)

ADMINISTRATOR. 1. An "apostolic administrator" is a priest or bishop appointed by the Holy See to administer a diocese for an indefinite or specified time, because of the inability of the bishop to so administer, or during the vacancy of the diocese until another bishop is appointed. **2.**

The priest placed in charge of a cathedral parish by the bishop of the cathedral. **3.** In the United States a priest appointed to administer a parish but having no canonical privileges concerning the parish. **4.** One assigned to administer the affairs of an ecclesiastical institution. Usually this is a priest who has care of both the spiritual and material concerns of the institution. A layman may be appointed an administrator of a church institution, but usually handles only the business affairs and is subordinate to the priest administrator.

ADMONITIONS, CANONICAL, paternal admonitions, usually three in number, given as quasi-severe warnings, in secret or in a confidential manner, by a prelate or ecclesiastical superior to a subordinate cleric who is suspected of or charged with misconduct of a scandalous nature. Following the third paternal admonition, a formal canonical or legal admonition is given which amounts to a summons to judgment. In a religious order or congregation the admonitions are given by the superior before beginning a judicial process of dismissal.

ADONAI, Hebrew word for "Lord," attributed to God out of reverence for the majesty and "unspeakably" great name, *Jahweh.*

ADOPTION, CANONICAL. Legally, adoption is the taking as one's own the child of another, with the consent and co-operation of the civil authorities. Traditionally, in law, this creates a legal relationship based on the natural relationship, and does not permit marriage in the following instances: between the adoptive father and his adopted daughter; between the adopted children and the natural children of the same parents;

between the adoptive father and the adopted son and their respective widows. Church law (c. 1059) provides that in those places where adoption constitutes an impediment to marriage in civil law, such a marriage is likewise canonically illicit. In the United States, adoption is regulated by statute of the various states and is usually undertaken only in the manner decreed by law. It is thus difficult or impossible to determine the precise manner in which legal relationship would be established. Hence, in the United States, in civil law, adoption is not a diriment impediment of marriage as considered by the Church and, thus, is not preventive of marriage.

ADOPTIONISM, an 8th century heresy, derived from Nestorianism. It taught that Christ was only an adopted and not the "natural" Son of God. Over the years this early erroneous teaching changed to the extent that it was claimed Christ was by this adoption somehow "divinized," in short, that He was not truly God. The Nestorian adoptionism was condemned by a council of bishops of Asia Minor in 268 A.D. and the later heresy, which might be called neo-Nestorianism, was first condemned by Pope Adrian I in 785, then at the Second Council of Nice (787 A.D.), the Council of Frankfort (794 A.D.), and in the eleventh and twelfth centuries.

ADOPTION, SUPERNATURAL. The act by which God takes us as His children and thereby makes us heirs of His kingdom—heaven. By sanctifying grace our souls are constituted in the likeness of Christ, the Son of the Father, and thus we are made co-heirs with Christ (Rom. 8:15 and Eph. 1:5).

ADORATION, the external act of worship or honor given to a thing or person of excellence. **1.** As an act of religion it is the honor offered to God alone because of His divinity, infinite perfection, supreme dominion over creatures, and the dependence of all creatures upon Him. Adoration is *internal* when we acknowledge God as possessing this divine excellence and our own subjection, and intend this acknowledgment and subjection; it is *external* when we act to manifest our acknowledgment and subjection. It is an act of the intellect and will expressed by signs of humility in our bodies. **2.** *Perpetual adoration* is the continuous exposition of the Blessed Sacrament and the day and night adoration by persons who take turns as adorers. The object of such worship is usually reparation to God for past or present offenses against Him. The Forty Hours' Devotion is a plan of such continual adoration. Adoration of the Blessed Sacrament is the highest form of worship, *latria* (*cf.* LATRIA). **3.** *Adoration of the Cross* is an act of veneration which takes place in the ceremonies of Good Friday. **4.** *Adoration of the Magi* is the Worship of the Three Wise Men in recognition of the divinity of the newborn Christ, commemorated on the Feast of Epiphany.

ADULTERY, sexual intercourse of a married man or woman with another than the own wife or husband. It is a diriment impediment to marriage between the two who, while legitimately married to someone else, commit the act and pledge a later marriage; or who commit the act while one or the other is legitimately married and causes the death of one of the married parties. Adultery is always a mortal sin.

ADVENT, the liturgical season beginning the Church year. It includes the four weeks opening on the Sunday nearest to the Feast of St. Andrew the Apostle. It is a time of preparation for the Feast of the Nativity, and is observed with some fasting, prayers and meditation to dispose all to welcome Christ. The time was observed in the Church as early as the 4th century, being mentioned in 380 A.D. at the Council of Saragossa. The season, while penitential, is not without a spirit of joy, hope, and anticipation. On the third Sunday, known as *Gaudete* Sunday, a special note of joy is introduced into the liturgy, indicating the assurance of everyone in the redemption of mankind by Christ.

ADVENT OF CHRIST. The millennium. (*Cf.* MILLENNIUM.)

ADVOCATE, a defense lawyer, one who pleads a cause. Originally, this translation of the Greek word *parakletos* is applied to Christ as a title by St. John (1 Jn. 2:1). The evangelist points out that we have one who intercedes for us and all men by stating, "We have an advocate with the Father." (*Cf.* PARACLETE.)

ADVOCATE OF GOD, the person assigned to promote the cause of one whose life is being examined in the process of beatification or canonization. The *advocatus Dei*. (*Cf.* CANONIZATION.)

ADVOCATE OF THE CHURCH, a layman who in the Middle Ages or feudal times was appointed to defend the Church in civil courts when its holdings were challenged; literally a champion of the Church. Because of abuses it has long been discontinued as a title.

ADVOCATES OF ROMAN CONGREGATIONS, lawyers, either laymen or clerics, who are trained in both civil and canon law and have a broad knowledge of dogmatic and moral theology and Church history, who plead cases before Roman tribunals. They serve under a fixed salary and no charge is made for handling cases of the poor. There are seven senior and five junior advocates in the consistorial college.

ADVOWSON, the right of filling a vacant ecclesiastical benefice. Formerly this right belonged to the one who created, or built, or endowed the benefice, but later it was attached to the place. The right may be exercised by nomination to the authority doing the appointing; where the property belongs to the bishop or diocese, a direct appointment is made. Since such patronage now is rare, it is chiefly of historic significance.

AEON, in Gnosticism, a representation based upon the Greek concept of "elements," Platonic "ideas," and mythology which became to Gnostics descriptive of divine attributes, and sometimes was referred even to Persons of the Trinity. It led to confusion even within the heresy.

AESTHETICS, the science of the fine arts based on philosophical principles. It leads to the perception, the recognition, the execution, and the judgment of beauty as it conforms to the ideal of beauty existing in God. This is supernatural beauty, order, harmony, symmetry, and proportion not perceived by the senses but nevertheless a metaphysical reality. Since beauty consists of intuitive knowledge and delight, it is seen that the intellect is the proper perceiving power of the beautiful. In being presented to the intellect, beauty elicits delight which is the excellence in proportion and balance of things in the highest faculty of man. With a knowledge of the principles, these principles may be applied in perceiving through the senses, in recognizing the degree, in executing through creative urges, and determining the proportion in judgment. This in turn provides the critical estimate of a person, object, literary composition, poetry, painting, sculpture, architecture, or musical composition, which is an evaluation of the degree of beauty possessed by or the absence of beauty in the object. The aesthetic sense may be extended into the moral sphere where it judges the conformity of the conduct of human life with the idea in the mind of God as to how He wishes us to follow the life of Christ.

AËTIANS, followers of Aëtius of Antioch who ascribed to the heretical teaching that the Son was unlike the Father. Its founder and the heresy were condemned in 360 A.D. As such it was a form of Arianism.

AFFECTIONS. As used by spiritual writers, this term refers to the emotions and dispositions flowing from the intellectual recognition of the love, desire, and enjoyment of what is good, and the repulsion, disgust, and rejection of what is evil. The training of these "affections," the correct method of eliciting them, is basic to the training in virtue and asceticism and the understanding of mysticism in the spiritual life.

AFFECTIVE PRAYER, the kind of prayer in which devout affections predominate, or wherein acts of the will are continually made to express love of God and the desire of glorifying Him. In such prayer there is more of an emotional than an intellectual motive, yet it follows the conviction of the mind as a habitual response on the part of the person praying without conscious effort. As prayer it leads to closer union with God, since it perfects the virtues arising from charity or love. It affords spiritual consolation and, as it concentrates by focusing the emotions to a more single purpose, it leads to the "prayer of simplicity" which is preliminary to contemplation.

AFFINITY, a diriment impediment to marriage arising from a valid marriage (c. 97), existing between the man and the blood relations of the previous wife and likewise between the woman and the blood relations of the previous husband. Affinity in the direct line annuls any such marriage, and no licit marriage can be contracted in the direct line in any degree (c. 1077). The direct line is of ancestors or descendants, and no dispensation can be given. Affinity in the collateral line annuls any such marriage, and no licit marriage can be contracted to the second degree inclusive. Dispensation may be given for either the first or second degrees of the collateral line.

AFRICAN CHURCH, the Church established by Christians of the second century in the Afro-Roman colonies comprising what is now Tripoli, Algeria, and Morocco. The chief see was that of Carthage and in the time of its greatest son, St. Augustine (d. 430), the bishop of Hippo, there were 400 diocesan sees. The Church was bitterly persecuted by Decius in the third century. Many fell away and were termed "*lapsi*," others who admitted some collaboration were called "*traditores*;" both caused much trouble to the Church. One of the effects was the rise of the Donatist and Arian heresies in the fourth century. When the Vandals of Spain conquered that portion of Africa, the orthodox Christians were again persecuted; after the defeat of the Vandals in the sixth century, Christianity was not strong enough to recover and the country fell to Mohammedanism. Only recently has there been achieved a return to Christianity by the mission work following the colonization by the French and Spanish.

AFRICAN COUNCILS, the 17 councils of religious leaders, notably SS. Cyprian and Augustine, held for the most part at Carthage, the last in 646 A.D. These councils contributed much to discussion of the doctrine and discipline that were the marks of Christianity in the world. In the main, the councils dealt with the Donatist and Arian heresies, the rebaptism of heretics, notably the *"lapsi,"* the Pelagian heresy, and matters of discipline as given by Rome for the African Church. After the last council the Caliph Othman brought about the ruin of both the Roman and Christian civilizations in Africa.

AFRICAN RITE, a development of the original Roman rite. It is no longer used.

AGAPE. The *agape*, or love feast, was a memorial of the Last Supper. Its thought was somewhat analogous to the Jewish Passover dinner or the Greek custom of having a "brotherhood" meal before a solemn event. As practiced by the early Christians, it merely recalled the Last Supper. It did not, as has been charged, have a relationship to the Eucharist, being merely an eating before or after the celebration of the Eucharist. Abuses arose and it was discontinued, even as a non-liturgical act, by the sixth century.

AGDE, COUNCIL OF, held in 506 A.D. at Agde (Agatha) in Languedoc, and presided over by St. Caesarius of Arles; it published fifty canons, or rules on Church discipline.

AGE, CANONICAL, the age, reckoned from the day of birth and not from the day of baptism. According to canon law it fixes the time when members of the Church can receive obligations or enjoy special privileges. Thus the age of reason is determined to be seven years for the reception of penance. Marriage contracted by males under sixteen and by females under fourteen is null and void. Fasting is of obligation for all over 21 years of age and under 59. Godparents at baptism must normally be at least 14 years of age. Those in religious life are likewise governed by a determined age as to when they may receive profession, make vows, receive Holy Orders, and be consecrated a bishop.

AGE, IMPEDIMENT OF. In matrimony, this means that the person attempting to contract marriage is too young for valid reception of the sacrament, having not yet attained the canonical age. (*Cf.* AGE, CANONICAL.)

AGE OF REASON. 1. The time when one, by legal definition of the Church, is capable of distinguishing right from wrong, begins to incur obligations such as abstinence, and takes on moral responsibility. **2.** In history, the period of the 18th century when in France and England the Encyclopedists and Deists were influential.

AGLIPAY SCHISM, a movement organized in 1902 by a priest of the native clergy as the Independent Philippine National Church with himself as archbishop. He nominated twenty assistant bishops, and achieved quite a following among the native clergy and the baptized Catholics. The church property seized by the Aglipayans was restored to the Catholic hierarchy by order of the United States Supreme Court in 1906. The movement had been supported by American money. Aglipay died, reconciled to the Church, in Sept. 1940. The movement is now minor and has but few followers in the Islands.

AGNOSTICISM, a philosophical theory which holds that it is impossible to arrive at a knowledge of reality either because by its nature it is unknowable or because of limits of the human mind. In effect it denies that man by reason can come to knowledge of God and the truths of religion. The correct doctrinal teaching was presented by the Vatican Council, reasserting the traditional claim of the Church as being in accord with reason.

AGNUS DEI (2)—A wax *Agnus Dei* from the pontificate of Leo XIII.

AGNUS DEI. 1. A prayer of petition in the Mass just before the Communion, invoking Christ as the Lamb of God. **2.** Oval disks of wax blessed by the pope on which the figure of a lamb is stamped. The wax is the remainder of paschal candles and solemnly blessed by the pope on the Thursday after Easter in the first and seventh years of his pontificate. On the reverse side is impressed the coat-of-arms of the pope. They are sacramentals and are not indulgenced and are worn as medals about the neck in leather cases or may be carried in any suitable manner. They are intended as protection against Satan, sickness, sudden death, temptations or tempests, and as a medium of divine help for expectant mothers. They were used as early as the 4th century.

AGONY OF CHRIST, THE. These words manifest the anguish suffered by Christ in the Garden of Gethsemani prior to His apprehension by the Jews and Roman soldiers before His crucifixion. The word "agony" is used (Lk. 22:43) to describe the phenomena of the bloody sweat which is medically not impossible. The suffering was most intense because of the two wills in Christ, His divine will and His human will. Instinctively, in His human will and nature, Christ shrank from suffering and death, yet in His divine, deliberate will He welcomed both death and suffering for the redemption of man as God willed it.

AGRAPHA, deeds or sayings of our Lord which find no mention in the Gospels but which have been kept and handed down by tradition (Jn. 20:30; 21:25). They are found in writings of the fathers, in some biblical manuscripts and papyri fragments but few of them are considered authentic.

ALAIS, TREATY OF. Signed in 1629 between the royal forces of France and the Huguenots, the treaty ended the religious wars, renewed the Edict of Nantes, and granted amnesty.

ALB. 1. Vestment of white linen, reaching from neck to feet, with full sleeves, which the priest puts on after the amice in vesting for Mass. The word comes from the Latin word *albus*, "white." The vestment is an adaptation of the tunic worn by early Romans and Greeks and is a full garment which is secured or "taken in" at the waist by a cincture. Dating from very early times, the alb symbolizes the purity of soul with which the sacrifice of the Mass should be offered. The surplice is a shortened alb as is also the rochet worn by prelates. **2.** Long white garment or robe worn by newly baptized persons from Holy Saturday until Low Sunday, from which the title *Dominica in albis* or "Sunday in white" is derived for this first Sunday after Easter.

ALBIGENSES, a sect of neo-Manichaean revolutionaries, also known as Catharists, who held an extreme view on purity. They came into Europe by way of Bulgaria, became numerous in Languedoc, Southern France, Italy and Spain. They borrowed from both paganism and Christianity. They repudiated the sacraments, especially marriage, promoted sexual promiscuity, and were vegetarians. They also promoted actions inimical to state authority and, because they were doubly dangerous, the barons of France, Germany and Belgium waged a crusade against them. They were also in the same century, the 11th, condemned by Councils of the Church. The Albigenses disappeared by the 14th century.

ALEXANDRIA, CHURCH OF, founded by St. Mark, the evangelist, at the port city of Egypt which became a great center of trade and learning. The church was administered by great bishops including SS. Athanasius and Cyril. However, it also gave rise to serious defections from the Church, and heresies such as Arianism in the 4th century, and Monophysitism, widespread in the 5th and 6th centuries. Under this latter heresy, which held but one nature in Christ, and rejected the Council of Chalcedon, the Church of Alexandria was severed from Rome.

ALEXANDRIA, SCHOOL OF. From its contact with Christianity in apostolic times, this distinct school of theology flourished in the ancient city of Alexandria. Already a center of Greek and Jewish learning, a famed catechetical school was founded which attained distinction for its instruction of catechumens, its zeal in the study of Scripture, and its interest in apologetics. One of the first works coming from there is the Septuagint, the translation of the Hebrew Scriptures into Greek. It also contributed much to the allegorical interpretation of Scripture, and fostered such great writers as Clement, SS. Athanasius and Cyril. While Christian philosophy was strong, it remained a leader among Christian thought, but the rise of the confusion of Arianism caused it to suffer and go into decline.

ALEXANDRINE RITE, one of the rites of the East used throughout the Patriarchate of Alexandria, Egypt. It has three forms: the Greek liturgy of St. Mark, which is no longer used; the three Coptic liturgies, and that used by the Abyssinian Church.

ALIMENTATION, the provision of whatever might be necessary to maintain life, as food, clothing, and shelter. Sometimes referred to the support of members by religious orders; also referred to the maintenance offered to diocesan priests. (*Cf.* BENEFICE.)

ALITURGICAL DAYS, days on which the sacrifice of the Mass is not permitted to be celebrated, as Good Friday in the Latin rite and all Fridays of Lent in the Ambrosian rite.

ALLEGORICAL INTERPRETATION, BIBLICAL. This is a part of the spiritual or mystical sense of Scripture. It is the interpretation of words or portions of Scripture where persons, things, and events as described, signify other persons, things, or events. The former are called types, the latter antitypes. Hence there are antitypes in the O.T. which prefigure the Church on earth and this sense is called the allegorical sense which derives from the manner of expression as a sustained metaphor such as is exemplified in the Canticle of Canticles.

ALLEGORY, a sustained metaphor. One sense of the allegory is really what the metaphor means literally, the other what it represents. Allegory as a literary device should not be confused with allegorical interpretation which is a kind of sense found in Scripture, by prefigurement or allusion.

ALLELUIA, the liturgical call of praise in the Bible, taken from the Hebrew and meaning "all praise to the God who is." In the liturgy of the Mass it is repeated as an expression of joy or thanksgiving.

ALLOCUTION, a solemn speech or statement made by the pope to the cardinals in a secret consistory.

ALL SAINTS, FEAST OF. The feast was instituted in the west by Pope Boniface IV (d. 615), and is celebrated in the Church to honor all the saints, especially those who have not been assigned a day in the Church calendar. It has been celebrated on Nov. 1, since about 731 A.D. when Pope Gregory III consecrated a chapel in St. Peter's Basilica in honor of all saints and set the date of the feast. It ranks as a double of the first class with an octave and is a holyday of obligation in the United States.

ALL SOULS' DAY, day of solemn prayer for all the souls in purgatory which the Church observes on Nov. 2. The Mass on that day is always a *requiem.* By a decree of Aug. 10, 1915, issued by Pope Benedict IV, a priest is granted the privilege of saying three Masses on this day: one for all the faithful departed; one for the intention of the Holy Father; and one for his particular intention.

ALMA also **ALMAH,** word used in the Messianic prophecy (Is. 7:14) referring to the Blessed Mother of God.

ALMONER, originally the person named by a prince or lord to dispense alms or monies to indigent subjects. Now, the member of a religious institution whose duty it is to distribute alms is so called; more rarely the chaplain of such an institution. The place where such alms are given out is referred to as an almonry.

ALMS, the material goods or moneys which are given to the needy as a corporal work of mercy. It arises as an obligation out of the natural law and divine precept to give alms. It is a serious obligation of charity and not of justice, and hence the goods or moneys are to be given out of one's surplus. It is not required that one give unless: his obligations to his family are first satisfied, his needs for reasonable comfort and social position are met, or the money is not otherwise owed in debt. Services of professional people are considered alms when extended to the poor without charge. However, alms are not to be confused with other works of charity such as fraternal correction or acts of a spiritual nature.

ALMUCE, an ecclesiastical garment formerly used to cover the head and worn in choir by chanters. Since the biretta has come into use, the almuce is more of a hood, hanging down in back of the head; the hood of a mozzetta.

ALOGI, literally "against the word." A name given by St. Epiphanius to all heretics who denied the doctrine of our Lord, the Word, and who rejected the biblical writings of St. John.

ALPHA and **OMEGA.** *See A–Ω.*

ALPHABETIC PSALMS. In the Hebrew text, these are the psalms whose successive verses begin with successive letters of the Hebrew alphabet.

ALTAR, a word from the Hebrew, meaning a "place of sacrifice." The Christian altar is a table on which the sacrifice of the Mass is offered. It is the center of dignity and importance in the church building. In the early days of the Church, the Holy Eucharist was celebrated in a home or any private place on a table. Pictures in the catacombs show these tables to be of a variety of shapes, round, square, or semicircular, but now the essential feature is a stone slab, called an altar stone, which may form the entire table top and which contains the relics of martyrs and is consecrated by a bishop or an abbot who has faculties. This idea of a stone with relics follows from the early practice of celebrating Mass on or near the tombs of martyrs in the catacombs. There are two kinds of altars: the *fixed* altar, a table (the *mensa*), with a support or base (the *stipes*), conse-crated as a unit. The *portable* altar, a smaller stone, incised, as is the *fixed*, with five crosses at the corners and center, consecrated alone or apart from its support. Also permitted is a compromise between the two types, made up of a wood or stone permanent structure into the top of which a consecrated stone or portable altar is inserted in the sepulcher (*sepulchrum*), a small, square cavity in the top of the mensa. Rubrics govern the erection, consecration, and fittings of the altar.

ALTARAGE, a seldom used term for the stipend offered to a priest for the intention of a Mass. It formerly meant the support of a chaplain as payment for his services.

ALTAR BOYS, boys or young men, privileged to serve the priest at Mass and other ceremonies, who take the place of the acolyte yet are not in minor orders. (*Cf.* ACOLYTE.)

ALTAR BREADS, thin, round wafers of unleavened wheat bread which are used as the Eucharistic elements in the Latin, Maronite and Armenian rites. Also the communion hosts.

ALTAR CARDS, the three printed cards or charts which are placed in the center, under the crucifix, and at each side of the altar. Printed on the cards are fixed prayers said during Mass, and their purpose is to aid the memory of the priest. The center card has the *Gloria, Credo*, the Offertory prayers, the *Qui pridie*, the prayers of consecration, the prayers before Communion, and the *Placeat* or final prayer. The card at the epistle side has the prayer said while pouring water into the chalice, and the *Lavabo*, said while the priest washes his fingers. The card at the gospel side has the prologue of St. John's Gospel, 1:1–14.

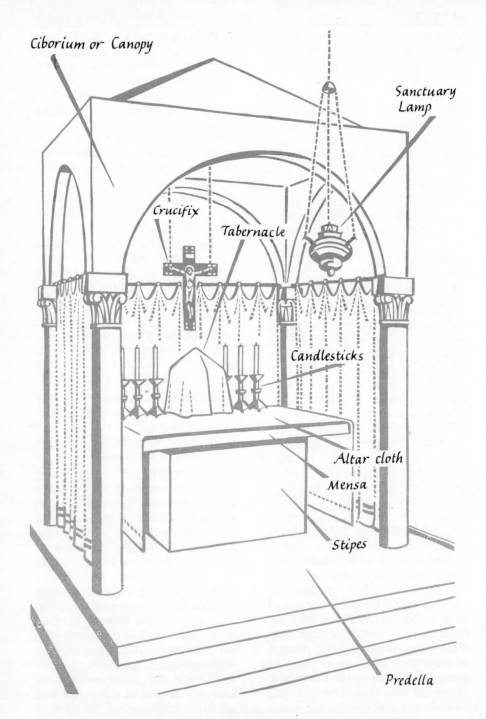

Ciborium or Canopy

Sanctuary Lamp

Crucifix

Tabernacle

Candlesticks

Altar cloth

Mensa

Stipes

Predella

ALTAR

ALTAR-CLOTHS. Strictly speaking, these are the three cloths of linen or hemp which cover the altar. The top cloth must cover the entire surface of the *mensa* and its two ends must hang down to the ground, or floor, but not on it. The two undercloths or, permissibly, one large cloth folded in two, should cover only the actual surface of the *mensa*. An extra cloth should be placed on the altar if candles are placed on the altar surface during Benediction or exposition of the Blessed Sacrament. This does not mean the dust-cover which is non-liturgical and serves only a practical purpose.

ALTAR SOCIETIES, groups of devout persons, usually women, who give their service to the church in preparing vestments, altar-cloths, etc. Many also perform similar work for missions and poorer churches. They are semi-social service organizations of the parish.

ALTAR STONE. *See* ALTAR.

ALTAR, STRIPPING OF. This is the ceremony performed on Holy Thursday after the Blessed Sacrament is removed from the main altar to the place of reposition. It consists of removing the altar cloths, antependium, and tabernacle veil in memory of Christ being stripped of His garments before the crucifixion.

ALTERNATION, the response to alternate verses in singing, or alternate responses to prayers as in the recitation of the Rosary or litanies.

AMA or **AMMA**, a Hebrew word applied in the Eastern Church to deeply religious women. In the early Church, the name of the vessel in which wine was brought to be used in the sacrifice of the Mass.

AMBO, a raised platform, with steps leading up to it from both sides and surrounded by a low rail, placed in the nave of early Christian churches. From it the Scriptures were read, all announcements made, and sermons preached. It has been supplanted more recently by the pulpit. In the Greek Catholic Church the ambo is a table in front of the iconostasis at which baptisms, confirmations, and marriages are celebrated.

AMBO

AMBROSIAN CHANT, hymns, written by St. Ambrose or his contemporaries in the 4th century, in iambic dimeter verse form. They were syllabic in form (a single note to each syllable of text) and originally of a simple rhythm but underwent many changes leading up to the later developments which were forerunners of the Gregorian chant in use today.

AMBROSIAN HYMNOGRAPHY, also called "Ambrosiani." This refers to all hymns having the metric and strophic measure found in the authentic hymns of St. Ambrose. More broadly, it is a poetical form or a liturgical use to which the hymns are applied. As introduced by St. Ambrose into Milan, it was of oriental origin, but was the first use of antiphonal psalmody or the singing of the psalms by two choirs.

AMBROSIAN RITE, the liturgy of the Mass used in the churches of Milan, Italy, so named because St. Ambrose (d. 397) introduced a revision of usage. Its origin is unknown although it is generally held to be an old Roman or Antiochene form. At present it is much like the Roman rite with these exceptions: a procession before the Offertory is made presenting the oblations of wine and bread; a litany is chanted by the deacon; the Creed is read after the Offertory. It is used in the archdiocese of Milan today but not in every church.

AMBRY or **AUMBRY,** a box-like closet or cupboard attached to either the gospel or epistle side of the sanctuary wall. It may be built into or hang against the wall. In the ambry the holy oils are kept. The ambry should have a door which must be kept locked, and the words *Olea Sacra* (Holy Oils) should be inscribed on this door. The ambry may have a white or violet veil hung before it. If the sacristy adjoins the sanctuary physically, the ambry may be kept there.

AMBULATORY, a covered passage or walk around a cloister and open on the side toward the courtyard. Also the passage around the apse of a church building from which chapels radiate.

AMEN, a Hebrew word meaning "truly," "certainly." According to Pope Benedict XIV it means assent to a truth, as when used at the end of a Creed. It is used in its original meaning in both Scripture and the liturgy of the Church. When in the N.T. (Jn. 3:3) it is used double, it is considered more solemn. As used at the end of prayers, "Amen" signifies our desire to obtain our request and is commonly translated "So be it."

AMERICAN BOARD OF CATHOLIC MISSIONS, an organization founded at Cincinnati, Ohio, in 1920, by a committee appointed by bishops of the United States. Its purpose is to distribute 40% of the annual collection of the Propagation of the Faith to archbishops and bishops of missionary dioceses of the U. S. and its dependencies. It consolidates missionary activities in the U. S., coordinates them with Catholic missions of other countries under general jurisdiction of an international board chosen by the Vatican, and operates under the direction of the National Catholic Welfare Council.

AMERICANISM. In Catholic history, this refers to a controversy which attracted attention near the end of the 19th century. It arose over French theologians who protested the missionary methods of Father Isaac Hecker, the American priest-convert, and the support given to American institutions. The charges included protests that methods of conversion used were heterodox, that American missionaries were placing the faith secondary and distorting Catholic doctrine, not following Church authorities, and belittling humility and obedience, the latter in regard to religious vows. In 1899, Pope Leo XIII in a letter, *Testem benevolentiae,* "Proof of affection," condemned the alleged practices which were included in the word "Americanism," and drew a clear distinction between the lawful and unlawful in the dispute. Notably the declaration made the following points clear: the necessity of spiritual direc-

AMPULLA

tion; the subordinate position of the natural virtues to the supernatural; the relative place of the active and passive virtues; and it refuted the claim that liberty is limited in religious vows. It further set forth the methods of treating with non-Catholics. The discussion continued for a few years, giving way to the issue of modernism.

AMICE, the vestment put on first by a priest in vesting for the celebration of Mass. It is an oblong linen cloth which is touched to the head before being placed over the shoulders. It is worn under the alb. While putting the amice on, the priest prays, "Put on my head, O Lord, the helmet of salvation, in order to repel the assaults of the devil."

AMMONIAN SECTIONS, divisions of the four Gospels made in the margins of early Greek and Latin manuscripts of the Scriptures. These sections, so named after Ammonius of Alexandria (circa 220), were an indication of the harmony of the four Gospels.

AMOVABILITY, canonical term describing the method and prerogative of a bishop of a diocese in moving a cleric from an office, which the bishop can do in prudent judgment, except in the instances of an irremovable office or a removable parish (c. 192, sec. 2, 3; c. 2147–61).

AMPULLA, a bottle or small jar which was used by early Christians to hold holy oils. Some were thought to contain the blood of a martyr. Later in the Middle Ages people making pilgrimages to holy wells carried water from the place of pilgrimage in small *ampullae* tied about their necks.

AMRA, an elegy written in prose or verse and recited to proclaim the virtues and life of a native saint of Ireland.

AMULA. *See* CRUETS.

ANAGNOSTES, the one who reads the Epistle in the Greek Church.

ANAGOGICAL SENSE, BIBLICAL. In the interpretation of Scripture, this is a division of the spiritual or mystical sense. It derives from the "subject matter" and, as St. Thomas points out, truth may be conveyed to us through Scriptures with (a) a view to right belief or (b) right conduct. When this is by "right conduct" it is a moral or tropological sense of Scripture. When it is directed to right belief then we have either the *allegorical* or *anagogical* senses. In the first, the allegorical, we have examples of types in the O.T. which prefigure persons in the N.T. In the second there are types in both the O.T. and N.T. which foreshadow the Church triumphant in heaven, and this we term the anagogical sense, e.g., St. Paul (Gal. 4:26) using Jerusalem as a type of the city of heaven.

ANALECTA, literally "gatherings" or gleanings from the writings of authors, such as the fathers, which may appear as part of the title of the book.

ANALOGY, an argument from the lesser to the greater; a demonstrated form of reasoning. Analogy is used in the sense that by noting the degree of perfection in creatures we may come to know, however imperfectly, the infinite perfection of God (Wisd. 13:5).

ANAMNESIS, something done in memory of someone or something, as is stated after the consecration in the Mass.

ANAPHORA, from the Greek, meaning an "offering." In the Latin rite, the term refers to the Canon of the Mass, including the Preface.

ANASTASIMATARION, a liturgica book of the Greek Church which contains the text and notation sung during the Sunday office.

ANATHEMA. The ban as used in the O.T. meant that which is or must be set aside or separated, especially whatever would bring danger to the people because of inherent evil. In practice, the ban was the sacrifice of living creatures and offering them up to God. This was governed by the law of Moses. In the N.T., St. Paul (Gal. 1:8) used the term "anathema" in the sense of utterly excluding a person from the kingdom of God. In this it is understood as an excommunication, a cutting off, or destruction. Later in the Church, the term was applied to one solemnly pronounced excommunicated or expelled from communion with the Church by the pope.

ANCHOR. This mariner's aid in keeping a boat safe has been used from earliest times in the Church as a symbol of hope. It appears several times in St. Paul (Heb. 6:19; 1 Tim. 1:1), where hope is portrayed as the "anchor of the soul." Later, the symbol appeared frequently in the catacombs as an emblem of hope. In art the symbol has also been representative of several saints who were steadfast in hope.

ANCHOR-CROSS, the symbol of the anchor representing hope, as used in the catacombs but, with its crosspiece, a veiled image of the cross. In this understanding it portrayed both faith and hope.

ANCHOR-CROSS

ANCHORHOLD, a hut or cell built beside a church wall having two openings, one leading into the church and one through which food was passed to the hermit who lived within.

ANCHORITE, a man who withdraws from the world to live as a hermit and in so doing devotes his life to penance and prayer. Women doing this are called anchoresses. Usually such persons are for some time a part of monastic life, spending preparatory years in monastic living or returning from time to time to a monastery.

ANCREN RIWLE, a code of conduct, rather rigoristic, drawn up in the 13th century for the direction of anchoresses. It is no longer considered except as a curio.

ANGEL. The name "angel" is taken from the Greek translation of a Hebrew word meaning "messenger." The angels are spiritual beings, created by God, and superior in nature to man. They are immortal beings whose role is to minister to God and to do the will of God in obedience. They are bodiless, spiritual intelligences who have their knowledge, not as man who acquires knowledge through his senses, but by intuition. Thus they do not arrive at conclusions following upon principles by a process of reason, but immediately know the principles as truth. Their intelligences are continually, eternally exercised and while much is hidden from them they understand and know much more than man. They have swiftness of movement, free will and communication among themselves. The number of angels is exceedingly great. Theologians and early writers, basing their reasoning upon an enumeration given in Scripture by Isaias, Ezechiel, St. Paul (Col. 1:16, Eph. 1:21), list three hierarchies, in each of which there are three orders, making nine types or classifications. The first threesome are: Seraphim, Cherubim, Thrones; the second, Dominations, Principalities, Powers; the third, Virtues, Archangels, Angels. The classes or choirs of angels differ in the degree of perfection of their nature and of grace, and this in a descending order in the listing above. It should be pointed out that all are called "angels," yet it also is the name applied to the lower choir from which the "guardian angels" are usually chosen. Veneration is given angels because of their dignity, relation to God, and excellence of nature, and petition is made to them because they minister to God and may, if God so wills, minister to man.

ANGEL, GUARDIAN, the angelic representative and unseen companion of every person on earth (Mt. 18:10; also Acts 12:15). This teaching is held by the Church not as a defined article but as a "proximate" teaching of faith. As such, the angel assigned to the person represents him before God, watches over him, defends him, helps in prayer and in thought, and presents the soul of the just person to God after death. Devotion to one's guardian angel is encouraged.

ANGELICAL SALUTATION

ANGELICAL SALUTATION, the Hail Mary prayer. More properly it is the greeting given to the Blessed Virgin by Archangel Gabriel at the annunciation, which is repeated in the first portion of the prayer (Lk. 1:26–38).

ANGELIC DOCTOR. *See* DOCTOR ANGELICUS.

ANGEL-LIGHTS, an architectural term for the small windows separating the structural tracery of arches in church windows.

ANGELS, EVIL. *See* DEVIL.

ANGELS OF THE CHURCHES. As mentioned in the Apocalypse (1:20), these were thought of by the Greek or Eastern Church fathers as referring to the guardian angels of seven cities (Ephesus, Smyrna, Pergamum, Thyatira, Sardis, Philadelphia, Laodicea) of the Asiatic Roman Empire. However, following the interpretation of the Western Church fathers, they usually are held to be the bishops of these cities to whom St. John addresses himself in writing.

ANGELUS, the devotion consisting of praying three Hail Marys, versicles and responses, and a collect or prayer at morning, noon and night in honor of the Incarnation and in veneration of the Blessed Mother. Usually this is prayed at the ringing of the *Angelus* by the church bells at 6 a.m., 12 noon, and 6 p.m. The devotion began in 1318 when Pope John XXII called for the recitation of three Hail Marys in the evening for peace. Later, in France, it was used at noon and in the morning, and by the 16th century was made universal with indulgences attached. During the season of Easter the verse *"Regina caeli laetare"* ("Queen of Heaven, rejoice") is said instead of the above prayers.

ANGER, a strong emotion which when aroused leads to other sins. The "inordinate inclination to take revenge." As such it is one of the seven capital sins. It may be considered inordinate by reason of the object that causes the anger or the extent to which it is aroused or expressed. The contrary virtue is meekness.

ANGLICAN, name of the organization and members of the Established Church of England. It is used more by the high churchmen, but chiefly as an argument to identify the Established Church with that "Catholic Church" as named in the Magna Carta. It began with the break with Rome made by Henry VIII whose marriage problems were a scandal and against the law of the Catholic Church. The first step in this separation was not in the nature of reform but was given in the instance of the publication by Henry of the Acts of Supremacy (1535) which declared the crown supreme in religious affairs. Having started thus, Henry drew up Ten Articles which rejected the Catholic doctrine on the papacy, purgatory, relics and images. The Catholic Church was persecuted and its properties seized; not always because of these teachings, however. Later, in the reign of Edward VI, the Book of Common Prayer was published. This first printing in 1549 was tainted by protestant errors, but a later edition was strongly Calvinistic. Elizabeth, during her reign, adhered to this second edition but made certain amendments to appease and make the book useful to both the moderate members (Episcopalians) and the extremists (Calvinists). Parliament in 1563 set up the Church of England with the publication of the Thirty-nine Articles and established the heresy by the repudiation of many Catholic doctrines. Elizabeth then brought forth her Acts of Supremacy and Uniformity which led to legalized persecution of Catholics for nearly two hundred years under the nationalistic belief that the patriotism of those outside the Established Church was questioned and those recognizing papal authority were accused of committing treason. Elizabeth was excommunicated in 1570 by Pius V.

ANGLICAN ORDERS. The validity of holy orders of the ministers of the Anglican Church is a disputed question. It follows that their rejection of holy orders as a sacrament would put succeeding administrations in doubt because of faulty intent. Certainly the effects of ordination rest in authority from the apostles, and the ordaining bishop intends to confer the right and duty to offer the sacrifice of the Mass in accord with that succession. Rejection of the sacrifice, the Eucharist, and the real presence makes it impossible to intend the effects of ordination. The question for Catholics was settled by the publication of the papal bull, *Apostolicae Curae*, (Sept. 13, 1896) which declared Anglican orders to be "absolutely null and utterly void," and this because of defect in (a) the form in the rite of ordaining and (b) the intention of the one ordaining.

ANGLO-CATHOLICS, name of the Anglicans who are so-called "high" church, and who claim to celebrate Mass, use the Latin Missal, etc. They favor union or identity with the Greek and Russian orthodox churches.

ANIMALS IN CHURCH ART. From the earliest days of the Church, animals were used as symbols representing animate and inanimate persons, e.g., the lamb as the soul, the lion for the evangelist St. Mark, etc. This use continued in Byzantine art and was carried into the later Gothic art as can be seen in the Cathedral of Notre Dame in Paris. The use now has vanished with the exceptions of symbols of the older and classic representations.

ANNATES, the revenue, in whole or part, paid to the papal Curia and derived from a benefice, usually figured on a one-year basis. The revenue is now paid on appointments made to dioceses other than those subject to the Congregation of the Propaganda. Support thus given to the Holy See is small and the chief source of revenue is the annual Peter's Pence collection.

ANNIVERSARY. In the Church, days of commemoration known as anniversaries are celebrated in many instances. The anniversary of the consecration of a bishop is celebrated with a Mass in the liturgy. The anniversary of the consecration or dedication of a church is celebrated with a Mass and Office on the feast. More frequently the anniversary of a person's death is commemorated annually, and may also be celebrated on the third, seventh and thirtieth day after the day of death, and a special requiem Mass is designated for celebration of these anniversaries.

ANNUAL PONTIFICAL, an annual statistical publication, (*Annuaire Pontifical Catholique*), giving data on the personnel, the dioceses, the Holy See, and the Church throughout the world. Each volume is added to the first twenty volumes, begun in 1898 by Msgr. A. Battandier and published in Paris, France, which covered basic information of the Church, bishops, properties, etc.

ANNULMENT. In Church usage, this is the declaration by authorities that a marriage is null and void because it was never valid, not being contracted validly owing to the presence of an invalidating impediment. (*Cf.* IMPEDIMENTS OF MARRIAGE.)

Dove

Lamb of God

Brazen serpent (healing)

Hart panting after living waters

Lion of Juda

Peacock of immortality

Hare rising from the earth

Hen gathering her young

FABULOUS ANIMALS:

Unicorn

Phoenix rising from his ashes

Pelican in her piety

ANIMALS IN CHURCH ART—Some of the animal symbols used in Church art.

ANNUNCIATION OF THE B.V.M., the announcement made to the Virgin Mary by Archangel Gabriel (Lk. 1:26–38) that she was to become the Mother of Jesus and her acceptance of the will of God. The act of declaring the Incarnation of the Son of God. The event is celebrated by the feast of March 25 in the Church calendar.

ANOMEAN also **ANOMOEAN,** a member of the strict Arians who broke from the followers of Arianism. The name is derived from the Greek for "unlike" since they held the heretical belief that God the Father and God the Son were "unlike." Anomeans rejected consubstantiality. Sometimes they are called Eunomians.

ANTEDILUVIAN, a term referring to people or events before the time of the flood (Gen. 6 to 8).

ANTEPENDIUM. In early times this was a vertically hung cloth which went around the entire altar and was suspended from the four corners. It was called a "pallium" and was a vestment enveloping the altar. Later this was a single piece of rich silk or brocade which hung down in front of the altar from the edge of the mensa to the floor, although some were metal or wood and appropriately ornamented. It is now more often called *frontal*. The rubrics now direct that a frontal is to be hung on the altar front below the mensa, and is to be of the color of the feast or office of the day. It should be made of a suitable fabric, and have battens (*telaria*), or verticle lathes which strengthen and cause the material to hang without appearing tucked or folded. The color and use are governed by the rubrics.

ANTHEM. *See* ANTIPHON.

ANTHONY'S FIRE, ST. This nonmedical term applies to a type of erysipelas, so named because of cures attributed to the saint, and to the Order of Canons Regular of St. Anthony that was founded partly to care for those afflicted with the disease.

ANTHROPOMORPHISM, BIBLICAL, references in the Bible wherein God is spoken of, in metaphor, as being in human form or having human attributes.

ANTICHRIST. There is no specific one person or thing indicated by the term. Rather the title of antichrist may be given to any person, idea, or group of persons who opposed, are opposing, or intend to oppose Christ and His Church. In particular this title is applicable only to the one enemy who will appear before the last judgment and draw many faithful away before being defeated by Christ. St. Paul calls this enemy "the man of lawlessness" (2 Thess. 2:3); this is not to be considered literally but as apocalyptic language in keeping with St. John (12:12). In brief, it is the one who will attempt to substitute himself for God.

ANTICIPATE. To anticipate means to read in private the hours of the Divine Office before the hours assigned to them, e.g., reading Matins, which should be read before Mass in the morning, during the previous evening.

ANTIDICOMARIANITES, literally, those opposed to Mary. Historically, it is the name given by Epiphanius (4th century) to those who denied Mary's motherhood of God and her perpetual virginity..

ANTIDORON, the fragments of bread remaining after the wafers have been cut from the baked mass and which are passed out, unconsecrated, to be consumed by the faithful before leaving the church. This is still the practice in the Greek Church. The *pain bénit* of the French.

ANTILEGOMENA, name given to the disputed writings of Scripture as referred to by Eusebius of Caesarea.

ANTIMENSION, a substitute for an altar stone as used in Greek churches. It is an oblong piece of silk, 10 by 14 inches, into which are sewn relics of saints and on which the instruments of the Passion are represented, and is spread on the altar top for the celebration of Mass. (*Cf.* ALTAR STONE.)

ANTINOMIANS, heretics who followed the false idea that Christians did not have to follow the commandments. It broke out anew under the "justification by faith" teaching of Luther since some held that evil acts did not hinder one's salvation if good acts did not help one. Even Luther repudiated this. The teaching was condemned by the Council of Trent.

ANTIOCH, the ancient city of Asia Minor, located in Syria on the Orontes river which was held one of the three great episcopal cities of apostolic times. It was there that the name Christian arose (Acts. 11:26), and there St. Peter was bishop for a time before going to Rome. It was in early times a center of theology and scriptural studies.

ANTIOCHENE RITE. In its original form this liturgy of the Mass differed chiefly because it omitted the *Pater Noster* and the saints' names. Later it was adapted to the Liturgy of St. James, a Greek form which was translated into the Syriac language. It is used in this form throughout the patriarchate with the exception that twice a year the Greek form is used by the Orthodox Church. Another form of this is the Maronite rite.

ANTIPHON, a word derived from the Greek, meaning the alternate recitation or singing of verses as practiced by the ancient Greek dramatists. It was introduced into the Latin Church in the 4th century. Later development brought it into what it is at present, namely, a phrase or verse immediately prefixed to and following a psalm or psalms or a canticle which gives the key to the mystery the Church wishes to indicate in that particular portion of her Office. A double antiphon means that the antiphon is prayed both before and after the psalm. On minor feasts the antiphons are not doubled but are said to be "announced" which means the words are prayed only as far as the asterisk (or indicated break) at the beginning of the psalm, but recited entirely at the end. The term may also indicate any psalm or hymn sung in alternate responses by choir members or by the choir and congregation.

ANTIPHONARY, the book containing all of the antiphons of the Divine Office together with the proper musical notation.

ANTIPOPES, the false claimants to the Holy See from the 3rd through the 14th centuries. Over the years there were 37 antipopes who sought to seize the power of the papacy against the canonically elected pope. Usually these men were supported by (a) fractional or dissident groups of the faithful and clergy; (b) by political, schismatic, or heretical groups; (c) by the ruling barons or kings who demanded the right of investiture.

ANTISTES, a title often applied in history or in prayers as a prefatory term of honor of a bishop or prelate.

ANTITRINITARIANS, name given to those who hold and promote the heretical teaching which denies the three Persons of the Trinity. The Arians were so named in the early history of the Church; more recently, the Socinians and Unitarians.

ANTITYPE. Through interpretation and a recognition of the economy of Scripture and the wish of God that both the O.T. and the N.T. together present a fullness of teaching, we find that persons, things and events of the O.T. signify persons, things or events in the N.T. It is the typological or mystical sense of Scripture. Thus persons, things, or events as described in the early writing are the *types* while the persons, things or events they signify in the later writing are antitypes. Discovery of these continues through interpretation, but they were always present in Scripture, placed there by God through inspiration.

ANTWERP BIBLE, a six-volume polyglot Bible published in Antwerp, Belgium, in 1573 by the Plantin press.

APOCALYPSE, the last book of the N.T., entitled "The Apocalypse of St. John the Apostle." The word "apocalypse" means *an unveiling* and indicates that the writing is classed as prophetic. It is also declared that it is "of" St. John, i.e., written by St. John. There has been some dispute over whether St. John was the author, but internal evidence, the method of its outline, and other numerous factors indicate without doubt that he was the writer. The book itself is difficult to interpret since it contains teaching, instructions, direct and indirect prophecy, visions, and all presented in symbolical language. It is divided into three parts: a prologue, the main book itself, and an epilogue. Its single theme is the final triumph of Christ in an antichrist world and the assurance of resurrection in Christ for those who are faithful.

APOCALYPTIC NUMBER, a mystical number, especially 666 as stated in Apoc. 13:18, which is the "number of the beast." It was an ancient practice to have the letters of the Greek or Hebrew alphabets stand for a number (thus A = 1). Using this formula, a name could be stated as the sum of its letters, as the name of Jesus in Greek amounted to 888. The number 666 is explained thus, that 777 being the perfect number and 888 meaning Christ or each unit of 7 augmented by 1, then 666 or each unit lessened by 1, was that of antichrist. In the derived name then, it could be the sum of Nero. However, the number, apart from the many conjectures, might stand for any "antichrist" or anyone who in time would stand against Christ.

APOCATASTASIS, a term from the Greek, applied to the false teaching that in the end all men will be saved, or their state restored as though there were no consequence to the goodness or evil of their lives.

APOCREOS, in the Greek rite that day when meat may be eaten for the last time before the lenten season.

APOCRISIARIUS, title of a legate to the court of an emperor used from the 4th to the 9th centuries.

APOCRYPHA. The meaning of the word is "hidden," and thus has been applied to a number of writings of spurious or at least highly doubtful books of Christian thought. As applied by the Church, apocrypha means that body of writings on religious matters which are outside of the canon of Scripture and which are not inspired but at one time claimed the authority of Scripture. In protestant circles the term is used to denote those books which Catholics hold to be canonical and inspired, e.g., the deuterocanonical books, the Prayer of Manasses and 3 and 4 Esdras. The Catholic use of the word includes all uncanonical writings, of uncertain origin, which were written anonymously or under the assumed name of some apostle or church leader. The Protestants call these writings *Pseudepigrapha*.

The term apocrypha originally was applied to writings of the first centuries which held "secret" teachings for the initiate. Later, when the heretics were putting out their "secret" writings and claiming authorship by patriarchs, prophets or apostles, the term became, among Christian writers, one of disdain. Finally, it was applied to Jewish and Christian writings which were written in the first centuries but were judged to be outside the canon. There are apocrypha of the O.T. which are broadly grouped under three headings: apocalyptic, historical and didactic; these number more than 28 in number, some of which are pre-Christian. The apocrypha of the N.T. are gospels, acts, epistles, apocalypses and the *agrapha*. In all, these number more than 40. These writings while spurious still contain value: notably in the historical knowledge they offer, in the inducement they give to appreciation of the genuine Scriptures, and in the insight they afford into the early doctrinal disputes and the items the early followers found important. From a theological standpoint they are of slight value.

APODEIPNON, the final daily part of the Greek Breviary.

APODOSIS, in the Greek Church, the final day of prayer commemorating a feast day.

APOLLINARIANISM, the heresy advanced by Apollinarius the younger, bishop of Laodicea in the 4th century. It taught that Christ had a human body and a human sensitive soul but not a rational soul, thus that Christ's human nature was incomplete. The heresy was condemned by the first Council of Constantinople in 381 A.D.

APOLOGETICS. Originally this meant any apology (defense) of the reasonableness of any revealed religion. It is now that branch of the science of theology called "fundamental theology" which is a division of dogmatic theology whose special field is to prove religious truth has been revealed. Its object is that revelation has been made by God and that the Catholic faith is that revelation. More broadly, apologetics has been inclusive of all writings and investigations in science, history and Scripture which have defended or explained the truth of Catholic teaching.

APOLOGIST, a title of honor given in the early days of the Church to writers among the fathers who defended the Church and its teachings. Now it is applied to one versed in fundamental theology, or one who teaches, speaks, or writes in defense or clarification of the teachings and practices of the Church.

APOLOGY or **APOLOGIA,** literally a writing in defense of a teaching, often also a "vindication" wherein one presents a reasoned viewpoint.

APOLUSIA, in Eastern rites the washing of those about to be baptized which is performed eight days before administration of the sacrament. During the 8 days of preparation those so washed wear white garments as a mark of their catechumenate.

APOLYSIS, the final blessing given in the Greek Church, either that at the end of Mass or after reciting certain parts of the Divine Office.

APOLYTIKION, the final prayer or hymn, spoken or sung at the conclusion of Mass, Matins, or Vespers, in the Greek Church.

APOSTASY. In the early Church this meant the going over permanently to paganism; the rejection, after an initial acceptance and baptism, of the graces of the faith (Heb. 6:1-8). Now it is defined as the complete repudiation of the faith of the Church by one who has been baptized (c. 1325, 2). It is a grievous sin since it is a denial of the truth of God and the Church. Also this is applied as apostasy from religious life which is the unauthorized departure from his place of assignment by one in perpetual vows who does not intend to return (c. 644).

APOSTLE, literally, "one sent." In the Church the apostles are the twelve men originally chosen by Christ to be the bearers of His teachings to the world. It was Christ who first called them "apostles" (Lk. 6:13). The Hebrew word *"saliah"* which is the translation for the word "apostle" means "one who is entrusted to fulfill a task, acting in the name of the sender." Before Pentecost, the apostles received the teaching and thereafter they gave the teaching as from Him who sent them. They are referred to as twelve by our Lord. St. Peter defined an apostle as one who

is "a witness with us of His Resurrection." (Acts 1:21-22). They are listed as follows: Simon Peter, Andrew, James the Greater (son of Zebedee), John the brother of James, Philip, Bartholomew, Matthew, Thomas, James the Less (son of Alpheus), Thaddeus (or Jude), Simon the Cananean, and Matthias, elected to replace Judas Iscariot (Acts 1:23-26). The title also is given to St. Paul and to St. Barnabas. To the apostles were entrusted the teachings of Christ, the jurisdiction and the authority to found and further the Church of Christ. They were the first bishops, and their successors, the bishops of the Church today, receive their fullness of authority to teach the faith directly from them. Also certain men who were the first missioners of the founders of the true religion in certain countries or places are called apostles of that country or place. (*Cf.* APOSTOLIC SUCCESSION.)

APOSTLES' CREED, a prayer in the form of a profession of faith containing twelve articles or fundamental doctrines. It is true that even in apostolic times, a profession of faith was required of persons before receiving baptism (Acts 8:36). Its name is due not to the fact that it was written by the apostles, but it is so called because it is a summary of apostolic teaching. In its present form it is an extension of a form used in apostolic times. This latter is evident from similarities found in its expression by very early writers such as Irenaeus and Clement.

APOSTLESHIP OF PRAYER, the League of the Sacred Heart, a pious association founded at Vals in France in 1844 by Francis Xavier Gautrelet, S.J. Its object is to promote prayer and devotion to the Sacred Heart and join the prayers of members in a single monthly intention. It serves in the U. S. to aid local centers of devotion in parishes, schools, and homes. Its publication is the *Messenger of the Sacred Heart.*

APOSTLES, TEACHING OF THE TWELVE. *See* DIDACHE.

APOSTOLATE OF SUFFERING, a pious association founded in Milwaukee, Wis., in 1926, to teach to the sick, invalids and shut-ins the moral value of suffering, and to promote the offering of sufferings for the spiritual good of all.

APOSTOLICAE CURAE, the title of the papal bull of Pope Leo XIII, in 1896, on the validity of Anglican orders.

APOSTOLIC CANONS, teachings claimed to have been dictated by the apostles to St. Clement of Rome. They are attached to the eight books of the Apostolic Constitutions and contain regulations pertaining to ecclesiastical persons. They cannot be ascribed to the apostles and have no substantial doctrinal value.

APOSTOLIC CONSTITUTIONS, eight books which, it was claimed, were written down by St. Clement of Rome at the dictation of the apostles. They are spurious in this claim and date from the 4th century. Largely they were compiled from other writings of the time.

APOSTOLIC DATARY, a lesser branch of the Roman Curia, though it formerly was the office for handling and countersigning all papal documents and granting favors such as benefices. Since Pope St. Pius X revised procedures, the Datary has the supervision of the conferring of non-consistorial or minor benefices which are reserved to the Holy See. Its staff is a commission of three theologians presided over by the Cardinal Datary of the Pope.

APOSTOLIC DELEGATE, a representative of the Vatican who has no diplomatic standing since he is not appointed to deal with the government of a country. Instead this delegate treats with the hierarchy of the country of his appointment in the supervision of ecclesiastical business, Church announcements of new bishops, etc. Delegates are themselves usually bishops. The United States has an apostolic delegate residing in Washington, D. C. At present there are 23 countries with such delegates. (*Cf.* NUNCIO.)

APOSTOLIC FATHERS, the Christian writers of the 1st and 2nd centuries whose writings were at one time considered as possibly belonging to the canon of Scripture, but which were classed as apocrypha.

APOSTOLICI, name given to a group of followers of the Gnostic heresy who pretended to imitate the apostles by absolutely renouncing the world, e.g., they rejected marriage as a sacrament. Other like groups having a similar name have arisen from time to time, most claiming all material goods to be evil and impure.

APOSTOLIC INDULGENCES. These are indulgences attached to religious articles when blessed by the Holy Father or by the person he so authorizes. The articles should, if possible, be carried on one's person or be kept in a suitable place and the prescribed prayers should be recited.

APOSTOLICITY, a mark of the Church, setting the Church apart as that founded by Christ directly upon His apostles. It is seen through the *mission* of the Church in being sent, through the apostles and their successors, to teach and baptize all men in Christ's name; it further is recognized as a mark in the *doctrine*, which has been preserved throughout all time by the Church, and her infallible prerogative. (*Cf.* APOSTOLIC SUCCESSION; MARKS OF·THE CHURCH.)

APOSTOLIC SEE. Sometimes a see founded and ruled over by one of the apostles was so named, but now it refers to Rome, the see city of the pope which he rules as bishop of the diocese of Rome. Also loosely applied to the Vatican.

APOSTOLIC SIGNATURE. Dating back to the 13th century, this was an important court and office handling papal affairs. Today, its full title is "The Supreme Tribunal of the Apostolic Signature" and it is a supreme court acting as a court of appeal from the decisions of the Roman Rota, especially those cases appealed because of defective juridical procedures. It is made up of six cardinals under a cardinal prefect and minor officials. It also serves the government of Vatican State regarding certain concordats.

APOSTOLIC SUCCESSION, the sequence, following from the apostles themselves down to the bishops of the present time. This is marked (a) by lawful, valid ordination conferred on bishops of the Church; (b) by the giving over or delegating directly the powers entrusted to the apostles of ordaining, of ruling, and of teaching, which powers were given by Christ to the apostles; (c) by the historic and scriptural truth that the apostles did confer this power on others; (d) by the intrinsic truth that the Church in all ages could not have·preserved its identity and unity as intended by

Christ ("I am with you all days, even to the consummation of the world") unless there were a giving over of such powers to others who would carry on the work of Christ's Church.

APOSTOLIC UNION, an association of diocesan clergy who live a rule directed to their religious life, assist mutually in the duties and effectiveness of their ministry and aid their work by conferences. It was begun in the 17th century in Bavaria by Venerable B. Holzhauser, and was commended by Pope St. Pius X who became a member.

APOSTOLICUS, a seldom used word, originating from the 11th century and applied to the Holy Father.

APPAREL or **PARATURA,** a piece of colored brocade or other rich material, usually the same color as the vestments, which was attached to the neckband edge of the amice and could be removed when washing the amice. It served to form a collar on the vested cleric. Though still in use in some places, as Milan and Spain, it is not recognized for liturgical use.

APPARITION, a vision or supernatural manifestation which God permits and which thus is seen by the person witnessing. It may be called corporeal, that is, it strikes the senses as reality, or it may be sensible, that is, appearing real because of luminous qualities. In both these senses it is not to be considered as a ghost or preternatural manifestation, but rather of a mystical nature as arising from God.

APPEAL, in canon law, recourse to a superior court from an inferior court in a case of justice. It is judicial when the appeal is made from the sentence of a judge sitting in a court.

It is extra- judicial when the appeal is from the injurious action of a superior in a question of rights. It does not imply injustice in the sentence rendered but rather a correction of the decision upon the entry of new facts into the testimony. There can be no appeal from a decision of the pope, because as Vicar of Christ he has no recognized superior.

APPELLANT CONTROVERSY, a quarrel which arose in England over the appointment of an archpriest by the crown after the death of Cardinal Allen in the late 16th century. The controversy was terminated in 1602 by a papal bull, but resentment followed for many years.

APPELLANTS, name given to a group of French clergy who, under Cardinal de Noailles and four bishops, appealed to a future general council against a papal constitution condemning Jansenistic writings in 1713.

APPETITE, the inclination of a being to seek its proper end or perfection. Used in a specific sense it means the inclination or seeking of any faculty or power of man of the proper object: thus the eye is inclined to see. In spiritual language, it may mean the desire of the Good (God) taking precedence over the natural inclination to evil due to original sin.

APPROPRIATION, in theology, the attributing of one quality, name, or operation to a single Person of the Holy Trinity. This does not mean that the other Persons of the Trinity do not possess these qualities, names, or operations, since all three possess all in an infinite degree. It is a man-

ner of human reference on our part, e.g., referring to Christ as the "God of love." (*Cf.* TRINITY.)

APSE

APSE, in church architecture the semicircular, vaulted end of the church building in the center of which the altar is placed. This was found in the tribunals of 4th-century Rome and was where the judges sat. Later when adapted to church use it became the place where the bishop's chair was placed. Improperly the sanctuary is sometimes referred to as the apse, probably because an apse often contains the sanctuary, and today may be either square, polygonal, or semicircular and need not be vaulted.

APSIDIOLE also **APSIDIALE,** a small apse or a lesser apse on either side of the main apse of a church, sometimes forming small chapels or places for side altars.

AQUAMANILE, an early name, rarely used today, for the basin in which the water is poured when the priest washes his hands in the celebration of Mass.

AQUARIANS, a sect of the 2nd-century Gnostics who held that the use of wine in the Mass was sinful.

AQUILEIAN RITE, an early liturgy of the 4th century which developed in the province of Aquileia and was abandoned in the 13th century in preference for the Roman liturgy.

ARAMAIC, the earliest liturgical language of the Church. It was the language spoken in Palestine, a west Semitic language, of which Hebrew and biblical Aramaic are dialects of Canaanite and true Aramaic, and was in use from the Babylonian captivity until apostolic times. Christ spoke Aramaic. It, along with Hebrew and Greek, is one of the three languages of the Bible.

ARCA, a box in which the early Christians kept the Eucharist in their homes, thus an early tabernacle. Now sometimes referred to as a place where special offerings are kept.

ARCANI, DISCIPLINA. *See* DISCIPLINE OF THE SECRET.

ARCHAEOLOGY, CHRISTIAN, a branch of the science of archaeology. It studies, investigates, explores and judges the remains of early Christian monuments, including literature, objects of art, inscriptions, etc. It is interested not alone in the discovery of early records and their classification, but also in the scientific cataloguing and the integration of such Christian records into the entire historic record of the science of archaeology.

ARCHAEOLOGY, COMMISSION OF SACRED, one of the papal commissions of study, founded in 1851 by Pope Pius IX. Its purpose is to promote the exploration and study of the Roman catacombs, the excavations of the Vatican, and to care for the museums of Vatican State.

ARCHANGEL. *See* ANGEL.

ARCHBISHOP. This title, used in the Western Church from the 9th century, is given to a bishop who governs one or more dioceses which form an ecclesiastical province. As such he presides over the metropolitan see, which is usually that of the principal city of the territory. Bishops of other dioceses within the province are called suffragan bishops; their dioceses are suffragan sees. The title archbishop may be *titular*, and then the archbishop is not known as a metropolitan. An archbishop has a wider jurisdiction, having the right to summon provincial councils (of the suffragans), and serving as an appeal court to the suffragan sees. The office of archbishop is marked by the *pallium* with which he is invested by the Holy See, and by the "cross with double bar" or archiepiscopal cross. (*Cf.* TITULAR BISHOP; JURISDICTION.)

ARCHCONFRATERNITY, an association of confraternities or sodalities established in many places. Enjoying certain privileges over and above those of the confraternity or sodality, it is a special affiliation of confraternities sanctioned by the Church. Most prominent among the archconfraternities are those of: the Blessed Sacrament; the Holy Name Society; and the Christian Mothers. (*Cf.* CONFRATERNITY.)

ARCHDEACON, in the early Church a deacon appointed by the bishop to assist him in certain jurisdictional details. Some abuses arose and the office was abolished upon the demand that the deacon take the order of priesthood. Today it does not exist as a rank in the Church and the work of aiding the bishop is done by the vicar-general and vicars-forane of the diocese.

ARCHDIOCESE, the territory, ecclesiastical province of jurisdiction, governed by an archbishop. (*Cf.* JURISDICTION; PROVINCE.)

ARCHIEPISCOPAL CROSS

ARCHIEPISCOPAL CROSS also **PATRIARCHAL CROSS,** cross with two cross-bars. Its upper bar is shorter and is portrayed as part of the coat-of-arms of an archbishop. Mounted on a long staff, it is carried before the archbishop in processions.

ARCHIMANDRITE, the superior of a monastery in the Oriental Churches; also an honorary title of a chancery official of certain Oriental Churches.

ARCHITECTURE. The ecclesiastical design and erection of Catholic and Christian buildings received its great-est impetus in the 11th century, although it dates back to the 4th century. The first phase followed the edict of Constantine (313 A.D.) and was adapted from Roman and Greek building. It is known as the Latin or Basilican. The progress then was through the Byzantine, the Romanesque, Gothic, Renaissance, which followed the styles of the several countries, thence to the Baroque or Rococo, and finally to the modern revival which is chiefly Gothic but with various adaptations. In the 20th century there is an emphasis upon a departure from the traditional to a more functional design, centering on liturgical simplicity, and marked by the uses of new materials, as concrete, etc. In the 11th century, architecture broadened to include the allied religious arts, as mosaics, bronze work, enamel work, stained glass, and woodwork. Ecclesiastical architecture extends to churches, monasteries, convents, chapels, bell towers and, less properly, schools and some hospitals.

ARCHIVES, term for both the place and the contents. As contents, they are records pertaining to the spiritual and temporal affairs of the Church; as place, it means where such records are kept. The archives may be *diocesan* or *papal.* They are maintained under lock because of the nature of the documents; the chancellor of the diocese has the key, and permission of the bishop or of both the vicar-general and the chancellor is needed for admission. Canon law requires that a catalogue or index be kept of all documents.

ARCHIVIST, the chancellor of a diocese or the one who has care of the archives of a diocese.

ARCHPRIEST. 1. Formerly a title conferred on one who took the place of the bishop in civil affairs or public worship. Now it is applied to a *dean*. **2.** The priest who assists the newly ordained priest at his first Mass or who assists at the solemn Mass of major prelates. As such he is vested in a cope.

ARCOSOLIUM, an arched recess over the sepulcher of one buried in the catacombs. Within this arched area, Mass was celebrated on the stone slab above the tomb.

ARCULAE, the small boxes used for carrying the Blessed Sacrament in the early persecutions of the Church. A primitive form of the pyx. (*Cf.* ARCA.)

AREOPAGITE, name applied to one who practiced or spoke in the outdoor court of Areopagus, located on a hill near Athens.

ARGIA, literally inactivity, but in Church usage applied to the refraining from servile work on Sundays and holydays, and to other practices of a spiritual nature.

ARIANISM. This heresy was condemned at the Council of Nicaea in 325. It took its name from Arius, a priest of Alexandria who was trained at Antioch. The heresy was probably based in part on Judaism, Eclecticism, and the Sophists. It taught that the Son of God is not of one nature or substance with God the Father, nor equal to Him in dignity and not co-eternal.

ARIEL, name given to the city of Jerusalem (Is. 29:1), meaning "hearth of God."

ARK. 1. The boat built by Noe at the time of the flood (Gen. 6) and which later was cited as a type of the Church (1 Pet. 3:20). **2.** Sometimes referred to the basket in which Moses was placed after being born and which was found by Pharaoh's daughter (Ex. 2:1–22). **3.** The "Ark of the Covenant" (Ex. 37:1–9) which was a chest of acacia wood overlaid within and without with gold. Its cover was of pure gold and was the place of propitiation on which the blood of the sacrificial victims was sprinkled on the Feast of Atonement. The word is referred to Christ in Rom. 3:25 in this sense of having offered Himself for our sins. The ark contained the Decalogue, a lasting testimony of the Sinaitic covenant; it was also to serve as the throne of Yahweh. Ark of the Covenant is a title given to the Blessed Virgin to signify her divine motherhood.

ARLES, COUNCILS OF. The first of these councils of the Church assembled in this city of southern France in 314 to settle the Donatist dispute. Later there were seventeen more councils convened there, the last in 1273.

ARMAGEDON, the place mentioned in Apoc. 16:13–16 where the beast and the false prophet will meet in final combat with Christ. The place is identified as the "mountain of Megiddo" which was in the plain of Esdraelon; the plain was vulnerable to attack in Jewish history, especially with the forces descending from Megiddo.

ARMENIAN CHURCH. In Armenia, in northern Asia Minor, the Church was outstanding until the Council of Constantinople (381). After the defeat of the Armenians by the Persians in the 7th century, the people gave way to heresies. At the time of Chalcedon (593), the Church was split; some followed Rome but the majority set up a separate church. Efforts for reconciliation have failed.

ARMENIAN RITE, the rite of the Armenian Church which originally was in the Syriac language but is now in ancient Armenian. It is used by the Uniat and Gregorian churches, both separated from Rome.

ART, CHRISTIAN. The fine arts were used by the Church from earliest times. Their Christian character is found in their expression and in the use to which they are put in service of the Church. Many examples of primitive Christian art are found in the catacombs. From here more than any other place came the use of symbols which were both a religious and a "guarded" method of expression. Once the Christians were given freedom of worship, art became an expression in the decoration of churches and a means of teaching, since reading was enjoyed only by the scholars. It became the means of expressing Christian ideas and doctrines, in mosaics, paintings, stained glass, calligraphy, illumination of manuscripts, work with metals for vessels of the Mass, woodcarving, and textiles. It became a part of church architecture and centered around the doctrine and teaching of the Church. It allied later with the whole of the fine arts, influencing writing, music and sculpture as well as painting. It remains a part of the life of the Church, depicting the truths of faith. Art as such must be theologically sound in expression, because of its tradition, while at the same time being governed by dignity in approach. Esoteric forms have consistently been discouraged.

ARTICLES OF FAITH. *See* DOGMA.

ARTOKLASIA, the final service of Vespers in the Greek Church at which five loaves of bread and measures of wine and oil are blessed and incensed.

ASCENSION OF CHRIST, the "going up" into heaven of Christ by His own power, in the presence of the apostles, the Blessed Mother, and His disciples, forty days after His Resurrection (Acts 1:6–12). St. Thomas asserts that He ascended, not indeed by the power proper to a natural body, but by the virtue proper to Him as God and by that which belongs to a blessed spirit. The feast commemorating the event was celebrated in the Church from earliest times. It is a holyday of obligation occurring forty days after Easter.

ASCETAE, the false teaching that through bodily exercise, discipline of the senses, and moral faculties of man, one could rise to spiritual heights; a form of Christian stoicism. It is paralleled today in the beliefs of yoga and some of the Christian Science beliefs. The term also applies to followers of the practice, who held themselves to be a group between the laity and the clergy, or semi-religious.

ASCETERION also **ASCETERY,** name given to a monastery or home for religious where they could retire for the practice of spiritual exercises; in some respects a retreat-house.

ASCETICAL THEOLOGY, that branch of theology which is strictly a part of moral theology, or an intermediate study between moral theology (the study of God's laws, and right and wrong acts) and mystical theology (the study of the extraordinary ways of perfection). Thus ascetical theology rises a step above moral theology and considers the methods by which we may make progress in the pursuit of perfection by study and practice of the ordinary means of self-discipline, prayer, and the sacraments, by which we bring ourselves gradually more in harmony with the will of God and progress to our end—personal salvation. It has been variously named: the science of the saints; the spiritual science; and the science of perfection. (*Cf.* THEOLOGY.)

ASCETICISM, a term from the Greek, meaning exercise or effort. It is the name given to the "science that deals with the efforts necessary to the acquisition of Christian perfection." It is the practice of principles learned through a study of ascetical theology.

ASEITY, the characteristic of a being that exists by virtue of its own nature, independent of all else. It affirms absolute existence; it excludes any external causality. It means a being whose existence proceeds from a nature which is in itself its own existence—thus, only God is such a being. It is the prime attribute of God from which we infer all other attributes, and it expresses the very essence of God.

ASH WEDNESDAY, the first day in the present Church calendar of the observance of the forty days of Lent. It takes its name from the solemn ceremony of the liturgy of the day wherein the ashes of palms are blessed and then marked on the foreheads of the faithful in the form of a cross with the accompanying words, "Remember, man, you are dust and to dust you shall return." It is thus a solemn call to penance so that one may enjoy eternal life.

ASPERGES, term applied to the sprinkling with holy water of the altar, clergy and people by the celebrant before a high Mass. Its name is taken from the first words of Psalm 50 which is recited by the celebrant and sung by the choir. During the Easter season the antiphon *"Vidi aquam"* replaces the Psalm.

ASPERGILLUM

ASPERGILLUM, the instrument, with handle and container, used to sprinkle holy water during liturgical ceremonies, blessings or consecrations.

ASPIRATIONS, short prayers expressing sentiments of charity or petition. Many aspirations are indulgenced, e.g., "My Jesus, mercy." (*Cf.* EJACULATION.)

ASSESSOR, a consultor to a judge in an ecclesiastical court.

ASSOCIATIONS LAW. Enacted in 1901 by the French government, the law forbade the forming of religious groups of men or women without an act of legislation by the civil government. As such it limited the Church and deprived it of rights. It became inoperative in 1928.

ASSUMPTION OF THE BLESSED VIRGIN MARY, the doctrine of the taking up of the body and soul of the Mother of God into heaven after her death. It was an early teaching of the fathers and was of special interest to all Christians. Tradition and theological reasoning show that the privilege of the Assumption was revealed implicitly. In 1951, Pope Pius XII declared the Assumption of the Blessed Mother of God a doctrine of faith. The feast is celebrated on Aug. 15 and is a holyday of obligation.

ASTROLOGY, the practice of attempting to determine actions by the influence of the stars on the bodies of men. It is based upon probabilities, but in no way can such prediction of the future be made, since the will of man is free. It was condemned in 1586 by Pope Sixtus V and by Urban VIII in 1631.

ASYLUM, historically, a place where one could enter to escape harm or avoid pursuit from the law; also called *sanctuary*. Now it refers to an institution where dependents or orphans may be given the best of care and enjoy the benefits of social supervision until such time as placement may be made in a normal environment.

ATHANASIAN CREED, an approved expression of the beliefs of faith, said to have been written by St. Athanasius. It is recited in the Divine Office on Trinity Sunday.

ATHEISM, the opinion that God does not exist. It can be a denial of God as a first cause; or the substitution of some lesser object in the place of God. It is moral atheism when it is held that human acts have no morality with reference to a divine lawgiver, sometimes called practical atheism. (*Cf.* GOD.)

ATONEMENT. Through His Incarnation, suffering and death on the cross, Christ reconciled sinners to God. Atonement was the essential element of the redemption of mankind by Christ. This was the promise of God the Father who reconciled humanity to Himself through His divine Son, and Christ by His perfect obedience gave back to ·His Father the worship that was violated by sin. Christ is thus the Mediator of men because He won for Himself the glory to which He was destined by the Father, and also pardon for men. Through Christ we have remission of sins, reconciliation with God, the graces of salvation and justification (2 Cor. 5:18f).

ATTENTION, the directing of our mind and senses to the accomplishment of some task which is undertaken. In a spiritual sense, it is the care we have in prayer, the receiving and administering of the sacraments. Thus in vocal prayer, we should say the prayers with correct pronunciation so that we may be led to think of what the words mean; in mental prayer we should concentrate on the subject of our meditation without distraction so that the most beneficial affections or response may be aroused; and in the reception or administering of the sacraments we should be aware without distraction so that there may be no mistake and that our intention may be of the highest order.

ATTRIBUTES OF GOD. Everything which distinguishes God from His creatures may be called an attribute of God. The Jews placed emphasis on three attributes of God, majesty, spirituality, and holiness. However, we mean more basic concepts which arise out of the understanding of God's nature by reason when we speak of His attributes. God's essence is one with His existence (*cf.* ASEITY).

His attributes also are identical with His nature and are infinite and perfect because nothing can be less in one whose nature is in itself infinite and perfect. In speaking of the attributes of Christ we recognize three classes of properties: (a) those which are His because of His divine nature, e.g., omnipotence; (b) those which are His because of His human nature, e.g., His capacity for suffering; (c) those which are His because of the union of His two natures in one divine Person, e.g., His Mediatorship. (*Cf.* GOD.)

ATTRITION. As used by spiritual writers, this means an imperfect sorrow for sin; an imperfect contrition because it is wanting in motive. Thus the sorrow, hatred of sin committed, and the resolve of not sinning again and sorrow for having offended God, not because of pure love of God, which would be perfect contrition, but because of a lesser reason such as the fear of hell. This is nevertheless good, and results from the grace of God.

AUDIENCES, PAPAL, the visits or conferences with major and minor officials of the Roman Curia or an official of the Holy See or of the diplomatic corps whereby the Holy Father carries on the work of the Church. These are· arranged in a regular schedule. Besides these the pope receives in private conference the great majority of bishops of the world. There are also interviews with the press, dignitaries, or individuals which are granted, whether in public (many people at one time) or private (one person), in a reception parlor of the Vatican palace. Such visits and interviews for lay persons are granted upon letters of recommendation of their bishop or upon appeal to the Vatican master of the chamber.

AUGSBURG, DIET OF. *See* DIET OF AUGSBURG.

AUGUSTINISM, term sometimes applied to the philosophical and theological teachings of St. Augustine (354–430), especially his theories on grace.

AUMBRY. *See* AMBRY.

AUREOLE

AUREOLE, the golden blaze often seen around the sun which was borrowed by artists of the Middle Ages to portray the heavenly glory of the saints. It is usually represented by a gold-colored haze or shafts of gold surrounding the figure of the saint in an oval shape. However, it is depicted also by a halo or nimbus. The aureole of the saints in theology is defined as a certain accidental reward of happiness and merit over and above the usual which is given to saints in heaven to distinguish them because of their special degree of sanctity in overcoming the world. St. Thomas says that this mark of excellence is given to virgins, martyrs, doctors of the Church and preachers.

AURICULAR CONFESSION, the declaration by voice of one's sins to the priest in receiving the sacrament of penance. It is so called because it is spoken "to the ear" and, thus, distinguished from public confession. In the early days of the Church, public confession and public penance were frequent, but since the 4th century auricular confession has been the accepted method.

AUSTERITIES, the rigorous practices of self-mortification imposed on oneself in the attaining of perfection. Many of the saints practiced various austerities such as: unusual fasts, abstaining from sleep, use of flagellation, wearing a hairshirt, etc. Such practices while they are commendable should not be lightly undertaken, and usually only upon the advice of a spiritual director or confessor.

AUTHENTICITY, BIBLICAL. Though often referred to the inerrancy of the Bible, it is directed primarily at the trustworthiness of the text, its official recognition by authorities and the exactness with which it expresses the known thought of the Scriptures. The Scriptures derive their authenticity first from the authors of the books and second from the studied declaration of the Church.

AUTHORITY, the power of self-government in the Church, derived from its foundation by Christ and from His teachings. In action, it means the co-operation of all members toward their ultimate sanctification in Christ. Inasmuch as the Church is a society, its authority has a corresponding subordination, that is, the ministers and those ministered to, or as St. Paul expresses it, a "blending of authority and humility," as interpreted from his Epistles. This authority of the Church, possessed by the Church as a society, may not be usurped by others, for example, the state, since it is the purpose of the Church to sanctify all. The authority

of the Church in her accredited officials, her ministers, is to be exercised within the "body of its followers," the faithful. Hence, such as have a ministering role exercise that also in a humble co-operation, realizing that theirs is the responsibility of proclaiming the Word, Christ, to all men. It is through this *authority* that organic harmony is had within the Church not only in the spiritual mission of the Church but also in maintaining the firmness of the human structure which derives first from Christ and second from the apostles.

AUTOCEPHALI, a name given in the Greek Church to archbishops or metropolitans who are not subject to a patriarch, but instead are responsible to a provincial synod or the Holy See.

AUTO-DA-FE, the public ceremony of the 16th century, especially in Spain wherein the decision of a court of the Inquisition was proclaimed. This gradually evolved into a semi-religious and official action of the Church and state authorities. It consisted of a procession, condemnation of the guilty, reconciliation of the penitent, the pardoning of those previously sentenced or "paroled." After the ceremony the guilty were turned over to authorities of the state for the carrying out of the sentences.

AUTOS SACRAMENTALES, religious plays, like the earlier "miracle and morality" plays, put on during the season of Corpus Christi in Spain in the late 17th and early 18th centuries. They were intended to instruct the people in the doctrine of the Eucharist, but were suppressed because they departed from their purpose.

AUXILIARY BISHOP, a titular bishop appointed by the Holy See who does not have jurisdiction but a fullness of holy orders, and who assists a ruling bishop of a diocese in carrying out the work of that diocese. Because they are not appointed to a diocese in a jurisdictional capacity, they are named titular bishops and, unless by special privilege, do not have the right to succeed to the governance of the diocese should it become vacant.

AVARICE or **COVETOUSNESS,** one of the capital sins. It is the inordinate love of temporal or earthly things, particularly riches. It need not be the direct possession of money or wealth. It is inordinate when one is not guided by reason, or by suitableness or need, or when one goes to unusual lengths for attainment or is selfish or miserly in giving. This vice leads to failures of charity through hardness of heart, a worried state of mind over possible loss or failure to obtain, and dishonesty and unjust practices in acquiring wealth. Its opposite virtue is liberality, a balanced attitude toward wealth, and the control or moderation of one's desires. (*Cf.* ALMS.)

AVE MARIA, literally "Hail Mary." (*Cf.* ANGELICAL SALUTATION.)

AVERSION, the opposite of desire. Theologically, it is said to be directed against the good, the useful, or the pleasurable. (*Cf.* DETACHMENT.)

AZYMITES, a name, not always derogatory, applied by Greek schismatics to members of the Roman Church because the latter use unleavened bread in the Eucharist.

BABEL, TOWER OF, a structure near the site of ancient Babylon, probably at what is today Bias-Nimrud. The inhabitants started to build this great stage-tower or ziggurat but could not complete it (Gen. 11:1–9). The popular story is that by miraculous intervention, God introduced different languages among the population and thus effected the stopping of the work, which was one of pride and arrogance together with a will to intimidate enemies. The tower had arisen to a height of 60 feet. It is more accurately accepted that because of discord and lack of harmony in settling on a policy, the work was halted and a migration started. As early as the 4th century, St. Gregory of Nyssa was emphatic in declaring that God did not impose a variety of languages upon mankind. Etymologically, the name *babel* means "Gate of God."

BABYLONIAN CAPTIVITY. This was a period of exile of 70 years which began in 605 B.C. with the first deportation of the Jews and continued until 537 B.C. when the 42,-360 Jews and 7,337 slaves were led back to Judah by Zorobabel after a decree by Cyrus the Great permitting their return. The Jews had been induced, under Sedecias, against the inspired counsels of the prophet, Jeremias, to revolt against Nabuch-odonosor in 587 B.C. after having suffered two defeats and the partial deportation and enslavement of their people. This was the final blow and upon defeat the temple was destroyed, Jerusalem laid waste and all but a few taken into captivity (3 and 4 Kings).

BALDAQUIN (2)

BALDAQUIN also **BALDACHIN** and **BALDACCHINO. 1.** A lesser civory or *ciborium*, which is a smaller, lighter structure of metal, wood, or cloth-covered framework which is projected over the altar and its footpace. It consists of the canopy which is a roof-like projection supported by chains from above or from brackets, or by two posts; with this, descending from the canopy behind the altar is a dossal. This baldaquin has a symbolic meaning since it is representative of the *arcosolium*, and has a practical purpose since it protects the Eucharist from falling dirt. However, this latter use in modern construction might be said to be symbolic also (*cf.* CIVORY; TESTER). **2.** The canopy supported on four poles which is carried above the priest who carries the Blessed Sacrament in procession. **3.** The canopy which is projected above an episcopal throne.

BALM or **BALSAM,** an aromatic resin derived from the terebinth tree or certain West Indies trees which is mixed with olive oil and then blessed as Holy Chrism. (*Cf.* CHRISM.)

BALTIMORE, COUNCILS OF. A series of provincial councils and plenary councils held at Baltimore, Maryland, by the bishops of the United States. The first provincial council was convoked in 1829 by Bishop England to settle problems confronting the Church in America and published decrees to promote religious life among the twenty-eight states and territories. Some of the problems were: providing Catholic literature, dispelling Protestant prejudice, and amendment of the trustee system. Six other provincial councils followed the first. Then there was convoked the first plenary council in 1852 whose main objectives, following rapid growth of the Church, were to unify the Catholics, to check the trend toward mixed marriages and promote Catholic education. It was here that the bishops decreed that parochial schools should be started

wherever possible, that catechism instruction be given to children and seminaries created in each diocese or province. After the Civil War, in 1866, the second plenary council convened. It was one of consolidation. In 1884 the third plenary council was called. It is designated the great educational council, for at this parents were commanded to see that their children receive a Christian education, parochial schools were to be erected near churches, a uniform catechism was prepared, annual collections for Negroes and Indians were prescribed, a wide distribution of Catholic literature called for, and secret societies censured. These Councils laid the groundwork for the Church and its missionary work in the growing United States. Now the work of the N.C.W.C., the administrative boards of the hierarchy, and the bishops' annual meeting in Washington, D. C., carries the Church's program to its expanding membership.

BANGOR ANTIPHONARY, an old Latin manuscript codex which was at the library of Bobbio and later sent to the Ambrosian library at Milan.

BANNER. 1. The ornamental cloth supported on a crossbeam above a single upright which during a sermon is placed before the exposed Blessed Sacrament. **2.** Any such banner, or mounted cloth, which is carried in procession as an emblem of a society or an order of knighthood in the Church.

BANNS, the public proclamation of an intended marriage, given on three successive Sundays or holydays of obligation during Mass or at a service where the attendance is large. The banns are for the purpose of helping to determine if any impediments exist to the proposed marriage, and should be published by the pastor of the two parties or where they have legal residence or a domicile. If the marriage does not take place before the expiration of six months, the banns must be repeated. This question of banns is governed by canon law which permits exceptions and dispensations according to the decision of the ordinary (c. 1023–1030).

BAPTISM. Christ gave His command to baptize universally to the apostles: "All power in heaven and on earth has been given to Me. Go, therefore, and make disciples of all nations, baptizing them in the name of the Father and of the Son, and of the Holy Spirit" (Mt. 28:18f). And baptism was the normal conclusion of the apostolic preaching and teaching (Acts 2:37f). The effects of this sacrament are: (a) it cleanses us from original sin; (b) it makes us Christians through grace by sharing in Christ's death and Resurrection and setting up an initial program of living (1 Cor. 6:9–11); (c) it makes us children of God as the life of Christ is brought forth within us (Rom. 8:15–17); (d) it makes us heirs of heaven for through baptism we "walk by the Spirit" whereby we will possess the Kingdom of God (Gal. 5:21–25). The ordinary minister of baptism is the priest, but in cases of necessity any person may baptize by pouring ordinary water on the forehead, saying while pouring: "I baptize you in the name of the Father, and of the Son and of the Holy Ghost." Infants should be baptized as soon as possible (c. 770), and whoever would defer it without reason for more than three weeks to a month would sin grievously. Baptism is the sacrament of mystical union with Christ which creates a

new society, the "glorious Church" which is the body of Christ (1 Cor. 12:13ff).

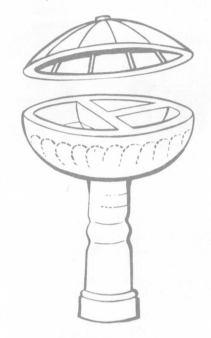

BAPTISMAL FONT

BAPTISMAL FONT, the permanent or semi-permanent basin where baptism is administered.

BAPTISMAL NAME, name given to the one baptized. It is taken from the list of the saints of the Church. The saint then is the person's patron, whose virtues it is hoped the person will imitate.

BAPTISMAL ROBE. See CHRISMAL.

BAPTISMAL VOWS, the three renunciations required of all adults before the sacrament of baptism is conferred, and spoken in behalf of infants by the sponsors. They are given in the form of three questions addressed to the one to be baptized and ask for the renunciation of Satan, all his works, and all his pomps.

BAPTISMAL WATER, the water, blessed in the baptismal font on Holy Saturday, which must be used in solemn baptism.

BAPTISTERY, the portion of the church set apart for the administering of baptism, wherein the baptismal font is located. It should be near the main entrance of the church.

BAREFOOTED FRIARS, name given to any discalced monks.

BAROQUE STYLE IN ART. This style of architecture and art expression is characterized by sweeping imagination, picturesqueness, immensity, and harmony between the building and environment by the suggestion of movement. Baroque arose in the 16th century and is generally considered as an expression of the Counter Reformation. It was flamboyantly aristocratic, international and unified; while it produced some excellent architecture it often degenerated into showiness and a straining after effect merely for effect's sake. For this reason it is said to be the end of the Christian content of art and was generally condemned without always receiving recognition for its merits.

BASILIAN RULE, the method of religious life propounded by St. Basil the Great (d. 379) who was a founder of the religious life and the first to insert the obligation of a vow. His rule prescribed poverty, chastity and placed great emphasis on obedience, required fasting five days a week, set hours of meditation, study, work and community prayers. It was the basis of many religious rules which were to follow. The monks were called Basilians.

BASILICA, formerly a place of justice or civic hall which consisted of a long hall with an apse at one end. Later Christian churches built over the tombs of martyrs were so named. Today it is merely a title of honor given to various kinds of churches. There are two classes of basilicas, *major* and *minor*. There are four *major* basilicas, all in Rome: St. John Lateran—the Cathedral of Rome, St. Peter's of the Vatican, St. Paul's outside the Walls, and St. Mary Major. The basilica of St. Lawrence outside the Walls at one time held the title and privileges of these four. The title of *minor* basilica is granted to certain churches by the pope, their clergy have precedence in rank and certain decorative insignia which indicates their dependence on the pope, and the papal arms may be displayed on the churches' exteriors.

BASILIDIANS, followers of the Gnostic heresy who practiced magic.

BASLE, COUNCILS OF, councils of the 15th century (1423, 1431) which followed the great schism of the papacy. These councils adopted measures for reform of the Roman chancery, and regulation of official fees, etc.

BEADS, popular, descriptive name given to the rosary. (*Cf.* ROSARY.)

BEADSMAN or BEDESMAN, a title of the Middle Ages for one who prayed for the soul of another.

BEATIFICATION, the declaration made by the pope that one of the faithful because of a life of virtue or the heroic death of martyrdom is entitled *blessed*, i.e., is living in the happiness of heaven. This permits veneration of the person, not throughout the Church, but only in those places where the beatified lived or in the houses of the religious community which he or she founded. Beatification is formally the final phase in the cause of one who is being considered for ultimate canonization. The pope's declaration states that the cause may proceed and fixes the date for the ceremony in St. Peter's which is the reading of the decree of beatification, the unveiling of the picture of the "Blessed" above the chair of St. Peter, the singing of the *Te Deum* and celebration of the newly beatified. The pope does not take a personal part in this ceremony, only assisting at Benediction in the evening and veneration of the relics of the beatified. (*Cf.* CAUSE; CANONIZATION.)

BEATIFIC VISION. By definition of Pope Benedict XII, this is an act of the intellect of the blessed in heaven which is the clear, intuitive, immediate sight of the divine essence which is God. Its clarity is the dispelling of the knowledge we have of God either as reflected in created things, by reason or by faith. Its intuitive and immediate character is found in its immeasurably superior knowledge to any knowledge we might have otherwise and is the supreme reality of the living God giving intrinsic evidence of the Trinity. The blessed "see" because they are elevated by the "light of glory" of the higher faculties of intellect and will arising from the consummation of sanctifying grace which being fully developed makes the blessed able to see God as He sees Himself. It is the fulfillment of men's happiness, seeing all in the light of supreme Truth.

BEATITUDE OF HEAVEN, the good which satisfies perfectly and completely the desire of created things. It is (a) essential, consisting of the vision of God and is consummated in the love which follows the vision; (b) accidental, which is the aggregate of the things we possess in possessing God, as glorified bodies, society of the blessed, etc. One's beatitude in heaven will be the eternal preservation in souls of all they have by nature and grace and the degree of beatitude will be according to merit, hence each shall not have the same degree of beatitude in heaven.

BEATITUDES, THE EIGHT. These are the blessings spoken by our Lord at the Sermon on the Mount (Mt. 5:1–12). The place where our Lord spoke was probably a hill near Capharnaum, above the plain of Genesar. The qualities meriting the blessings as given in the pronouncements of Christ outline a single, consistent spiritual outlook. They assure entry, or possession of the kingdom of God (heaven), and are guarantees to: the poor in spirit, the meek, the mourners, the seekers of justice, the merciful, the peacemakers, the clean of heart, the persecuted. Some theologians acknowledge only seven, eliminating that of the justice-seekers. Also there are some who name an additional "beatitude," the "evangelical beatitude" of believing without seeing as given in Jn. 20:29.

BEAURAING, OUR LADY OF. This title of our Blessed Mother derived from the village of Beauraing in Belgium where the Blessed Virgin appeared thirty times during a period from Nov. 29, 1932 to Jan. 3, 1933, to five children: Fernande, Gilberte, and Albert Voisin; Andrée and Gilberte Degeimbre. Final approbation of the apparitions was given July 2,

1949. The message given was a promise to convert sinners. It was, next to the apparitions of Fatima, the most significant mystical occurrence of the twentieth century.

BEAUTIFUL GATE, THE. This is the name of one of the entries of Herod's temple (Acts, 3) which is not identified clearly by archaeology but is believed to be the same as the Corinthian Gate of Josephus located on the east side of the inner enclosure leading from the outer court to the Women's Court.

BEAUTY. Philosophically, beauty consists of intuitive knowledge and delight. It is received through the intellect as its power or sense and has three integral elements: integrity, proportion or consonance, and radiance or clarity. (*Cf.* AESTHETICS.) Spiritual beauty, however, is the shining forth in the soul of a person of the reflected virtues of Christ.

BEFANA, a fair or carnival held at Rome during the season of Epiphany.

BEGUINES and **BEGHARDS,** associations of laymen of the 13th century who followed the religious rule of St. Francis or St. Dominic but who did not take vows. They were suppressed because of heresy.

BEING, in philosophy, that which is or has the notion of reality. It embraces all essences of the actual and conceptual order, the latter having existence in their causes. Being, reality, essence are synonymous.

BELFRY, an extended structure above a church as a steeple where church bells are housed. It also applies to the frame supporting the bells. When such a tower stands independent of the church proper it is called a *campanile.* (*q.v.*)

BELL, BOOK, and **CANDLE,** a symbolic act of medieval times. With the reading of a sentence of major excommunication the book was being closed, the lighted candle thrown to the ground while the bell tolled.

BELLS. When blessed (incorrectly called a "baptism") or consecrated, bells are sacramentals of the Church and used in the service of religion. Thus they may be a large church bell, a carillon of many bells, or the small sanctuary bell used during Mass. They have been used since the 6th century.

BEMA, literally, a step. In the Greek Orthodox Church it is the space surrounding the Holy Table behind the iconostasis.

BENEDICITE, the Latin title of the Canticle of the Three Children (Dan. 3:51–90). It is a hymn of praise in the form of a litany psalm.

BENEDICTINES, followers of the rule established by St. Benedict shortly before his death in 543. He is called the "Father of Western Monasticism." His rule cultivated the family spirit of the community, established moderation as an ideal, and exacted no unusual austerities. The monks were to be self-supporting and spend their lives under an abbot with full authority. The rule began in Monte Cassino in 529 and the movement spread and became a great force in the development of Europe.

BENEDICTIONALE, a non-liturgical book containing a collection of blessings from the Ritual, Missal, and Pontifical.

BENEDICTION OF THE BLESSED SACRAMENT, a devotion to the Eucharistic Christ in the Roman rite. It consists of exposition of the Blessed Sacrament in the monstrance, adoration of the faithful, hymns, the blessing where the priest makes the sign of the cross with the Blessed Sacrament over the people, and the recitation of Divine Praises.

BENEDICTION WITH CIBORIUM, a less solemn form of Benediction of the Blessed Sacrament. It consists of opening the tabernacle door so that the ciborium containing the Blessed Sacrament can be seen, hymns, and the blessing of the people in the form of the cross with the ciborium containing the Blessed Sacrament.

BENEMERENTI MEDAL—Bestowed by Pope Pius XII.

BENEDICTUS, Latin title of the canticle of Zachary as recorded in Lk. 1:68–79. It marks the recovery of Zachary's speech, and is in the form of a prayer for the people. Its chief feature is that the Messias, born of the house of David, is hailed as a divine being.

BENEFICE, the juridical right established by competent Church authority in favor of an ecclesiastical person, for the life of the person, whereby the revenue from some Church property is received by the person for the discharge of his spiritual office. These are controlled now by canon law with certain exceptions permitted because of concordats between governments and the Vatican.

BENEFIT OF CLERGY, the privilege granted to persons in holy orders to be tried in the diocesan court rather than the civil court, except in cases of treason or arson. The benefit was denied by Congress in 1790 in the United States.

BENEMERENTI MEDALS, pontifical decorations originated by Gregory XVI. They are awarded for exceptional military or civic service and are worn suspended about the neck by ribbons of the papal colors.

BERRETTA. *See* BIRETTA.

BESTIARIES, books of the Middle Ages having descriptions and pictures of animals, both real and fabled. They served to instruct, were often the basis of animal symbols, and were sources for the use of animals in decoration, as the gargoyles in Gothic architecture.

BETROTHAL also **ESPOUSAL,** the formal mutual promise of future valid and lawful marriage. Made in due canonical form, a betrothal must (a) be in writing; (b) the date and year must be given with the day and month indicated; (c) it must be attested by the signatures of the persons betrothed, by either the parish priest, the ordinary, or two witnesses. It can be rescinded by mutual consent (c. 1318).

BIBLE. Holy Scripture, the Scriptures, or the Bible are the names given to the sacred books of the Jews and Christians. The Bible is the inspired word of God written under inspiration of the Holy Spirit and gathered in the order of the providence of God, which destined man to a supernatural end. In keeping with that divine decree, there follows that it is necessary that God's purpose be supernaturally revealed, that God be known, and His counsels and goodness be made manifest. This heavenly knowledge is the written portions of the divine tradition which is formed of Scripture and historic tradition, and makes up the font of doctrine and teaching in the Church. The Bible has been called the Book of Spiritual Perfection, for to be ignorant of the Bible is to be wanting in the knowledge of Christ. Pope St. Pius X lists three rewards to be gained in the reading of the Bible: spiritual delight, love of Christ, and zeal for His cause.

The Bible is divided in two chief parts: the books of the Old Testament and those of the New Testament. In all there are 72 books in the Bible. In the O.T. there are 21 historical books whose contents tell of the early history of the world, man and the Jewish nation, and are: Genesis, Exodus, Leviticus, Numbers, Deuteronomy, Josue, Judges, Ruth, 1, 2, 3 and 4 Kings; 1 and 2 Chronicles; 1 and 2 Esdras (Nehemias); Tobias, Judith, Esther, and 1 and 2 Machabees. In the O.T. there are seven didactic books: Job, Psalms, Proverbs, Ecclesiastes, Canticle of Canticles, Wisdom and Ecclesiasticus; and finally 17 books of prophesy: Isaias, Jeremias and Lamentations, Baruch, Ezechiel, Daniel, Osee, Joel, Amos, Abdias, Jonas, Micheas, Nahum, Habacuc, Sophonias, Aggeus, Zacharias and Malachias. In the N.T. there are: five historical books: the Gospels of Matthew, Mark, Luke and John, and the Acts of the Apostles; 21 doctrinal books: the 14 epistles of St. Paul and those of James, 1 and 2 of Peter, 1, 2, and 3 of John, and that of Jude; and one prophetical book, the Apocalypse (*cf.* CANON OF SCRIPTURE; INSPIRATION). Spiritual favors or indulgences may be gained, by decree of Leo XII, Dec. 13, 1898, as follows: "The faithful who spend at least a quarter of an hour in reading Holy Scripture with the great reverence due to the Word of God and after the manner of spiritual reading may gain an indulgence of 300 days, and a plenary indulgence may be gained monthly by those who make this reading a daily practice."

BIBLE SOCIETIES, biblical associations founded to spread the reading, study, and meditation of the Scriptures. The encyclical *Divino afflante Spiritu* treats of this modern biblical study. Such groups should be under the direction of competent religious authorities.

BIBLIA PAUPERUM, literally "Bibles of the Poor." These were popular picture books of the Bible of about 40 pages, each with short explanatory texts used in the 15th century.

BIBLICAL COMMISSION. The official title of this group is *Pontificia Commissio de Re Biblica.* It was established as a commission under the Holy Father by Pope Leo XIII when he issued his apostolic letter *Vigilantiae* on Oct. 30, 1902. Its stated purpose is to procure "that Holy Writ should everywhere among us receive that more elaborate treatment which the times require and be preserved intact not only from any breath of error but also from all rash opinions."

BIBLICAL INSTITUTE OF JERUSALEM, a biblical school founded at Jerusalem by the Dominicans, especially Lagrange, in 1889. It publishes a quarterly, *Revue Biblique.*

BIBLICAL INSTITUTE, PONTIFICAL. Established by apostolic letter, *Vinea Electa*, of May 7, 1909, the Institute is directed to the promotion of the reading and understanding of the Bible. It publishes a biblical quarterly, *Biblica*, which is a scientific treatise, and a less technical bimonthly called *Verbum Domini.*

BILL OF RIGHTS. In the United States the first ten amendments of the Constitution. The bishops of the United States declared at Washington, D. C., Nov. 16, 1952: "The concept of man which they set forth in the Declaration of Independence and on which they based the Constitution and our Bill of Rights, is essentially a religious concept—a concept inherited from Christian tradition."

BILOCATION, the actual presence of one finite person in two places at the same time. This is not impossible according to reason, since it does not mean the extension of the body or increase of its substance but rather the multiplication of the person's bodily relations to other bodies.

BINATION, also called "duplicating." This is the permission given to a priest to celebrate more than one Mass on a single day, granted by the ordinary and limited to two Masses, except by apostolic indult. Its purpose is to provide a sufficient number of Masses to give all the faithful a chance to fulfill their obligations.

BIRETTA, a stiff square cap having three or four projecting "leaves" or prominences rising from the ridges of its top, and usually having a pompom at the top center. It is worn by the clergy: a cardinal's being red, a bishop's purple, and black for other clerics. The pope does not wear a biretta, but instead wears a more loose headpiece called *camauro.*

BIRTH CONTROL. The willful perversion of the natural gifts of God for the engendering of children, whereby conception is prevented: by interrupted or arrested coition, by contraceptive instrument, or by surgery which prohibits the functioning of otherwise healthy organs. The effects of such actions are to limit the number of offspring, to prevent births, and thereby to escape the responsibilities of parenthood. It is essentially wrong because: to employ the sexual function for self-gratification in a manner to prohibit the natural purpose of that function is to pervert the function; to defeat the primary purpose of the marriage relation is to oppose the divine will; the committee of the bishops of the United States stated the position of the Church in a statement of Jan. 30, 1922: "The Church condemns all positive devices and methods of birth control as necessarily immoral because they are perversions of nature and violations of the moral law. Moreover, they lead inevitably to weakening of character, degradation of conjugal relations, decline of population, and degeneracy of national life. As a remedy for social and economic ills, birth control is not only mistaken and futile, but tends to divert attention from genuine methods of social betterment."

BISHOP, a supreme, divinely instituted member of the Church hierarchy. He has received the highest of the holy orders, is invested with the authority to govern a diocese, and is a successor of the apostles. Bishops are responsible directly to the Holy Father for the affairs of their diocese (*cf.* HIERARCHY; JURISDICTION). The sacrament of holy orders, through consecration, confers on a bishop spiritual power in its fullness and he may administer confirmation and holy orders, and consecrate other bishops. Besides administration of the temporal and spiritual affairs of a diocese, it is the bishop's duty (a) to teach, that is to guard the purity of doctrine and see that it is given to others; (b) to guard the morals of the faithful under his care, to maintain discipline, and to provide that the faithful receive the sacraments, and insure divine worship; (c) to reside in his jurisdiction; (d) to visit the parishes of his diocese regularly.

BISHOP, AUXILIARY. *See* AUXILIARY BISHOP.

BISHOP, COADJUTOR. *See* COADJUTOR BISHOP.

BISHOP IN PARTIBUS INFIDELIUM, a bishop consecrated to a diocese which at one time existed in the Church but which, because of the loss of faith in that part of the world, no longer exists as a distinct diocese. He is thus a "titular" bishop and because his diocese as such does not exist he need not make an *ad limina* visit.

BISHOP OF ROME. His Holiness the pope is the bishop of Rome, with the Eternal City as his diocese. He is also: Vicar of Jesus Christ, Successor of St. Peter, Supreme Pontiff, having primacy of honor and supreme power of jurisdiction over the Universal Church, Patriarch of the West, Primate of Italy, Archbishop and Metropolitan of the Province of Rome, and Sovereign of the State of Vatican City (*cf.* PAPACY).

BISHOP, SUFFRAGAN. *See* SUFFRAGAN BISHOP.

BISHOP, TITULAR. *See* BISHOP; BISHOP IN PARTIBUS INFIDELIUM.

BLACK FAST, the strict abstaining from meat, eggs, butter, cheese, and milk.

BLACK FRIARS. 1. Name applied to members of the Dominican order. **2.** Places, notably in England and Scotland, where the Dominicans had monasteries.

BLACK MONKS, name given to members of the Benedictine order.

BLASPHEMY. While originally in English this meant any injurious words or statements, it has come to mean explicitly words or actions dishonoring God; words or actions of irreverence against God. Primarily it means verbal attacks on God, but it includes also thoughts, writing and actions, and is divided into two categories: (a) heretical blasphemy, which is a denial of God's providence, etc., and is more grave because it is also a sin against faith; (b) imprecatory blasphemy which is an imprecation against God that evil may follow. Blasphemy may be indirect in that it is directed against God's attributes, His angels, saints, etc. All blasphemy against God is a grievous sin, the most serious against religion, and transgresses the second commandment (Ex. 20:7).

BLESSED, official Church title conferred on one at the pronouncement of the judgment of beatification.

BLESSED SACRAMENT. *See* EU-
CHARIST, HOLY.

BLESSING. In a scriptural sense,
blessing is always opposed to *cursing*
and means placing a thing or person
under the favor of God, dedicating or
giving something or someone to God.
In its liturgical meaning it is the ceremony and prayer by which an authorized cleric sanctifies persons or things
or invokes God's favor upon them.
The ceremony includes the naming of
the object and the signing of the cross
over it. This latter may be accompanied with a sprinkling of holy
water.

BLESSING, APOSTOLIC, benediction or blessing given by the pope
at the close of liturgical functions at
which he presides and sometimes at
the close of papal audiences. To this
blessing a plenary indulgence is attached. This blessing may also be
delegated by the pope to be given by
others; priests attending the sick at
the moment of death may give the
apostolic blessing. Also this is referred to the blessing or solemn benediction *Urbi et orbi* given by the
pope from the balcony of St. Peter's
after his election and on other solemn
occasions.

BOAT. 1. A symbol in art which
represents the Church, or the boat of
St. Peter as a fisherman. **2.** The container in which incense is kept and
used during liturgical ceremonies. It
is usually accompanied by a small
ladle.

**BODY, RELATION OF SOUL
AND,** the substantial union which is
a human person. Body and soul are
incomplete substances which complete and perfect one another, forming a union of one complete substance. Thus it is the human composite united in one substance and
nature which constitutes the human
person and to which all actions of
which man is capable are ascribed.

BODY, RESURRECTION OF THE,
the conversion whereby the body of a
person, separated from the soul by
death, is reunited with the soul and
restored to its complete condition.
The resurrection is a dogma of faith.
This teaching, first revealed and
found in numerous scriptural texts,
and defined by the Church, is that the
body will live again, will be a part of
the accidental beatitude of heaven
and will be glorified (1 Cor. 15:53).
It is a restoration of our nature, since
body and soul being incomplete without each other, should not be separated from each other (Mt. 5:29; Jn.
5:29; Acts 17:31). (*Cf.* BODY, RELATION
OF SOUL AND).

BOLLANDISTS, name given to the
writers and editors who, led by John
Bolland (d. 1665), a Jesuit of Antwerp, following the plan of the Flem-
ish Jesuit Rosweyde, undertook to
compile a complete lives of the saints.

BOLSHEVISM, the historic forerunner of atheistic communism. The
term was applied in 1903 to the movement of the radical leftists in the
Social Democratic Party in Russia.
They were revolutionaries who moved
into power on Nov. 6, 1917, when
Nicolai Lenin became dictator of
Russia. The aim of bolshevism was:
(a) a so-called liberation of the
people; (b) the overthrow of capitalism and substitution of communism
under the dictatorship of the proletariat; (c) nationalization of all resources and industries. (*Cf.* COMMU-
NISM.)

BONA MORS, name of the Happy
Death Confraternity, founded in the
church of the Gesu in Rome by Fr.

V. Caraffa, in 1648. It was later raised to an archconfraternity and has for its objective the preparing of its members for a good death in grace, through a well-regulated life, and meditation on the Passion of Christ and the suffering of Mary.

BOOK OF HOURS, book used in the Middle Ages, containing prayers, Psalms, antiphons, etc. to be recited at the canonical hours. It was a form of breviary for common use in a monastery.

BRANCH THEORY, THE. This is the misconception, advanced chiefly by Anglicans, that the one, true Church is composed of the Anglican, Catholic and Orthodox Churches. It is opposed to the "oneness" of the Church as a mark of its authority.

BRASSES, engravings on incised sheets of heavy brass, called latten. They were used as memorials of the dead and placed over sepulchers or as ends of sepulchral niches used from the 13th to the 18th century. They were often inscribed with pertinent details or carved with figures of the person buried and so became valuable records.

BREAD OF LIFE, name given to the eucharistic Christ, the sacrament of the body and blood of Christ under the appearances of bread (Jn. 6:35–40). The name was given to Himself by Christ: "I am the bread of life" (Jn. 6:48).

BREAKING OF BREAD, name of a famous fresco in the catacomb of St. Priscilla, in Latin called the *Fractio panis*, depicting the early (2nd century) celebration of the Eucharist. It is also the sign of recognition wherein the apostles at Emmaus knew it was the Lord who spoke with them (Lk. 24:30).

BRETHREN OF THE LORD. Reverence is made in several instances in the Bible to "the brethren" of our Lord (Mt. 12:46; Jn. 7:3). These were not full brothers of our Lord, that is, sons of Joseph and Mary, nor were they half-brothers, that is, sons of Joseph by a former marriage. They were at most cousins of Jesus. Only four of the "brethren" are named in the Gospels: James, Joseph, Simon and Jude.

BREVIARY, liturgical book containing the Divine Office assigned to the canonical hours which must be recited by all persons in major orders and by certain religious. The Breviary is divided into four parts, usually printed as four separate books, for the four quarters of the year, winter, spring, summer and fall. Each part contains: (a) the Psalms arranged for each day of the week; (b) the Proper of the season, the hymns, antiphons, chapters and lessons with responses and versicles for each day of the Church year; (c) the Proper of the saints, prayers, etc. for the immovable feasts of the Church year; (d) the Common of the saints, for feasts of a particular class, e.g., of the Blessed Mother. Each day the office is made up of 8 hours: Matins and Lauds, Prime, Tierce, Sext, None, Vespers and Compline—all governed in the mode of recitation by specific rules. In addition to this Roman Breviary there are other special breviaries used by religious orders in certain places, or monasteries.

BRIDE OF CHRIST, term applied in a figurative sense to (a) the Church (2 Cor. 11:2); (b) a woman who dedicates her virginity by vow to God; (c) a state of mystical union enjoyed by certain saints.

BRIEF, PAPAL, also **BREVE,** a letter issuing from the chancery of the pope, less solemn and formal than a bull, to which has been affixed a seal marked with the Fisherman's Ring.

BROTHERS. Generally, those members of a religious community or society of men who are not priests are called "brother." It may be that some of these may be preparing for the priesthood and prior to ordination are so-called. Others, who have no intention to receive ordination are, properly speaking, brothers who live according to the rule of the religious order, dedicate their lives to service of religion within the purpose of the order, and are frequently referred to as "lay brothers." There are also religious communities of men whose members do not intend to enter the priesthood, but who serve a special purpose of religion in particular fields as education, hospital work, etc.; e.g., Christian Brothers; Brothers of Mary, etc.

BULLARIUM, term applied to any collection of papal bulls.

BULL, PAPAL, a major decree from the Apostolic Chancery. These bulls take their name from the lead seal affixed to them by the official known as the *Plombator.* Formerly all such documents were known as "bulls," but now they are chiefly the Apostolic Bulls for the appointment of bishops, erections of dioceses and decrees of the Sacred Congregations or the pope. The bulls are signed by the Cardinal Chancellor and by two of the Prothonotaries Apostolic of the College of Notaries of the Roman Curia.

BUREAU OF INFORMATION. *See* NATIONAL CATHOLIC WELFARE CONFERENCE.

BURIAL, ECCLESIASTICAL, the interment of the body of a deceased person in consecrated ground after the funeral rites of the Church. This honor is conferred by the Church and can be withheld from some because of grave reasons, as: public life of sin and dying unrepentant; deliberate suicide; membership in forbidden societies; apostasy; heresy or schism; excommunication; interdiction; cremation or dueling. Final determination of such cases is referred to the bishop (c. 1204; 1239–1240).

BURSE

BURSE also **BURSARY, BURSA, PERA. 1.** Known in medieval times as the "corporal case," this is a square (9″ by 9″) case, usually made of two stiff pieces of cardboard, bound at three sides, covered with silk to match the vestments, ornamented with a cross, and lined with linen into which the corporal used at Mass or Benediction is placed. It is carried to the altar above the veiled chalice. **2.** The leather, silk lined purse in which the pyx is carried when the Blessed Sacrament is brought to the sick. To this there are usually attached two tie-bands with which the priest may secure the burse to his person while carrying the host.

BURSE, FINANCIAL, the fund or endowment, in whole or in part, which is invested to provide for the expense of educating one or more aspirants to the priesthood. Such funds may vary according to need and are of no fixed amount as a rule.

BUSKINS, ceremonial stockings, reaching to the knees, worn over the ordinary violet stockings by a bishop when celebrating a pontifical Mass. Buskins are ornamented with embroidery and are usually of silk, matching the color of the vestments, but they are not worn when black vestments are used.

BYZANTINE ART. This form of art, developed in Constantinople in the 4th century, was a combination of early Greek and Christian art, centered on lavish color and somewhat florid decoration. It was protected by the Church, and followed the norms laid down by the Church for art to be used in the expression of religious truths. In architecture, it is characterized by rejection of wood in construction, the use of vaulting, and a balance of thrust and counter-thrust; in sculpture, it did not carve in the round but used flat surface and incised the design; in painting, it was expressed by painting on wood, in miniatures and reached its greatest expression in mosaic work.

BYZANTINE RITE. A development of the Antiochene rite, this is the liturgy followed in the celebration of the Mass, administration of the sacraments and other Church functions, by the Greek Church of the Patriarchate of Constantinople. Next to the Roman, it is the second most used rite. As of now it is a combination of the modifications introduced by St. Basil the Great and St. John Chrysostom after whom the two Greek Mass books are named.

C

CAEREMONIALE EPISCO-PORUM, liturgical book containing the rites and ceremonies to be observed by bishops and certain lesser prelates in performing episcopal acts. It also contains the order of rank to be followed in determining precedence of clergy and lay persons.

CAEREMONIARIUS, an officially appointed master of ceremonies.

CAESAROPAPISM, term applied to the interference of rulers of states or civil authorities with the authority and control of Church affairs exercised by Church officials. Originally this arose at the time of the Roman Empire in the 4th century and as a policy was first called Byzantinism, later caesaropapism. It began when the emperors assumed religious jurisdiction, deciding theological questions by order of the throne, appointed bishops and treated them as officials of the court. It meant a divided authority in the handling of heretics, erroneous teachings and the control of internal affairs of the Church. It led to a division into spheres of influence between the East and the West. Since that time various other leaders of countries have attempted to seize the spiritual rule of the Church, and only by vigilance and strong diplomatic policies has the authority of the Church in executive and doctrinal matters been maintained.

CAGOTS, name given to a group of Christians, of a presumed lower class of people, of the 10th century in Southern France. They were limited to country living and could only be trained as butchers or carpenters and were not welcome in the main part of the churches. This attempt at establishing a caste system in Christian circles failed and does not exist today.

CALATRAVA, ORDER OF, one of the three military orders of Spain founded in the 12th century which were under the direction of the Cistercians and espoused a rigorous rule of life in carrying out the pledge of knighthood. All were done away with by Isabella and Ferdinand in the 15th century when they attached all such orders to the crown. However, the title now exists as an honorary distinction.

CALEFACTORY. 1. A heated room in early monasteries. **2.** A form of hot-water bottle, being a hollow metal globe, filled with warm water and used in early medieval times by the priest to warm his fingers so he could distribute Communion more securely in cold churches.

CALENDAR, ECCLESIASTICAL. This is also sometimes referred to as the "Church" calendar or, more appropriately, the *liturgical* calendar. It provides the sequence of feasts in the Church founded on the Julian-Gregorian calendar of the civil year and marking each date of a particular religious celebration. Determining that Easter is to be celebrated on the Sunday after the first full moon of the vernal equinox causes a variation as to the dates on which feasts will fall. Thus, since the calendar of the Church depends upon this determination of when Easter is celebrated, the feasts from about the middle of January to the third week of November are liable to variation from year to year. Changes in the calendar of the year proposed in keeping with the establishment of a "universal" calendar would not affect the liturgical calendar, except in minor details.

CALIFORNIA MISSIONS, the missionary work carried on in the territory of California by Franciscans from the middle of the 18th century till 1834. It included the conversion and instruction of the native Indians, and the building of religious institutions. When the far southwestern portion of continental United States became a part of Mexico in 1822, the missions were exploited and plundered by the state-appointed commissioners. This led to a great loss of faith among the Indians. Many of the sites and the mission buildings remain as memorials of the missionary activity of the time and are examples of skillful architecture and adaptation to a difficult terrain by Church missioners.

CALIXTINES also **HUSSITES,** name given to those who demanded Holy Communion under both species.

CALUMNY. This is a more serious form of detraction, in that it is lying as well as an injustice against another. Thus calumny is the uttering or publishing or otherwise relating to others of false statements, which are known to be false, which harm the character or reputation of another. It is a grave sin depending upon the nature of the statements and the damage that may follow to the good name of the person. It demands retraction and repair of the damage in so far as the resulting damage was foreseen. An oath disclaiming calumny is given, under canon law, by both sides in a litigation. (*Cf.* DETRACTION.)

CALVARY. In Aramaic, Golgolta, in Greek, literally, "the place of the skull," and translated into the Latin equivalent *calvarium*, this was originally the name given to a place of execution that was customarily located on a rocky site or a small rise. Calvary was the place near Jerusalem where Christ was crucified. Also called Golgotha (Mt. 27:33–38).

CAMAURO, the headpiece worn by the pope instead of the biretta, and which is a loose, full cap of red velvet trimmed with white fur. It has no brim. Permitted only on extra-liturgical occasions, it is seldom used today but is frequently seen in paintings of the popes.

CAMERA, literally a room. *See* CURIA, ROMAN.

CAMERLENGO also **CAMERARIUS,** an official of the Holy See who is always a cardinal. The office is largely honorary today, although previously the office called for wide financial dealings. However, with the death of a pope, the interim administration of the Holy See is carried on by the cardinal camerlengo. His duties are limited to the temporal affairs of the Church. He issues the official notice of the pope's death, closes the papal apartments and places the documents and effects of the dead pope under seal. His authority ceases with the election of a new pope.

CAMISIA, name infrequently applied to the alb. Originally this referred to the place where the book of Gospels was kept in the early Church.

CAMPANILE

CAMPANILE, a tall, slender structure erected adjoining a church building or standing apart from it, in which bells are kept. This bell tower differs from the steeple. The leaning tower of Pisa is a campanile.

CANA MOVEMENT. This movement, also called Cana Conference Movement, is established in many dioceses of the United States under a priest-director appointed by the bishop. It is under the patronage of the Blessed Mother, being named after the marriage feast of Cana (Jn. 2:1–11). It operates through conferences which offer instruction and discussion under the leadership of the priest-director. There are two divisions, but both have a single purpose: first, the Pre-Cana Conference which is to instruct those who are preparing for receiving the sacrament of marriage; second, the Cana Conference, which aims at instruction in the true, dignified and happy conduct of life in the married state. Its program of instruction is directed primarily at the married state as a spiritual state of mutual work toward the salvation of the married parties and the responsible execution of obligations to promote the salvation of their children. It is also directed to the physical, moral, economic, psychological relationships of the married state or any subjects which are salutary to this state. Its chief aim is the formation of family life in Christ and to this end it seeks to promote retreats for the family, understanding through reading and instruction, Holy Hours for the family, and frequent reception of the sacraments.

CANCELLI, literally, the communion railings separating the sanctuary from the nave of the church. (*Cf.* CHANCEL.)

CANDLEMAS, name sometimes applied to the feast of the purification of the B.V.M. celebrated on Feb. 2. It is so called because candles are blessed on this day.

CANDLES. Blessed candles are sacramentals used in the liturgy of the Church. They were used from very early times and according to St. Jerome were symbols of joy. There are no hard and fast rules concerning the size or shape of candles. However, those used during liturgical functions and exposition of the Blessed Sacrament must contain more than 50% of pure beeswax. So-called vigil or votive lights are not blessed as a rule.

CANDLESTICKS. These belong to the furnishings of any altar and, as the word indicates, they should be single, i.e., on one base and not a part of a branch. They may be made of wood or metal but should not stand higher than the base of the crucifix at the altar's center.

CANON. 1. Either the rule or law of guidance, or standard or norm which follows reason; or it may be the sum total (Kant) of all such principles in the correct application of our knowledge. In art, it means an established rule directive to a reasoned standard. (*Cf.* CANON OF THE SCRIPTURE; CANON OF THE MASS.) **2.** Title of members of a cathedral chapter. These clerics are appointed by the bishop to assist in divine services and Church government. They are governed by special legislation since the office grants the spiritual right of a voice in the chapter and a share of the revenue of the chapter. As a title it is seldom used in the United States.

CANONESS, a woman following the religious rule comparable to that of a Canon Regular. Originally they were women following a religious life in common who were permitted to hold private property.

CANONICAL HOURS, THE. The division of the prayer of the Church into several hours or periods (*cf.* BREVIARY; DIVINE OFFICE) was probably derived from Ps. 118:164, "Seven times a day I give praise to thee." The seven denoting "completion," thus making for a continuing and yet complete prayer for each day.

CANONICALS, vestments required by Church law to be worn by a priest officiating at a liturgical ceremony.

CANONIST, a person trained in canon law, usually holding a doctorate in canon law, a J.C.D. Sometimes applied to the ranking canon lawyer of a diocese.

CANONIZATION. This is the final declaration, the seal of approval, whereby the soul of a person is declared to be in heaven. It follows the process of beatification. Through this declaration, veneration of the person as a saint is not only permitted but ordered for the entire Church. The title of "saint" is given to the person. The process of beatification and canonization is conducted by the Sacred Congregation of Rites, but the declaration of canonization is made only by the Supreme Pontiff and he acts and is protected under his prerogative of infallibility. The initial step of the process is a formal inquiry instituted by the bishop of the diocese wherein the person lived. This inquiry is accomplished by a tribunal of three judges, a notary, and the "promoter of the faith," more commonly called the "devil's advocate." This is then reported to Rome and the examination is made as to whether or not a "cult" has been begun before the pronouncement of the Church. Following these reports, the Sacred Congregation opens the process, enlarging on the previous inquiries, with a promoter of the faith again presenting the flaws or weak points in the evidence. Only thereafter is the apostolic process authorized by commission directly to the Sacred Congregation, and investigation is made of the "reality and nature of the virtues and miracles ascribed to the person to be beatified." Extensive precautions are taken, and the "cause" once introduced proceeds slowly. Two fully authentic miracles are required before beatification and two distinctly different miracles must be attested to and proven before canonization. (*Cf.* BEATIFICATION.)

CANON LAW. The official body of ecclesiastical law for the Latin Church is gathered in a single volume known as the *Code of Canon Law*. (In Latin: *Codex Juris Canonici*.) There always existed in the Church groups of laws, collections of canons which were formally recognized. In 1234 Pope Gregory IX issued five books of "Decretals" and later additions were made. However, there was great necessity for a codification of laws which would contain the regulating decrees and application of legal thought to the administration of the Church. Under Pope St. Pius X the monumental task of codification was begun late in 1903. In a little less than fourteen years the work was completed, examined by the bishops throughout the world, and promulgated on Pentecost Sunday, 1917, by Pope Benedict XV. After one year of study, it was decreed that this code would have the force of law beginning on Pentecost, May 19, 1918. In the Code the whole

of canon law is reduced to 2414 canons, divided into five sections or books. There are 86 canons on the general principles under which the Code is applied; 639 canons on categories of persons in the Church; 826 canons on the means employed by the Church to achieve its purpose; 643 canons on procedures and rules governing Church tribunals; and 220 canons on the penal code of the Church. It is this body of law which is exercised in behalf of the faithful by the Roman Curia and all Church courts and regulates the functioning of all Church affairs. At the time of promulgation, a special Pontifical Commission was set up to interpret, clarify, and pronounce on the meaning of any disputed part of the law.

CANON OF THE MASS, also called "Action" of the Mass, the main part, the "heart" of the sacrifice of the Mass. The Canon begins immediately after the *Sanctus*, opening with the prayer *Te igitur* . . . and ends at the Lord's Prayer. This is followed by the lesser canon or "action," the canon of the Communion. The Canon of the Mass is the portion of the Mass where the liturgy of the Mass, by representation and repetition, reenacts the Last Supper and the sacrifice of Calvary.

CANON OF THE SCRIPTURE. The word "canon" comes from the Greek and means "a measuring rod." It later came to mean a rule or standard. In adaptation the term came to be used in the Church for the decrees, pronouncements, and decisions, enacted as to a "standard" doctrine, and men began to speak of the Canon of Scripture as the "standard" source of faith. However, the term as commonly used and understood today means the collection or list of books acknowledged and accepted by the Church as inspired. Thus they conform to the "rule" or "standard" required for classification as inspired. (*See* BIBLE for list of books so accepted.) Likewise a "canonical" book of the Scriptures is any book that forms a part of the Canon (*cf.* INSPIRATION OF SCRIPTURE). Extensive study and research have confirmed the list of books of the Bible as contained in the Canon.

CANON PENITENTIARY, title of that member of a chapter of a cathedral or collegiate church who is appointed according to canon law by the bishop to hear confessions. He is the confessor extraordinary who is delegated to absolve, in the internal forum, censures and sins reserved to the bishop.

CANON, PRIVILEGE OF. *See* IMMUNITY.

CANON REGULAR, a cleric who lives in a community under the governance of one of his own order. Most follow the rule established by St. Augustine.

CANONS, CHAPTERS OF. These are groups of clerics assigned to a cathedral church who live a community life of religion, recite the Divine Office in choir, and live off the revenue of the church, each being allotted a share called a *prebend.* They serve the church in the dignity and solemnity of the divine services, and the bishop in his duties of governing. The Council of Trent calls the chapter an "ecclesiastical senate," and recognizes their services in keeping up the dignity of the cathedral, setting examples of pious lives and giving assistance to the bishop.

CANONS OF THE APOSTLES also **APOSTOLIC CANONS,** a collection of early decrees of the Church on matters of discipline.

CANON THEOLOGIAN, a member of a cathedral or collegiate chapter, versed in theology who serves as consultant to the others of the chapter. It may also be applied to a priest-theologian who is trained in canon law, usually having a doctorate of canon law, J.C.D.

CANOPY. *See* BALDAQUIN; CIVORY; OMBRELLINO.

CANTATE SUNDAY, name given to the fourth Sunday after Easter from the Introit of the Mass, dating back to the 12th century.

CANTICLE, a sacred prayer or song of praise or love directed to God as found in Scripture, excluding the Psalms which many consider canticles. Canticles have been incorporated into the Divine Office of the Church and there are 14 from the O.T. and 3 from the N.T. Those from the N.T. are also known as the "evangelical canticles." The canticle is a sacred chant or hymn of praise in poetic form.

CANTICLE OF CANTICLES, the 24th book of the O.T. in the Catholic Bible. Its authorship has always been popularly attributed to Solomon, but it was most likely written much later. It is a love poem whose interpretation is that God's love of Israel was a parallel figure of Christ's love for His Church.

CANTOR also **PRECENTOR,** title of a seldom named semi-official who is the chief singer and often director of a church choir.

CANTORAL STAFF, an ornate staff carried by the cantor of a choir as a mark of dignity and authority in the Middle Ages.

CAPITAL SINS also **CAPITAL VICES** or **DEADLY SINS.** Properly, these are vices in the sense that each has many facets any of which may be a sin. Seven in number, the capital vices are the sources of other sins, but the chief or first is the origin of all the others and is found in all sin to some degree. The seven are: pride, covetousness, lust, anger, gluttony, envy, sloth. (See listings under individual titles.) They are considered as deadly because they lead to mortal sin, and vices because in themselves they are passions or habits that dispose one to sin and even prompt the occasions for sin instead of being distinct acts of sin themselves.

CAPITULARY, a collection of rules or laws. Seldom used in the ecclesiastical sense as a collection of canons passed by a provincial council.

CAPPA MAGNA

CAPPA MAGNA, full long cape with a train, made of purple wool (for bishops) or red (for cardinals). It has a full cowl which is lined with silk for summer use or fur for winter use. The cowl portion which fits over the neck and shoulders in front and back may be detached. It is worn by bishops, cardinals, and certain prelates.

CAPPA PLUVIALIS or **PLUVIALE.** *See* COPE.

CAPTIVITY EPISTLES, the four epistles written by St. Paul while he was imprisoned in Rome in the years 61–63. They are: to the Ephesians, to the Philippians, to the Colossians, and to Philemon. All are concerned with the union of Christ and the Church.

CARDINAL, a prince of the Church appointed solely by the pope. In the Code of Canon Law (c. 230), the place of the cardinals in the Church is stated: "The cardinals of Holy Roman Church constitute the senate of the Roman Pontiff and aid him as his chief counselors and collaborators in the government of the Church." There are three orders or categories of cardinals: (a) Cardinal bishops, the six cardinals living in Rome, are bishops over seven small dioceses adjoining that of Rome, and serve as major officials of the Roman Curia. (b) Cardinal priests, who are usually bishops or archbishops, being fifty in number, and who are given title to one of the major churches of Rome. In these churches, the cardinal titular exercises the authority that he has in his own diocese. (c) Cardinal deacons, ordinarily 14 in number, who act as deacons when the Holy Father pontificates solemnly, and serve in a special way in the Roman Curia. These too are assigned to a church of Rome, called their "deaconry," by title. Today according to canon law only ordained priests may be elevated to the cardinalate. All cardinals are members of the College of Cardinals and enjoy a wide variety of privileges.

CARDINAL LEGATE. *See* LEGATE.

CARDINAL PROTECTOR, a member of the College of Cardinals who represents at the Holy See the people of a nation, a religious institution, or a pious association by solicitude and interest in their affairs.

CARDINAL VICAR, the cardinal appointed to assist the pope, who is the bishop of the diocese of Rome, in the spiritual and temporal administration of that diocese. (*Cf.* BISHOP OF ROME.)

CARDINAL VIRTUES, the four chief moral virtues: prudence, justice, fortitude, and temperance. (See listings under individual titles.) All other moral virtues may be considered under aspects of these four.

CARLSRUHE FRAGMENTS, two portions of early manuscripts, four pages each, containing portions of Masses. They date back to the early 9th century and are retained in the Carlsruhe library in Germany.

CARMEL, MOUNT. This mountain, or high hill, frequently mentioned in the Scriptures, is to the east of the plain of Esdraelon on the Mediterranean sea to the south of Acre. It was there in a cavern that the prophet Elias took up his abode, and later a community of men must have established an early monastery or hermitage because ruins were found in the 12th century. Thus it was and is one of the earliest places where religious life was followed according to any kind of a regimen.

CARNIVAL, time of celebration before a religious feast day, but usually the three days preceeding lenten season.

CAROLINGIAN SCHOOLS, system of education, in the nature of a reform, which followed the issuance of the capitulary of Charlemagne in the late 8th century. It was the first establishment of free church schools. This influenced the spread of Christian doctrine and gave a broader scope to the training in monastic and cathedral schools.

CARTHAGE, COUNCILS OF. The first of these councils of bishops at Carthage in North Africa was held in 220. Of importance was the council of 397 because it published a list of "canonical" Scriptures; the one in 404 condemned the Donatist heresy, and the council of 411 was notable because St. Augustine there refuted the Pelagians.

CASES OF CONSCIENCE, term applied to real or imaginary instances or examples in canon law or moral theology which are gathered to exemplify and teach practical application of principles to problems. Usually each such case is discussed in detail and is a basis of pedagogy or learning such as in study clubs. The applications are sometimes given in a question and answer pattern and in some instances have been applied to catechetical instructions.

CASSOCK also **SOUTANE,** an ankle-length gown worn by clerics, usually of black cloth. The sleeves generally have a deep cuff. There are two styles in use: one buttoning down the full front length from the collar to the hem, called "Roman style;" the other being open and fastened by hooks and eyes at the collar and waist, usually worn with a black band-belt of cloth, called "Jesuit style." Cassocks are worn by acolytes serving Mass or assisting at other services. The Holy Father wears a white cassock.

CATACOMBS—Gallery in the catacombs with *loculi* cut into the wall.

CASTEL GANDOLFO, the summer residence of the Holy Father. It is located 14 miles southeast of Rome and is held as extraterritory of Vatican State by concordat with the Italian government.

CASUISTRY. This is the method of studying causes of conscience or solving questions of obligation by application of general principles in ethics or moral theology in regard to concrete problems of human conduct. This form of inquiry requires an extensive knowledge of law, precepts, interpretation of like cases and skill in analyzing conditions effecting motive and consent. (*Cf.* CASES OF CONSCIENCE.)

CASUS, literally, case. An example that is used to point out a problem, be the case a real or imaginary one.

CATACOMBS. These were subterranean cemeteries which served a double purpose: that of burial for Christians who had died or been martyred; and a place to which Christians could resort to conduct devotions, administer sacraments, and celebrate the Eucharist in secrecy. There are some twenty-five catacombs which have been excavated, the majority located along the Via Appia and the Via Ardeatina, all within two and a half miles of the old Roman walls of Aurelius. The catacombs were dug into hill areas by burrowing into a mid-stratum called *tufa granolare*, a soft stone. The practice was to excavate a stairway and then open a narrow gallery. Off this gallery there were *loculi* cut into the wall, capable of holding from one to three bodies. These were sealed with a slab of stone

CATACOMBS—An *arcosolium* or vault atop a tomb.

when the bodies had been placed within. Also leading off the gallery there were a number of *cubicula*, chambers or vaults. Along the walls, there were occasionally cut into the wall above a single tomb (*loculus*) an *arcosolium*, a vault above a tomb. In these *arcosolia* it was customary to celebrate the mystery of the Eucharist, the Mass, using the top of the tomb for an altar surface. When a gallery became full, it was customary to cut lateral galleries and continue on with each as above. In the 4th century, after the end of the persecutions, the catacombs became places of pilgrimage and remain so until the present. The catacombs, however, are most notable because of the testimony of art and practice which they supply to modern ages. Chief of these testimonies are: that of the sacramental religion observed by these early Christians; the purity of the spiritual truth that is manifest. These facts are deduced from the art, the carvings, artifacts and inscriptions with which the catacombs are replete.

CATAFALQUE

CATAFALQUE, a bier on which rests a mock coffin. Covered with a black cloth called the pall or hearsecloth, it is used at requiem Masses when the corpse is not present.

CATECHISM. Among early Christian writers this meant both the subject matter and the method of instruction. However, today it is more frequently applied to the text or manual which is a summary of Catholic doctrine presented in question and answer form. The word comes from the Greek word "catechesis" which means oral instruction. Today the word catechism is applied to a wide variety of booklets, texts, question and answer forms and study notes relating to various aspects of Christian doctrine. The basic work, however, in the United States is the Baltimore Catechism, the compilation of instructions authorized by the third plenary council of Baltimore and first published in 1885 and variously presented since that time. Revisions are undertaken, not with the purpose of changing teaching, but solely for clarification and improvements in the teaching method.

CATECHIST, originally the title given to the one who instructed those about to receive baptism. Now it is loosely applied to any instructor versed in Christian doctrine who teaches others, especially in missionary schools.

CATECHUMENS. In the early Church when a pagan sought to become a Christian he was basically instructed and became an "inquirer" and was permitted to be present only during the first part of the Mass. Thereafter, having been given additional instruction and become versed in doctrine, he was called a catechumen and allowed to remain at Mass up to the beginning of the Mass of the Faithful. After more instruction, the catechumens were baptized and became "competents" and were received into the "body of the faithful."

CATEGORICAL IMPERATIVE, a term introduced by the philosopher Immanuel Kant (d. 1804). He stated: "Act on maxims which can at the same time have for their object themselves as universal laws of nature." It is an absolute moral law of reason, acting for the sake of law itself, making man a law unto himself. However, it must be recognized in contradistinction that reason does not manufacture moral law, but only recognizes it and interprets application, and that only God is the supreme lawgiver and is Himself the end of morality, being the supreme good.

CATHARI or **CATHARISTS,** a sect of Neo-Manichaeans. *See* ALBIGENSES.

CATHEDRA

CATHEDRA, chair-throne of a bishop. It is always located in the sanctuary against the left wall on the gospel side in the cathedral church of the diocese. *Cathedra* is the Latin word for chair or throne from which is derived the word cathedral. (*Cf.* EX CATHEDRA.)

CATHEDRAL, the official church of a bishop who has jurisdiction over a diocese. It is located within the diocese, generally in the see city, in which the bishop exercises his authority and conducts worship for all under his jurisdiction.

CATHEDRATICUM, small dues or tax exacted of all churches and benefices under a bishop's jurisdiction as a symbol of their subordination to the bishop and for his financial support, stated as a right of the bishop under canon 1504.

CATHOLIC. The term meaning "universal" was first applied to the Church of St. Ignatius of Antioch (d. 107) writing to the Church at Smyrna: "Wheresoever the bishop shall appear, there let the people be, even as where Jesus is, there is the Catholic Church" (Smyr. VIII, 2). It was later used by many writers referring both to the Church and to individual members of the Church, the most famous being perhaps that of St. Pacianus, a bishop of Barcelona in the 4th century, "Christian is my name; Catholic is my surname." The term as used by the fathers of the Church means the true Church as distinct from all other religious groups. It is thus used today and applies to the body of the faithful, the creeds, churches, institutions, clergy and hierarchy who follow the same teachings of Christ as given to the apostles. (*Cf.* MARKS OF THE CHURCH.)

CATHOLIC ACTION. Catholic Action as defined by Pius XI is, "The participation of the Catholic laity in the apostolate of the hierarchy." Catholic Action has four essentials which help to explain it more fully: (a) it is an apostolate, working toward the conversion and salvation of souls; (b) it is formed by the laity, who are called by the bishops to work for the salvation of souls; (c) it is organized, that while an individual may be engaged in Catholic Action, it is in organized lay associations that the work will be most successful since the work is social in nature; (d) it is under the direction and control of the bishops who have the direct responsibility of teaching and ruling the Church. Such Catholic Action may be effected through a variety of means, cultural, physical, or spiritual. It calls particularly for informed leaders of personal ideals of sanctity who can clearly state the position of the Church on essential questions of doctrine, moral, or practice. In practice, for the majority, Catholic Action may be no more than the co-operation with the bishop in the enterprises he sets forth. It is not a political activity; its work is in the religious circle, the moral, and those border areas where religion or morals are directly or indirectly related to the good of the individual or the community, or the universal good of the Church. The sacrament of confirmation is sometimes called the sacrament of "Catholic Action," meaning that all the faithful through the Holy Spirit are made co-operators in the work of the bishops, teachers and leaders of the community. However, in its popular use it must be distinguished from "Catholic Activity." The bishops of the United States, in Nov. 1935, issued the qualifying statement: "The bishops remind all groups according to the instruction of our Holy Father, Pope Pius XI, that there is no such thing as Catholic Action until there is an episcopal commission. For a diocese there must be a commission from the bishop of a diocese, for a province from the bishops of a province, and for the country from the bishops of the United States. The Holy Father only can give a commission for the universal Church on Catholic Action. When His Holiness does so he communicates with the bishops."

CATHOLIC CHURCH. The Church founded by Jesus Christ, which was first taught and governed by the apostles, is taught infallibly by the successor of St. Peter, the pope, the vicar of Christ on earth, and by the bishops, and is formed by the society of the faithful. This divinely founded society extends to every nation and race, is neither national nor ethnic, but is truly universal. Those members composing this society are of one faith, profess one doctrine found in the Creed, participate in the same seven sacraments, and are governed by the pope. St. Paul writing to the Ephesians spoke clearly of the Church from which we derive the distinct marks of this Church: It is *one*, having one body to the single head that is Christ; it is *holy*, since its members are in Christ and through Him are made holy and are saved; it is *universal*, extending to the Gentiles and Jews, all in the household of God (2:19); it is *apostolic*, its doctrine being direct from Christ through the apostles (2:20).

CATHOLIC EPISTLES, name given to those 7 Epistles of the N.T. which were directed by certain apostles to the Church as a whole rather than to particular areas or groups. They are: that of St. James; 1 and 2 of St. Peter; 1, 2, and 3 letters of John; and that of St. Jude.

CATHOLIC FOREIGN MISSION SOCIETY OF AMERICA. This society of the Maryknoll Fathers was founded in 1911 and incorporated under the laws of the State of New York, U. S. A., in 1912. Its aim is to train priests to conduct foreign missions.

CATHOLICOS, name of distinction given to certain patriarchs of the churches of Mesopotamia, Armenia, and Persia, signifying their wide jurisdiction.

CATHOLIC TRUTH SOCIETY, a group organized first in England in 1872, reorganized in 1884. Its purpose is the spreading of the means of wider information of their faith among Catholics and true information of the Church among Protestants. It aids and promotes the writing, printing and distribution of inexpensive printed matter. In the United States its official title is International Catholic Truth Society.

CATHOLIC UNIVERSITY OF AMERICA, the foremost Catholic school of higher education in the United States. It was founded in Washington, D. C., in 1889 by the bishops of the United States and is maintained as an institution by them. It has canonical value, conferring degrees by apostolic faculty (c. 1378). The University is both undergraduate and graduate and consists of the Schools of Sacred Theology, Canon Law, Philosophy, Law, the college and graduate school of Arts and Sciences, schools of Social Service, Nursing Education and Social Service. Its student body is both male and female, religious and lay. In conjunction with the University, many religious orders have houses of study for the training of their members or which serve as residences for their members while studying at the University.

CAUSE. As used in its religious, non-philosophic sense, this is the process or procedure of investigation and justification. (*Cf.* BEATIFICATION; CANONIZATION.)

CELEBRANT, term applied to either the priest who celebrates Mass or the bishop pontificating.

CELESTIAL HIERARCHY. While there is no degree of authority in heaven excepting that of God, this term is applied to the three categories of angels according to rank. (*Cf.* ANGELS.)

CELIBACY, the ecclesiastical law in the Western Church imposed on clerics forbidding those in the married state from being ordained and those in Holy Orders from marrying. It includes the obligation of observing perfect chastity under vow. The reasons for this are: that those being ordained may serve God with a greater singleness of purpose (1 Cor. 7:32), and that so living a life of continence they observe the state of virginity which is holier and higher than that of marriage. While celibacy was practiced by the majority of clergy in the first three centuries of the Church's history, it was after the Council of Elvira in 305 that the law became more definite. A council held at Rome in 386 and two later councils at Carthage imposed continence on all bishops, priests and deacons.

CELL. 1. A numerically smaller group of monks who formed a colony apart from some large monastery. **2.** The individual room or living quarters of a monk, friar, nun, or hermit. **3.** A small, effective group set up for work or study as a part of a Catholic

Action program. **4.** In early ages, the name of a small chapel usually erected over a tomb.

CELLARER, in early monastic life the title of the one who saw to the provision of food, drink and clothing for all members of the community. Today the title is procurator.

CELTIC CROSS

CELTIC CROSS, ancient cross of Irish origin, having a circle about the juncture of the cross arms.

CELTIC RITE, term applied to a variety of liturgical features which were used by the early British, Scottish and Irish churches, based upon French and Roman forms. It was used until the 13th century but is no longer in use.

CEMETERY, the place set apart for burial of the bodies of Christians and consecrated for this purpose. Solemn blessing or consecration can only be performed by the ordinary of the diocese, while simple blessing may be either by the bishop or a delegated priest. It is not necessary to bless the individual graves but rather the area as a whole is consecrated.

CENACLE, the upper room where Christ and His apostles ate the Last Supper at which the Eucharist was instituted (Lk. 22:12). It was here also that Christ appeared to the as-

sembled apostles eight days after His death (Lk. 24:36), and where the Holy Spirit descended upon the apostles (Acts 2:1–4, 1:13–14). Romantically this has been called the first Christian church. While it is not known where this room was located, tradition places it in the house of St. Mark's mother in the southwest quarter of Jerusalem.

CENOBITE, the equivalent of our word monk, meaning one who lives in a religious community life rather than as a hermit or anchorite. This was the name given to the individual member in the first centuries of the Church, derived from the "Cenobium" or group. The earliest rule for cenobites was written by St. Pachomius (d. 346) who is commonly called the "Founder of Monasticism."

CENSER, cup or bowl, usually of metal, having a perforated cover, the whole suspended on chains, in which lighted charcoal is placed. Onto this charcoal, grains of incense are sprinkled to provide the scented smoke used in liturgical functions. Also called a thurible.

CENSER

CENSOR, the cleric, appointed according to canon law by the bishop of a diocese, whose duty it is to examine, read, and judge a writing before publication to assure that there is nothing contained in the writing contrary to the teaching of the

Church regarding faith or morals. When a book has been censored and approval given in writing by the censor, this is signified by the term *Nihil obstat*. The writing and *Nihil obstat* are then submitted to the bishop who attaches his *Imprimatur*, or permission to publish. Together these assure that the writing can be read without harm to faith or morals, but are not an approval of the contents otherwise. The Church requires censorship of the following writings: (a) Those books of holy Scripture as well as commentaries or annotations on any part of Scripture. (b) Those books treating of Scripture, theology, Church history, canon law, natural theology and ethics. (c) All prayer books, devotional, catechetical, moral, ascetical, and mystical books or pamphlets. (d) All books which treat particularly of religion, faith or morals. (e) All sacred images or pictures when printed, whether or not a prayer is printed with them. (c. 1384–1405.)

CENSURE. A Church censure is a penalty by which a baptized person, being delinquent and contumacious, that is, conscious and obstinate, is deprived of certain spiritual benefits until that individual has ceased being obstinate or is absolved from the censure. The state of being delinquent is defined (c. 2195) as one who has committed an external and morally imputable violation of a canonically sanctioned law. It must thus be a seriously sinful act, both from the internal and external aspects. Such Church penalties are primarily corrective and secondarily seek to punish the crime. Excommunication, suspension and interdict are three types of censure. A censure may be inflicted by law (*a jure*), i.e., when it is contained in the law or precept as written

or promulgated; or inflicted by an individual having jurisdiction (*ab homine*) when it is expressed as part of the penalty or imposed by a judicial sentence. A censure which is incurred by the very fact of being deliberately delinquent is said to be "*latae sententiae*," or incurred *ipso facto*, i.e., without a pronounced sentence. A censure which must be imposed by a judge or competent superior is said to be "*ferendae sententiae*." The following can inflict censures because of their office: the pope, an ecumenical council, congregations and courts of the Roman Curia, bishops in their dioceses, a plenary or provincial council, cathedral chapters before election of a vicar capitular, the vicar capitular, apostolic administrators, abbots and prelates with episcopal jurisdiction, vicars and prefects apostolic, higher superiors in clerical exempt religious orders and their chapters. Absolution from a censure may be reserved to the bishop or to the Holy See, but in danger of death any priest may absolve from all censures.

CERECLOTH, a linen cloth, more properly called *chrismale*. It is waxed on one side and should be spread upon the entire top, the *mensa*, of an altar before the altar cloths are spread as long as any traces of the holy oils may remain on the surface of the altar after its consecration.

CEREMONIAL, THE, the book which contains the procedure to be followed in religious ceremonies and solemn worship as prescribed for church functions. There are two such official publications: the "Roman Ceremonial" (*Caeremoniale Romanum*), and the "Ceremonial of Bishops" (*Caeremoniale Episcoporum*). In the United States the "Ceremonial

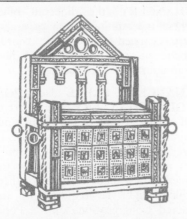

CHAIR OF ST. PETER—The portable chair (*sedia gestatoria*) of which the earliest parts have been used by St. Peter. The ivory ornaments date from the ninth century.

for use of Catholic Churches" as approved by Cardinal Gibbons is in general use.

CEREMONY, in the wide sense any external act, gesture, or movement made in the worship of God. Such actions may be of two classes: (a) Essential, as the ceremonies which are part of the matter and form of the sacraments. (b) Accidental, when they are not a part of worship as such.

CERTITUDE, the firm assent and adherence of the mind to any proposition without possible fear of being mistaken. There is implied a quietness or satisfaction of the intellect in the thing known either because of evident truth, or because a sufficient reason is seen to exist.

CHAINS OF ST. PETER, the bonds which were forged to keep St. Peter a prisoner, as recorded in Acts, Ch. 12. The feast is celebrated on August 1.

CHAIR. In the church, besides the throne of the bishop, chairs are used in one form or another. (*Cf.* CATHEDRA; FALDSTOOL; SEDILIA.)

CHAIR OF ST. PETER, a portable chair preserved in the Vatican and believed to be that used by St. Peter in Rome. Evidence for this dates back to the 2nd century. The feast is celebrated on Jan. 18, and commemorates the first service held by St. Peter in Rome.

CHAIR OF UNITY OCTAVE. This term refers to the eight days of prayer, from the feast of St. Peter's Chair (Jan. 18) to the feast of St. Paul's Conversion (Jan. 25), a devotion begun by Father P. J. F. Watson at Graymoor, N. Y., in petition that all Christians may be united in the true faith. A plenary indulgence is granted, under the usual conditions, on the first or last day of the octave.

CHALCEDON, COUNCIL OF. *See* ECUMENICAL COUNCILS.

CHALDEAN RITE. Also called the East Syrian, Assyrian, or Persian rite, this is a liturgy of the Uniat East Syrians written in old Syriac. Communion is given by dipping a bit of Consecrated Bread into the chalice of Consecrated Wine.

CHALICE. 1. The most important of the sacred vessels, it is the type of cup used in the Mass to hold the wine to be consecrated. Formerly it was a cup on a low base, but it has now come to be a cup supported on a stem and base, usually 8 inches in overall height. The chalice cup must be of gold or silver, and if the latter, then the inside must be surfaced with gold. The base and stem may be of any metal. The base should be sufficiently heavy to provide firmness to avoid upsetting; the stem has a knob or node beneath the cup to provide a more secure grip in handling. Chalices are consecrated with chrism by a bishop or one delegated by him. The chalice should not be touched directly by anyone not in holy orders. **2.** The "chalice" or cup spoken of by Christ in the agony in the garden (Mt. 26:42) and after His arrest (Jn. 18:11) is interpreted as the "portion" accepted by one voluntarily.

CHALICE VEIL also **PEPLUM** and **SUDARIUM.** This is the cloth, made of the·same material and color as the vestments of the Mass, which is used to cover the chalice when carrying it to or from the altar and before the unveiling following the Creed in the celebration of Mass.

CHAMBERLAIN, title of several classes of officials serving at the papal court. Also the title of those who serve in the apartments of the pope, usually honorary.

CHAMBRE ARDENTE, literally "burning room," a court or commission established by the French government in the 16th century which put heretics on trial. It was so named because the court was lighted by burning torches.

CHANCEL, that part of the sanctuary which specifically is the area between the high altar and the nave of the church. It was formerly marked by a screen, but derives its name from the *cancelli*, the railings which came to separate the area from the body of the church. Today the separation is made by the communion rail.

CHANCELLOR, in the Church, the priest appointed in accord with canon law by the bishop of a diocese. His title is "diocesan chancellor" and he serves as an ecclesiastical notary. His duties include the supervision of the diocesan archives, the authentication of documents and the drawing up of written reports on the official government of the diocese.

CHANCERY, the diocesan office where the administration of a diocese is carried on and where records, documents, and proceedings of diocesan courts, etc., are kept.

CHANCERY, PAPAL also **APOSTOLIC CHANCERY,** the oldest of all official groups of the Church administration. At present its task is to prepare and send all apostolic bulls for appointment of bishops or the erection of a diocese and any others which might be required by the Sacred Congregations or the Pope. (*Cf.* BULLS.)

CHANT, the official music used in the liturgy of the Roman rite, made up of Ambrosian chant, plain chant, and Gregorian chant, but largely referred to today as Gregorian chant or music. It is official in the sense that ecclesiastical authority prescribes that those parts of the liturgy which are to be sung require the officiating clergy to sing according to this chant. It is distinguished from other musical notation or composition permitted in hymns. In make-up, chant is monodic, usually diatonic, and ranges from simple recitation of a text in a slightly variated tone to the more elaborate melodies. The notation is upon a four line staff, using a concise form of notation printed in square or diamond shapes with a variety of combinations and elisions. Gregorian chant was derived from several sources going back to the earliest days of the Church—the Hebrew, represented in the Psalm tones; the Oriental, with its singular rhythm; the Greek and Latin in its choral makeup; and the Frankish which was chiefly syllabic. The part that St. Gregory the Great (d. 604) played in the founding of the chant bearing his name has been disputed, but a collection of chants called the Antiphonal was prepared by him or caused to be published by him in the late 6th century. He also introduced a school of Church music and fostered its development toward use in the divine services. In the 9th century when this "Gregorian" type was introduced among the Franks, they found the compositions somewhat elaborate and wrought a modification which led to the adaptation called "plain chant." More recently, the monks of Solesmes in a work begun under Dom André Mocquereau, have done much to authenticate the early versions and to provide editions of restored texts of the Church's chant.

CHANTRY, an endowment. It is set up to provide: (a) the upkeep of one or more priests; (b) the place for saying Mass, or (c) both priest and place, with the provision that the priest offer Masses for a deceased person in that place. Chantries were common in England in the Middle Ages, but were done away with entirely under the Acts of 1545–1547.

CHAPEL, either a small church other than the parish church, or a small area or part of a larger church set apart for special devotions. It was customary to call the small churches erected on palace grounds where divine worship was conducted by the name chapel. Today it is more frequently applied to the small rooms where the Blessed Sacrament is kept, and established for convenience as in convents, schools, etc. These may be designated as public or semi-public oratories. (*Cf.* ORATORIES.)

CHAPELLE ARDENTE, name applied to the chapel or room in which the body of a deceased person lies in state, derived from the candles burning around the bier.

CHAPEL OF EASE, a chapel or small church built in a remote part of a parish territory to accommodate parishioners living a considerable distance from the parish church.

CHAPLAIN. 1. The priest appointed to conduct liturgical functions for a lay association or group, a religious institution or public institution such as a hospital or prison. The appointment is made by the ordinary or a religious superior of exempt religious orders. The chaplain does not have parochial rights over the community unless by special privilege, and serves to accommodate those in the place of his assignment. **2.** A military chaplain is a priest permitted by his diocesan or religious superior to enter military service, in the army, navy or air force, to have charge of religious services in the place of his assignment. As such he is subject to either the ordinary of the place wherein he serves or the bishop-ordinary of the Armed Forces.

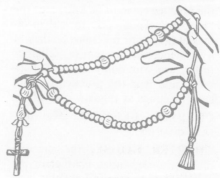

CHAPLET (2)—A late medieval specimen.

CHAPLET. 1. Originally, a wreath worn about the head as at religious professions, etc. **2.** Name applied to the rosary of five decades. **3.** More commonly today a string of beads, varying in number, upon which prayers or ejaculations of special devotions are said.

CHAPTER, CATHEDRAL. In the Middle Ages, it was the practice to join the priests serving a cathedral into administrative groups who were to assist the bishop. These groups became autonomous and usurped the authority of the bishop in some areas of his jurisdiction and, as a consequence, special rules were made to curtail their activities. Today in England, every diocese has a chapter, usually numbering ten canons (*cf.* CANON, 2.) and presided over by a provost. These serve under rules prescribed by the Council of Trent, as aids to the bishop in the performance of divine services and in the execution of the temporal affairs of the diocese. In the United States this practice is not followed.

CHAPTER, CONVENTUAL. It was the custom in certain religious houses for the members of the community to gather each morning to hear the reading of a part of their religious rule. Both the place of meeting and the practice came to be known as the "chapter." Today any formal meetings of monks or religious, be they of a province or an entire religious order, are commonly called "chapters," and it is the practice to hold such meetings at regular intervals.

CHAPTER, GENERAL. *See* GENERAL CHAPTER.

CHAPTER HOUSE, the meeting place of a conventual chapter or the members of a cathedral chapter.

CHARACTER. 1. The collective qualities, emotional, intellectual and volitional, which distinguish the mind and personality of an individual. **2.** In a religious sense, the indelible, invisible, seal or mark impressed upon the soul of a person through reception of the sacraments of baptism, confirmation, and holy orders. It is a spiritual mark which consecrates and dedicates the person to Christ in a singular manner and thus these sacraments can be received but once.

CHARISMATA also **CHARISMS,** the gifts or graces of an extraordinary type, called *gratis datae*, given to individual Christians for the benefit of others. They may be defined as functions which are present continuously and exercised at a particular time and which, whether or not they are extraordinary, by their very nature tend to aid the faithful either locally or universally. St. Paul (1 Cor. 12:8–10; 12:31) lists nine of these graces *gratis datae*, including prophecy and the working of miracles, etc., and declares them to be given by the Holy Spirit. Also in Rom. 12:6ff, he includes other gifts that are not so extraordinary in themselves, as "he that exhorteth" and "he that showeth mercy." St. Thomas groups these graces as: those pertaining to knowledge, those pertaining to speech, and those pertaining to miracles.

CHARITY, a supernatural virtue infused, with sanctifying grace, by which we love God above all as the greatest good and for His own sake, and ourselves and our neighbors for the love of God. It is the greatest of the three theological virtues and of all other virtues. The object of the virtue is our union with God through love; the act itself is the giving of ourselves to God. Charity is given as the greatest commandment (Mt. 22:34–40) and it is joined inseparably by the command to love one's neighbor. St. Bonaventure points to charity as "a life which unites the lover with the beloved." While charity may be manifested in many ways, it is not to be confused with almsgiving as such, nor is it only good deeds which may arise out of natural virtue and the emotion of good will. Rather charity is the very basis, the foundation which prompts and is the motivating force by which all acts of good directed toward ourselves or our neighbors are performed for love of God. St. Thomas states: "Essentially the perfection of the Christian life consists in charity, first and foremost in the love of God, then in the love of neighbor" (S.T. IIa IIae, q. 184, a3). (*Cf.* LOVE OF GOD.)

CHARITY, HEROIC ACT OF. This act includes the offering to God of all the merits of good deeds performed during life and the benefits or suffrages gained after death in one's behalf, and making this offering for the souls suffering in purgatory. It is advisable to consult one's confessor as spiritual guide before making the act; however, it is revocable at any time.

CHARITY, WORKS OF. These are the actions of a social nature which are resultant from the love of God, and are more than emotions, feelings or sentiment. They are actions directed primarily toward our neighbors and are of a social nature. Thus social justice is a work of charity. (*Cf.* CORPORAL WORKS OF MERCY.)

CHARTOPHYLAX, title in the Eastern Church, corresponding to Chancellor in the Western Church.

CHARTRES, OUR LADY OF. This title was given to the famous Gothic cathedral consecrated in 1260 at Chartres, the capital city of Ense-et-Loir in France. Besides the beauty of the church and the fame of the blue color in its stained glass windows, the church was erected as a singular devotion to the Blessed Mother and fostered veneration to her through (a)

the statue of Our Lady under the Earth, from an ancient Druid figure; (b) the "Black Virgin" in the upper church; (c) and the "Veil of the Virgin" enshrined there.

CHARTREUSE, THE GREAT, the original founding house of the Carthusians, set up by St. Bruno 14 miles northeast of Grenoble, France, in 1084.

CHASTITY, a moral virtue. The exercise of it checks, controls, moderates or excludes the desire and pleasure of carnal or sexual thoughts or actions. It is called the "angelic" virtue because the angels are pure by nature. There are two kinds of chastity: *conjugal* chastity which is exercised in the control and moderation of legitimate acts of the sexual relations of married persons; and *continence* or *purity* which is chastity exercised by youths and the unmarried, and includes more essentially the control and exclusion of sexual or voluptuous desires, thoughts and acts. Chastity differs from celibacy and virginity while being an essential virtue of both. Chastity is the virtue contrary to lust, and is exercised by (a) refraining from thoughts, fancies, daydreams and imaginings of sexual matters; (b) by restraining the temptations of lust by practical, energetic means; (c) by directing one's thoughts by prayer and reason to a love of God who made the senses for His own glory. (*Cf.* MODESTY.)

CHASUBLE, the vestment worn by priests or bishops over all other garments or vesture when they celebrate Mass. Originally the chasuble was a full, semicircular cloak and is so mentioned by St. Paul in the Second Epistle to Timothy (4:13). Through gradual development the chasuble evolved into two forms which are common today, though no particular shape is prescribed. The first and more common is the Italian or "Roman" style which is rectangular at the back extending to either side beyond the shoulders and cut away in front in a fiddle-shape with a square-shaped opening for the neck. It is decorated with a T-shaped cross in front and a broad orphrey in back. The second style is called "Gothic" or "Gothic Revival." This is more the cloak type, being cone-shaped with a semi-circular cut causing it to rest more loosely on the shoulders. Recent liturgical studies have brought about a trend toward use of the Gothic style. Among many symbolisms attributed to the chasuble, the most popular is that it is a figure of the love of God, charity being the greatest of all virtues.

CHERUBIM, the angels of the second highest of the nine hierarchies or choirs. The word from the Assyrian means "great, powerful," and St. Gregory says the name signifies "the fullness of knowledge." They were revealed as the angels who guarded the gate of the garden of Eden (Gen. 3:24) and formed the throne of God in heaven. (*Cf.* ANGELS.)

CHESTER PLAYS, a series of miracle plays performed at Chester in England during the early 15th century during the Pentecostal season. They were intended particularly to teach the Scriptures.

CHEVET, the French architectural term for that part of a church which is at the easternmost end of the building where the apse is closed over by a screen. Behind the screen there is an aisle leading to an area opening into three or more smaller chapels.

CHILDERMAS, the medieval name for "Children's Mass." It is the Feast of the Holy Innocents, celebrated on Dec. 28.

CHILD OF MARY, a member of a confraternity of the Blessed Virgin Mary. Originally begun by the Jesuits in the 16th century for the instruction of children, the movement was taken up again in 1847 by the Sisters of Charity to promote the devotion of the miraculous medal. Since then, various sodalities have been founded to promote devotion to the Blessed Mother among youth.

CHILDREN, DUTIES OF, the obligations required of children by the fourth commandment. The obligation to honor one's parents includes the giving of respect, love, and obedience. The same duties are to be extended by children to authorities, superiors and teachers.

CHILDREN'S COMMUNION. By his decree of August 8, 1910, Pope St. Pius X granted that children who have reached the "age of discretion" (declared to be seven years) may receive first Holy Communion.

CHILDREN'S CRUSADE. Under the erroneous belief that the Holy Land would be captured by the pure of heart, forty thousand children were gathered in 1212 for this purpose. Following the Fourth Crusade, the children were marched as far as Brindisi, but many died on the way, some were sent home, and others were sold into slavery by treacherous Christian traders.

CHILIASM, the belief of early Christians in the reign of a thousand years as recorded in the twentieth chapter of the Apocalypse. (*Cf.* MILLENIUM.)

CHINESE RITES, various religious practices of a superstitious character which the early missionaries permitted the Chinese converts to retain in ceremonies. These were forbidden by an apostolic constitution of Pope Clement XI in 1715.

CHI-RHO—Three forms of the monogram.

CHI-RHO, the monogram or christogram formed of the Greek letters *Ch* and *R*, which are an abbreviation of the Greek word for Christ. They resemble the Roman letters *X* and *P* and are usually represented as one imposed upon the other.

CHIROGRAPHUS, a personal papal letter, usually addressed to a church dignitary on a serious current problem. Also called an "autograph letter."

CHIROTONY, the sacrament of orders in the Byzantine rite. The term is derived from the Greek and means "stretching forth of the hands."

CHIVALRY, the system of ideas which formed the ideals of conduct of the medieval knight. It was the basis of his conduct in both civil and church society and at peace and war. At the core was honor and devotion under a discipline that governed his personal life and developed a spirit of Christian service for others. As such it arose in the 9th century as a means of saving the Christian West.

The knight was invested and dedicated himself to a life of valor in protecting the weak and upholding the cause of Christ. Chivalry has made a notable contribution to romantic literature of an inspiring nature.

CHOIR. 1. A degree in the hierarchy of the angels. **2.** The place in cathedral or collegiate churches set aside for the recitation of the Divine Office by canons, monks, priests or religious. Each place occupied by these is called a stall. **3.** A group of singers who sing the portions of the liturgy in response to the celebrant and represent the people. Also the place in the church occupied by such singers, usually where the organ is erected.

CHORAL VICAR, the choir director of a group of canons of a cathedral chapter.

CHRISM, a mixture of pure olive oil and balm, or balsam, which is blessed by the bishop on Holy Thursday and used in the administration of baptism, confirmation, holy orders, and at the consecration of bishops. It is also used in the consecration of churches, altar stones, chalices, patens, the solemn blessing of bells, and baptismal water. The two elements together signify a "fullness of grace."

CHRISMAL also **CHRISMATORY.** These words have been applied to a variety of objects in the history of the Church and are now seldom used. Most commonly is meant a jar or vessel, usually larger than an oil stock, for holding a holy oil. Formerly the words were used for: a small container for the Holy Eucharist similar to a pyx, a corporal, a reliquary, the head-covering of a newly baptized child, the first cloth covering a consecrated altar.

CHRISMARIUM, an area once set aside in a cathedral where the sacrament of confirmation was customarily administered. It is sometimes used for the name of a container of chrism.

CHRISMATION, term sometimes applied to an anointing where holy oils are used.

CHRISOM, an old English word for a baptismal garment.

CHRIST. The use of "Christ" (not "the Christ"), meaning "the Anointed," the "Messias," as a proper name became common after the death of our Lord, particularly in the writings of St. Paul (Phil. 1:1–2). It might be used either before or after the name "Jesus." Its use by St. Paul declared the apostle's belief and affirmation of the divinity of Jesus, explicit in Phil. 2:5–11. However, the word "Christ" in Greek is a translation of the Aramaic equivalent of "the prophesied king." Thus Jesus fulfilled in His Incarnation the promise made to Abraham, as given in the genealogy found in the first chapter of St. Matthew's Gospel. (*Cf.* HOLY NAME OF JESUS; SON OF MAN; TRINITY, THE MOST HOLY.)

CHRISTENING. *See* BAPTISM.

CHRISTIAN BROTHERS, a religious order, properly called "Brothers of the Christian Schools," founded by St. Jean Baptiste de la Salle (d. 1719). The order is devoted to the Christian education of youth.

CHRISTIAN DEMOCRATS, followers of the political philosophy of Christian Democracy which adheres to the inalienable rights of individuals and society in regard to the civil authority of the state, whereby individuals may act in accordance with Christian principles. Christian Democracy, established as a party in France, Belgium, Holland, Germany, and Italy, opposes socialism, but seeks no political objective in the governance of property. It is composed of two groups: the radical seeks its purpose through republican government; the mild or less radical permits monarchial government but with representation of the people in executing government.

CHRISTIAN DOCTRINE, the teachings and instructions which are applicable to all Christians. In the Catholic Church this is a broad term embracing primary instruction as well as the most advanced theology. It is progressively systematic and may be applied to the entire course of learning from the child's first learning of simple prayers to catechism, religion courses, and theology, and may include Church history and allied subjects. In its basic meaning it is the developed form of the early teachings given by the apostles to the Christians of the first century of the Church.

CHRISTIAN DOCTRINE, CONFRATERNITY OF. In 1905, Pope St. Pius X decreed the canonical establishment of the Confraternity of Christian Doctrine in every diocese and parish of the Catholic Church. This was incorporated in the New Code of Canon Law in 1917. Its purpose is to extend and improve education in the faith for converts, youth, and those unable to attain knowledge through the Catholic school system. In 1934 a committee of the Catholic hierarchy of the United States was set up to organize the work of the

Confraternity. The work of the Confraternity in spreading knowledge and practice of the faith is accomplished in the following manner: religious training of Catholic children attending non-Catholic grade schools through classes of instruction either during the school term or vacation times; the instruction of Catholic high school students who are attending public high schools or vocational schools through study clubs or other means; by aiding parents in the religious instruction of their children at home; the providing of instruction for non-Catholics. The discussion club has been the most commonly used means of instruction of the Catholic laity. It is also the objective of the Confraternity to provide through a publications department books, texts, manuals, graded courses of study, discussion club aids, catechetical aids, pamphlets and leaflets.

CHRISTIANITY. The establishment of the Christian faith is essentially a part of history. While it has been a rejuvenation of the human race, influencing ages of men in government, social living, the arts and sciences, it had its origin in the religion and the Church established by Jesus Christ. It cannot be understood apart from knowledge of the history and development of the Catholic Church. As such Christianity is the embodiment of the teachings of Jesus Christ, the founding of His Church, and the inspiration and authority found in Scripture. It follows with the continuity of that teaching through the apostles, the expansion and dissemination of that teaching in opposing and conquering the pagan world and through the overcoming of obstacles to its introduction. Following the founding and the introduction of this teaching, there is the organization and the erection of the hierarchical order, the bishops as successors of the apostles, and the continuing of the administration of the seven sacraments which Christ instituted. With organization and growth there followed the great consequences of that teaching, notably its effect upon the family, society, especially the overcoming of slavery, the dignifying of the human personality, new concepts of property rights and duties and the understanding of poverty, and influence on the thinking, actions, and expression of authority by civil authorities. It is the whole of revealed religion in content and execution.

CHRISTIAN MOTHERS, ARCHCONFRATERNITY OF. Societies of Catholic women established in many parishes whose purposes are: spiritual advancement for each member, particularly through the introduction of Christian ideals into their homes, and the works of Christian leadership in their parishes and communities. Their patronesses are: Our Lady of the Seven Sorrows and St. Monica.

CHRISTIAN NAME. *See* BAPTISMAL NAME.

CHRISTIANS, the name of those who follow the faith of Christ. They are of no particular nationality but very early were recognized as a distinct group (Acts 11:26). St. Luke's names for Christians are "saints" (Acts 9:13), "disciples," "brethren," "those of the way," "those who invoke the name" (Acts 9:14), and "believers." In later days the name has been more widely applied to those who imitate Christ in their lives; to Catholics as a single group; to all baptized persons who believe in Christ; and to all who were baptized whatever their belief might be.

CHRIST OF THE ANDES

CHRISTIAN SOCIALISM, the political and economic system which espouses the objectives of socialism as to social reorganization, but seeks to bring them into effect through the application of Christian principles. Thus it stresses private ownership and social duties. In organizations, Christian socialism operates in England, Austria and Germany.

CHRISTMAS, the day on which is celebrated the Nativity of Jesus Christ. In the Church calendar, the feast is commemorated on December 25. Following the celebration of the Church, the world as a whole honors this day as the anniversary of the birth of Christ. On this day, by special privilege, priests are permitted to celebrate three Masses. (*Cf.* IN-CARNATION.)

CHRIST OF THE ANDES, an heroic statue of Christ erected to commemorate the friendly settlement through arbitration of a boundary dispute between Chile and Argentina in South America in the last years of the 19th century. It was cast from the metal of guns intended for the possible war and was placed on the border between the two countries on a mountain 14,000 feet above sea level. An inscription on its pedestal reads: "He is our peace who hath made both one."

CHRISTOLOGY, name of the body of theology dealing especially with the nature and personality of Jesus Christ, the Scripture concerning Him, and His life and teachings. It is the theology centered on Jesus simply rather than on Christ as the Second Person of the Trinity.

CHRISTOPHERS, name given to the followers of the Christopher movement, founded in 1946 by the Rev. James Keller, M.M., in the United States. The purposes and ideals of the Christophers are attained by no closely-knit, dues-paying membership, but by allying oneself with the movement to bring Christian principles to American public and private life. This program is one of positive thought and action in the fields of government, education, trade-unions, and the fields of drama and writing or in any walk of life. While the membership is largely Catholic, it is not limited to those of a particular religious affiliation. The work is done on a purely individual basis, by being first an exemplar and second a responsible leader, willing to take the initiative in Christian action. It is supported entirely by voluntary contributions.

CHRIST, SUPREME ORDER OF, a papal decoration, with one class of knights. The order was founded in the 14th century by Pope John XXII in Portugal. Now called Militia of Our Lord Jesus Christ.

CHRONICLES, BOOK OF. *See* PARALIPOMENON.

CHRONOLOGY, BIBLICAL, the record by years of the history of Israel, but more particularly that record of the reigns of the Hebrew kings under the divided monarchy. This history is divided briefly into three periods: that of hostility (931–885 B.C.), that of alliance (885–841 B.C.) and that of their independent development (841–721 B.C.). Upon these dates there is general historical agreement, but the accord between dates in the Jewish history and that of secular history is attained only after extensive research.

CHURCH. 1. When speaking of *the* Church, it is that visible religious society, founded by Jesus Christ, under one head, St. Peter, and continuing under the governance of his successors, the popes. In its founding, Christ promised protection of the Church until the end of time (Mt. 28:20), and gave as its commission the preservation and extension of His teachings in His name. It is thus the role of the Church to present the means of salvation given by Christ, i.e. the sacraments and sacrifice (*cf.* MARKS OF THE CHURCH). **2.** The Church is the mystical body of Christ. This is described by Pope Pius XII in his ·encyclical, "The Mystical Body of Christ," thus: "If we would define and describe this true Church of Jesus Christ—which is the one, holy, Catholic, apostolic, Roman Church—we shall find no expression more noble, more sublime or more divine than the phrase which calls it 'the mystical body of Jesus Christ' " (*cf.* MYSTICAL BODY OF CHRIST). **3.** In a limited sense, the word Church may mean a particular Church of a country, nation, or city, usually stated as such, e.g., the American Church. This is not to be confused with "national Churches" which are those circumscribed by the country and are governed by a separate jurisdiction, as the Armenian Church. **4.** In its most limited sense, a church is a building set apart and dedicated to the public worship of God, the celebration of Mass, the singing of the Holy Office, the administration of the sacraments, and for the use of all the faithful.

CHURCH AND STATE. While this is customarily presented as a problem, it need not be if proper understanding of the two entities is pursued. Both the Church and the state are perfect societies in themselves, each with a purpose and so endowed with rights and powers to attain that purpose. However, each, while operating in its own sphere, must also overlap the activity of the other since both exercise authority over the same individuals as subjects. Stated as principles we see: the Church is supreme in spiritual affairs, the state in temporal and material affairs. Each is separate and distinct in juridical activities and legislatively, but the state must foster and preserve in a positive manner the purposes of the Church, since the spiritual sphere is greater than the temporal, and the Church must teach the recognition and acceptance of the authority of the state and teach the practices which further the good qualities of citizenship. The Church likewise has a right to the temporal things which are necessary for her to carry out her mission, as church property, schools, etc. Lastly the Church's rights must have precedence over those of the state in affairs where the two spheres of activity are in conflict. The bishops of the United States have stated: "Authoritative Catholic teaching on the relations between Church and state, as set forth in papal encyclicals and in the treatises of recognized writers in ecclesiastical law, not only states clearly what these relations should normally be under ideal conditions, but also indicates to what extent the Catholic Church can adapt herself to the particular conditions that may obtain in different countries. Examining, in the full perspective of that teaching, the position which those who founded our nation and framed its basic law took on the problem of Church-state relations in our own country, we find that the First Amendment to our Constitution solved the problem in a way that was typically American in its practical recognition of existing conditions and its evident desire to be fair to all citizens of whatever religious faith. To one who knows something of history and law, the meaning of the First Amendment is clear enough from its own words: 'Congress shall make no laws respecting an establishment of religion or forbidding the free exercise thereof.' The meaning is even clearer in the records of the congress that enacted it." (Letter of Nov. 21, 1948.)

CHURCH HISTORY. The record of the activity of the Church since its founding by Christ usually presented in the concurrent setting of secular events which are the accounts of mankind's course since Christianity became the major influence upon that course. The history of the Church is a recounting of the events which mark the progress of an imperishable society. This society has unusual features, namely, a divine Founder, supernatural powers, the promise of enduring, the inspired wórd of Scripture, and infallibility in doctrinal matters of faith and morals. Together with these there is the completeness of revelation, to which nothing is or can be added, but which from the apostolic deposit of faith, may be presented in its development and unfolding. Moreover, the Church's history spans more than nineteen hundred years and reaches into every nation and race and is included in every known language of those years. Because of the complex nature of this history, there are many approaches made to encompass the record. This may be accomplished by making an arbitrary division of the time into centuries, into periods. This latter system is usually followed thus: (a) First period: from apostolic times to the time of Charlemagne, crowned emperor in 800 A.D. (b) Second period: from Charlemagne through the Middle Ages to the rise of the Protestant religion. (c) Third period: from the 16th century to the present day. Strictly speaking, since the Church is universal, its history cannot be considered nation by nation, except in special studies. The study of Church history is unique in that there is a necessary distinction to be made between the divine and human factors.

CHURCHING OF WOMEN, the blessing given to a woman after childbirth. It is not mandatory that women receive this blessing or make the act of thanksgiving accompanying this, since there is no taint attached to childbearing; it is simply recommended. The blessing is not given when the child is illegitimate.

CHURCH PROPERTY, legally the movable and immovable possessions of the Church which she has by right. The Church as a society has the right of purchasing and possessing property, personal or real, in order to carry on the work she is commissioned to do. Just as the state may tax its citizens, so the Church has the right to assess its members for the means of functioning.

CHURCH UNITY OCTAVE. *See* CHAIR OF UNITY OCTAVE.

CHURCHYARD, the property or land surrounding a church building. It may or may not be enclosed, but it often specifically refers to a cemetery when this adjoins church property.

CIBORIUM. 1. The metal vessel similar to a chalice but having a cover in which small hosts or particles of the Blessed Sacrament are reserved in the tabernacle for distribution in Holy Communion to the faithful. When containing the Blessed Sacrament, it is covered with a silk veil. **2.** A baldaquin. (*Cf.* CIVORY.)

CILICIUM, literally cloth of hair. This is a penitential garment, a hairshirt, sometimes worn next to the skin.

CINCTURE or **GIRDLE,** a cord 12 to 14 feet in length, with tassels at each end, used to bind the alb at the waist when the priest is vesting for Mass. It is usually white but, properly, should be the same color as the vestments. It may be of any material, but that of prelates is of silk.

CIRCUMCELLIONES, a wandering group of fanatic Donatist heretics of the early 4th century.

CIRCUMCISION, FEAST OF. This feast is celebrated on Jan. 1, to commemorate the submission by Jesus to the rite of circumcision (Lk. 2:21–24) as prescribed by the Law and by which Christ comes forward as the heir of the promise made by God to Abraham in the institution of the rite. It is a holyday of obligation.

CIRCUMINCESSION, the inexistence of the three distinct Persons of the Blessed Trinity, the Father being whole and entire in the Son and in the Holy Spirit, and each one in the other as well as in the Father. (*Cf.* TRINITY, THE MOST HOLY.)

CITATION, in canon law (cc. 1711–1725), the summons of a defendant to an ecclesiastical court.

CITY OF GOD, the book *De Civitate Dei*, written by St. Augustine between 412 and 427 A.D. An apologetic work defending the Church against paganism, it portrays a "city" or group of men ruled by the love of God, free of self-love and self-interests and, perhaps more important, it presents a philosophy of history for universal man.

CIVIL ALLEGIANCE. This is the Christian's duty to the state to which he is bound by loyalty and, as a citizen, by obedience to its laws. It is the acceptance of the civic obligations, as secondary and necessary following as they do the higher obligation to God, in recognition of the fact that the state has its authority from God. (*Cf.* CHURCH AND STATE.)

CIVIL LAW, broadly, the body of laws and governing legislation of the state as distinct from the canon law of the Church.

CIVIL MARRIAGE, the pronouncement of the marriage vows and the execution of the contract by which a man and woman are declared to be husband and wife by a representative of the state, as a justice of the peace, a judge, or other official. The state does not have the juridical right in the case of baptized persons, nor has it the power to dissolve the bond of any marriage. The Church alone is competent in all matters pertaining to the bond of baptized persons (c. 1960). A Catholic who goes through a ceremony of marriage before a minister or official of the state contracts no marriage. Further, a Catholic marrying before a Protestant minister incurs excommunication reserved to the bishop (c. 1063). Non-Catholics are exempt from this law and their marriages before ministers and state officials are valid unless otherwise null. Questions concerning the civil effects of matrimony, registration, legal residence, etc., are the province of the state and the marriages of Catholics must be registered with the civil authorities. In countries where civil marriage is demanded by the state, Catholics are allowed to fulfill this requirement but understanding that no act of marriage is intended. (*Cf.* MARRIAGE.)

CIVORY also **CIBORIUM,** a solid structure of stone, metal or wood, erected over the altar and its *predella* or footpace, and supported by columns or posts, usually at the corners. (*Cf.* BALDAQUIN.)

CLANDESTINITY, an impediment to marriage. It is illegal secrecy or an agreement affecting the form of marriage. Thus for a marriage to be valid it must be contracted before the pastor of the parish, or the ordinary

of the diocese (or before a priest delegated by either) and at least two witnesses (c. 1094). Clandestine marriages may be made valid by a remarriage under the proper form.

CLAPPER

CLAPPER also **CLEPPER** or **CROTALUM,** a wooden device, with a handle and swinging hammer which strikes two surfaces, making a clapping noise. It is used in place of bells in ceremonies from Holy Thursday till the *Gloria* of the Mass on Holy Saturday.

CLAUSURA. *See* ENCLOSURE.

CLEMENTINE INSTRUCTION, THE. This is the title of the regulations governing Forty Hours' devotion, so called because they were first set down by Clement XII in 1736. The regulations were revised by Pope St. Pius X in 1914.

CLERGY, collective term for male persons who administer the rites of the Church through holy orders and jurisdiction. It includes all bishops and priests, and more broadly those having received the four minor and first two major orders; yet anyone who has received tonsure is properly classified as a member of the clergy. (*Cf.* CLERIC.)

CLERIC. In England and some other countries called "clerk," a cleric is: **1.** A member of the diocesan clergy. **2.** Anyone who has received tonsure. **3.** Anyone who may incur clerical penalties, bishops excepted.

CLERICALISM, the claim on the part of the clergy, or the charge by others, that priests or bishops exercise jurisdisdiction pertinent to the state. It is usually a derogative term for any attempt to apply religious principles to questions of society, morals, economics, or political life. Historically, certain movements begun by churchmen were branded as clericalism in order to defeat their good purposes.

CLERICAL PRIVILEGE. The clergy, besides certain obligations arising from their state, have privileges which are set forth in canons 118–123. More specifically this means (a) that clerics are not under the jurisdiction of the lay courts, and are not to be tried before a lay judge, but before an ecclesiastical court, unless by specific exception set forth in the law, (b) that clerics have freedom from military service or the bearing of arms and from the imposition of secular occupations or duties.

CLERKS REGULAR, a term for those groups of men in religious life who live under community rule but are engaged primarily in the activities of the diocesan clergy, as the care of parishes, teaching, etc., rather than the monastic life, e.g., Jesuits, Redemptorists, etc.

CLINICAL BAPTISM, a term, no longer used, which in early times referred to baptism given to one who was ill.

CLOISTER also **CLOSE. 1.** A covered passageway around the quadrangle (or garth), usually open on the quadrangle side, with the opposite side formed by the walls of the buildings of a monastery. **2.** A term signifying the restrictions from egress of members of a monastic order of religious and the prohibition of outsiders from entry. **3.** The enclosure itself. **4.** Sometimes referred to the life led by members of an encloistered convent or monastery.

CLOTHING, THE, name given to the formal admission of a candidate to a religious order at which he is solemnly clothed in the habit of the order.

COADJUTOR. 1. One who assists another, as in church use the one appointed to assist a bishop or a priest. **2.** A coadjutor bishop is one appointed by the Holy See as an assistant to a bishop governing a diocese. As such he may be given either to the person of the bishop governing and either have or have not the right of succession to the diocese upon the death of the governing bishop, or he may be given to the diocese, in which case he continues in office after the death of the incumbent bishop until the diocese is again filled. A coadjutor given to a bishop who is incapacitated usually has all the rights and duties of a residential bishop. (*Cf.* AUXILIARY BISHOP.)

COAT-OF-ARMS. In Church heraldry an arms insignia may be that of religious corporations, schools, etc., or that of religious rank or dignity, sometimes the emblems or devices of saints, and the orders of knighthood. Most frequently seen are the coats-of-arms of dioceses or bishops. That used by bishops is marked by the use

COAT-OF-ARMS—The coat-of-arms of His Holiness Pope Pius XII.

of the miter, the crosier and the ecclesiastical hat. The hat is low-crowned, flat, wide-brimmed and has cords and tassels hanging from either side. For example, a cardinal's coat-of-arms is shown surmounted by a scarlet hat with fifteen tassels on each side. The hats of a patriarch, an archbishop, or a bishop are green as depicted above the coat-of-arms, the patriarch's with fifteen tassels with gold interwoven in the cord and tassels; an archbishop's has ten tassels and a bishop's six. The hat above a priest's coat-of-arms is black and has two tassels. The papal coat-of-arms consists of the tiara above the crossed keys of St. Peter, one key being gold, the other silver.

COAT, THE HOLY. *See* HOLY COAT.

CO-CONSECRATORS, the two bishops who assist the presiding bishop at the consecration of a newly appointed bishop.

CODE OF CANON LAW, the compilation and codification of the common law of the Church. (*Cf.* CANON LAW.)

CODEX. In biblical use, a codex is a manuscript of the Sacred Scriptures. In the absence of original manuscripts and the first copies of the N.T., the text is dependent upon manuscript codices of a later date. Codices are grouped as to their contents as either pure or mixed. Pure codices provide only original Greek texts, while the mixed give, in addition to the original text, commentaries or versions in Latin, Greek, or Syriac. Some codices are named according to their past or present place of storage or their former owners. The oldest and most important codices are: *Vaticanus*, of the 4th century, probably of Egyptian origin, containing the entire Bible from Gen. 46:28 to Heb. 9:14; *Sinaiticus*, probably of the 4th century, discovered in the monastery of Mt. Sinai and now in the British Museum; *Alexandrinus*, 5th century; *Codex Ephraemi Rescriptus*, 5th century, now in the Paris National Library; *Codex Bezae*, 6th century, in the possession of Cambridge University; *Claromantanus*, 6th century, now in the Paris National Library.

COENOBITE, an early term, equivalent to monk, used by St. Jerome to distinguish one of a religious life from an anchorite or hermit. Later listed by St. Benedict as one type of monk who lives in a community under an abbot.

COENOBIUM, a monastery or convent. The place where monks or coenobites live in community life. Sometimes it refers to the church building of a monastery as distinct from the other buildings.

COLLATERAL, term for the blood relationship in the indirect line, as brother or sister, uncle or aunt, nephew or niece, first or second cousins. Such relationship is an impediment to marriage, rendering it invalid to the third degree inclusive (c. 1076). Also called cognate line.

COLLATION. 1. Name applied to the light meal taken on a day of fast, other than breakfast and the main meal. The amount of food is not specified but must be less than a full meal. The name derives from the *collationes*, the spiritual reading from the Fathers, which was customarily read aloud in monasteries at meal time. **2.** The act of appointment of a new incumbent to an ecclesiastical benefice.

COLLECT. The *Collect* of the Mass consists of short prayers which are said just before the Epistle is read. They are of three kinds: first, that of the feast of the day which changes with the feast; second, that of a second feast falling on the same date, more specifically called a commemoration; third, various prayers or orations which are said for a special intention; e.g., for the pope, or for the Church, and which do not change with the feast. The name is derived from "assembly" and was the prayer said in the early Church while the people gathered for the celebration of the Eucharist.

COLLECTION, OFFERTORY, the custom of accepting voluntary contributions from the faithful. The practice now is to accept money donations, frequently in envelopes of the parish, which are used for various church expenses. Formerly, such collections were of food or coin and were to support the priest.

COLLEGE. 1. An association, corporation, or organized society or group of persons with a common purpose, forming a moral body. Such are the College of Cardinals and the colleges of collegiate churches. Every Church college must be canonically erected. **2.** A pontifical college is a seminary, directly subject to the Holy See, for the training of priests and missionaries. **3.** Apostolic college designates the group of the apostles under St. Peter as their head (Lk. 22). **4.** A national college is a seminary established at Rome for the education of priests of a particular country, e.g., North American College for the United States. **5.** An institution of higher learning, distinguished from a university.

COLLEGIATE CHURCH, a church served by a group of clerics, called a chapter. The members of the chapter are called canons. (*Cf.* CHAPTER.)

COLLEGIUM CULTORUM MARTYRUM, the Latin title of the "Association for Venerating the Martyrs in the Catacombs." It was founded in 1897 by the Commission of Sacred Archaeology to further devotion to the martyrs, to aid in excavation work, and to extend learning of the early Church.

COLORS, LITURGICAL. The use of color in the Church as an added aspect of its symbolism in the liturgy is of early origin, although in the days of the Roman empire white was most commonly used. Color as such became a mark of distinction in dress, and in the Middle Ages there was added the sequence of colors in vestments to be used for various feasts. The modern sequence of colors are five: white, red, green, violet and black. Any shade of these colors is permitted, while cloth of gold (never yellow) may be used in place of white, red or green on major feast days. Cloth of silver may replace white. Rose vestments may be worn on the fourth Sunday of Lent and the third Sunday of Advent.

COLOSSIANS, EPISTLE TO THE, one of the "captivity epistles" written by St. Paul. It was intended for the people of the Lycus valley and was to correct certain errors in their teaching; it is thus a polemical treatise. The epistle lays great emphasis on the divinity and manhood of Christ, stating that Christ is supreme over all creation, He rules the world because of this fact of creation, He is the Redeemer of the world and He is the Head of the Church, His mystical body.

COMES, name of the compiled book containing the lessons of the Breviary, the Epistles and Gospels.

COMMANDMENTS OF GOD also **DECALOGUE** or **TEN COMMANDMENTS,** the moral commands or laws given by God to Moses (Ex. 20:1–21) on Mount Sinai. It is certain that the Decalogue was made up of ten distinct commandments (Deut. 5:2–33) no matter how they may be grouped. These commands are interpreted by Christ in the N.T. (Mt. 5:17–47). The first three are concerned with the love and true worship of God, and the other seven are directed to the love and justice due our neighbor. The wording varies in either the original or translation, but the substance of the law remains. The order traditional in the Church is: First table, or group: **I.** I am the Lord, your God, you shall not have false gods before Me. **II.** You shall not take the Lord's name in vain. **III.** You shall keep holy the Sabbath day. Second table: **IV.** Honor your parents. **V.** Do not murder. **VI.** Do not commit adultery. **VII.** Do not steal. **VIII.** Do not lie. **IX.** Do not have adulterous desires. **X.** Do not covet your neighbor's goods.

COMMANDMENTS OF THE CHURCH. While these might be taken to include all the legislation of the Church as a teacher and governing body, it is accepted more generally as applying to the six precepts of a moral and ecclesiastic nature which are directed to the observance of religion in practice. In the United States as presented by the third plenary council of Baltimore these are: **1.** Keep the Sundays and holydays of obligation by assisting at Mass and desisting from servile work. **2.** Fast and abstain on the days appointed by the Church. **3.** Go to confession at least once a year. **4.** Receive the Blessed Sacrament during the season of Easter. **5.** Contribute to the support of the Church and its pastors. **6.** Do not marry within certain degrees of kindred nor solemnize marriage during a forbidden time.

COMMEMORATION OF FEASTS. In the celebration of feast days in the Church, some feasts are movable (i.e., vary in date because of the date of Easter changing), and thus two feasts may fall on the same day. In these occurrences, the Church does not celebrate the two feasts but recites in the Office of the day that of the major of the two feasts and commemorates or includes part of the Office of the lesser feast. Applications of this principle are made both in the Divine Office and in the prayers of the Missal.

COMMEMORATION OF THE LIVING AND THE DEAD IN THE MASS. At the prayer of the Mass, the *Memento, Domine,* the priest silently commends to God benefactors, friends, etc., who are living. At the fifth prayer of the Canon the priest mentions by name the one or many who are dead for whom he is to pray. Such commemorations may be made by anyone attending Mass at the reading of these prayers, and they may include anyone of their choice for whom they wish to pray.

COMMENDA, formerly the custody of a church or institution exercised by one not the regular incumbent.

COMMENDATION OF THE SOUL, the prayer for the dying said by a priest or other as contained in the Roman Ritual. It includes the last blessing, the plenary indulgence, a short form of the Litany of the Saints, three prayers of farewell asking the forgiveness of sins and commending the soul of the dying person to God and the saints, a prayer in the form of a litany beseeching deliverance, followed by three more prayers of forgiveness and commendation.

COMMENTARIES, BIBLICAL, explanatory writings on the books of the Bible. Strictly speaking these are not works of biblical criticism, but are for the study and understanding of the texts of Scripture. They are grouped as: Jewish, patristic, medieval and modern.

COMMISSARY. 1. Apostolic commissary is one delegated by the pope to take evidence and pronounce judgment in an important case, or to serve as an administrator. **2.** Provincial Commissary is the superior of a province of Friars Minor and Conventuals where there are insufficient members to form a real province, and hence it is dependent upon another established province. **3.** Simple commissary is any ecclesiastic with delegated jurisdiction from a bishop. **4.** Commissary of the Holy Land is the Friar Minor who receives and collects alms for the upkeep of the Holy Places of Palestine. It may also refer to the place where this friar resides.

COMMISSIONS, ECCLESIASTICAL. 1. A group of persons lay or cleric legally appointed to perform some duty or special work. **2.** Pontifical commissions are those set up to aid the Holy Father. Principally, these commissions are: for study of the Scriptures; for interpretation of the Code of Canon Law; for the revision of the Vulgate; of sacred archaeology; for the protection of historical and artistic monuments; and for the heraldry of the papal court.

COMMIXTURE, LITURGICAL. In the celebration of Mass the priest, after the prayer *Libera nos quaesumus,* breaks the host in two halves, and from one half breaks a smaller fragment. After making the sign of the cross three times over the chalice with this particle, he drops it into the chalice as he begins the prayer *Haec commixtio.* This is a symbol of Christ's union with the Church, His mystical body.

COMMON. 1. Common life is the community or group living of members of a religious order. **2.** Common teaching of theologians is a doctrine which all theologians hold is true, is taught as true doctrine, and is binding in the doctrine of the faith. **3.** Common of the Mass is the collective name for the ceremonies and prayers of the Mass which remain the same, the ordinary. **4.** Common of the Saints is the division of prayers into groups, e.g., apostles, martyrs, etc., which are found in the Missal and Breviary and said where no Proper is assigned to these saints.

COMMUNICATIO IDIOMATUM, the "interchange of properties," whereby the divine attributes of Christ as God may be affirmed of Christ as Man and *vice versa.* The reason for this is that, for example, in speaking of the God-Man, or God the Son incarnate, we imply not only the human nature of Christ but also the divine Person united with it. Care must be exercised that no detraction or distortion is wrought in this interchange. Thus it is wrong to say "Divinity suffered," but correct to say, "God suffered."

COMMUNION. 1. Holy Communion is the body, blood, soul and divinity of Christ which is received whole and entire under the form of bread or wine alone and consumed by the recipient. All persons who are baptized, have the right intention, are free of mortal sin (in the state of sanctifying grace), and observe the proper fast from food, may receive the sacrament of the Eucharist. Exceptions are: infants and children who have not reached the age of reason, those who are notorious public sinners, those who have been legally separated from the Church by censure, and those who because of mental or bodily illness cannot receive with reverence. The rules for the Eucharistic fast are: 1. Water may be taken up to any time before receiving Communion, but it must be plain, with no other food element added, e.g., sugar as in soft drinks. Alcoholic drinks, coffee, tea and milk are forbidden. 2. The sick, with the permission of a confessor, even though not confined to bed may take liquids and medicine, in addition to water, before receiving Holy Communion. 3. Persons who are not sick, but are in one of the following groups may take liquid nourishment up to one hour before receiving, upon advice of a confessor: (a) one who can only receive Communion at a late hour; (b) one who must perform exhausting labor; (c) one who must travel some distance to go to church. 4. At an evening Mass, permitted by the bishop (not earlier than 4 P.M.), one may receive Communion providing he abstains from solid food for three hours before the time of receiving. No alcoholic beverages are to be taken during that day and only wine or beer are permitted with meals on the day of receiving. Other beverages may be taken up to one hour before receiving. Fasting from food is ordinarily required from midnight when one intends to receive Communion in the morning. **2.** Manner of receiving Holy Communion in the Roman rite is under the species of bread, the priest placing a eucharistic host (or particle) on the tongue of the one receiving. In the Byzantine rite, reception is by receiving the consecrated bread by spoon after the bread has been dipped into the consecrated wine (known as intinction). Those of the Ethiopian rite receive under both species. **3.** Spiritual Communion is the desire to receive Communion when one is not able to do so, and the expression of this desire by acts of love, thanksgiving, etc., when one is not able to receive in actuality. **4.** Communion in the Mass is the title of that antiphon, varying with the feast, which is read right after the Communion of the Mass when the priest returns to the epistle side of the altar.

COMMUNION OF SAINTS. The ninth article of the Apostles' Creed declares the spiritual union which exists between the saints in heaven, the souls in purgatory and the faithful living on earth. This union is one of grace and good works, and in recognition of this the faithful imitate, venerate, and pray for the intercession of the saints in heaven, and pray for the souls in purgatory.

COMMUNISM, the extreme form of socialism based upon the theory of state absolutism as propounded by Karl Marx (1818–1883). As such, communism seeks to set up a world-wide collectivism under dictatorship of the proletariat. It is a doctrine of totalitarianism whereby the state becomes the supreme authority, answering to no other. As a system its aims are: world control; the elimination of (a) private property and rights; (b) production for profit; (c) the rights of the individual; (d) belief in God. As a political and economic system, the Communist party repudiates Christianity and belief in God and advocates a policy of violence—even toward its own members and allies. In 1935 at the Seventh Congress of the Third International, there was begun a new program aimed at world domination: (a) party affiliates in other countries were freed from the strict practices of the Russian party except in adherence and recognition of the Russian leadership; (b) local groups were to oppose fascism even by the means of joining other Socialist, Laborite, or even Christian parties. This was a method of strategy and propaganda. The Church has been opposed to communism because of its atheistic materialism, its promotion of class war, and denial of human rights. Pope Pius XI in his encyclical *Divini Redemptoris*, published in March 1937, condemned communism and instructed Catholics of the world not to co-operate with communists in either social or political activities. In 1949 the Church issued a decree by which the sacraments are denied to nominal communists or their supporters, and this applies even to those who, without authorization, read communist literature or who freely and knowingly perform actions aiding the communists. A further more dire penalty of excommunication is applied "by the very fact" to Catholics "who profess, defend and spread the materialistic and anti-Christian doctrine of the communists." Today not only the Church but all peoples of freedom-loving nations oppose communism.

COMPARATIVE RELIGION, the science or study of the teachings, founding, practices, and development of the known religions.

COMPLINE, the final hour of the Divine Office, following Vespers. It is composed of a short lesson, the Our Father, Confiteor, three Psalms with their antiphons, a hymn, a little chapter and responsory, the Canticle of Simeon (*Nunc Dimittis*) with its antiphon, a collect and a blessing. In the Byzantine rite, the Apodeipnon.

COMPOSTELA, PILGRIMAGE OF, the practice of making a penitential visit to the shrine of St. James the Greater, at Compostela, Spain, begun in the 8th century.

CONCELEBRATION, the simultaneous celebration of Mass by more than one priest, consecrating the same bread and wine. This is done at the Mass of ordination of priests and the consecration of bishops in the Roman rite.

CONCEPTION, IMMACULATE. *See* IMMACULATE CONCEPTION OF THE B.V.M.

CONCILIAR THEORY, also **CONCILIAR MOVEMENT.** This movement sought to make the pope subordinate to a general council and arose in the 14th century. It lost force when the danger to unity was seen and was finally condemned in 1870 at the Vatican Council.

CONCLAVE, the assembly of the cardinals and the place where they gather to elect a new pope. In the conclave an area or small cell is constructed and allotted to each cardinal with accommodations for two of his companions. The strictest enclosure separates this area from the rest of the Vatican allowing no communication between the cardinals and the outside world. Extreme caution and special rules govern the conclave.

CONCOMITANCE, in philosophy, the act or state of being associated. In theology, by natural concomitance, the whole Christ is present in the Eucharist under each species of bread and wine, meaning that both *body* and *blood* are present together with His soul, or by virtue of the fact that soul, body and blood of a living being cannot be separated. Thus also by supernatural concomitance the divinity of Christ is also present under each species of the Eucharist as understood by the hypostatic union.

CONCORDANCE OF THE BIBLE, an alphabetical index arranged to give the leading words of passages of Scripture and references to book, chapter, and verse. It also supplies the location of principal words of the Bible and the number of times they were used, thus being indispensable to anyone seeking to locate a certain text of Scripture.

CONCORDAT, a special agreement, compromise or treaty drawn up between the Holy See and the civil government of a country, nation, or dominion. Its sole objective concerns spiritual matters, in particular the spiritual welfare of Catholics residing as nationals of the country. These concordats usually arise in the Sacred Congregation for Extraordinary Ecclesiastical Affairs, but the Supreme Tribunal of the Apostolic Signature has special competence regarding certain of these agreements. Concordats are means of better regulation of religious life in certain countries and in no way are a capitulation to dominance by the state.

CONCORDAT OF WORMS, an agreement made in 1122 between Pope Callistus II and Emperor Henry V which ended lay investiture. Also called the *Pactum Calixtinum.*

CONCUPISCENCE. The word is used in two senses: (a) the passionate desire of a person inclining the sensitive appetite toward sensible good or away from sensible evil; (b) the inclination toward evil, particularly the inclination toward impurity. In both instances concupiscence arises in the imagination and arouses the sensual appetite. In the second sense it is an inclination against right reason and a giving way to the propensity of human nature toward sin.

CONCURSUS. 1. A competitive examination by which candidates to ecclesiastical offices are chosen. **2.** The divine concursus is the act by which God as the first cause operates through secondary or created causes.

CONDITIONAL ADMINISTRATION OF THE SACRAMENTS. Under certain circumstances, the sacraments of baptism, penance, and holy orders may be administered on condition as stated, e.g., in the words of the form, "If you are not baptized, I baptize, etc."

CONFERENCES, CLERGY, meetings of the diocesan clergy, usually held monthly in the principal city of the diocese, or in each deanery. Their purpose is to discuss pastoral problems, cases of conscience, particularly questions of liturgy or moral theology. These meetings are also called pastoral conferences.

CONFESSION. 1. Sacramental Confession (*See* AURICULAR CONFESSION; PENANCE, SACRAMENT OF). 2. Annual confession. The obligation is imposed on all who have reached the age of reason to confess at least once a year (c. 916). This may be done at any time or place and to any authorized priest. Properly, the obligation does not extend to those who have not committed mortal sin; but it is recommended to them. 3. Sacrilegious confession. In the case that a penitent willfully withholds the confession of a known mortal sin, or willfully fails in sorrow for sin or purpose of amendment, or does not intend to make satisfaction or restitution if required, the sacrament of penance is made void, absolution is not effective, and the confession must be repeated and the fact of the sacrilegious confession confessed.

CONFESSIONAL, the enclosed place where the priest behind a screen hears the confession of a penitent and administers the sacrament of penance. It may be single or double, that is, in the single the priest sits in one side of the enclosure while the penitent kneels on the other side with the screen between them; in the double, the priest sits in a compartment between two screens with the penitents on either side. The priest then alternates, hearing the confession first from one side and then from the other, alternately sliding soundproof panels across the screens.

CONFESSION OF A MARTYR also **CONFESSIO.** This originally was the tomb of a martyr, particularly those in the catacombs where Mass was celebrated. Now it refers to the crypt where the remains of a martyr are kept beneath the main altar of a church, e.g., the crypt beneath St. Peter's in Rome containing the body of the first pope.

CONFESSOR. 1. Title of a canonized male saint, being one whose life gave testimony to the faith. There are two groups, those who were bishops and those who were not. **2.** A priest, having the required faculties or jurisdiction from the bishop of the diocese, who hears the confession of penitents and administers the sacrament of penance. His role is not only to act in the place of Christ as judge and impart sacramental absolution, but also to serve as counselor and spiritual guide. **3.** An extraordinary confessor is the priest appointed to hear the confession of men or women religious over and above their regular confessor.

CONFIRMATION NAME, the name of a saint, chosen by the one confirmed and imposed by the bishop, and which is added to the Christian name. It is recommended that the person confirmed imitate the virtues of the saint whose name is chosen. It is optional as to whether one wishes to use the name since it is not a legal name as such.

CONFIRMATION, SACRAMENT OF. Confirmation is a sacrament of the New Law by which grace of the Holy Spirit is given to one baptized by anointing with chrism in the form of a cross on the forehead, the imposition of hands and saying the words: "I sign you with the sign of the cross and confirm you with the chrism of salvation, in the name of the Father, and of the Son, and of the Holy Ghost." The effects of the sacrament are: an increase of sanctifying grace and the gifts of the Holy Spirit; imparts a seal or character on the soul (so this sacrament may not be repeated), and so strengthens actual grace that the recipient is enabled to fearlessly profess the faith and fight against temptation. The bishop is the ordinary minister of confirmation, while the extraordinary minister is a priest to whom the power has been granted by office, as a cardinal, or by apostolic indult. It is the custom of the Church to have each one confirmed presented by a sponsor. We learn much about the sacrament of confirmation in the Acts of the Apostles (1:5; 11:16; 2:38). It was early called "the baptism of the Spirit" and the Council of Trent declares confirmation a "true and proper sacrament."

CONFITEOR, literally, "I confess," the title and the first Latin word of a prayer. It is said by the priest and acolyte in the prayers at the foot of the altar before the celebration of Mass. In wording it is an open confession and petition for prayer and forgiveness. It is recommended that it be said in preparation for receiving the sacrament of penance.

CONFRATERNITY, in canon law a voluntary association, generally of the laity, established under Church authority, for the promotion of some work of devotion, charity or instruction undertaken for the love of God. Confraternities are not free-acting groups but are subject to the assent of the bishop and their statutes are subject to his approval.

CONFRATERNITY EDITION OF THE BIBLE, a revision of the Challoner-Rheims Version of the N.T. produced in 1941. It is a new version, retaining the "thou" of the original, but the wording and grammar have been modernized and all archaic forms have been eliminated. Basic sources were the Vulgate and Greek editions. The Confraternity edition of the O.T., translating from the Hebrew into modern English, was begun in 1948.

CONFRATERNITY OF CHRISTIAN DOCTRINE. *See* CHRISTIAN DOCTRINE, CONFRATERNITY OF.

CONGREGATION. 1. Religious: a community of religious whose members are bound together by a common rule and take only simple vows. **2.** Monastic: one or more monasteries under a single superior. **3.** A group of Catholics who are members of a parish, usually living within the territory designated as the parish by the bishop. Also members of a parish assembled in the parish church for divine worship. **4.** Sacred Congregations. These are departments of the Roman Curia and are the highest ranking bodies serving the pope in the administration and government of the Church. They are: Congregation of the Holy Office; the Sacred Consistorial Congregation; the Sacred Congregation for the Oriental Church; the Sacred Congregation of the Sacraments; the Sacred Congregation of the Council; the Sacred Congregation of Religious; the Sacred Congregation for the Propagation of the Faith; the Sacred Congregation of Rites; the Sacred Ceremonial Congregation; the Sacred Congregation for Extraordinary Ecclesiastical Affairs; the Sacred Congregation of Seminaries and Universities; and the Sacred Congregation for St. Peter's Basilica. **5.** Congregations are appointed at general councils and are made up of bishops appointed or approved by the pope for the carrying out of the program.

CONGRESSES, EUCHARISTIC, gatherings of the clergy and faithful for the purpose of giving glory to

God in the Holy Eucharist by public adoration and general reception of Holy Communion. They also serve to promote the spiritual, social and intellectual welfare of the faithful especially through discussion and means of furthering devotion to our Lord in the Blessed Sacrament. They may be (a) international when all countries of the world participate or (b) national when they are held for one country.

CONGRUISM, a theory of grace originated by Molina and developed by Suarez and others. It maintains that efficacious grace is adapted to suit (*congruus*) the person receiving the grace and in proportion to the person's future co-operation once the grace is given. This degree of co-operation they maintain God knows because of His *scientia media*, mediate knowledge. St. Thomas' teaching is: the good use of grace by free consent is itself an effect of grace and it would be contradictory to say that the grace of God is only efficacious by the consent of the recipient, since this would detract from the divine causality in giving the grace.

CONSANGUINITY, a diriment impediment to marriage, being blood-relationship in either the direct or collateral line. Consanguinity renders marriage invalid in the direct line in all degrees (i.e., parents-children-grandchildren, etc.) and no dispensation can be granted (Lev. 18:6:18). In the collateral line it extends to the third degree inclusive. In the first degree of the collateral (side) line, that of brother and sister, no dispensation can be granted because of the natural law forbidding; the second degree (first cousins) and third degree (second cousins) may be dispensed. (*Cf.* DIRIMENT IMPEDIMENT.)

CONSCIENCE, the judgment of our reason with regard to the morality, the goodness or badness of an act. This judgment is called the "dictate" of conscience. Conscience is the proximate rule of moral action, that is, it resides in the mind and proposes to the will the morality of a given course of action. Hence, conscience binds and must be followed. However, one must strive to form a right conscience (Rom. 14:22).

CONSECRATION. 1. The act and ceremony by which a person or thing is dedicated to sacred service or set apart for sacred use. The ceremony is more solemn than a blessing; once consecrated the object cannot be consecrated again and any profanation is a sin of sacrilege. **2.** Consecration at Mass is the solemn portion of the Canon at which time the celebrating priest, in commemoration of the act of our Lord at the Last Supper, changes bread and wine into the body and blood of Jesus Christ. By this the bread and wine lose their substance, retaining only their appearances (*cf.* TRANSUBSTANTIATION). **3.** The consecration of a bishop is the act and ceremony conferring the fullness of holy orders on the one consecrated and imprinting on his soul the episcopal character. Three bishops, the one consecrator and two co-consecrators perform the ceremony, imposing hands, anointing, blessing and giving the insignia of a bishop (crosier, ring, miter and gloves), and enthroning the one appointed by the pope.

CONSECRATION CROSS, one of the twelve small crosses which are painted or sculptured directly on the inside walls of a church when it is consecrated. These mark the twelve places where the chrism was signed

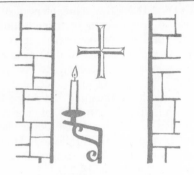

CONSECRATION CROSS

in the form of a cross during the consecration, and they may never be removed. On the anniversary day of consecration each year a lighted candle is burned before each of the twelves crosses.

CONSISTORIAL CONGREGA-TION. *See* CONGREGATIONS, 4; SACRED ROMAN CONGREGATIONS.

CONSISTORY, an ecclesiastical court. Formerly the consistories were governing bodies of the Church, meeting regularly three times a week to weigh questions of faith, discipline and policy. Today these have been replaced by the Sacred Congregations of the Roman Curia. However, the pope may call an assembly of the cardinals and this would be a consistory, with its function chiefly that of promulgation of an official decision or announcement.

CONSTANCE, COUNCIL OF, the sixteenth ecumenical council, held at Constance (Baden) in Germany from Nov. 1414 to April 1418. In its forty-five sessions it effected: repair of the schism of rival popes and rival emperors; reform of the Church; legislation on Holy Communion; pronouncements on the forty-five errors of Wyclif and thirty errors of Huss. (*Cf.* ECUMENICAL COUNCILS.)

CONSTANCY, a moral virtue by which one learns to persist in the struggle and suffering of life to the end without giving in to weariness, discouragement or indolence. It is attained by prayer, understanding that perseverance is a gift of God; by concentrating on the everlasting reward awaiting us; and by courage supported by God's grace and our love of God.

CONSTANTINOPLE, COUNCILS OF. There were four ecumenical councils held at Constantinople situated in the Bosporus, the seat of the Byzantine empire. The first (second ecumenical) was held in 381 and endorsed the Nicene Creed, condemned the Arian and Macedonian heresies and formulated the Catholic doctrine concerning the divinity of the Holy Ghost. The second, in 553, condemned the "Three Chapters" (writings of three anti-Monophysites) and the Nestorian heresy. The third, in 681, confirmed the doctrine set forth at Chalcedon, namely, that Christ possesses both a divine and human will, and condemned the Monothelite heresy. The fourth, in 869 condemned Photius and his followers and Iconoclasm and affirmed the unity of the human soul. (*Cf.* ECUMENICAL COUNCILS.)

CONSTANTINOPLE, PATRI-ARCHATE OF. Formerly a great jurisdictional power in the Church, claimed to be "second to Rome," the patriarchate fell into definite schism in the Middle Ages and formed the Orthodox Eastern Church. There have been since that time fractions falling away from its power and the patriarchate today is minor, embracing only a few thousands of faithful. The patriarch of the Orthodox Church resides there, but there is no Catholic patriarch with jurisdiction in Constantinople.

CONSTANTINOPLE, RITE OF, a liturgy developed from the ancient Antiochene. It used the Greek, Arabic, Old Slovenian and Rumanian languages and followed the Old Style (Julian) Calendar (the liturgical year beginning on Sept. 1). Today it is commonly referred to as the Byzantine rite.

CONSTITUTIONAL CLERGY, those clerics who took the oath to uphold the civil constitution set up for the Church by the National Assembly of France in 1790. It was a political scheme proposed by "liberal" Catholics in the interest of "liberty" as set up by the Revolution. It served to suppress many dioceses and brought persecution on priests who did not sign. The constitution was condemned by Pius VI. It ended with the Concordat of 1801. However, one salutary effect was that emigrant priests, fleeing from being forced to uphold false legislation, helped to carry the faith to the new world.

CONSTITUTIONS. 1. Papal: a decree or pronouncement, being a type of bull usually issued in the pope's name. Also called "Apostolic letters *sub plumbo*" or apostolic constitutions. **2.** The applications of the general rule of a religious order developed as principles to govern a particular society.

CONSUBSTANTIAL, being of one and the same substance, as the three Divine Persons of the Trinity are of but one substance as set forth at the first ecumenical council of Nice in 325.

CONSUBSTANTIATION, heretical teaching of the Lutherans which maintains that the substance of bread and wine exist *together with* the substance of the body and blood of Christ after consecration. This was condemned by the Fourth Lateran Council and the Council of Trent.

CONSUETUDINARY, title of a book setting forth the liturgical customs of a monastic order.

CONSULTORS. 1. Technicians or specialists who serve the Roman Curia. They supply the initial study of a problem and formulate possible solutions. They are prelates, priests or religious versed in theology and canon law and serve the various sacred congregations at the request of the prefect or secretary of a particular congregation. **2.** In the United States, in place of cathedral chapters, four to six diocesan consultors must be appointed by the bishop of a diocese to assist and advise him in administrative affairs.

CONTEMPLATION, a higher form of affective prayer, above meditation, in which the mind and will are engrossed in viewing truth above reason and joined with profound admiration. It is accomplished not by reasoning or vocal expression but by a deep, sincere concentration on God, a loving knowledge of Him and His works, which aided by grace is a simple, wordless act of love of God. It is the perfection of prayer. It is the prayer proper to the contemplative life but may be practiced by anyone. St. John of the Cross states: "Contemplation is the science of love, which is an infused loving knowledge of God." Generally, authors distinguish two types of contemplation: acquired and infused. However, while acquired contemplation may attain to a degree of mystical union with God which is the height of "infused and loving knowledge of God," it is more a prayer of simplicity or developed meditation. Acquired contemplation is, according to St. Teresa, "acquired prayer of recollection." In contradistinction, infused contemplation is a simple and loving knowledge of God and His works which results not from human activity aided by grace but only through inspiration of the Holy Ghost. It is always passive and if this infused contemplation persists and becomes frequent the result is mystical union, or the mystical state.

CONTEMPLATIVE LIFE, an austere, religious life adapted to foster contemplation as in a contemplative order. In the religious life it is the highest form, for not only does it encourage the members to seek union with God through love, but by seclusion and freedom from the worldly spirit, the objective worship of God is perfected. In purpose it is a continuous life of prayer to God "that His kingdom may flourish," and of mortification or atonement for sinners. This life calls for a generous vocation of a special degree of love of God and should not be considered lightly.

CONTINENCE. 1. The virtue, derived from that more profound virtue of chastity, which in practice preserves the mind from impure thoughts and desires and restrains the will from actions following aroused sexual desire. **2.** Voluntary abstinence from marital intercourse, for any period of time by the mutual consent of husband and wife. (*Cf.* CHASTITY.)

CONTRACT. In the Church, the civil laws and contracts are adopted (c. 1529), except when they are in opposition to the divine law or to special prescriptions of canon law.

CONTRITION, the sorrow which arises in the soul, making one's mind repent past sins and resolve not to sin again. There are two divisions: (a) Perfect contrition is when the motive of one's sorrow is the love of God, the highest Good, and for God as God. With this are all the elements of contrition including the desire to confess. (b) Imperfect contrition is had when the motive is other than God but is supernatural in that it refers to God, e.g., through fear of God's punishment, etc. In the reception of the sacrament of penance, contrition must be genuinely present, that is, at least implicitly in preparation for receiving the sacrament and virtually during the time of receiving absolution.

CONTUMACY, in Church law, contempt of court. It is the failure to appear in an ecclesiastical court when summoned, or failure to carry out an order of this court. This presupposes that the transgression is with knowledge of the law and its attached punishment. Censure follows upon the fact of one being contumacious, and contumacy is presumed in censures *latae sententiae* (q.v.). One is "purged of contumacy" when it is proven in court that one was lawfully hindered from answering the summons or order.

CONVENT. 1. When the term is used to mean the entire corporate capacity of a religious community, that is, its director and effects, it is used of both male and female communities of monks or nuns. **2.** Popularly, the establishment, similar to a monastery, where sisters or nuns live in community life. **3.** Less precisely, the word convent is referred to the parochial residence of the teaching sisters of the parish school.

CONVENTUAL MASS, the daily Mass celebrated publicly every day in churches where professed religious live in a community. Also that Mass celebrated in churches of religious who daily recite the Divine Office publicly.

CONVENTUALS, those members of the Fransciscan Order who, by approval granted in 1322, possess and use property in common. They are called: Friars Minor Conventual.

CONVERSION. The word is used in several different ways, philosophically and theologically, by Church writers. The word is from the Latin and means "to turn toward." **1.** Total physical conversion is the passage or "turning into," the transmutation, of the matter and form of one entire substance into another substance already existing, without any change in this latter substance. This is transubstantiation (q.v.). **2.** Conversion also is taken to mean a turning toward God (on the part of a sinner), or a turning toward the Church of God, that is accepting its doctrine and discipline as true and of faith. This latter is to become a convert. There are according to St. Thomas three phases of this conversion: preparation, merit, and glory. To each of these there is a corresponding grace: first, the operation of divine grace through God; second, the habitual state of grace; and third, the consummation or fulfillment of these graces and all other graces. **3.** In philosophy, logical conversion is the transposition of the terms of a proposition without the loss of the truth of the proposition. **4.** The "conversion of manners," spoken of in the religious life, is both the process and the accomplishment of doing away with vices that afflict one and the acquiring of virtues.

CONVERT, anyone who has made a conversion to God. Precisely, a person who has not been baptized, is of the age of reason, is instructed and receives baptism. Also one who having been baptized, but brought up as a non-Catholic, abjures his error, submits to the Church and by conditional baptism, profession of faith, and confession and absolution becomes a Catholic.

COPE, in Latin *pluviale*, literally a "raincoat." It was used in the early Church for a practical purpose. It is now a vestment, used for other ceremonies than the Mass itself, made in a semicircular shape, worn draped around the shoulders full length, and fastened in front across the upper chest by a clasp called the morse. On the back it is necessary that the cope have a flat hood or shield which may be round or pointed, falling almost to the waist. The orphreys or embroidery, usually of a markedly different color from that of the vestment, are customarily not too broad. The morse may be of cloth or metal. A jeweled morse may be worn only by prelates.

COPT, an Egyptian Christian, a member of either the Catholic or dissident Coptic Church.

COPTIC RITE, THE. Its liturgy and administration of the sacraments is followed by both Catholic and dissident members of the Coptic Church. The liturgical language is the early Egyptian (Coptic) with Greek and Arabic. The dissident church followed the Monophysite heresy after the Council of Chalcedon (451 A.D.). They deny the supremacy of the pope, and while their orders are valid they administer the sacraments in a different manner and there is question about the validity of baptism as they administer it (by immersion). This Church is governed by the Patriarch of Alexandria. The Catholic Coptic Church was reconciled in the 18th century and under Pope Leo XIII was given a patriarch who is located at Alexandria and appointed by the Holy See.

CORAM CARDINALE (EPIS-COPO), literally, "in the presence of a cardinal" (or bishop). A Mass celebrated *coram cardinale* is one at which a cardinal, not being the celebrant, assists from either the throne or faldstool.

CORDELIERS, a name given in France in the Middle Ages to the Franciscan Recollects because of the knotted cord worn about their waists.

CORINTHIANS, EPISTLES TO THE. The letters which St. Paul wrote to the Christians of Corinth, the ancient capital city of the Greek province of Achaia, form two books of Scripture. St. Paul arrived at Corinth in 49 or 50 A.D. and remained perhaps a year and a half. In the First Epistle the apostle answers certain questions which had arisen due to the erroneous doctrines of the "false apostles or false teachers." Its doctrinal message is St. Paul's fullest teaching on the make-up of Christ's Church as His mystical body, teaching on the Resurrection, on the Eucharist, and on Christian chastity. It is a writing of spiritual counsel and is probably the most valuable historical document of all the Epistles of the N.T. The Second Epistle was written about 57 A.D. to confirm those who had remained loyal, but also to set forth in plain language the issues by which the true doctrine was to be recognized. Its doctrinal content again speaks of the unity of Christ with His Church and also of the authority of the Christian minister. Its spiritual message is: the good of suffering with Christ and the hope of immortality.

CORNETTE

CORNETTE, the large, spreading white linen headdress worn by the Sisters of Charity. It had its origin in a French type of head-covering of the 14th century.

CORONA. 1. The band of hair about the head of a religious, the crown of whose head is shaved after receiving tonsure. **2.** A circle of candles or vigil lights used in the church, also the circular candlestick holding the lights. **3.** A seldom used word for any five mysteries of the Rosary.

CORONATION OF OUR LADY. 1. The name of the fifth glorious mystery of the fifteen meditations which are the subjects of mental prayer during the recitation of the Rosary. **2.** The representation in art or literature of the arrival and reception of the body of the Blessed Mother assumed into heaven. Also called the Coronation of Mary as Queen of Heaven.

CORONATION OF THE POPE, the ceremony taking place after the newly elected pope celebrates Mass, following shortly after his election. It is the official act of his becoming pope, but not of receiving the jurisdiction over the Church which is received immediately after his election. During the coronation, the new pope is solemnly blessed by three cardinals and the tiara is placed on his head by the senior cardinal-deacon.

CORPORAL, the small linen cloth, about 20 inches square, upon which the sacramental species rests during the Mass. Upon it both the chalice and sacred host are placed. It is folded in three folds, overlapping inwardly so that no fragment of the consecrated host may be dropped. It is carried to and from the altar in the burse. The corporal also is placed on the altar before the tabernacle when the Blessed Sacrament is placed in the monstrance at Benediction, or when the tabernacle is opened to transfer consecrated hosts from the ciborium to the pyx.

CORPORAL

CORPORAL WORKS OF MERCY, the seven acts of charity, in practice directed as relief to the physical needs of our fellow man. They are: to feed the hungry, clothe the naked, give drink to the thirsty, shelter the homeless, tend the sick, visit those in prison, and bury the dead. (*Cf.* MERCY, SPIRITUAL AND CORPORAL WORKS OF.)

CORPUS CHRISTI, literally, from the Latin, "the Body of Christ." The feast of *Corpus Christi* is celebrated on the Thursday following Trinity Sunday in honor of Christ in the Blessed Sacrament and to recall the

institution of the Blessed Sacrament. It is customary to carry the Blessed Sacrament in procession about the church, often stopping at temporary altars to give benediction, with final benediction at the main altar of the church. The office of this feast was written largely by St. Thomas Aquinas and is considered one of the most beautiful of the Roman Breviary.

COSMOLOGY. This division of the formal study of philosophy studies in particular the characteristics and basic principles of the material universe. Based upon the findings of the physical sciences, it examines chiefly the causes of material bodies. It is called special or applied metaphysics, embracing psychology, the study of the soul, and theodicy, the study of God.

COSTUME, CLERICAL. According to canon law, the ordinary dress, that is suits, hats, etc., of those in minor and major orders is black (c. 136, 2379). By special permission white may be used in certain missionary countries. Dress also includes the Roman collar and the cassock.

COTTA, a white vestment with full sleeves reaching just below the elbow, and its hem descending just below the hip line. This short kind of surplice is worn by priests over their cassocks and by acolytes and altar boys. (*Cf.* SURPLICE.)

COUNCIL, a group of church officials, scholars, hierarchy or clergy, called together in assembly to discuss, deliberate, or study doctrinal or disciplinary matters pertaining to the Church. 1. *Diocesan*: referred to as a synod, which is a gathering of the chief clergy of a diocese called together by the bishop, at least every ten years, at which the position of the faith in the diocese and matters of government are examined. As a group, this is only advisory. 2. *National Council:* an assembly either plenary or provincial, called by the bishops and representing an entire country. The last in the United States was the 3rd plenary council of Baltimore in 1884. 3. An *Ecumenical Council (q.v.)* is one to which all the bishops of the Catholic world and all other prelates or dignitaries entitled to vote are invited to gather under the presidency of the pope or his representative. The decrees of an ecumenical council, when ratified by the pope, are binding in conscience upon all Christians. Now sometimes called "general" council. There have been twenty ecumenical councils to date. 4. A *plenary council:* the hierarchy having jurisdiction of a nation. 5. *Provincial council:* the meeting of the suffragan bishops of a province called by the metropolitan.

COUNCIL, SACRED CONGREGATION OF THE. *See* SACRED ROMAN CONGREGATIONS.

COUNSELS OF PERFECTION. *See* EVANGELICAL COUNSELS.

COUNTER-REFORMATION. This movement, more correctly called "The Catholic Reform," and recently termed by historians the "Catholic Reaction" or "Catholic Restoration," began as a reaction to the defection from the Church, the Protestant revolt at discipline and authority, and the political and social upheaval which stemmed from the new type of religion based upon individual interpretation of the Bible. In length of time it was not much longer than one hundred years, but the effects are still present. The reform for the Church began with the Council of Trent (1545–63) which, in twenty-five sessions, gave a definite

statement on Catholic doctrines denied by Protestants. It was a revitalizing period for the Church when her great leadership was expressed in the Baroque in art, in great endeavor, as Lepanto, and in great development in expression and mystical devotion, as seen in the writings of St. Robert Bellarmine and SS. Teresa of Avila and John of the Cross.

COVETOUSNESS. *See* AVARICE.

COWL, name commonly given to the hood of a religious habit. More properly, a cowl is the sleeveless garment worn by religious, covering their heads and shoulders. The confusion, resulting from translation difficulties, was early recognized and the Council of Vienne defined cowl as "a habit long and full, but without sleeves."

CREATION, act of God, bringing something into existence, or causing something to exist, which had no previous existence either in itself or in a subject. This means the production of something from nothing. The beginning of the world is given in the first two chapters of Genesis; that God created out of nothing is declared in 2 Mac. 7:28. When speaking of creation no theory of evolution or transformism is meant. The act of creation is proper to God alone. It is also a part of the creative act to sustain a thing, once created, in its created state. This is also the work of God, and is described as being linked to the role of the Son of God in His work of Redemption. Since "all power in heaven and earth" belongs to "Christ enthroned," Christ's divinity is reflected, so to speak, in His Sonship and in the fact that He is the conserver of creation (Heb. 2:8, 10) and exercises power over it (Mt. 26:64).

CREATOR, title proper to God alone (Ps. 101:26ff.) who creates, sustains, and commands the universe by His will exercised through laws He develops.

CREDENCE, a piece of sanctuary furniture. It is a simple table large enough to hold whatever is needed for liturgical functions. On it also rests the chalice covered with the humeral veil at a solemn high Mass. The table should be to the right of the altar as usually viewed, and covered with a white linen cloth.

CREED, a summary of the principal truths of the Church written as a profession of faith. Quite literally creeds are prayers of belief. In the Church there are four "creeds" which are each expressions of the same truths which were developed historically: (a) the *Apostles' Creed*. This is a development of the practice of the apostles (Acts 8:37) of having persons who desired baptism profess their faith; (b) the *Nicene Creed*. This creed was put forth by the fathers of the Church at Nicaea in 325 A.D. and recorded by Eusebius of Caesarea in a letter to his people. It is popularly known as the "Creed of the Trinity"; (c) the *Athanasian Creed*. A creed attributed to St. Athanasius in a writing of the 7th-century Council of Autun where the reference states it as "the faith of the holy prelate Athanasius." However, the earliest known copy is contained in the Utrecht Psalter, a manuscript of the 6th century; (d) the *Creed of Pius IV*. It was published first in 1564 in the papal bull *Iniunctum nobis* and restates the truths of the Nicene Creed and the doctrines defined by the Council of Trent. Pius IX, in 1877, added a declaration of the Decrees of the Vatican Council, especially affirming the primacy of St. Peter and the infallibility of the pope. In 1910, Pope St. Pius X appended a solemn repudiation of the error of modernism, to be taken as an oath by all ecclesiastics when Church law obliges.

CREMATION. The Church forbids ecclesiastical burial to those who order that their bodies after death are to be burned, even if the act is not executed by the relatives. The Church opposes cremation because: the practice was historically an act of disbelief in immortality by members of certain societies and others; and because cremation does not show reverence to the human body, the temple of the Holy Ghost. For grave reason, e.g., plague, the Church permits the destruction of bodies by fire.

CRIB. 1. Name given to the manger where Christ was born. The term includes the immediate area of the stable, especially as applied below. **2.** A fabricated representation of the manger containing statuary figures of the Christ Child, the Blessed Mother, and St. Joseph. Tradition and custom also includes figures of the Magi, animals and sometimes angels. The crib is erected in churches during the Christmas season, from Christmas Eve until Epiphany. The practice arose in 1223 as a devotion founded by St. Francis of Assisi. Cribs may be erected in the home or elsewhere. In French, the term is *creche*, which is often used in English, also.

CRITICISM, BIBLICAL. Criticism in general and as applied to the Bible, may be defined as the art and science of distinguishing, in a literary work, what is genuine, false, authentic, from what is added, and evaluating and assessing the whole work in literary terms and according to other standards. Biblical criticism is divided into three types: (a) *textual* or *literary*, called "higher" criticism, which is the fundamental type. It is study directed to the material given through a manuscript tradition, and it seeks to eliminate accidental corruptions of the text, such as errors in copying, and determine the exact wording in the original. From this point textual criticism goes on examining the text as established, determining its origin, method or style of composition, the authors, their plan, etc. (b) *Historical criticism* is directed to a variety of questions, examining each after the basic findings of the textual criticism, and may be concerned with the history recorded, the theology propounded, the legal or moral context. (c) The third type, *evaluative*, which is commonly grouped with the "higher," judges the value and significance of the books of the Bible, the Bible's place and importance in history, and arrives at a synthesis of the general and particular information contained in it. This third type is not alone concerned with historical importance or sociological significance, but to a greater degree is directed to formulating a biblical theology, a systematic analysis of the doctrine or teaching of Scripture concerning God and religion. All of these types of criticism are fundamental and basic aids to exegesis which is the exposition of the text of Scripture (*cf.* EXEGESIS; INSPIRATION, BIBLICAL.) In the 20th century there has been great growth in Catholic critical work. A most important step was the publication, on Sept. 30, 1943, of the encyclical, *Divino afflante Spiritu*, which closed the era of modernism's attack upon inspiration and the history of Israel, pointed out what was dangerous doctrine, restored a "true free-dom" to Catholic exegetes, and gave tribute to textual criticism. It emphasized the importance of biblical theology and encouraged a continuing study of the Bible.

CROSIER

CROSIER also **CROZIER,** the "pastoral staff." It is a symbol of office carried by the ordinary of a diocese. It is an ornamental staff, shaped as a shepherd's crook, pointed at the lower end, of varying heights, usually a little taller than the crown of the head. It is made of metal tubing and the crook portion is carved (of wood, ivory, gold or silver) or ornamented. The shaft may be separated at the middle for convenience in handling. The crook itself is symbolical of the bishop's role in keeping the members of his flock, while the pointed end is a symbol of the possible prodding needed by the spiritually lax. The bishop in his diocese always carries the crosier with the crook pointing outward. Others entitled to the crosier carry it with the crook turned inward. The popes have not used the crosier since the 11th century.

CROSS, the most widespread and important of the Christian symbols. It is for the Catholic the sign of our redemption, being the instrument upon which Christ sacrificed Himself (*cf.* CRUCIFIX), and is also a symbol of faith. When blessed, the cross or crucifix is a sacramental. There is a wide variation of crosses derived from four basic types, the T (tau)-form, the Y-form, the X-St. Andrew's form (the cross saltire), and the Greek cross of four equal extensions, e.g., the Red Cross symbol. The shape of the cross upon which Christ died is not certainly known, but it is determined that probably it was the T-form with the upright (*crux immissa*) extending slightly above with room for an inscription (St. Irenaeus). The transverse beam was called the *patibulum*, and in Roman practice, the one condemned carried this beam. This was probably true in the case of Christ (Jn. 19:17). It was also the practice to have a small block or seat in the middle of the upright, but in Christian art this has become a foot support. Our Lord's feet were probably not nailed together as is derived from the fact that all representations of the Crucifixion up to the 12th century show them nailed separately. In the Church a variety of crosses are used: (a) the archiepiscopal cross, with two lateral beams, the top slightly shorter, (b) the hand cross, used by bishops of all Eastern rites, (c) processional cross, a crucifix mounted on a long staff, carried at the head of a procession, (d) pectoral cross, a small cross, jeweled and ornamented, often containing relics, worn on the chest by bishops and abbots, suspended about the neck by a chain or cord, (e) cross *pro Ecclesia et Pontifice*, a papal decoration instituted by Leo XIII.

CROSS, RELICS OF THE TRUE. The wood of the cross upon which Christ was crucified was found by the Empress St. Helena about 318. It was of pine wood, and portions have been sent throughout the world.

CROSS, VENERATION OF THE, the honor paid to a relic of the true cross. As a relic it may be carried under a canopy in procession, is genuflected to when on exposition, and is kissed as a mark of respect.

CROWN, EPISCOPAL, a tall rounded headdress, worn as a miter by Byzantine and other Eastern bishops.

EPISCOPAL CROWN

CROWN, FRANCISCAN. Also called the Seraphic Rosary, this is a rosary of seven decades recited in honor of the seven joys of the Blessed Mother.

CROWN OF THORNS, the plaited, thorny branches impressed upon the head of Christ as a mark of ridicule before the crucifixion (Mt. 27:29–30). In all probability it was fashioned of the *poterium spinosum* which is found about Jerusalem and which was used as firewood. It has a slender spike. The form of the crown is disputed; it may have been as a headdress (helmet), covering the entire top of the head as it is shown in the Catacomb of Proetextatus dating back to the 2nd century, or as a fillet, a rounded wreath form.

CROWN, PAPAL. *See* TIARA.

CRUCIFIX, properly speaking, a cross to which there is attached, in relief, an image of the body of Christ.

However, if the figure is painted, impressed or otherwise represented it is classed as a crucifix. A crucifix must be placed over an altar where Mass is celebrated; it is recommended that there be a crucifix in each home; and a crucifix is attached to the pendant portion of all rosaries. The skull seen upon some crucifixes is not essential to the crucifix, being a symbol of Calvary ("the place of the skull"). More proper is the tablet, or banner, called the "title," attached near the top of the upright, bearing the letters: I N R I, the initials of the Latin words for "Jesus of Nazareth, King of the Jews." Special indulgences are attached to the crucifix and to certain prayers recited before it.

CRUCIFIXION, the manner of execution by which Christ suffered and died and effected our redemption. It was a method used by Egyptians, Romans and others and embodied a degree of ridicule and mockery in the procedure besides being a mark of degradation. The condemned was either nailed or bound to the cross, remaining thereon until dead. In the case of Christ, He was nailed to the cross, both feet and hands. (*Cf.* CALVARY; CROSS.)

CRUET, a small vessel or jug. The cruets used during the celebration of Mass to carry water and wine should

CRUETS

be made of glass or crystal and should have a loose-fitting stopper to keep out dust. A glass saucer should be provided for the cruets to stand in as well as the shallow dish into which water is poured at the Lavabo. Sometimes one cruet is marked with the letter A, the other with V, to mark their contents (*aqua*-water; *vinum*-wine).

CRUSADES. In Christian history, a crusade was a major military expedition undertaken for an exalted purpose. They were promoted and partly financed for nearly two hundred years by the popes, and as such were internationally organized movements. The name is derived from the cross of cloth worn on the garments and inscribed on the pennants of those who participated. Once proclaimed, they were preached as a holy undertaking. All classes of people took part: kings, knights, soldiers, religious and peasants. As individuals they were inspired by a variety of motives: religious idealism, politics, economic reasons, adventure, or a hope of spoils. While crusades have been undertaken for many purposes, we include here only the eight major movements. The numbering is arbitrary, for they were an almost continuous series of expeditions directed primarily at regaining the Holy Land from the Turks and Moslems. The *First Crusade* (1095–1101) was announced by Pope Urban II at the Council of Clermont. It set out in four units, with the Christian army entering Jerusalem in 1099. The *Second Crusade* (1145–1148), began with the commissioning of St. Bernard by Eugene III to preach the expedition to recapture Edessa from the Moslems. It ended in disaster with the crusaders reaching Damascus in 1148 but never getting to Edessa. The *Third Crusade* (1188–1192), begun by Gregory VIII and Emperor Frederick Barbarossa, Philip Augustus of France and Richard the Lion-Hearted who effected a truce with Saladin in 1192. The *Fourth Crusade* (1202–1204) was undertaken at the plea of Innocent III. It ended with the leaders being excommunicated and abandoning their purpose. The *Fifth Crusade* (1212) was the so-called Children's Crusade (*cf.* CHILDREN'S CRUSADE). The *Sixth Crusade* (1228–1229) undertaken by Emperor Frederick II secured possession of Jerusalem by treaty with the sultan. The *Seventh Crusade* (1248–1254), led by St. Louis of France and proclaimed by Innocent IV, was unsuccessful, ending with the imprisonment of Louis and his being sent home. The *Eighth Crusade* (1267–1270), also led by St. Louis and by Charles of Anjou, ended disastrously with the death of St. Louis and the loss of the last Christian towns. The crusades failed to save Palestine. However, they had great effects upon history. They encouraged travel and commerce, broadened the outlook of Europe, fostered religion, established the conception of the papacy as the center of Christendom, developed a sense of freedom among peoples and played a part in the development of capitalism because of expanded financial activities. The bad effects were also numerous as far as the Church was concerned. It widened the gap in the Eastern schism, and permitted the entrance of heretical teachings into the West.

CRYPT, the lower, excavated portion of a church, similar to a cellar, used for divine worship in early times. Originally it was intended for the burial of martyrs. (*Cf.* CONFESSION OF A MARTYR.)

CUBICULUM

CUBICULUM, a hewn-out burial chamber in the Roman catacombs. (*Cf.* CATACOMBS.)

CULDEES, the name of religious men who lived a community life in Ireland and Scotland from the 8th to the 11th centuries, but never were established as a religious order.

CULT also **CULTUS,** broadly, honor to a thing or person. It thus includes worship and veneration. As such it is usually divided into: worship which is accorded to God alone; *hyperdulia,* which is the esteem and veneration given to the Blessed Mother; and *dulia* which is the veneration given the saints. It also refers to the liturgy in a loose sense and as such is controlled strictly in the Church by the Sacred Congregation of Rites. Canon law "On Divine Cultus" sets up specific laws concerning worship and veneration (canons 1255 through 1277).

CULT, DISPARITY OF, a diriment impediment to marriage. It means that a person baptized in the Catholic Church or converted to it from schism or heresy cannot validly marry a non-baptized individual (c. 1070).

CURATE, one ordained to the care of souls. In French, the *curé* or parish priest. More commonly in the United States it is referred to a member of the diocesan clergy assigned as an assistant to the pastor of a parish.

CURE OF SOULS. The *cura animarum*, properly "the care of souls," is entrusted by authority to a priest whose obligations are: the instruction, the administration of the sacraments, the celebration of the "Mass for the People," preaching, and the care of the poor and sick. It is actually a delegated authority, descending from the pope who has the universal cure of souls. In practice it is the assumption of pastoral duties and properly does not include the administration of physical or temporal affairs.

CURIA, ROMAN. The term *curia* is translated from the Latin as "court," but is broader in meaning. The Roman Curia, *Curia Romana*, is not to be taken in the sense of a "legal court" or as the "court" of a king. As used in the Church it means the center of government and includes all administrative groups together with the personnel. The present function and the make-up of the Roman Curia was established by Pope St. Pius X in 1908 and was a revamping of procedures in government which are embodied in the Code of Canon Law. The Roman Curia is thus the entire body of officially organized agencies who assist the pope in the government and administration of the Church, being the Sacred Congregations, the Tribunals, the Offices and Commissions. They make up in large part the "Holy See" in its popular acceptance (*cf.* SACRED CONGREGATIONS). Under Offices are included: the Apostolic Chancery, Apostolic Datary, Apostolic Chamber (*camera*), and the Secretariate of State. All units of the Curia exercise only delegated authority, being subject to the pope (c. 243), and they can initiate no action of importance without consulting the pope (c. 244).

CURSING, the calling down of evil, either spiritual or temporal, upon one's neighbor, oneself, or any other of God's creatures. It is a sin against charity, but if the evil is seriously wished, it can become more serious because of being against religion (irreverence) or against justice, and may include scandal, e.g., in the presence of children. Cursing and swearing are often popularly understood as being one or all of: profanity, blasphemy or abusive language.

CUSTODIA, name given to any temporary receptacle wherein the Blessed Sacrament is kept.

CUSTOM, a term meaning legalized usage which creates a right; unwritten law. If custom, having been a continued manner of acting, is invoked it must be proven and reasonable and continued without interruption. A regular usage, for forty years uncontradicted, establishes the usage as custom. In Church law, established usage gives custom the force of law only with the consent of competent ecclesiastical authority (c. 25).

CUSTOS, literally a custodian, one having restricted authority as in a religious community or a cathedral chapter.

CYCLE, a series of numbers or letters, standing for numbers, which are recounted again in the same order when the cycle is completed. The solar or cycle of Dominical Letters is a series of twenty-eight years, after which Sundays and weekdays again fall on the same days of the month. By calculation, the church calendar can be computed.

D

DALMATIC, an outer liturgical vestment with short open sleeves, an opening for the head, and open at the sides from the hem to the shoulders. It reaches to or below the knees and is worn by the deacon at solemn Mass and processions. It is so named because originally they were made from Dalmatian wool.

DANIEL, BOOK OF, a prophetical book of the O.T. named after its traditional author (Daniel, meaning "God is my judge"). In content the book treats of the "almighty, all-knowing God," and His rule. Its prophetic content speaks of the extension of the Messianic kingdom over all the earth, that it will be a spiritual kingdom not gained by the sword and that it will derive from God (4:14). It also has an eschatological aspect, in that it speaks of this kingdom of God which is the Church of Christ as being a prelude to the heavenly kingdom.

DARK AGES, a term applied variously to the period from the 5th to the 15th century but which scholarship has repudiated as inaccurate and non-descriptive. In Catholic circles this period is more appropriately called the "Age of faith."

DARK NIGHT OF THE SENSES, a period of transition spoken of by St. John of the Cross wherein one passes from meditation to contemplation (*cf.* CONTEMPLATION). It is a time when the soul seeks God by pure faith, and is given no assistance from the senses, when it may be difficult to make acts of prayer, when nature rebels against self-scrutiny and the effort demanded of all who would draw closer to God. This period may be accompanied by actual suffering of the spirit, as through scruples and temptations against faith, or physical suffering in the form of sickness, permitted by God as a trial.

DARK NIGHT OF THE SPIRIT. This term was applied by St. John of the Cross to that period of passive purification which the soul undergoes after having attained the grace of contemplation. It is a purification, a purging before being brought into the full joy of mystical union with God. St. John of the Cross says: "For this night is drawing the spirit away from its ordinary and common sense of things, that it may draw it toward the divine sense, which is a stranger and an alien to all human ways; so much so that the soul seems to be carried out of itself." It is a final purging, since no one can stand before or penetrate to the "deep things of God" (1 Cor. 2:10), effected while one merits and grows in charity. (The alternative is purgatory which is purification without merit, and the way of sanctity is to be purified in this passive manner before death instead of after.) St. John of the Cross further defines it: "The dark night is a certain inflowing of God into the soul which cleanses it of its ignorances and imperfections, habitual, natural and spiritual" (Bk. II, ch. 5). It is called a suffering of the soul in the sense that there is intense yearning for God while experiencing a desolation or feeling of being abandoned by God. It is a transitory state during contemplation, but once undergone it may return.

DATARY, APOSTOLIC. *See* APOSTOLIC DATARY.

DAY HOURS, the times, or parts, arranged in sequence in the Divine Office except the morning hours or matins. (*Cf.* DIVINE OFFICE.)

DEACON, literally, a "servant". In the Church the diaconate is the second of the major orders of holy orders, but the lowest in the hierarchical order. In the sacrament of holy orders the diaconate is received prior to ordination to the priesthood, with the conferring of the stole and dalmatic from the bishop and the words, "Receive the power of reading the gospel in the Church of God, both for the living and the dead, in the name of the Lord." The duties of the deacon are: assisting the celebrant of Mass, preaching, administering Holy Communion, and baptism with permission.

DEACONESS, title given to women in the first centuries who were appointed to assist the minister and perform other worthy duties, as caring for the sick. They were discontinued following the Council of Nicaea.

DEAD, MASS FOR. *See* REQUIEM.

DEAN, a minor official who presides over a deanery, called a *vicar forane*. He is appointed by the bishop and may be removed by him. His office includes these activities: to see that the clergy observe canonical and liturgical laws and follow instructions of the bishop; to summon deanery conferences and preside over them; and to make a yearly report to the bishop. Within the deanery he has precedence over the other priests.

DEANERY, a district of a diocese, usually a territorial division. A diocese must be divided into deaneries by canon law (c. 217).

DECADE, a section of the Rosary which consists of one Our Father, ten Hail Marys, and one Glory be to the Father. These prayers are recited while meditating on one mystery. The ten corresponding beads of the section are also called a decade.

DECALOGUE, THE. *See* COMMANDMENTS OF GOD.

DE CONDIGNO, from the Latin, meaning "out of worthiness." It is said of merit by which the reward is in justice, or the action is equal to the reward; or, in fidelity, where the reward is beyond the deserving of the action, as by a promise.

DE CONGRUO, from the Latin, meaning "out of suitability." It is said of merit where no reward is due, but where a reward would be becoming.

DECORATIONS, PONTIFICAL, honors conferred by the Holy See, usually on laymen, because of outstanding service to the Church, the Holy See, or the welfare of society. They are titles of nobility varying from prince to baron inclusive, six orders of knighthood, and medals (*Benemerenti*, etc.) and crosses (*Pro Ecclesia et Pontifice*).

DECREE, a decision or a regulation for a community or place issued by Church authority. Decrees are documents issued by a Sacred Congregation for a specific purpose. They are: (a) *general*, if applicable to the entire Church; (b) *particular*, if directed to only a part of the Church. The decrees are generally on questions of faith and morals, and those of the pope or a general council are binding on all the Church, while particular decrees bind those to whom they are directed. (*Cf.* RESCRIPTS.)

DECRETALS, decisions handed down by the popes, generally on questions of discipline, which preceded the Code of Canon Law. These were frequently in the form of letters and were also called "constitutions."

DECRETALS, FALSE, a collection of papal letters and councilar canons gathered in the 9th century in Gaul. The majority were forged and, while they were for a time considered genuine, they were chiefly issued as an attack upon the authority of the pope. Also called "Decretals of Pseudo-Isidore." *See* PSEUDO-ISIDORE.

DECRETIST, a name formerly given to one versed in canon law.

DECRETUM GRATIANI, a writing by Gratian (d. 1160), a professor of law in Bologna, published in 1140. These *Decrees of Gratian,* which mark the end of the first period in the history of canonical legislation, became the common text upon which canonists based their commentaries.

DEDICATION OF A CHURCH, the setting apart of a Church building for divine worship. This is often confused with the more solemn consecration. However, each public and semi-public oratory is to be dedicated by blessing of the bishop or a priest. The church may be dedicated by consecration, but this must be performed by a bishop, and as such the anniversary of consecration is observed by a feast ranking as a double of the first class.

DEFECT, IRREGULARITY OF. No one may be ordained a priest unless the state of irregularity is done away with or dispensed (c. 984). This refers to: illegitimates; those with bodily defects, e.g., a blind person, epileptics, the insane, the diabolically possessed, and these may not be ordained even if cured; bigamists; the infamous; i.e., infamy of law; judges who have pronounced a death sentence; executioners and all who are voluntary and immediate assistants in carrying out a death penalty. (*Cf.* IRREGULARITY FROM CRIME.)

DEFENDER OF THE BOND, in Latin, *Defensor vinculi.* The bishop of every diocese appoints a priest to serve as defender of the marriage bond (tie) and of sacred ordination. The one appointed must be a priest of good standing, learned in canon law and prudent and just. His duties are to act in all cases of solemn trial or simple process where the bond or contract of marriage is challenged or parties to a marriage seek a dispensation. He sees to it that the law is properly applied, offers reasonable objections, and when a court makes a declaration of nullity in the first instance he must appeal to a higher court (c. 1968–1969).

DEFENDER OF THE FAITH, a title conferred on King Henry VIII of England by Pope Leo X in 1521 for the king's writing in defense of the sacraments and the Sacrifice of the Mass against Luther. It is still carried as an official title by the sovereigns of England and appears on their coinage. A similar title was given to James V of Scotland by Pope Paul III.

DEFENSOR ECCLESIAE, title of one appointed by a ruler in the early days of the Church to take care of the temporal affairs of the Church.

DEFENSOR MATRIMONII. *See* DEFENDER OF THE BOND.

DEFINITION, PAPAL, a solemn and irrevocable decision, from which there is no appeal (c. 1880), rendered by the pope as the supreme head of the Church. When this directly concerns faith or morals and is made by the pope as universal teacher of the Church (*ex cathedra*) or by an ecumenical council acting with the pope's consent and sanction, it is infallable and binds all the faithful. As such this is not a definition, or decision as a sentence of law, but a statement of truth which always existed in the deposit of faith. (*Cf.* INFALLIBILITY.)

DEFINITORS, those who form the governing council of a religious order.

DEGRADATION, the most serious canonically vindictive penalty (c. 2305) which the Church can inflict upon a cleric. It directs that the cleric: (a) be deposed (*see* DEPOSITION); (b) suffer the loss of the right to wear ecclesiastical garb; (c) be reduced to the lay state (however, he is bound by celibacy and the obligation to recite the Divine Office). Its infliction is governed most rigidly by canon law.

DEGREES, ACADEMIC. According to canon law, no degree conferred by a school of higher learning has canonical value unless by apostolic faculty. Such schools would be: Catholic University of America,

Gregorian, etc. (c. 1377–1378). Persons with a doctorate or licentiate are preferred in making ecclesiastical appointments.

DEIPARA. This Latin translation of the Greek word *Theotokos*, which means "God bearing," was conferred as a title on the Blessed Mother by decision of the council of Ephesus in 431 A.D.

DEISIS. 1. A prayer of petition in the Byzantine liturgy. **2.** A representation in art of our Lord as judge, accompanied by the Blessed Mother and St. John Baptist.

DELATOR, one who denounced early Christians to the pagan authorities thereby causing their seizure and possible martyrdom.

DELEGATE, APOSTOLIC. *See* APOSTOLIC DELEGATE.

DELEGATION. One who has ordinary power or jurisdiction, that is the jurisdiction had by reason of his appointment to an office, e.g., bishops, etc., can delegate this power, totally or in part, to others unless restricted by law (c. 199). One delegated by the Holy See to an office of jurisdiction can subdelegate to another person, either for a simple act or habitual performance, unless restricted by law. That authority delegated by an office inferior to the Holy See may be subdelegated, but one having subdelegated power may not subdelegate again except when this is expressly granted by law.

DELUGE, the flood, the rain of waters for forty days visited upon the earth by act of God as narrated in Genesis (6:9 to 8:14). The idea of a world-wide flood, geographically universal, covering the entire earth has been abandoned by all scholars. The reasons for this are that a series of unheard-of miracles would have been required, e.g., bringing animals from all over the earth, housing them, and getting them used to a change of climate, etc. A new and accepted theory is that the flood was of mixed or relative universality. Thus, only a limited portion of the earth's surface was inundated but all mankind perished except those in the ark of Noe since the race of men had not spread beyond this region. The purpose of the flood was twofold: (a) it was a punishment of the wicked after they had failed to repent; (b) it was a means of freeing the "sons of God" from the corruption surrounding them and providing them the opportunity to bring up a new generation, the ancestors of the Chosen People, in virtue, which was the covenant of God with Noe. The ark was commonly held by early fathers of the Church, from apostolic times (1 Pet. 3:20), to be a type, a figure of the Church; as the ark saved Noe and his family by divine providence, so the Church is the divinely appointed means of mankind's salvation.

DEMIURGE, a term first introduced by Plato in the *Timaeus* to signify the intermediate creator of the material universe. It was borrowed by several heresies, notably Gnosticism, to refer to an imperfect God or an emanation from God, and by others as the personification of evil.

DEMON, a term for devil, used in the N.T. (*Cf.* DEVIL.)

DEMONIAC, a person possessed by a demon, a devil or evil spirit. Instances are narrated in the Gospels (Mk. 5:1–20; 9:13–34; Lk. 8:26–39) and demonstrate the power of Christ over the demons. (*Cf.* EXORCISM.)

DENUNCIATION, in canonical usage, the report made of wrongdoing on the part of another. This is only for serious cause as when the crime is in self-defense or for the public welfare. It should be made in writing, signed, and sent or read to the ordinary, chancellor, or dean.

DEPOSING POWER, PAPAL, the right by which the pontiff, out of spiritual necessity, releases from allegiance the subjects of a ruler who is flagrantly in opposition to religion, morality, and the pursuit of Christian life. While the right exists, it is no longer exercised and has not been since the 17th century.

DEPOSITION, a vindictive penalty of the Church. By it (c. 2303) a cleric is suspended from office, deprived of all offices, benefices, dignities, and functions in the Church, and forbidden to acquire these in the future. The cleric is not reduced to the lay state but retains his clerical privileges and by the law is bound to celibacy and the recitation of the Breviary. The reasons for imposing deposition must be serious and are governed by canon law.

DEPOSITION, BULL OF. The bull of St. Pius V, issued April 27, 1570, wherein Queen Elizabeth of England is named a tyrant and heretic, and declared anathema, has been given this name. The proper title, taken from its opening words, is *Regnans in excelsis.*

DEPOSITION, DAY OF. The anniversary day of the burial of a saint is often so named.

DEPOSIT OF THE FAITH. This comprises the body of teachings and commands given to the apostles and to their successors, the bishops, which are to be retained, taught, and offered to all mankind. The deposit is the sum of revelation and tradition and is entrusted to the Church that Christ founded and its *magisterium*, or teaching and defining role. It is attested to in Scripture (Jn. 16:13) that through the illuminating action of the Holy Spirit the Church will grow, and is recognized by the apostles (1 Tim. 6:20) as having been "committed" to them. The Vatican Council declares: "Faith's doctrines which God has revealed are not put before us as some philosophical discovery to be developed by human ingenuity but as a divine trust (depositum) handed over to the Spouse of Christ for her faithful safeguarding and infallible exposition (Vat. Sess. III, cap. 4, Dz. 1800). (*Cf.* MAGISTERIUM OF THE CHURCH.)

DESECRATION OF CHURCHES, the defilement, also called violation, of a blessed or consecrated church by which the blessing or consecration is lost, not totally as in execration, but partially. The church must be reconciled according to the Roman Ritual before it can be again used for divine services. The church is defiled by: homicide committed in the church, the sinful and serious shedding of blood, use of the church for sinful purposes, burying within the church one excommunicated by sentence.

DESIRE, BAPTISM OF. In its proper meaning, this consists of an act of perfect contrition or perfect love, and the simultaneous desire for baptism. It does not imprint an indelible character on the soul and the obligation to receive baptism by water remains. (*Cf.* BAPTISM.)

DESPAIR, the deliberate, willful distrust of God's goodness, fidelity and power, or the giving up of all hope of salvation and the means necessary to obtain it. As such it is a grave sin

against hope. It is not to be confused with anxiety, fear, or defection, which arise often from bodily ills, and are not sins against hope even though they cause a temporary abandonment of "seeking after God."

DETACHMENT. As a practice of the ascetical life of any Christian, detachment means a balance and proportion of attitude, in actual possession and desire for, relative to the natural goods of the world including honors, fame, wealth and degrees of success. As such it is an exercise toward perfection arising from the three theological virtues of faith, hope, and charity and the three counsels of poverty, chastity and obedience. It is a recognition that the things of the material world are not bad in themselves, but are "lesser goods" of relative unimportance in the light of perfection or salvation. Spiritual goods are of primary importance, involved in the love of God for Himself and in the abandonment to Him and His will in regard to us. Through detachment we overcome cupidity, the concupiscence of the eyes, the desire for riches, and forgetfulness of the poor, which distract us from God. We learn to follow Christ "in spirit" even when having these possessions. The basis for detachment can be found in Scripture, Mt. 5:3, and in the words of St. Paul we read of the spirit required: ". . . and those who buy, as though not possessing, and those who use this world as though not using it, for this world as we see it is passing away. I would have you free from care" (1 Cor. 7:30–32). Through the practice of detachment we are able to give alms ungrudgingly, be humble in acceptance of honors, and more essentially it enables us to desire God, the goods of heaven, and to rely upon God as our means of attaining our salvation. Through this we can concentrate upon our destiny and be recollected in God. (*Cf.* RECOLLECTION.)

DETERMINISM, the doctrine that every fact or effect in the universe is guided or caused entirely by law. The name was applied to the doctrine of Hobbes (d. 1679), stating that the physical universe and human history are dependent on and conditioned by their causes. It excludes free will and in the fashion of Leibnitz (d. 1716) denied the liberty of indifference, maintaining that the mind is compelled by the motive realized through any deliberation.

DETRACTION, usually associated with calumny, both being unjust injuries to the good name of another. Detraction is committed by revealing the true faults of our neighbor; calumny is by imputing false defects. Both include the sinful judging and censuring of one's neighbor and arise in resentment and envy. A detractor assumes that which belongs to God alone as judge (Jas. 4:11–12). Detraction and calumny are seriously sinful being sins against justice. Also listening to detraction and calumny is sinful if in so listening one is induced to commit either, if the one listening takes joy or satisfaction from the revealed defect, and if the one listening does not stop the defamation when he can do so. The sins of detraction and calumny demand restitution or repair to the neighbor's reputation and reparation of material loss suffered therefrom in so far as this was foreseen.

DEUTEROCANONICAL BOOKS. These books, some of the O.T. and some of the N.T., were all genuine and inspired, but their full canonical status was not universally acknowledged for some time. This hesitancy in acknowledgment was due to many circumstances such as the correlating of tradition regarding them, the difficulty in communication and transmission, and the necessity of eliminating possible errors due to copying of the originals. Those of the O.T. are: Books of Tobias, Judith, Wisdom, Ecclesiasticus, Baruch, 1 and 2 Machabees, parts of Esther (10:4 to 16:24), parts of Daniel (3:24–90 and chs. 13, 14). Those of the N.T. are: Hebrews, James, Jude, 2 Peter, 2 and 3 John, and the Apocalypse. Protestants do not accept these books as scriptural. (*Cf.* CANON OF THE SCRIPTURE.)

DEUTERONOMY, the fifth book of the Bible and last of the five books of which the Jewish *Tôrāh*, the Law, is made up; the last book of the Pentateuch. The name means literally "a second law." In content it is "a homiletic exposition of law in an historical setting," given with the persuasion of oratory. Christian tradition holds that Moses is the author. Doctrinally, Deuteronomy stresses practical theology, a firm fidelity to God, His love for the Chosen People, and the gratitude to be given to God.

DEVELOPMENT OF DOCTRINE. 1. Since the death of the last apostle, revealed truth is complete and is not added to or increased. However, revealed truth is unfolded gradually, in a sense being made more fully and explicitly understood. It is only by stages penetrated to the full depth of its meaning. The truth made known by our Lord and the apostles was received by the Church, made clearer in the following centuries, and, if demanded because of some obscurity, the truth was made explicit by definition. This continues, not as different doctrine or new revelation, but an enlargement toward deeper understanding of what is known. (*Cf.* DEPOSIT OF FAITH.) **2.** Title of a writing by John Cardinal Newman (d. 1890).

DEVIL AND THE EVIL SPIRITS. Christ opposes the devil, Satan and the evil spirits, with the Spirit of God. The name is applied to the chief of the fallen angels, Lucifer (Mt. 12:25), and to those other angels who followed his leadership in rebellion against God. Christ has power over the devil and evil spirits and can free souls and bodies from their domination (Mk. 5:1–20), and He empowered the apostles to drive out devils. The devils being like the angels pure spiritual beings have lost none of their powers except supernatural grace. It is of faith that the fall of man was due to Satan, and that the devils continue to tempt and persecute mankind (1 Pet. 5:8). (*Cf.* ANGELS.)

DEVIL'S ADVOCATE, the traditional name of the "Promoter of the Faith" whose duty it is, in the cause of canonization, to raise objections and possible difficulties against approval of the cause. The office was instituted early in the 11th century and is attached to the Congregation of Rites. His task is much like that of a prosecuting attorney, examining the evidence in favor of canonization for adverse arguments, and in so doing helping the Church to arrive at final certainty. (*Cf.* CANONIZATION.)

DEVOLUTION. 1. In canon law an appeal or recourse for judgment to a higher authority when a previous appeal does not suspend or alter the effect of a decision by a superior. **2.**

Also the filling of a vacant benefice by devolution on the part of the Holy See when the ordinary has not acted to fill it by appointment after six months (c. 1432).

DEVOTION. 1. Prayer, or a formula of pious practices devoted to the veneration of a particular saint, or in honor of the Trinity, the Sacred Heart, etc., or to the Blessed Mother under one of her titles, made in common or in private. **2.** Spiritual devotion is the sensible response or consolation felt in the service of God. While such feelings of joy have advantages, such as making it easier to pray or be recollected, etc., they have certain dangers which prompt one to be proud of accomplishment in spiritual things, to expect to be rewarded for every prayer, and to be presumptuous. The opposite of this spiritual devotion is aridity. **3.** Devotion is the voluntary giving of oneself to the service of God; assuming freely a life of devotion.

DIAKONIKON. 1. In the Byzantine church an annex or part of the sanctuary where the priest and deacon rest and where the necessary supplies for the altar are kept. **2.** A book of the liturgy containing the deacon's functions. **3.** A book of prayers to be recited by the deacon before the people.

DIASPORA, the dispersion; the name given to those Jewish communities which were settled outside of Palestine. These groupings of Jews were occasioned by deportations by the conquering Assyrian and Babylonian rulers in the 8th to the 6th centuries B.C., and during the next centuries by migrations of Jews to foreign countries for trade. The most important Jewish community outside of Palestine was at Alexandria, a successful group who spoke Greek and carried on cultural activity. In the Roman empire under the rule of Julius Caesar (d. 44) Roman citizenship was permitted to be conferred on Jews of the diaspora, e.g., St. Paul. Also these Jews contributed large sums to the support of the temple in Jerusalem.

DIATESSARON, the first Syriac version of the four Gospels in a harmonized form, written by Tatian probably in the years 160–180 A.D. It was written in narrative form ostensibly to provide a popular life of Christ. Also the name is applied to any harmony of the Gospels.

DIDACHE, a short treatise in two parts called "Doctrine of the Twelve Apostles," written about 65–80 A.D. The first part of it is moral and the second disciplinary, especially on the administration and ministry of the sacraments of baptism and Holy Eucharist. It was highly regarded by the early fathers of the Church and provides interesting insights into the early practices of the Church.

DIDASCALIA APOSTOLORUM, a 3rd century writing in Greek concerning doctrine and discipline, sometimes attributed to the apostles, but probably written by a bishop of Syria.

DIET OF AUGSBURG or **PEACE OF AUGSBURG,** the compromise reached with the Protestant states of Europe in 1555 under Charles V of Spain who as emperor signed. It established religious toleration by international law, it cleared the title of German Lutheran rulers to church lands and gave them equal status with Catholic rulers.

DIMISSORIALS, letters of authorization and testimonial issued by a bishop or religious superior regarding candidates for ordination under their jurisdiction to another bishop who is to ordain the candidates. This authorization testifies to the qualifications, etc., of the one to be ordained, and requests such ordination. Instead of by letter, it may be given validly by word of mouth (c. 958–967).

DIOCESAN CLERGY, those in holy orders, not being members of a religious order, society or congregation, who administer the temporal and spiritual affairs of a diocese by delegation of the ordinary and are attached to the particular diocese. Often loosely called "secular" clergy.

DIOCESE, the territory under the jurisdiction of a bishop, erected canonically only by the Holy See, which comprises the institutions and properties of the Church and the people within the area. The diocese in turn is divided into deaneries each with several parishes, these latter having their own proper pastor or administrator appointed by the Ordinary.

DIPTYCHS, term from the Greek meaning "folded double," which

A DIPTYCH

came to mean two leaves or tablets bound together by a hinge or thong along one edge. Diptychs were made of metal, ivory, wood or leather, and the inner surfaces were coated with wax so that they could be inscribed with a stylus. In Christian usage they contained lists of names, particularly those of benefactors, newly baptized, etc., and were considered "lists of approval." These were used in the liturgy, the deacon reading them during the Mass as a forerunner of what is now a "memento" of the living or dead. They also are in a manner the original of the Church calendar of feasts, preceding the "Martyrologies." Diptychs are still represented in church art. (*Cf.* TRIPTYCH.)

DIRECTION, SPIRITUAL, the guidance of souls to perfection. Spiritual direction, while it is not absolutely necessary for sanctification, is a normal means taken to assure progress since one's own judgment may be doubtful or erroneous regarding spiritual procedures. The spiritual direction of souls is not easy nor to be taken lightly. St Francis de Sales said of the spiritual director, "He must be full of charity, of knowledge and of prudence: if he lacks one of these, there is danger." Such a person must have knowledge of the spiritual way even before being a person of holiness himself. He must have insight and understanding, firmness in counsel, and detachment from emotion. On the part of the one receiving spiritual direction, there are certain basic requirements as: respect for the one giving counsel and docility in accepting advice. This spiritual direction is not to be confused with advice or admonitions which are customarily given in the confessional. Rather this is a program set up by the director, practices and counsel, which one undertakes as a more than ordinary means of arriving at a high state of virtue and the higher forms of prayer.

DIRECT LINE. In matrimonial legislation, this includes all ancestors and descendants, legitimate or natural. Marriage between any such is invalid (c. 1076). (*Cf.* CONSANGUINITY.)

DIRECTORIUM, an early term for the "Ordo" (q.v.).

DIRIMENT IMPEDIMENT. An impediment is an external fact or circumstance which prohibits marriage or makes it invalid or unlawful. These impediments arise from the natural and positive divine law or the general and particular laws of the Church, or they may be established by civil law. Impediments may be: (a) Prohibitive or diriment, rendering marriage unlawful or unlawful and invalid; (b) absolute or relative, according as they affect the person with or without regard to certain other persons; (c) public or occult, as they can be proven in an external court; (d) temporary or perpetual, as to whether they cease in time; (e) of major or minor degree, depending chiefly upon the relative difficulty of dispensation; and (f) of divine or human right. Diriment impediments which render a marriage invalid and unlawful are: Age, i.e., a boy who has not completed his 16th year and a girl who has not completed her 14th year, cannot validly marry; impotency (antecedent and perpetual); a previous and existing marriage (*cf.* PAULINE PRIVILEGE); disparity of cult, i.e., between an unbaptized person and one baptized in, or converted to, the Catholic faith; those in major orders; those in solemn vows of religion; abduction (holding a person in one's power with intent to marry the person); crime (certain cases of adultery combined with a promise of subsequent marriage, or murder); consanguinity; affinity; public decency; spiritual relationship (between person baptizing and the one baptized or between the baptized person and the sponsors); legal relationship. Inculpable ignorance of a diriment impediment does not make a marriage valid. Under certain circumstances and conditions governed by canon law dispensations may be had for some impediments.

DISCALCED, literally, "barefooted" or "without shoes." The term is applied to certain religious orders, both men and women, who by their rule wear sandals instead of shoes.

DISCERNMENT OF SPIRITS. 1. The grace, mentioned by St. Paul (1 Cor. 12:10), by which the saints and others can see and judge correctly if one is speaking or acting out of charity or only simulating the virtue. **2.** The particular grace of prudence infused by God, and acquired through the practice of the gift of counsel, granted to one, or to a spiritual director, to judge whether a spiritual activity is genuinely prompted by God or by the devil as a temptation to perplex the faithful (1 Jn. 4:1–6; Gal. 5:19–23).

DISCIPLE. 1. Broadly, this may apply to the apostles and the 72 "students" who received instructions from Christ (Lk. 10:1–24), and were in turn sent out by Him to instruct others. They have thus been likened to the hierarchy (the apostles) and the priests (the disciples). There were others added to the body of disciples by the apostles after the Ascension of Christ, for 120 are mentioned as gathered at Jerusalem in Acts 1:15. The mission of the disciples differed from that of the apostles, however, in this that they were sent out "two by two" by Christ and were specifically to prepare for the coming of Jesus Himself. (Mk. 6:7). **2.** The term "Beloved Disciple" is applied to St. John since he was called "the disciple whom Jesus loved" in the account of the Last Supper (Jn. 13:23).

DISCIPLINE. 1. Name of the small whip or scourge used by some austere religious orders in penitential practice as a means of bodily mortification. The prescribed use is called "taking the discipline." Voluntary use by individuals should only be undertaken on advice of a competent spiritual director. **2.** An instruction, or system of teaching.

DISCIPLINE OF THE SECRET or **DISCIPLINA ARCANI.** In her early days, it was the custom of the Church to withhold certain doctrines and aspects of worship from those seeking eventual membership in the Church, out of fear that there would be blasphemy, persecution or interruptions in divine service. Actually full instruction was given before one was baptized, but in the liturgy the "Mass of the Catechumens" was open only to those receiving instructions. Likewise there were various symbols employed as a "secret" representation of truths, e.g., the "fish" meaning Christ as a means of communicating without interference. This withholding at the beginning of certain teachings is still in practice among some missionary groups.

DISKOS, the paten used in the Byzantine rite. It is larger, dish-like, having a raised rim, differing from the paten used in the Roman rite.

DISPARITY OF WORSHIP, also called disparity of cult, a diriment impediment to marriage (c. 1070). Marriage is null and void if contracted between an unbaptized person and one baptized in or converted to the Church. (*Cf.* IMPEDIMENTS.)

DISPENSATION, the relaxation of the obligation of a law due to special circumstances of a case which can only be granted by the proper and competent authority (c. 80). Dispensations are given only by the Church for church laws and by one having jurisdiction. They are applied to particular laws of fasting, abstaining, to vows, or to certain marriage laws, as well as other laws. A dispensation can be recalled and thereby ceases.

DISSOLUTION OF A MARRIAGE. This question, covered completely in canon law, can only be briefly given here. 1. A person who is already married validly cannot enter into a second marriage validly until the bond of the first marriage is legitimately dissolved. This is of divine law, binding all persons. 2. In the event of desertion by one of the parties, most serious investigations must be made in accord with instructions laid down by the Holy See, should the party remaining wish to enter into contract of a new marriage. 3. The marriage bond between two baptized persons can only be dissolved if the marriage has not been consummated. 4. The Pauline Privilege can dissolve the marriage bond of unbaptized persons even though the marriage has been consummated. The bond of a non-sacramental marriage

can be dissolved by the Pauline Privilege or by the vicarious power of the pope in favor of the faith (*cf.* PAULINE PRIVILEGE; MONTANA CASE). 5. A non-consummated marriage between two baptized persons is dissolved by the solemn religious profession of one or both of the parties or by dispensation of the Holy See (c. 1119). It is to be understood that this is not divorce in a legal sense ("divorce" as such has no effect before God). The dissolution of the bond of marriage in the Church is an examination of the contract itself from the primary and secondary ends of marriage, its essential properties, its validity, and the spiritual welfare of the parties. While the civil law may claim to dissolve the bond of marriage, a Catholic can only go through the civil legal procedure of such dissolving of the bond (divorce) when one of the parties or both cannot otherwise obtain the civil effects. The parties in this case must obtain ecclesiastical permission, must promise in writing that only the civil effects are sought, and must intend not to remarry.

DISTRACTION, in its religious sense, a lack of advertence or attention when praying. Distractions are: voluntary, when one wilfully sets the mind to thinking about vain things or deliberately ceases to pray because of preoccupation (may be gravely sinful); involuntary, when fleeting thoughts, due to objects seen or mental fancies, turn one away from the prayer. Distractions are obstacles to prayer, and should be overcome by directing the attention. This may be done by: (a) making an effort to pronounce the words of prayer correctly, called verbal attention; (b) attempting to understand the meaning of the words of the prayer, called intellectual attention; (c) the mental sweeping upward of our thoughts to God in worship and love, called spiritual attention. This latter is recommended mostly for one who has achieved the first two.

DIVINE COMEDY, the title of a three-part allegory, written in a verse form called *terga rima*, by Dante Alighieri in 1321. It is composed of the *Inferno*, treating of hell; the *Purgatorio*, treating of purgatory; and *Paradiso*, treating of heaven, each in an imaginative manner but showing great insight into the theology of the fathers of the Church and the philosophy of the 13th century.

DIVINE OFFICE, the public, official and common prayer of the Church. It is offered daily in public or liturgically in union with Christ in adoration and supplication of God. It is the prayer of the mystical body. It derives from the authority of the Church, and its content is formulated by the Church. Thus by direction of the Church it is prescribed to members of the priesthood, deacons, subdeacons and all religious, under solemn obligation, to be prayed in the name of the Church and all the faithful who pray also in this recitation. (*Cf.* BREVIARY.)

DIVINE PRAISES, a litany of praises said after Benediction of the Blessed Sacrament. Each is said by the celebrant and repeated by the faithful. They are: Blessed be God; Blessed be His Holy Name; Blessed be Jesus Christ, true God and true Man; Blessed be the name of Jesus; Blessed be His most Sacred Heart; Blessed be Jesus in the most holy Sacrament of the Altar; Blessed be the great Mother of God, Mary most

holy; Blessed be her holy and Immaculate Conception; Blessed be her glorious Assumption; Blessed be the name of Mary, virgin and mother; Blessed be St. Joseph, her most chaste spouse; Blessed be God in His angels and in His saints.

DIVINITY OF CHRIST. This is the answer to the question of Scripture: "Who do men say the Son of Man is?" (Mt. 16:13). The answer is found in a twofold examination concerning first, the Messiasship of Christ; second, the Sonship of God. Subordinate but supporting these two is a synthesis of Christ's works, miracles, teachings, and associations. Concerning the first, Christ as Messias: In the Gospel of St. John we recognize Jesus as the Messias, "Him of whom Moses . . . and the prophets wrote" (Jn. 1:45). We further find it recorded that others recognized Christ in His role as Messias: "and they knew that He was the Christ" (Lk. 4:41). While Jesus did not proclaim Himself the Messias in words, it is revealed that He permits others to ascribe to Him the most popular of all Messianic titles "the Son of David" (Mt. 12:23), and that Christ knows Himself to be the Messianic Son of David in propounding the meaning of Ps. 109 (Mt. 22:41ff). Finally Jesus affirms explicitly the role of Messias when in answer to the high priest He replies, when asked: "Art thou the Christ, the Son of the living God?," saying, "I am" (Mk. 14:61). Concerning the second, Christ as the Son of God: This term "Son of God" is applied to Jesus frequently in the synoptic Gospels. For example, the confession of Peter, "Thou art Christ, the Son of the living God" (Mt. 16:16); and in the confession of the centurion (Mk. 15:39). More profoundly we find in the prologue of St. John's Gospel attestation of the "Word of God" His pre-existence, the action of the Word in the creation of the world, and the fact that the Word has become incarnate in Jesus Christ. Christ's becoming incarnate, "being made flesh," is no longer a matter of prophecy only, but actually is the fulfillment of the O.T. prophecies. And most conclusively, Christ is presented by St. John as the one who reveals the secrets of the Godhead, which is only possible to the "only-begotten Son" (Jn. 5:19–23). This is summarized in the protestation of faith by Thomas "My Lord and my God" (Jn. 20:28), and is the confession of Catholic Christianity in the divinity of Jesus Christ. Relative to and supporting these scriptural texts are further distinctions of Christ in the Gospels: His works which were to be done according to "the will of Him who sent Me" (Jn. 4:34); also His many miracles showing His power over demons (Mt. 9:32ff, etc.), over nature (Mk. 8:22ff, etc.), over cosmic forces (Mt. 8:26), and finally His triumph over death in His Resurrection (Lk. 24:1ff); His teaching, by which He identifies Himself as "the Way" (Jn. 14:6); and by His associations or His knowledge which was exclusively His, such as that of heaven, and intimacy with God the Father (Jn. 1:18), etc. All of these together present the personality of Christ and from this we know Him as the divine Christ (Jn. 7:17) who speaks with authority. Christ in virtue of the hypostatic union is a divine Person, the second Person of the Blessed Trinity.

DIVORCE. *See* DISSOLUTION OF A MARRIAGE.

DIVORCE FROM BED AND BOARD. In canon law, this compares to the civil judicial action called a "separation" (c. 1128–1132).

DOCETISM, a heresy of the 2nd century. It is not truly a Christian heresy, i.e., arising from a denial of a dogma by the faithful, but it arose from another heresy, Gnosticism. The Docetae taught that Jesus was not real, but only a phantom.

DOCTOR. 1. One who has received the highest of the university degrees (*cf.* DECREES, ACADEMIC). **2.** Doctor of the Church is a title conferred on eminent ecclesiastical writers because of their learning and holiness of life; they are always canonized. Thus as a "doctor" each has a feast of his own with Mass and Office or is celebrated in the Common of Doctors.

DOCTOR ANGELICUS, from the Latin, the Angelic Doctor, a title of St. Thomas Aquinas (1225–1274), the great scholastic theologian of the Dominican Order.

DOGMA, a teaching, a firm principle. In the Church, the word used today in its strictest sense as "dogma of the faith" or "Catholic dogma" means a truth revealed by Scripture or contained in tradition, and for belief proposed by the Church through solemn definition or arising from the magisterium of the Church as a teaching of divine revelation (c. 1323). The fathers of the Church used the term to designate revealed teachings of our Lord, and later a distinction was made between dogma and moral teaching.

DOGMATIC FACT, certain truths which, while not revealed by God, are proclaimed by the teaching authority of the Church. By infallible authority the Church judges and proposes these facts for belief.

DOGMATIC THEOLOGY. This division of theology has as its object to demonstrate the existence of dogmas, to show that they are contained in the deposit of faith, and to further show the causes, the connections, and logical conclusions of these dogmas. It thus differs from fundamental theology which demonstrates that these truths are revealed. Dogmatic theology receives the dogmas from the Church from whom the deposit of faith is received. Thus it takes the definitions of the Church, accepting the authority of the Church as infallible. Dogmatic theology then proves the existence of each dogma from Scripture and Tradition, showing the Church's teaching to be in agreement with the sources of revelation. It further proves that the Church's teaching does not change, that there are no new dogmas handed down, and that these truths were taught from the very beginning. Dogmatic theology is also called "special dogma."

DOLORS OF THE BLESSED VIRGIN. *See* SEVEN SORROWS.

DOM. 1. A title, being an abbreviation of the Latin word *dominus*, master, given to professed religious of the Benedictine, Carthusian, and Cistercian Orders. In Italy the term is "Don" and is applied to all clerics except mendicant friars and regular clerks. **2.** Formal title of a cathedral in Germany.

DOMESTIC PRELATE, an honorary title of rank and distinction conferred on priests by the Holy See which designates the recipient as a member of the pope's court and household. With the title go certain privileges: recipients are addressed Right Reverend Monsignor; they use a black biretta with a purple pompom; they have a cassock of violet with a rochet and mantellettum; they never let down the train of the cassock, and at solemn Masses they may use the bugia, or special candlestick.

DOMICILE, one's fixed residence. In canon law one has a domicile if he resides or dwells in a place with the intention of remaining there unless some unforeseen event occurs, or he has spent ten years in that place. A wife's domicile is that of her husband. By location of the domicile it is determined under which bishop's jurisdiction one is, making him subject to the bishop and the laws established for the diocese. (*Cf.* QUASI-DOMICILE.)

DOMINATIONS, one of the choirs of the hierarchy of angels. (*Cf.* ANGELS.)

DOMINICAL LETTERS. In the early method of reckoning the Church calendar, the first seven letters of the alphabet were used to indicate the days of the week and were called dominical letters. (*Cf.* CYCLE.)

DONATION OF CONSTANTINE, a forged letter falsely attributed to Constantine the Great, written probably as early as the 8th century, allegedly conferring supremacy of the pope over all bishops and temporal rulers.

DONATISM, a schism caused by Donatus in 311 A.D. at Carthage over the election of Caecilian as successor to Bishop Mensurius by appeal to the Emperor Constantine. It brought about the breakdown of the African church since it lasted for 300 years or until the conquest by the Saracens. Donatists also affirmed the heretical belief that the validity of a sacrament depends upon the spiritual condition of the minister. The schism and heretical teachings were answered and condemned by a council held in Carthage in 404.

DOORKEEPER, the first of the four minor orders in the Roman rite. Also called *Porter*. It is conferred after tonsure, and, while the office it entails is now more symbolical than actual, it literally entrusts the "entry" of the church to the recipient, granting the "ringing of bells, opening the church and sanctuary, and opening the preacher's book."

DORMITION OF THE B.V.M., the falling into sleep, rather than death, of the Blessed Mother. Also a name sometimes applied to the Assumption.

DOSSAL also **DORSAL,** a suspended curtain of rich cloth, tapestry or brocade, behind the altar, extending the length of the altar or beyond. It may serve to form the background of a large hanging crucifix.

DOUAY also **DOUAI** or **DOWAY BIBLE,** the standard translation of the Bible into English, in use for three and a half centuries. It is called the Douay-Rheims Bible, this name deriving from O.T. volumes published in Douay (France) in 1609-10, and the N.T. books published in Rheims in 1582. Both versions were translated by Gregory Martin at Rheims where the English college of Douay was temporarily removed for fifteen years (1578-1593) and where he was pro-

fessor of theology and Scripture. However, the text as we know it now has had several revisions, the first by Dr. Witham in 1730, and this was superseded by five revisions by Dr. Richard Challoner (1691-1781). Our present version is based upon these, so more exactly it should be referred to as the "Douay-Challoner," or "Rheims-Challoner." Since this work notably had some literary flaws in style, due perhaps to translation difficulties in rendering from the Latin, including many "Latinisms," revisions were necessary. It must be remembered that Catholics are bound to use a text approved by Church authority (*see* Leo XIII's encyclical, *Officiorum ac munerum*), and may not print a text without authorization (c. 1391, 2318), and hence any text so authorized may be considered as a Catholic text. In recent years many texts have so been printed and published in the United States. They are texts of the entire Bible or of Old or New Testaments, e.g., the Baltimore Bible (1899); Herder's Cardinal Farley's Bible of 1911; Benziger's "Red Letter Bible" of 1943; Sheed and Ward's N.T. of Dr. Arendzen—all of which are revisions and improvements of the Douay-Challoner. More sweeping changes have appeared in the Confraternity Edition of 1941 and that of Father Carey in 1935. In 1945 and 1949, an entirely new translation was made from the Vulgate by Msgr. Ronald Knox, and a rendition from the Greek by Frs. J. A. Kleist, S. J. and J. L. Lilly, C. M., of the N.T., in 1954. (*Cf.* BIBLE.)

DOUBLE, the highest rank of feast in the liturgical order. They are thus: doubles of the first class, e.g., Christmas; doubles of the second class, the major doubles and ordinary doubles (*cf.* FEASTS OF THE CHURCH). The term arose in the 4th and 5th centuries as a result of the then current practice of saying two, or "doubling," the offices on certain days, saying one for the fixed feast and one as a special office in honor of a saint.

DOVE. 1. A Catholic symbol of the Holy Spirit, used because of the form assumed at the baptism of Christ (Jn. 1:32f) and recognized and associated with the Pentecostal baptism of fire. Thus also it became a symbol of baptism for early Christians. **2.** A medieval pyx was shaped as a dove.

DOWRY OF MARY, a 14th century title of the "land of England." It included the islands of the realm.

DOXOLOGY, a prayer or tribute of praise offered to God or the Trinity. There are two classes: the greater, e.g., the *Gloria in excelsis* of the Mass; and the lesser, e.g., the prayer "Glory be to the Father, etc." There are frequent doxologies in the Scriptures (2 Peter, 3:18; Rom. 11:36; etc.) and the reason may be found for such prayers in the words of St. Paul (Col. 3:17).

DREAMS, activity of the subconscious mind during sleep. Dreams have been used by God as means of revealing courses of action and truths otherwise unknown (Gen. 37:1–11). However, it is gravely sinful to attempt to use dreams as a means of reading the future out of superstition or attempted diabolical aid.

DRESS, CLERICAL. *See* COSTUME, CLERICAL.

DUEL, a fight between persons conducted by previous agreement as to time, place, and weapons, with death or maiming of one of the parties as its outcome. Such are forbidden by the Church under grave penalties: excommunication reserved simply to the Holy See (c. 2351) together with infamy of law incurred by the very fact. Ecclesiastical burial is denied to those who die in a duel (c. 1240).

DULIA or **CULTUS DULIAE,** the special worship, generally called veneration, due to the angels and saints because as friends of God they share in His excellence. (*Cf.* CULTUS; HYPERDULIA; LATRIA.)

DUPLEX. *See* DOUBLE.

DUPLICATION. *See* BINATION.

DYING, PRAYERS FOR. *See* COMMENDATION OF THE SOUL.

E

EASTER CONTROVERSY. This was the dispute between the East and the West in the 2nd century (circa 155) wherein the Asiatic bishops protested against the Roman custom of celebrating Easter on Sunday, instead of on whatever day of the week the 14th Nisan might fall according to the old Jewish calendar. The dispute arose again in 325. The controversy points to the historic relationship of the bishops and the pope. It was settled finally with the 95-year cycle that was followed everywhere after the 9th century.

EASTER DUTY, the obligation of all the faithful who have attained the use of reason to receive Holy Communion at least once during the season of Easter. It is recommended that each fulfill this duty in his own parish church, or if he does so elsewhere, he should inform the pastor of his parish (c. 859). The Easter season in the United States extends from the first Sunday of Lent to Trinity Sunday inclusive. It is also recommended that the faithful fulfill their obligation of annual confession (c. 906) at this time out of practical considerations. (*Cf.* PRECEPTS OF THE CHURCH.)

EASTER, FEAST OF, the celebration in the liturgy of the Resurrection of Jesus Christ from the dead (*cf.* RESURRECTION OF CHRIST). The name Easter derives from the Saxon goddess Eastre, the ancient deity of the dawn. However, the Christian name of the feast is Pasch which is the Jewish feast of the Passover and this derives only because, in the providence of God, Christ's death and Resurrection coincided with the Passover of that year in the Jewish calendar. In present reckoning this date was probably the Sunday of April 9, 30 A.D. The feast is the greatest in the Church, going back to the early years. It is celebrated with the greatest solemnity and in the centuries immediately preceding the 12th, each day of Easter week was a holyday of obligation. In the Church calendar all movable feasts are calculated from Easter.

EASTERN CHURCHES. These are groups of Christians, Uniate (returned to Catholic unity from the corresponding non-Catholic church of their rite), or schismatic, who are either (a) Catholic or (b) dissident or non-Catholic. To the *Catholic* (a) belong those of the Byzantine rite as Catholic Armenians, Chaldeans, Catholic Copts and Ethiopians, Maronites, Catholic Syrians, and those of the Malabar rite. These are classified as Uniates (except the Italo-Greeks) and returned to Catholic unity. Each is as fully and completely Catholic as the Western Church. They retain their own liturgies, canon law and customs by right, differing among themselves and from the Western Church, but teach the same faith and morals and are obedient to the Holy See as is the Western Church. The *dissident churches* (b) are made up of two categories: those national churches which collectively form the Orthodox Eastern Church; and the Nestorian, Armenian, Coptic, Ethiopic, and Syrian Jacobite Churches. While these were at one time parts of the Catholic Church, they now deny the authority of the Holy See and variously teach erroneous or heretical doctrines. Each does teach the Real Presence, the Eucharistic Sacrifice, confession, veneration of the Blessed Mother and the saints, and other doctrines and, with the exception of the Copts and Ethiopians, have valid orders and sacraments.

EASTERN STUDIES, PONTIFICAL INSTITUTE OF. Also called the Oriental Institute, this house of study for oriental clergy, Catholic or dissident, is under the direction of the Jesuits. It was founded by Benedict XV in 1917 and is part of the Gregorian University in Rome.

EASTER WATER, holy water blessed on Holy Saturday in special ceremonies.

EBIONITES, an heretical sect which arose in the first centuries around Jerusalem (Acts15:1–3). They taught that the Jewish law still bound Christians, that Christ was a mere man, and considered St. Paul an apostate. The sect, its remainder having been absorbed into the Gnostic heresy, had disappeared by the 4th century. The name Ebionite comes from the Hebrew word for "poor."

ECCLESIA, a Latin word meaning "church." It applies both to a building and a group of religious believers.

ECCLESIASTES, a biblical book of the O.T., claimed to have been written by Solomon under a pseudonym, but critics today agree that this was a literary artifice. It was written probably toward the close of the 3rd cencuty B.C. Its theme is retribution, finding that the theory of earthly rewards is weighed and found wanting, and that the infinitely just God has a purpose which man finds unsearchable. It is asserted that God will intervene and right apparent injustices (3:17).

ECCLESIASTIC, a term applied to a cleric in major orders, but most frequently to a church dignitary.

ECCLESIASTICUS. In the Prologue to this O.T. book of the Bible we learn that the author is one, in the Hebrew idiom, named "Jesus, son of Sirach." He lived in Jerusalem, was probably a scribe, and was versed in the Scriptures. The book was written according to historical data referred to in the text between 190–180 B.C. The theme of the book centers upon moral teaching in relation to human life and man's relationship to God, that sin is evil, but that God draws good out of evil, and that God judges and punishes evil (17:13–19).

ECONOMICS, the branch of social science which is concerned with the exchange, production and distribution of goods and services in human society. It also investigates and studies the general laws which apply in any given society to the use and consumption of goods. In its strict moral sense, in the directive and application of general laws of both goods (production) and skills (means of production), economics is the science of justice in social life. (*Cf.* RERUM NOVARUM.)

ECONOMY, DIVINE, the providence, orderly plan, employed by God in the exercise of His divine will, which is the best possible since it arises from an omniscient being.

ECSTASY, an enraptured condition of the soul and body. In the mystical understanding of this condition, it follows the affective state, and entails a suspension of the activity of one's exterior senses. It attains to that state where the interior, intuitive senses are active within one. It is thus the highest form of spiritual union or direct transmission of divine mysteries and must be, over and above the sense suspension, an absorption of the soul in God. (*Cf.* CONTEMPLATION.)

ECTHESIS, a general term used in the early Church, meaning an exposition of doctrine.

ECUMENICAL COUNCILS. The Church has held 20 world-wide councils. They are with dates and primary actions: 1. Nicaea I, 325, condemned Arianism and declared the Son "consubstantial" with the Father. 2. Constantinople I, 381, condemned Macedonians, declared Holy Spirit consubstantial with Father and Son. 3. Ephesus, 431, condemned Nestorians and Pelagians and declared the divine maternity of the Blessed Mother. 4. Chalcedon, 451, condemned Monophysitism. 5. Constantinople II, 553, condemned the Three Chapters. 6. Constantinople III, 680, condemned Monothelitism and censured Honorius. 7. Nicaea II, 787, condemned Iconoclasm. 8. Constantinople IV, 869, ended the Greek schism and deposed Photius. 9. Lateran I, 1123, issued decrees on simony, celibacy, lay investiture and confirmed Con-

cordat of Worms. 10. Lateran II, 1139, ended the papal schism and enacted reforms. 11. Lateran III, 1179, condemned Albigenses and Waldenses and regulated papal elections. 12. Lateran IV, 1215, planned crusade, decrees on annual communion, repeated condemnation of Albigenses, enacted reforms. 13. Lyons, I, 1245, deposed Frederick II and planned crusade. 14. Lyons II, 1274, reunited Church with the Greeks and enacted disciplinary reforms. 15. Vienne, 1311–1312, abolished Knights Templars, enacted reforms. 16. Constance, 1414–1418, ended Great Schism, condemned Huss. 17. Basle, Ferrara, Florence, 1431–1445, effected union of Greeks, enacted reforms. 18. Lateran V, 1512–1517, treated of the Neo-Aristotelians and enacted reforms. 19. Trent, 1545–1563, condemned Protestantism, enacted reforms. 20. Vatican, 1869–1870 (not yet officially closed), condemned errors, defined papal infallibility. (*Cf.* COUNCIL, 3.)

EDICT OF MILAN, also called Edict of Toleration. This announcement in 313 was a political compromise between two emperors, Licinus of the East, a pagan, and Constantine of the West, soon to be a professed Christian, which made Christianity one of the recognized religions.

EDICT OF NANTES, an action of Henry IV of France (d. 1610), signed in 1598, which ended the seventh of the Religious Wars. It restored the rights and privileges of the Catholic clergy, and gave to the Huguenots freedom of worship in many parts of France, civil rights, and possession of 100 fortified cities. In 1685, Louis XIV (d. 1715), thinking he could bring about religious unity but chiefly for political reasons, revoked the Edict of Nantes, seized or destroyed the property of the Huguenots, and forced many to flee (thus actually aiding the spread of Protestantism). When Pope Innocent XI (d. 1689) expressed disapproval, strained relations began between France and the papacy and almost led to a French schism which was not settled until after the pope's death.

EDICT OF RESTITUTION. This document issued at the close of the Thirty Years' War in 1629 by Emperor Ferdinand II (d. 1637), gave an official interpretation of the Peace of Augsburg. It nullified privileges which Protestants had enjoyed for years and restored Catholic properties. However, the Holy See remained indifferent to this edict, perhaps foreseeing the resultant disturbance in this hazardous legislation.

EDIFICATION, CHRISTIAN, a term of metaphor, applied to the "building up" of the body of Christ, i.e., effecting the completion of the mystical body, the Church (Jude 1:20). This can only be done through the Holy Spirit. St. Paul uses it similarly in the sense of the Christians rebuilding the sanctuary of Christ's body being compared to the resurrection, and doing this by their influence of good on one another (Rom. 4:25; Eph. 4:12f). From this we arrive at the term "edifying" in regard to proper conduct, which is a far departure from the scriptural sense.

EDUCATION. Properly, education is the formal and general quest of wisdom. It is thus mentioned in the Bible (Eccu. 6, 21ff). However, we also learn that it is in vain if it does not prepare for a deeper spiritual life

and prepare for the happiness of the next world. This has been the centuries-long struggle of the Church, to instruct all toward their eternal salvation. For this the Church has developed systems of study as the Jesuit Code and that of the Christian Brothers. She has established schools from the 1st century at Antioch and Jerusalem to today's parochial and university institutes spread over the world. Likewise the Church has fostered the arts of drama, rhetoric and oratory as well as developing entire philosophies as that of Scholasticism. Among many pronouncements, the Church's attitude toward education may be re-stated in the words of the bishops of the U. S. (April 25, 1933): ". . . the unchangeable elements of education and its real purpose—to fit men for life in eternity as well as in time; to teach men to think rightly and to live rightly; to instill sound principles in our youth, principles not only of civic righteousness, but of Catholic faith and morality; to educate groups, according to their capacity, so as to make them the best men and the best women of our country—and all this with a thorough training in the secular branches of knowledge." To this end there continues to the present the use of means to instruct men to truth through parochial schools, high schools, universities, through the Confraternity of Christian Doctrine, through study clubs, through the radio and Catholic press.

EFFICACIOUS GRACE. This is the actual, effective grace, for the Church affirms *de fide* (of faith) that no act conducive to salvation can be performed without grace, which causes us to act for our salvation. As said in Ezechiel (36:27): "I will cause you to walk in My commandments, and to keep My judgments, and do them." And the Council of Orange states: "It is God who works in us both to will and to do." That grace which causes us to act is efficacious, effective not only as to powers in the supernatural order, but also effective in operation, producing together with us, through our will concurring with the grace, the good action. While efficacious grace is conferred, it is not the only kind of grace, nor is the liberty of the will taken away by it. It is the grace by which the hard heart is overcome and we yield to act being aided in our will to act by the efficacious forces of the grace. (*Cf.* GRACE.)

EIKON. *See* ICON.

EJACULATION, the name for short affective prayers of a few words, e.g., "Jesus, I love You." Many of these prayers are indulgenced and as such are listed in the Raccolta and they need not be said orally to gain the indulgences. They are sometimes called aspirations, perhaps because they can be uttered in one breath. Also called "invocations."

ELECTION, one of those methods of selecting a pope, recognized as valid by the Constitution of Pope Pius XII. Two-thirds plus one of the votes of the electing cardinals are necessary for a valid election.

ELEVATION OF THE MASS. In this ceremony that was introduced by Eudes de Sully, bishop of Paris (d. 1208) in the Mass of the Roman rite, the celebrant after the consecration of the host raises it briefly above his head for the adoration of the faithful. Likewise immediately after the wine has been consecrated, the chalice is raised. In the Middle Ages the people considered it most important that those attending Mass should look upon the Blessed Sacrament, and for this reason, so that no one would fail to see, the practice of ringing a handbell at the elevation was begun.

ELEVATION OF THE MASS

ELNE, COUNCIL OF, a minor council held in 1027, notable for introducing the "Truce of God," prohibiting armed hostilities from Saturday night *angelus* to Monday morning *angelus*.

ELOHIM, the *general* name for God, as Yahweh is the *personal* name by which God was known to the Israelites. The Vulgate renders Elohim as "God" while Yahweh is translated "Dominus" i.e. "Lord." The two together "Yahweh Elohim" appear 21 times in the O.T.

ELVIRA, COUNCIL OF, the first Spanish council of record, held about the year 300. It published the oldest known positive law concerning clerical celibacy, stated the Catholic rule concerning the indissolubility of marriage, and enacted 81 disciplinary canons.

EMBER DAYS, days of special penance which are intended to prepare the faithful for entry into the four seasons of the year. They are the Wednesday, Friday and Saturday which follow Dec. 13, the first Sunday of Lent, Pentecost and Sept. 14. (*Cf.* ABSTINENCE, FASTING.)

EMBOLISM, an added or inserted prayer, e.g., the prayer said immediately following the "Our Father" in the Mass which is an extension of the last part of the Our Father and expands the petition beyond the prescribed wording of the prayer.

EMINENCE, term of address to cardinals only, by decree of the Congregation of Rites. Thus, "Most Eminent"; "His Eminence"; "Your Eminence." The sole exception to the above is that "eminence" may be given in titles of address to the Grand Master of the Knights of St. John of Jerusalem.

EMPIRE, HOLY ROMAN, the empire of single rule founded by Charlemagne with the aid of the Roman Pontiffs. It collapsed for a time through dissension, but was revived in 962 with the coronation of Otho (Otto) I as king of Germany by Pope John XII. It lasted for more than eight centuries. The addition of the adjective "Holy" appeared for the first time in the reign of Frederick I (d. 1190) and became customary after Charles IV (d. 1378). For the states involved, chiefly Germany and Italy, it became an extension of an aristocratic system, feudalizing the old Roman empire. It held advantages for both the states and the Church, but actually brought the Church into sharp contrast with the temporalities and created a number of problems as lay investiture, etc. The Holy Roman Empire dissolved in 1806 when the Hapsburg Emperor Francis II was defeated in the war with Napoleon. Succeeding attempts at confederation failed, but the Church was not party to their make-up or failure, the times having changed the political aspect of the world and democratic principles altered the protective necessity of the empire as it once existed.

ENCHIRIDION, the title of the best known writing of H. J. D. Denzinger (d. 1883). It is a compilation of the chief conciliar decrees together with a list of propositions they condemned, and is frequently quoted as a source book.

ENCLOSURE also **CLOISTER.** This is the enclosed place reserved to religious, including the physical barriers which surround it, together with the special laws governing admission to it or exit of religious from it. This enclosure is either papal or by the bishop of the diocese in which the monastery or convent is erected: (a) in regard to male religious (regulars) with solemn vows, the enclosure is papal and must be observed strictly. The area of the enclosure must be clearly indicated; e.g., certain public rooms or visiting parlors and the nave of the monastery church are excluded generally. Laymen may enter a monastery of men, but women are strictly prohibited under penalty of excommunication for the woman and him who permits her to enter, reserved to the Holy See; (b) in monasteries of nuns, those taking solemn vows, the law of enclosure is equally strict, though exceptions of diocesan sisters, episcopal enclosure, are made. It is not to be taken that nuns who wish to return to the world permanently may not do so. Laws governing the enclosure, entrance and egress, dismissal and voluntary leaving are contained in canon law with full provisions (cs. 597–606; 2342).

ENCRATISM, a rigid moral and ascetic doctrine practiced by certain Christians of the 2nd century. It was based on the misconception that matter is evil. Those practicing this were called Encratites, a sect of the Gnostic heresy.

ENCYCLICAL. The term comes from the Latin description of these letters, *literae encyclicae*, literally "circular letters." An encyclical is a profound letter addressed by the pope to all the patriarchs, primates, archbishops, bishops and prelates nullius of the entire world-wide Church. An encyclical may also be addressed to the hierarchy of a single country or confederation of nations. Each is written in Latin. The purpose of an encyclical is not personal but is to condemn certain current errors, to inform the faithful, through the hierarchy, of adverse legislation or government administration interfering with the mission of the Church, or to explain conduct that should be followed by Christians. They are intended for all the faithful, and in turn the faithful are to give the message of these letters assent, obedience and respect because of the weight and truth they contain. Each is titled usually by their first words in Latin. Recent notable encyclicals are: Pius X, 1904, on the Blessed Virgin Mary, Mediatrix of Graces; Pius X, 1907, on Modernism (*Pascendi*); Pius XI, 1922, on Church and State (*Ubi Arcano Dei*); Pius XI, 1929, on Catholic Education (*Divini illius Magistri*); Pius XI, 1930, on Christian marriage (*Casti Connubi*); Pius XI, 1931, on the social and industrial order (*Quadragesimo Anno*); Pius XI, 1937, on atheistic communism (*Divini Redemptoris*); Pius XII, 1943, on the mystical body (*Mystici Corporis*); Pius XII, 1954, on the state and merit of virginity.

ENCYCLICAL EPISTLE. An encyclical epistle differs only slightly from an encyclical letter. It is primarily directed to instruct concerning some devotion or special need of the Holy See, e.g., a world-wide charity, or some special event as a Holy Year.

ENCYCLOPAEDISTS, a group of rationalists and free thinkers who wrote articles for the French *Encyclopedie* (published 1751–1765) notably Voltaire (d. 1778), Rousseau (d. 1778), Diderot (d. 1784), and others. They attempted to inject a trend toward infidelity to the Church, prepared the thinking on irreligion preceding the Revolution, and opposed the pontificate of Pope Clement XIII (d. 1769).

END. In scholastic philosophy, end means "that object for the attainment of which the agent moves and acts." It is divided: a) the "end which" (*finis qui*), the good intended to be attained; b) the "end for whom" (*finis cui*), the person or subject for whom the "end which" is obtained; c) the formal end (the end by which or *finis quo*), the actual attainment of the thing intended. Further, the end of the work (*finis operis*) is that to which an act is ordered, or tends, by its own nature, e.g., study is to enlighten the mind; and the *end of the one working* (*finis operantis*), that toward which one directs an action, e.g., study a science because it is useful. Ends may be proximate, intermediate, or ultimate; also, *primary end* is that which is sufficient for prompting one to act, and *secondary end*, one not sufficient but auxiliary in prompting the act.

END OF MAN, the final, ultimate goal to the attainment to which all other actions are subordinate, which can only be God, or beatitude in God. (*Cf.* HEAVEN.)

END OF THE WORLD. At no place in Scripture, the teaching of the Church, mystical revelations or otherwise is the time of the world's end set forth. The only certainty refers more precisely to the final or last judgment (Mt. 25:31–46) described by Christ. The judgment at which the kingdom of the Son, all the individuals of the faithful, is purified before coming into the kingdom of the Father is settled ultimately on religious grounds: Christ is to be the judge. Human history will be at an end and man continues in eternal life of happiness or loss. (*Cf.* ESCHATOLOGY.)

ENDOWMENT, a fund set apart for the support of an institution of the Church, either a church building, school or hospital. Sometimes the term is applied to a house or fund for the education of candidates for the priesthood.

ENDS OF THE MASS, the four solemn intentions for which every Mass is offered: a) adoration, the worship of God; b) thanksgiving; c) reparation for the sins of the world; d) petition for the needs of all men.

ENERGUMEN, term applied to one possessed by evil spirits; a demoniac.

ENGLISH MARTYRS, those who were put to death for the faith in England between the schism of Henry

VIII and 1681. Of record these are 602, of whom some have been canonized and petitions for others started with the Holy See, but this does not include all who suffered death in persecution during this time. The feast is celebrated in England on May 4.

ENKOLPION

ENKOLPION, a medallion worn suspended from the neck and resting on the breast by bishops of the Byzantine rite. They bear either a representation of our Lord or the Blessed Mother and sometimes contain relics.

ENVY, one of the capital sins. It is the willful grieving or sadness because of another's spiritual or temporal good, looked upon or considered as a lessening of one's own goods, e.g., if he didn't have such and such, I could have it; or an honor paid to another being considered a disgrace reflected upon oneself. It is begrudging of what one's neighbor has and wishing seriously that he did not have it so that the envious person would not feel at a disadvantage.

EPARCHY, a term corresponding to diocese in Eastern churches, notably the Russian.

EPHESIANS, EPISTLE TO THE, one of the four captivity Epistles written by St. Paul about 63 A.D. It was not addressed exclusively to the Ephesians, for while Paul was there for about three years, critics agree it was intended for a broader group, e.g., the "Church in Laodicea." The Epistle is a non-controversial exposition on mankind being one with Christ and God's purpose in the world through His Church (1:15-23). It is also directed at the development of a Christian life, particularly of the Christian family (5:22-28; 6:1-4).

EPHESUS, COUNCIL OF, an ecumenical council held in 431, summoned by Theodosius II. It condemned Pelagian and Nestorian heresies. Most notable is this council for having defined the Catholic dogma that the Blessed Virgin Mary is the Mother of God. (*Cf.* DEIPARA.)

EPHESUS, ROBBER SYNOD OF. Also called *Latrocinium*, this was a meeting in 449 presided over by the heretical Dioscurus of Alexandria. The synod advanced Nestorian doctrines, ignoring the pope and his rights.

EPIEIKEIA also **EPIKEIA.** This term, meaning equity, is applied to the interpretation of a law. Reasonably taken for granted that the lawgiver does not wish to bind in some particularly difficult case because the exercise of the law would work an unforeseen hardship, this is an examination of the law and a judgment of the intent of the lawgiver in the spirit of the law but against its rigor in application. Epieikeia may not be used in the following cases: when the lawgiver may be approached directly for an interpretation or dispensation; in the case of laws which make an act invalid; in the case of one being incapable of undertaking legal action; divine law, positive or natural, or where the lawgiver could not oblige, e.g., where one in following the law would commit sin.

EPIGONATION, a eucharistic vestment of all Eastern Church bishops, archimandrites, and other dignitaries. It consists of an oblong of embroidered silk, stiffened with cardboard, which is worn suspended at one corner, attached to the cincture (girdle) or hung from one shoulder, falling to the right knee. In the West, it is worn only by the pope, called then the subcinctorium. It symbolizes the spiritual sword of justice.

EPIKLESIS also **EPICLESIS,** a prayer found in all the liturgies of the East. It is said immediately after the words of consecration by the celebrant, and is addressed to God the Father and God the Son, asking that the Holy Spirit be sent down upon the sacred species and that the recipients be thereby filled with grace.

EPIMANIKIA, a liturgical vestment of all Eastern rites. It consists of an over-sleeve which binds the fuller sleeve of the *sticharion* or alb at the wrist.

EPIPHANY, the feast celebrated on Jan. 6 commemorating especially in the West the visitation of the Magi and Christ's manifestation of His glory to them. The feast arose in the Eastern Church and remains there one of more broad significance, celebrating not only the above but also Christ's glory manifested to the Gentiles through the Magi, and His divinity manifested at His baptism in the Jordan, as well as at the miracle of the marriage at Cana. It is sometimes called Twelfth Night, being twelve days after Christmas.

EPISCOPACY. 1. The full group of the hierarchy known as bishops. **2.** The completion to fullness of the sacrament of holy orders conferred through consecration. By this completion the recipient is consecrated bishop, is given the power to ordain and consecrate others, to confirm, to consecrate objects for divine worship and to wield jurisdiction under delegation from the pope. This fullness of the sacrament of holy orders is an article of faith defined at the Council of Trent (sess. 23, c. 7). The existence of bishops was confirmed in apostolic times (1 Tim. 5:19–22), but at first the right of jurisdiction was not fully theirs. However, from the beginning of the 2nd century the title *episcopos* was reserved to the superior now known as bishop. (*Cf.* BISHOP.)

EPISTLE. 1. A letter. In a broad sense a letter of instruction, information or command from a superior addressed to subordinates. **2.** Biblical Epistles are the books of the N.T. named either by reference to the people to whom they are addressed or by name of the writer. The authenticity of these writings is guaranteed by the fact that all Councils of the Church which treated of the Canon of the Scripture included these. The form of these letters, and undoubtedly there were many others written but now lost, follows that of ordinary secular letters of the times. As a rule therefore they consist of three parts: an introduction giving the name of the writer, the name of the party to whom it is addressed and a greeting; the middle portion or main message; and a concluding paragraph of farewell. In those of St. Paul the greeting is characteristically Christian, being "grace and peace" instead of the pagan "health." Often all of these Epistles have been called "Catholic" in the sense that rather than being directed to a particular group they were addressed to the universal Church. This can be determined from their wide doctrinal content and internal evidence. This term also appears in this sense in a portion of the Muratorian Canon, as well as in the writings of Eusebius (d. 340). It is from the Epistles that the first scriptural lesson read in the Mass is taken.

EPISTOLAE ECCLESIASTICAE, literally, Church letters. Each letter written by Church dignitaries has taken on special classifications which are included under this title. They are: (1) Apostolic letters, written by authority of the pope. (2) Commendatory letters. (3) Letters of communion, or those authenticating one's affiliation with the Church. (4) Confessorial letters, those asking that one be reunited with the Church. (5) Decretals. (6) Dimissorials. (7) Encyclicals. (8) Letters of enthronement, or orthodoxy addressed from a bishop to other bishops. (9) Paschal letters, issued at Easter (formerly those that declared the date of Easter as a feast). (10) Pastoral letters, those of instruction sent by a bishop.

EPISTOLARY, a book containing authentic texts of the biblical Epistles. Written in Latin, sometimes with tonal notation, it is the book from which the subdeacon chants the first lesson in solemn Masses.

EPITRACHELION, a vestment corresponding to the stole of the Roman rite worn by priests of the Byzantine rite at liturgical functions. It differs only in that the strips of cloth are fastened together from the loop at the neck to the ends and it reaches almost to the feet.

ERASTIANISM, a system of subordination founded by Thomas Leiber (d. 1583) in Switzerland, whereby the Church is subservient, even in its teaching role, to the state. Contrary to the Church teaching as laid down by Leo XIII in his encyclical, *Immortale Dei.*

EREMITE, a hermit.

ESCHATOLOGY, the part of theology which treats of the final things: death, judgment, heaven, and hell. More specifically this is concerned with a study of the Resurrection of Christ and His teaching to the disciples concerning His second coming (the parousia). The time of Christ's coming is known only to the Father (Mt. 24:36–39); we do not know the hour of His coming (Mt. 24:42–51); but we are assured of a last or final judgment which will reward or condemn eternally the faithful (Mt. 25: 31–46). The summation of this study is that mankind must prepare for the second coming of Christ (Phil. 1:6) at the end of time when Christ will judge the living and the dead.

ESPOUSAL also **BETROTHAL,** an engagement of marriage, or a promise of marriage. In early times this was equivalent to a binding contract of marriage.

ESPOUSALS OF THE BLESSED VIRGIN, a feast celebrated in previous times and still observed in some countries on Jan. 23. Its observance was never extended to the universal Church.

ESSENCE. Essence is that which tells us what a thing is, answers the question: What is it? It strictly tells the nature of reality, and indicates its genus and species. Like being, essence defines the nature of the thing or that which makes it something. This must be extended to the things that are, but also to the innumerable possible things or realities which could be brought into existence.

ESTABLISHED CHURCH, the religion recognized, established, and/or fostered by a civil state as the official religion. It places other religions on a "tolerated" basis. The most notable example is the Church of England.

ESTHER, BOOK OF, a book of the O.T. by an unknown author and probably written a short time after the events narrated (5th century B.C.). It is an historical book telling of God's providential care of Israel in protecting the nation from peril while it was in exile during the reign of Assuerus, king of Persia. The book is named after Esther who was made queen in the seventh year of his reign by Assuerus after the king deposed Queen Vasthi. It also records the beginning of the Hebrew feast of Purim.

ETERNITY. We understand eternity only from the standpoint of time, and thus it is an infinite extent of time considering every event, at the same time, as past, present and future. In a more profound sense we may consider this as an instant *now* with neither beginning nor end. It is in this sense that we may say God's essential Being is an eternal Now. At the same time putting this in accord with our understanding we find St. John speaking of Christ as He "who is and who was and who is coming" (Apoc. 1:4). On the other hand, we speak of a thing which is not subject to change or something founded in time which will continue forever, e.g., the laws of nature, as eternal, i.e., without end. (*Cf.* IMMORTALITY OF THE SOUL.)

ETHIOPIAN CHURCH. *See* ABYSSINIAN CHURCH.

EUCHARIST, HOLY. The word Eucharist is derived from the Greek and means "good grace." The term is applied to the sacrament and sacrifice of the New Law in which Christ Himself is present, is offered and received under the species of bread and wine. The Church teaches and believes that in the Holy Eucharist the body, blood, soul and divinity of Christ, the God-Man, are truly and substantially present under the appearances of bread and wine. This presence of the entire Christ is by reason of the transubstantiation of the bread and wine into the body and blood of Christ which is accomplished in the unbloody sacrifice of the Mass. Jesus Himself instituted the Eucharist and requested its repetition (Lk. 22:19ff). That this was accomplished and continued we know from the many references in the Epistles (Heb., 1 Cor., etc.). (*Cf.* TRANSUBSTANTIATION.) The sacrament of the Eucharist is a true sacrifice, a representation of the sacrifice of Christ on the cross, for the ritual elements of the sacrifice are identical with the body and blood of Christ (Heb. 9:12, 14). As a sacrament the Eucharist is most excellent, first, in *dignity;* second, *in the grace it contains,* for it is Christ Himself, the source of all grace; third, *in its permanency,* being a perfect sacrament when we receive it and also when it is retained in our churches. The Holy Eucharist is known by many titles of truth and esteem: it is called the Bread of Life; the Most Blessed Sacrament; Holy Communion; the Sacrament of Life (Jn. 6:58); the Sacrament of Love; the Sacrament of Unity. (*Cf.* HOLY COMMUNION.)

EUCHARISTIC CONGRESSES. *See* CONGRESSES, EUCHARISTIC.

EUCHITES, an heretical group of the 4th century, also called Messalians. They rejected all religious practices except prayer and were the forerunners, so to speak, of the Quietists.

EUCHOLOGION, a liturgical book of the Byzantine rite containing the prayers of the eucharistic liturgies, the prayers of the Divine Office, and the ceremonies of blessings. A combination of the missal, ritual and breviary of the Roman rite. Also called the Euchology.

EULOGIA, unconsecrated bread given to those who could not communicate but wished to join in early Church rites. Now obsolete.

EUNOMIANISM, a branch heresy, begun in the last half of the 4th century by Eunomius of Cappadocia, as an offshoot of Arianism. It denied the divinity of the nature and will of Christ.

EUSEBIANS, followers of the Arian heresy among the West Goths who were converted from paganism to Arianism by Eusebius of Nicomedia in the latter part of the 4th century.

EUTYCHIANISM or **MONOPHYSITISM,** an heresy developed by Eutyches, an influential monk at the court of Constantinople, in opposition to Nestorianism. It is most confused in its early writings, but it maintained that there was only one nature in Christ following the Incarnation. This was condemned by the Council of Chalcedon (451).

EVANGELIARIUM, book containing the Gospels to be sung at solemn Mass by the deacon. Also a lectionary.

EVANGELICAL COUNSELS. These are: voluntary poverty, chastity, and obedience. St. Thomas teaches that there are two essential procedures to the attainment of perfection: first, the keeping of the commandments and, second, the observance of certain counsels. The commandments are absolute and rest upon all. The counsels are not absolutely necessary for salvation, but essential for perfection. Such counsels may be undertaken by anyone, and every counsel, being rooted in charity, helps remove the obstacles to the practice of charity and makes possible the perfection of love of God and neighbor. The counsels are specifically related to one's facility and exercise of carrying out the requirements of a particular state of life. Thus the evangelical counsels are willfully assumed as vows by priests and religious, either as vows or promises, in order to enable themselves more readily to ·attain sanctification. By *poverty*, religious free themselves of worldly wealth and attachments so as to concentrate more fully upon God; by *chastity*, they renounce the pleasures of the flesh, even those legitimate to the marriage state, that they may be even naturally centered on God; by *obedience*, the pride of will is overcome and subjection to the will of God is attained.

EVANGELISTS, THE. Originally this term was applied to the one who preached. Since the 3rd century it has been referred to the four writers of the Gospel books of the Bible: SS. Matthew, Mark, Luke and John. Traditionally these four have been distinguished in symbols derived from the vision of Ezechiel and the creatures spoken of in the Apocalypse: thus St. Matthew by the human head, St. Mark by the lion, St. Luke by the ox, and St. John by the eagle. (*Cf.* GOSPELS.)

EVE OF A FEAST. *See* VIGIL.

EVIL. There is not a "principle" of evil by which it can be defined. Evil can best be observed and realized in its effect. Evil is not to be solely identified as sin which is evil in the moral order only. According to St. Thomas who based his argument on St. Augustine who in turn derived much from Plotinus, evil is not a reality. Rather, evil is the lack of perfection that should be present in a person, action or thing as a part of its reality, e.g., it is evil for one to be blind since sight is an integral part of the natural sense of seeing. Thus this lack may be present in either a) the physical order as in the above example or b) the moral order, or may be extended to both at the same time.

EVOLUTION. In the Catholic understanding, the theory of evolution, or transformism from lower forms of life through a sequence to man, remains a theory. However, should proof be eventually produced, the teaching of Genesis and its inspired narrative would remain, for it tells that the world was created for man and that man himself came from God no matter what course was followed by divine wisdom in forming man's frame. More essentially, man has a spiritual rational soul and as a spiritual substance could not have his origin in a material source. It is in the spiritual part of man that he differs from brute beasts. Apart from the field of natural science we are cautioned by revelation. Pius XII, in *Humani generis* (1950), speaks on the current aspect of the theory, namely, polygenism, and warns that the faithful may not believe that after Adam there were true men who were not generated from Adam "since it is not at all clear how such an opinion can be reconciled with what the sources of revelation and the acts of the Church's teaching authority put forward concerning original sin."

EXALTATION OF THE CROSS, a feast celebrated in the Roman rite on Sept. 14. It originated in commemora-

THE EVANGELISTS—Symbols of the four Evangelists.

tion of the recovery of a portion of the true cross of Christ from the Persians by Emperor Heraclius in 629.

EXAMEN, an examination of conscience made daily or at special intervals as a devotional practice (not by necessity as before confession). It enables one to eliminate faults and imperfections by recognizing them as well as their causes, and helps to develop practicing the opposing virtues. It is *particular* when directed against a single fault; *general* when it is concerned with a complex or variety of similar faults or all faults.

EXAMINATION OF BISHOPS, questions put to a bishop-elect before his consecration concerning obedience to the authority of the Church, the episcopal life, the faith, and the rejection of errors.

EXAMINATION OF CONSCIENCE, act of recalling, in so far as possible, the number and seriousness of sins made by one in preparation for reception of the sacrament of penance. This is in reality an examination of oneself as a spiritual exercise wherein one remembers what sins are to be mentioned in his confession. It also serves the following spiritual purposes: it elicits the necessary sorrow for sins and offenses against God, and affords one the occasion of thanking God by recognizing the ingratitude expressed by one's sins; it enables one to make a resolve not to sin again, a necessary requirement in the reception of the sacrament. (*Cf.* EXAMEN; CONFESSION; PENANCE, SACRAMENT OF.)

EXAMINERS, SYNODAL. When a vacancy arises between synods (c. 385), at least four members of the clergy, proposed and approved by the clergy in the diocesan synod of a

diocese or appointed by the bishop, are to carry out the following functions: examine the fitness of the clergy for the care of souls and advise the bishop on the subject.

EXARCH, historically, the title of a ruler of a province of the Roman empire. In Church use, it is a title of limited jurisdiction, usually appointed temporarily, to carry out some mission. In the Western Church, the title has been supplanted with that of "vicar apostolic" or "primate." In the Eastern Church, the title is conferred on the head of a Church whose position is neither that of a patriarch nor a metropolitan. Bishops of the Ukrainian rite in North America are called exarchs.

EXCARDINATION. It is required that a cleric belong to a diocese, vicariate, etc., or be a member of a religious community. Excardination is the formal transfer of a cleric from one diocese to another or from the jurisdiction of one bishop to that of another. A cleric can be excardinated by formal letters of perpetual and unconditional excardination, signed by the cleric's bishop and followed, necessarily, by letters of incardination (cs. 111–118). (*Cf.* INCARDINATION.)

EX CATHEDRA, literally, "from the chair." (*Cf.* INFALLIBILITY.)

EXCELLENCE, the polite and official term of address used in the Roman Church for all archbishops, bishops, and prelates nullius. Thus: "Your Excellency"; "His Excellency."

EXCLUSION, a claimed right, no longer recognized by the Church, whereby nations, as France, Austria, Spain, and Germany, vetoed the election of a cardinal elected as pope.

EXCOMMUNICATION. This is the most serious censure of the Church. By excommunication a person is excluded from the communion of the faithful, loses the right of attending divine services, except at preaching; is forbidden the reception of the sacraments (c. 2260); loses the suffrages of the Church and public prayers and all participation in indulgences; may not act as sponsor, or perform other ecclesiastical acts; loses the right of plaintiff in Church trials except according to canon 1654; may not fill ecclesiastical offices, e.g., trustee, organist, etc.; may not receive Christian burial. In the case of clerics, in addition to the above, they may not administer the sacraments except under specified circumstances (c. 2261), or be appointed to ecclesiastical offices. Excommunication may be imposed: *ipso facto*, that is, as a very consequence of the commission of an act calling for the imposition of the censure, if that consequence is known; or by a condemnatory or declaratory sentence, that is, by imposition of the censure by authority. There are two degrees of excommunication: 1. excommunicates *vitandi* are those so named by sentence and with whom members of the faithful are forbidden to associate, etc. 2. excommunicates *tolerati* are those with whom the faithful may associate. Absolution may be received by an excommunicate from any priest, even from a priest who himself is under censure, if in danger of death. Absolution otherwise depends upon to whom the censure is reserved, e.g., excommunication may be reserved to the Holy See in a very special manner; reserved to the Holy See in a special manner; simply reserved to Rome; reserved to the ordinary; or non-reserved (cs. 2347; 2352). (*Cf.* CENSURE.) Excommunication is imposed according to the reservation as follows: (a) Acts reserved to the Holy See in a very special manner are: throwing away, taking or retaining for evil purposes the consecrated species; striking the Roman Pontiff; absolving or pretending to absolve one's accomplice in sin; violating the seal of sacramental confession. (b) Reserved in a special manner to Rome: heretics, apostates and schismatics; publication of books of formal heretics, apostates or schismatics wherein these sins are defended; reading or retaining such books or other books condemned in apostolic letters; forcing cardinals or one's ordinary to appear as defendants in civil courts without permission of the Holy See; pretending to say Mass or hear confessions when not a priest; falsely accusing a confessor of solicitation, either personally or through others in a solemn manner. (c) Simply reserved to Rome: fighting, accepting or aiding a duel; joining the Masons or societies that plot against the Church or state; practicing simony in regard to ecclesiastical offices, dignities or benefices; presuming to absolve from excommunication cases reserved very specially or specially to the Holy See, except in urgent necessity; bringing suit in civil courts against bishops other than their own ordinaries; clerics who attempt marriage and those who contract marriage with them even by civil action; anyone who steals, destroys, conceals or vitiates a document of a diocesan curia or causes another to do so. (d) Reserved to the ordinary: all who procure an abortion, including the mother and all co-operators; marrying before an heretical minister acting as a religious agent; all who strike clerics, sisters or others who enjoy the privilege of the Canon; commission of certain crimes in the education of children, e.g., agreeing to bring up the children outside the Church (c. 2319); selling, making or distributing false relics. (e) Non-reserved: unlawful alienation of property without apostolic indult; using force to induce a person to become a cleric or religious; writing or publishing books of Scripture or commentaries on it without due permission.

EXEAT, the formal letter of excardination.

EXECRATION. *See* DESECRATION.

EXEGESIS, the study whereby the investigation and exposition of Sacred Scripture is presented. In general it seeks through tradition, archaeology, history and criticism to expound the true meaning of the Scriptures. In particular it concerns itself with the various senses of Scripture, the literal, spiritual senses and the accommodation of Scripture. The Church sets forth no restriction upon the extent of investigation regarding the Scriptures, teaching only the absolute truth of inspired Scriptures, and disallowing any restriction of inspiration to certain parts of the Bible, such as doctrinal parts, and forbids the concession that the sacred writer may have erred. (*Cf.* INSPIRATION; INTERPRETATION, BIBLICAL.)

EXEGETE, a biblical scholar, versed in exegesis.

EXEMPTION, term used in canon law to denote the position of a subject or thing in relation to the jurisdiction or law of a superior. An exempt religious, for example, is one not under the jurisdiction of the bishop of the diocese wherein he resides, except in certain specified laws (c. 615). An exempt diocese is one not subject to a metropolitan but is directly under the authority of the Holy See.

EXEQUATOR, the right claimed by rulers to examine and judge papal bulls and constitutions before the regulations contained within them may go into effect in the territories over which they govern.

EXEQUIAL MASS, the requiem Mass said at a funeral where the body of the deceased is present and the absolution is given.

EXERCISES, SPIRITUAL, the name given by St. Ignatius of Loyola (d. 1556) to the meditations, counsels and exhortations which form a spiritual guide. Broadly, any course of spiritual precepts or counsels which are presented to be practiced by religious or laymen.

EXISTENCE, the first or prime act of essence in being. It is the perfection of being whereby what was possible becomes actual through the operation of an efficient cause outside of the being. In God, since He has no efficient cause, existence and essence or pure actuality are identical.

EXISTENTIALISM. Existential philosophy as propounded by the Danish scholar, Soren Kierkegaard (d. 1855), and developed by others, notably Heidegger, Jaspers, and Marcel, declares that the source and elements of knowledge are not in relation to truth as demonstrated but are parts conditioned by the *concrete existence* of the individual, or by his consciousness of them. As a philosophy it is a cross between realism and idealism, confusing the internal and external realities, having an agnostic attitude toward God, a denial, for the most part, of the supernatural, and accepting the problematical as a quasi-absolute. Thus it tends to pessimism since no definite solution to life's problems seems possible. In the area of psychology, existential philosophy treats of experiences of the mind as separate *existences*, which become unified in the individual, hence it must deny imageless thought.

EXODUS, BOOK OF. This second book of the O.T. is one of religious history. Its author is undoubtedly Moses but the time of its writing is uncertain. Two dates are usually given, both uncertain according to interpretation, either in the 15th century B.C. or in the 12–11th centuries B.C. The narrative tells the oppression of the Israelites under their Egyptian masters, the call of Moses, and the deliverance of the Israelites, their march through the desert to Sinai, God's miraculous care of them, the Sinaitic Covenant and the giving of the Decalogue. The teaching of the book is that God chose the Hebrew people in the execution of His plan of redemption. There are also many teachings and a variety of parallels to the N.T., e.g., the release from bondage is a type of the redemption; the manna of the desert is a type of the Eucharist.

EX OPERE OPERANTIS, a term from the Latin, meaning "from the work of the one working" or more loosely "from the action performed." (*Cf.* EX OPERE OPERATO.)

EX OPERE OPERATO, a technical phrase first used in 1205, then defined by the fathers at the Council of Trent and thereafter by theologians, to declare that the grace of the sacraments is caused by the sacramental rite *validly performed.* Translated, it means, "from the work of the work itself," or more loosely, "from the act

itself." This is to say that grace is the result of the objective act. It is thus opposed to the subjective *ex opere operantis.*

EXORCISM, the rite administered properly now by a priest whereby devils are expelled from possessed persons or *energumeni.* This rite may be exercised only with permission of the bishop and in accord with formulas of the Roman Ritual. The authority over evil spirits was given by Christ to the apostles and Christ manifested His own power over devils by driving them from a possessed person (Mk. 6:7). Lesser exorcisms are frequent in Church liturgy, as in the baptismal ceremonies and the blessing of holy water, etc. However, these lesser exorcisms are directed at placing the objects beyond the use of evil spirits and preserving their use for holy purposes.

EXORCIST, one who performs an exorcism. As the third of the minor orders, also called *exorcistate*, it confers, on the one receiving, the power to impose hands on the possessed and to recite prayers to expel devils. This office as a minor order dates back to the 3rd century, but in present-day discipline is only exercised by a priest. (*Cf.* EXORCISM.)

EXPOSITION OF THE BLESSED SACRAMENT, the ceremony, either private or solemn, whereby the Blessed Sacrament is removed from the altar tabernacle by a priest for the adoration of the faithful. Private Exposition, i.e., without the use of the ostensorium, may be merely an opening of the tabernacle so that the faithful can see the Blessed Sacrament in the ciborium or lunette and this can take place any time for a sufficient reason and without the permission of the bishop. Solemn Exposition with the monstrance used (c. 1274) is permitted on the feast of Corpus Christi and within its octave by all churches where the Blessed Sacrament is reserved. However, other public and solemn Exposition requires a just cause and permission of the ordinary. Solemn Exposition is governed by laws of the liturgy to preserve the dignity of the occasion and show reverence, e.g., the *O Salutaris* is sung, the host is incensed, and the *Tantum Ergo* is sung. Today such solemn Exposition is usually followed with Benediction.

EXTERNAL GRACE, name applied to those facts or events which aid individuals because of moral influence. It is a type of sufficient grace, and may include the Scriptures, preaching of the gospel, miracles, the examples of Christ and the saints, etc. (*Cf.* GRACE.)

EXTREME UNCTION, THE SACRAMENT OF. This sacrament is conferred on baptized Catholics who are seriously ill, in danger of death. As a sacrament of the New Law, we learn all its elements in the text: "Is any one among you sick? Let him bring in the presbyters of the church, and let them pray over him, anointing him with oil in the name of the Lord. And the prayer of faith will save the sick man, and the Lord will raise him up, and if he be in sins, they shall be forgiven him" (James 5:14–15). The sacrament may be conferred by a priest or bishop. The purposes of receiving this sacrament are found in its effects: its reception completes the effects of the sacrament of penance; removes the remnants of sin, brings grace to the soul; disposes the recipient to undergo his sufferings with the conscious joining of these with the sufferings of Christ; and it sometimes brings health to the body. The sacrament is conferred in a brief ceremony consisting of the recitation of the *Asperges*, three prayers for health, safety and peace, and beseeching the care of the angels, followed by the *Confiteor* and a brief exorcism. The priest then touches his thumb to the Holy Oil (oil of the sick) and anoints the recipient on eyes, ears, nostrils, the closed lips, the hands and feet, saying at each anointing a prayer asking forgiveness to the person for any sins which may have been committed through these senses. There follows three prayers for the health of the soul and body of the sick person. The form of the sacrament is the prayer and its matter the Holy Oil.

EZECHIEL, BOOK OF, the historical-prophetical book of the O.T. written by Ezechiel, the son of Buzi and priest of the line of Sadoc. He became one of prophetical vocation in 593 B.C. We only learn of him from his own writings and do not have the dates of his birth and death. His book is concerned with the period between the death of Josias (609), and the destruction of Jerusalem (587 B.C.).

F

FABRIC also **FABRICA**, term applied to the church building and its fittings, but it also means the funds for repair, reconstruction, or maintenance as distinct from the funds of the benefice or those for the living of the priest and curates. However, the term is sometimes applied to one who has charge of maintenance, usually a layman.

FACULTIES, CANONICAL, explicit powers, granted as authorization to enable a person to act validly or at least licitly. Such powers are granted by the Holy See or by a bishop or prelate and must be authenticated. Faculties are understood to include all the necessary power or authority for their use, and may be granted for varying lengths of time or may be designated to cover a single or numerous cases. Most commonly we hear "faculties" referred to the permission given to priests to administer the sacrament of penance.

FAITH. 1. The assent given to a truth. **2.** An entire body of dogmas or truths to which one gives assent, e.g., one is of the Catholic faith. **3.** The theological virtue by which one, through grace, adheres in intellect to a truth revealed by God because of the authority of God rather than the evidence given. **4.** The faith which is called "justifying", i.e., the belief necessary for personal justification (Mk. 16:15–16). In its Catholic interpretation, faith is in the mind as a *habit* and as an *act*, and so is in the mind and will. It is described as divine or supernatural. It is habitual when it is an infused habit, assisted by grace, wherein the mind assents to a truth revealed by God, making the assent because God is Himself the essential truth, who cannot be deceived in His divine knowledge and cannot deceive when He reveals a truth. When such habitual faith is informed by charity or the love of God it becomes a "living" faith. Faith is actual when, again aided by grace, the mind assents and together with the will prompts one to both the internal and external expression of faith, e.g., when we recite the Creed. Divine faith and Catholic faith demand that we believe all those points of doctrine which are contained in the Scriptures, in the unwritten word of God and all those proposed to our belief as revealed by God or by the solemn definition of the Church acting as the ordinary and universal teaching authority of Christ on earth. According to the Council of Trent, faith is necessary for sanctification and salvation.

FAITHFUL, THE, in early days of the Church those who were baptized and instructed and who were admitted to communion. Today all those who are members of the Church, addressed as such by the pope, and who have not been excluded by declaration or by their own acts.

FALDA, garment of white silk with a train. It is worn by the pope over his cassock on solemn occasions.

FALDSTOOL

FALDSTOOL, movable folding chair of wood or metal, with arms at the side but no back. It is used at pontifical functions by a bishop outside of his cathedral or when he is not at his throne. The seat of the chair is made of cloth or leather and has a cushion corresponding in color to that used in the liturgy of the day.

FALSE DECRETALS. *See* DECRETALS, FALSE.

FAMILIAR, name given to a lay attendant who lives in and works for

a monastery; also the title of the priests in the household of a bishop.

FAN. *See* FLABELLUM.

FANON, a vestment worn over the alb at pontifical ceremonies by the pope only. It is circular or cape-like in shape, made of two pieces of white silk, with an opening at the center where it slips over the head. It is ornamented with two stripes of gold and red and an embroidered cross on the center front.

FASCISM, a form of state absolutism. Fascism professes a philosophy of economic and social practicality, but in reality it is a political theory which seeks to establish the dictatorship of a single political party to the exclusion of all others and with distinct limitations of personal freedom. In this sense it is totalitarian. In application, fascism is national or racial and seeks to gain its ends by party means while keeping the party in power. It may differ from country to country. In June, 1931, Pope Pius XI denounced the fascist ideology in his encyclical, *Non abbianno bisogno*, calling it a "pagan worship of the state" and declaring it destructive of the natural rights of the family.

FAST, an ascetic practice, limited in duration, undertaken as a means of mortification or penance for one's spiritual welfare; the act of fasting. The Eucharistic fast is the complete foregoing of food and drink (water excepted) for a prescribed period of time before receiving Holy Communion.

FASTING, a limitation of the quantity of food eaten, as distinguished from abstaining from foods (*cf.* ABSTINENCE). The Church, both in its traditional practices and its present legislation on fasting, asks its members to fast, not because she considers certain foods as evil, but because she wishes her members to mortify their appetites, to progress spiritually, and to overcome self-indulgence. The essence of fasting consists of taking only one full meal each day. By custom, and since the Church does not require that the faithful injure their health or be wanting in the necessary strength for daily work, it is permitted to eat two other meatless meals each day. No specific amount is prescribed for these two meals except that together they should not equal one full meal in amount. In practice, the breakfast is the lighter with a consideration that the normal amount would be about two ounces. Meat may be taken at the principal (full) meal on a day of fast, except on Fridays, Ash Wednesday, and the vigils of the Feast of the Assumption and Christmas. No eating between meals is permitted, but liquids including milk and fruit juices, are allowed. Under the term meat as forbidden are included: the flesh of mammals (whale meat excepted by interpretation) and birds, broth or bouillon made from these, the marrow, blood, brains, meat extracts, mince pie, beef tea, mutton soup. The law of fasting binds everyone over 21 years of age and under 59 years completed. The law may be revoked because of personal needs by permission of one's confessor. Exceptions are: fasting is not required when a vigil falls on a Sunday or holyday, or a holyday falls on a Friday; members of the Armed Forces while on active duty are dispensed from the Church's law of fasting except on Ash Wednesday, Good Friday, Holy Saturday and the vigil of Christmas. This dispensation applies wherever the individual may be and is extended to his wife, children, parents and servants if he is habitually living with them. In the United States, the days of fast are: the weekdays of Lent; the Ember days; the vigils of Pentecost, Assumption, and Christmas. (*Cf.* EMBER DAYS.)

FATHER, the title extended to all priests of the English-speaking world. Holy Father is a title of the pope alone. God the Father is the First Person of the Blessed Trinity.

FATHERS OF THE CHURCH also **APOSTOLIC FATHERS.** As a title of excellence this refers to the writers and bishops of the early Christian centuries who either had direct contact with the apostles or were sufficiently close to them and the influence of the apostles' teaching to have expressed their teaching most clearly. Sometimes they are referred to as *Latin* or *Greek* Fathers because of their locations and area of operation, but Christendom, while divided into two great parts, was one in thought. At first the title was conferred only on the heads of churches, that is, the bishops who were both responsible for discipline and doctrine. Later, it was conferred on those who were defenders of the faith and notable for the purity of their doctrinal teachings. Thus the title of father of the Church connotes orthodoxy and is extended to include many early writers of the Church. An author in order to be considered a father of the Church must have lived during the first ages of the Church, his doctrine must be true, he must be known for holiness of life and have merited the approval of the Church. (*Cf.* DOCTOR, 2; PATROLOGY.)

FATIMA, APPARITIONS OF, the most well-known appearances of the Blessed Mother during the 20th century. Following three preliminary visitations by a being who identified himself as the Angel of Portugal, the Blessed Mother appeared first on May 13, 1917, to three children, Lucia dos Santos, aged ten, and her two cousins Jacinta and Francisco Marto, seven and nine years old. The apparitions took place, with the exception of that of August, at the Cova da Iria, a grazing ground near the village of Aljustrel, within the parish of Fatima, north of Lisbon, Portugal. In this series there were six monthly apparitions, May through October 13th. (A seventh took place June 18, 1921 to Lucia.) On the October occasion an attested miracle of confirmation took place, called the miracle of the sun, wherein the sun appeared to plummet to the earth, spin, and give a multi-colored light. The message of Fatima as declared by the Blessed Mother of God is constituted of the following: The performance of penance; the frequent recitation of the Rosary; the practice of prayer and mortification for the conversion of sinners; devotion of the world and all peoples to the Immaculate Heart of the Blessed Mother; and the offering of Holy Communion of reparation on the first Saturday of each month. The promised result of following these requests of devotion would be: the saving of many souls, the avoidance of a more terrible world war, the conversion of Russia and world peace. In Oct. 1942, Pius XII consecrated the world, with special reference to Russia, to the Immaculate Heart of Mary. The site has become a world-famous place of pilgrimage with the erection of a church, a chapel of the apparitions, hospitals, hospices, and religious institutions.

**THE APPARITION OF
OUR LADY OF FATIMA**

FEAR OF GOD. This embraces two forms: (a) *servile*, which is the mental anxiety and emotion arising from the knowledge of the punishment that God may inflict; (b) *filial*, which is the dread of offending God who is all-good, and the fear of being separated from God by offenses which incur the loss of sanctifying grace. Filial, also called reverential fear, is a particular means of sanctification, a gift of the Holy Spirit, since it enables one to acknowledge God's greatness, have sorrow at any offense against God, and avoid occasions of possible offense, while at the same time teaching one to avoid familiarity with God and presumption. (*Cf.* GIFTS OF THE HOLY SPIRIT.)

FEASTS OF THE CHURCH, the sequence of festivals in the calendar of the liturgical year to commemorate a teaching or event of religious importance, or saints' days. Feasts are divided into: (a) holydays of obligation on which the faithful are required to attend Mass; (b) feasts of rank or classification as doubles and simple feasts; (c) feasts classified as doubles are subdivided into doubles of the first class, doubles of the second class, greater doubles, and ordinary doubles. According to this division, it is determined which of two feasts is celebrated when two feasts fall on the same day; (d) feasts are also either movable or immovable, those being movable whose date in the calendar is determined by the date on which Easter is celebrated, while immovable feasts have a fixed date, e.g., Christmas; (e) those feasts are called "cardinal" which have a series of Sundays following them and are so listed in the calendar, e.g., those following Epiphany or the Feast of Pentecost.

FEBRONIANISM, a theory which first appeared in a book published in 1763 by Bishop John von Hontheim who wrote under the pen name "Febronius." It primarily expressed opposition to the jurisdiction of Rome in ruling the affairs of the Church, in favor of the state or secular ruler, and it favored ecumenical councils as the courts of last appeal. These teachings were condemned by Popes Clement XIII and Pius VI. The movement was paralleled by Josephism which was named after Emperor Joseph II and was an attempt to make the Church in Austria independent of the pope. Both were exaggerated forms of Gallicanism and were strains upon Church and state relations.

FERENDAE SENTENTIAE, term used to describe the punishment of censure which is added to a law or precept by the sentence of a judge or a proper ecclesiastical superior. The penalty is thus not automatic (*cf.* LATAE SENTENTIAE) but is yet to be inflicted following the crime.

FERIA, a weekday of the Church calendar on which no feast or vigil is observed. The Mass said on a ferial day is normally that of the previous Sunday. However, there are certain "greater ferias" which have their own assigned Masses as Ash Wednesday and the first three days of Holy Week. No other feast may be celebrated on these days. The lesser ferias are the weekdays in Advent and Lent, Ember days, and the Monday of Rogation week. When these lesser ferias occur on feasts of higher than simple rank they are merely commemorated.

FERRAIOLA, short cape, attached to a cassock and reaching halfway down the upper arm.

FERRAIOLONE, literally, "big cape," a cape of black cloth worn over the cassock, reaching to midcalf or of floor length. It must be worn by diocesan priests attending papal audiences.

FERRARA. *See* FLORENCE, COUNCIL OF.

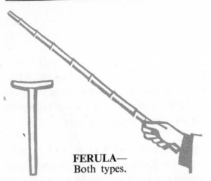
FERULA—
Both types.

FERULA. 1. A small rod with which a penitent, usually in a religious community, is lightly struck to signify acceptance of a penance. **2.** In former times, before sitting was permitted at Church functions, a T-shaped staff used to support one as a crutch during lengthy ceremonies. It is still used in choir by Maronite, dissident Ethiopian, and Coptic monks.

FEUDALISM, a system of class distinctions of the Middle Ages which seriously affected the Church. As a system it essentially was the organization of the land-owning aristocracy into a sort of hierarchy with lesser lords serving overlords in a mutual agreement. Beneath these were the masses of people, soldiers, farmers, craftsmen, etc. The aristocrats and freemen fought battles and offered protection to the serfs and villeins. The clergy also fell into classes, higher and lower, with higher Church offices going to members of noble families. From the standpoint of the Church, one of the evils of the feudal system was the lord's claimed right of appointment to Church offices, thus placing ecclesiastics under lay control, and this gave rise to the practice of "lay investiture" with its attendant evils.

FILIOQUE. This Latin word, translated "and from the Son," is used in the Nicene Creed to declare the two-fold procession of God the Holy Ghost from the Father "and from the Son." It was a word of controversy, not because of the question of its doctrine, but because since its first use in the 6th century and acceptance by the Western Church it became a source of contention with the Greeks who objected to its insertion in the Creed. It was settled, with the Greeks accepting the dual procession, at the Council of Florence (1438–1445).

FINAL PERSEVERANCE, the gift from God whereby one may remain in the state of sanctifying grace until death. The grace to persevere can come from God alone, and implies that sufficient grace will be given to aid one not to fall in seeking salvation.

FINDING OF THE CROSS, the feast celebrated on May 3 in commemoration of the finding of the true cross of Christ by St. Helena in the year 326. (*Cf.* CROSS, RELICS OF THE TRUE.)

FIRE, BLESSING OF, ceremony of the liturgy of Holy Saturday wherein fire is blessed. Stemming from an early Celtic practice, it has been adapted to the preliminary ritual in celebration of the Resurrection of Christ.

FIRE OF HELL. *See* HELL.

FIRST COMMUNION, the reception of the consecrated host for the first time. This event is traditional after a child has been suitably instructed and has reached the age of reason. The recipients sometimes, by custom, carry a candle, and the event is often solemnized in various ways.

FIRST FRIDAY, the devotion of receiving Holy Communion on consecutive first Fridays of nine months in honor of the Sacred Heart. This practice arose following one of the promises made to St. Margaret Mary Alacoque (1647–1690) by Christ, by which one gains the grace of repentance, an assurance of receiving the last sacraments, and the consolation of the love of Christ's Sacred Heart at the time of death.

FIRST-FRUITS. According to the law of Moses, the first produce of man, animals and "whatsoever was sown in the field," was to be given to the Lord (Ex. 23:16). This O.T. law has been ascribed to the physical support to be given to the Church and her priests in present times. However, it no longer refers to the substance given but rather to the monetary contribution made by the faithful.

FISCAL PROCURATOR, an official appointed to a diocese whose duty it is to start proceedings against criminal offenders and bring them to trial in Church courts.

FISH—Symbol from a fresco in the catacombs.

FISH, in Christian art, a symbol of Christ, our Savior. The use of this symbol is derived from the Greek word for fish (phonetically *ichthus*), its letters being the initials of the phrase, "Jesus Christ, Son of God, Savior."—Fishes are used (a) as a symbol of the faithful, referring to the miraculous catch of fish narrated in Jn. 9; (b) as a symbol of the apostles who by their missionary work were designated as "fishers of men" (Lk. 5:11).

FISHERMAN, THE RING OF THE. The official ring of the reigning pontiff, upon which is incised a semblance of St. Peter sitting in a boat, fishing, with the pope's name around it. The ring is emblematic of the pontiff's succession to the Chair of St. Peter.

FISTULA, term applied to the small gold pipette by means of which the pope receives the consecrated wine during a solemn papal Mass.

FLABELLUM

FLABELLUM, a large fan, usually with a leather haft supporting a spread of feathers, and mounted on a long staff. It is chiefly used in pontifical liturgical functions, serving only an ornamental purpose. Originally it was used to keep insects from the sacred species.

FLAGELLANTS. Self-flagellation was a common penitential practice among religious orders, but in the middle of the 13th century an Umbrian hermit organized a brotherhood which became known as the Flagellants. This group of fanatics made a custom of marching through the streets scourging themselves and exhorting the people to repentance for their sins. The group became heretical and had political leanings. They were prohibited by papal order in 1261, but after the Black Death plague (1346–1350) they were again active. The movement spread widely, and north of the Alps the Flagellants developed an organized religious ceremony and their own set of heretical doctrines. They were condemned by Pope Clement VI in 1349. Today any group who fanatically or excessively inflict, on themselves or others, scourging by rod or whip are referred to as "flagellants." However, the practices have been done away with, except for occasional instances among primitive peoples.

FLECTAMUS GENUA, a prefatory bidding, meaning "Let us bend the knee," given in chant to the people by the deacon during solemn Mass on Ember days and some days of Holy Week. To each bidding the subdeacon replies "levate" (arise!).

FLOOD. *See* DELUGE.

FLORENCE, COUNCIL OF. This Council is commonly known as the Council of Ferrara-Florence. As a continuation of the Council of Basle (1431), it first reconvened at Ferrara in 1438, but, because of the ravages of the plague, Pope Eugene IV transferred it to Florence. The Council discussed the reunion of the Latins and the Greeks and the insertion of the word *Filioque* in the Creed. A degree of union was agreed upon in 1439 (but rejected later in 1472 by Gennadius, the patriarch of Constantinople, who had been appointed by the sultan of the Turks). The Council was finally adjourned in 1445 at Rome. (*Cf.* ECUMENICAL COUNCILS.)

FLORIDA PASCUA, the Spanish name for Palm Sunday.

FONT. *See* BAPTISMAL FONT; BAPTISTRY.

FOOTPACE. *See* PREDELLA.

FOREIGN MISSIONS. *See* MISSION, 5.

FORM. 1. In scholastic philosophy, form is (a) *substantial*, that is the principle of reality which determines a being into what it is. Together with prime matter, form is the first act or potentiality determining a being in existence through the operation of an efficient cause. In a being, form determines the nature or cause. In a being it determines the nature or essence in existence. Form, however, may be designated as apart from matter, e.g., pure spirits; or by its nature, form may be made to inform matter, e.g., the human soul; or form may be constituted in the potentiality of matter (passive) e.g., animals; (b) *accidental* form is what is added to that which is substantially complete, e.g., roundness or firmness; in this sense, form has an aesthetic significance. **2.** Sacramental form, or the form of a sacrament, is that designated in theology as the words and signs which accompany the matter being used. As such these words are an established and authentic sign determining the sacrament and cannot be substantially changed without invalidating the sacrament. The matter of the sacrament, the physical element, is determined or signified only by what the words clearly express.

FORTITUDE, a cardinal virtue, and a gift of the Holy Ghost. Considered as a virtue, fortitude is the strength of soul, or the firm and assured practice of all other virtues practiced in the pursuit of good and the love of God. Thus it is expressed as a strength which overcomes fear of not doing the right and is manifest in the character of an individual who acts rightly and does not succumb to temptation. It thus aids in practice to place the effort demanded by a good act, helps to eliminate the fear of criticism, and provides the will to continue to perform good acts. As a gift of the Holy Spirit it is the action of the Holy Ghost within us, granting the impulse to act rightly, the will to do so, and the joy in so acting, and so it perfects the virtue of fortitude.

FORTY HOURS' DEVOTION, the solemn Exposition of the Blessed Sacrament held for the duration of forty hours. This devotion, which began in the 16th century, is held each year (c. 1275) in parochial churches, and in other churches that have the right to reserve the Blessed Sacrament, on days determined by and consented to by the local ordinary. Usually it is by continual progression, so that there is Exposition of the Blessed Sacrament each day throughout the year at some church of the diocese. Appropriate prayers and ceremonies accompany this devotion. By special grant of the Holy See, the United States is permitted a modified form of this traditional devotion, known as the "Thirteen Hours' Devotion."

FORUM. This term (plural form: *fora*) has a wide variety of meanings which have been adapted to the canonical language of the Church. Originally the word *forum* meant a public market place or a court of justice. It came to mean also the bench or tribunal and then the judge who exercised authority within the court. By wider application it came to apply to the entire territory wherein a judge had authority, and then it finally applied to judicial power as

such. In Church use it may refer to one or the other of these meanings but the word is always qualified, e.g., *competent forum* is the court or the judge who has authority to try and determine a case. Forum of the Church means the sphere in which jurisdiction is exercised, be that in courts or in the sacramental tribunal of the confessional. As such it is referred to as: *internal forum*, or the exercise of judicial acts in regard to matters of sacramental confession or those of a secret nature. *External forum* refers to the social and juridical effects of jurisdiction, e.g., a dispensation granted and recorded. A juridical act, such as the lifting of a censure, given in the external forum is valid in the internal forum, but the reverse is not, that is, a power of jurisdiction exercised in the internal forum has no acceptance in the external forum. A priest may receive power for both fora. The *Privilege of the Forum* refers to the right of clerics and religious, including sisters, to be tried before ecclesiastical courts in causes civil or criminal.

FOSSOR, one who served officially as a gravedigger in the catacombs, sometimes considered of minor clerical rank.

FRANCISCANS, members of the Order of Friars Minor that was founded by St. Francis of Assisi (d. 1226) in 1209. The rule written by St. Francis, like that of St. Dominic, was later to apply to three orders: one for men, one for women, and one for men and women living in the world. The rule was revised in 1221 and again in 1223 but basically was adapted to the changing social and religious structure of society at that time. The rule is now observed by three separate bodies of religious men: the Friars Minor, Friars Minor Conventuals, and Friars Minor Capuchins. The Second Order of Franciscans, the Poor Clares, used the basic rule as first written for them by the future Gregory IX in 1219, which was later adapted by St. Clare. The Third Order was not entirely a new application since the Benedictine Rule had been adopted to lay participation in religious life (tertians) as early as the 9th century. However, the Franciscan application was made in 1221 under the name of the Brothers and Sisters of Penance. From this developed the Third Order Secular and the tertiary order for lay persons. Later, other tertiary groups sprang from this application of the rule.

FRANKFORT, COUNCIL OF, a local council called by the Frankish bishops in 794. It was actually gathered to protest the Council of Nicaea. Due to incorrect translations, it was thought that Nicaea had approved "image adoration." Hence, the Franks sent a refutation of the error and condemned such practices. At the same time, besides confirming the Church's true teaching on the questions of images (actually set forth correctly at Nicaea) the Council of Frankfort attacked and condemned Adoptionism.

FRATERNAL CORRECTION, the practical application of the virtue of charity in which love of neighbor is extended to another to aid him to avoid sin and its occasion, or to refrain from further sin. By application it need not be given only in instances of sin, but may be given in instances where faults or imperfections exist. The method or manner of giving such correction may be by words, glances, or by refusing to support one by financial means in order to correct the error. Chiefly it is a matter of counsel. However, fraternal correction is not to be lightly indulged. There should be present, before one assumes the corrector's obligation, the following conditions: the one to be corrected must be in spiritual distress and this seriously; there should be a reasonable hope that the correction will be profitably received and it must be possible to bring about the correction without great personal detriment.

FREEDOM OF THE WILL, the exercise of the spiritual faculty or power of the soul, will, in making a choice. Through will, an individual seeks to perform an act or to attain an object proposed to it by the intellect. The will always has for its object the good, and even the choice of evil must be proposed to the will under the appearance of good. Freedom of the will has this essential: a freedom of contradiction, i.e., to act or not to act on something proposed by the intellect. It likewise possesses, but not essentially, the freedom of contraries, i.e., the choice of doing one thing or another.

FREEMASONRY, a secret society which arose in 1717 from Masonry, the international fraternity called the Free and Accepted Masons. Membership in Freemasonry is forbidden to Catholics under provision of canon 2335 with penalty of excommunication reserved simply to the Holy See. (*Cf.* MASONRY.)

FRESCO, a technique of painting frequently used in church decoration whereby the colors are put directly on the freshly applied, wet surface of plaster. It was used by the early Christians in the catacombs.

FRIAR, originally a term of address among Christians, applied after the

13th century as a title to any member of the mendicant order. The friar differs from the monk in that he does not remain within a monastery following a religious life in allegiance to an abbot and of an individual monastery, but exercises his ministry to the world in a variety of ways, being a professed religious working under a central director. Friars are considered under two divisions: (a) Mendicant orders of the common law, the Dominicans, Franciscans, Carmelites, and Augustinians; (b) the "lesser" orders, the Servites, Minims, Trinitarians, Mercedarians, Order of Penance, and the Brothers of St. John of God.

FRIARY, term applied to any residence of a group of members of the orders of friars, but usually referred to Franciscan houses.

FRIDAY. *See* ABSTINENCE.

FRONTAL. *See* ANTEPENDIUM.

FRUITS OF THE HOLY GHOST, collective name for the resultant acts which follow the practice of those supernatural graces infused into the soul by the Holy Spirit. St. Paul (Gal. 5:22–23) lists them as: charity, joy, peace, patience, kindness, goodness, faith, modesty, and continency. The Church includes: benignity, longanimity, and chastity.

FUNDAMENTAL ARTICLES, an inclusive term for those teachings of Christianity which Protestant theologians accepted from among the truths of faith, and considered essential. Dispute and differences in acceptance of these doctrines has marked the sectarian approach of Protestants to all true doctrines. The Catholic position is an acceptance of all truths or doctrines revealed by God, without consideration of their degree of importance in relation to each other.

FUNDAMENTAL THEOLOGY, that branch of the study of theology which follows progressively the study of philosophy in which the culmination is found in natural theology. Strictly speaking, fundamental theology is basic to dogmatic theology, perhaps to such an extent that it may be termed a first subdivision of dogmatic theology. The object of fundamental theology is to establish the fact that a revelation has been made by God, and that the Catholic faith is that revelation. It first establishes the possibility of revelation, examines the evidence underlying the fact of a revelation, and traces through the O.T. and the prophets this revelation and its culmination in the revelation of Christ and the apostles. It then proceeds to prove that this revelation was committed to a teaching body, that this body is the Catholic Church, that this Church is the authorized teacher and that this Church is assured of divine assistance and infallibility. (*Cf.* DOGMATIC THEOLOGY; THEOLOGY.)

FUNERAL, the rites and ceremonies accompanying the burial of a deceased person. In the Catholic Church this consists of the preliminary ceremony in which the priest sprinkles with holy water the coffin containing the body and recites the *De Profundis* and *Miserere*. Then the Office of the Dead is said, or the requiem Mass, or both. This is followed by prayers, the sprinkling of the body with holy water, the incensing, and the final prayers. When the body is committed into the grave, the ceremony consists of a blessing of the grave, the recitation of the *Benedictus*, the *Kyrie Eleison*, the Our Father, and additional prayers for the deceased and those present.

G

GABBATHA, the paved space occupying the highest point of the court at the eastern side of Jerusalem where Pilate tried Christ (Jn. 19:13).

GALATIANS, EPISTLE TO THE. This letter of St. Paul, addressed to the converts of his first missionary journey, was probably sent while the apostle was on his way to Jerusalem for the Council in 49 A.D. It is considered to be the earliest of St. Paul's Epistles (Acts 15:3). The writing was occasioned by the knowledge that the Galatians, mostly Gentiles (Acts 13, 14), were espousing the false teaching that circumcision and the Mosaic Law were necessary to salvation, leading to the conclusion that the redemption by Christ was insufficient. This Epistle sets forth many dogmatic teachings, notably the authority of the apostles (1:9); the doctrine of the Blessed Trinity (4:6); and especially the salvation for all according to faith in God's promises (1:4; 4:5).

GALLICANISM, term referring to the false teachings set forth in a writing called "The Gallican Liberties" (1682). Primarily, these teachings were an attack on the temporal power of the papacy. They demanded supremacy of ecumenical councils over the pope's authority; an independent position of the Gallican churches; and restriction of the pope's authority to matters of faith, this even subject to the consent of the Church.

The teachings were condemned by a constitution of Pope Alexander VIII (d. 1691) in 1690. The term Gallicanism has come to be applied to any instance where a national Church claims authority at the expense of the authority of the Holy See.

GALLICAN LITURGIES, rites developed in Gaul (France) in the 8th century, followed by a version of the Roman rite. These historic rites were full liturgies in many respects, but they were abandoned except for certain vestiges which still remain in use in certain dioceses, e.g., that of Bayeux.

GALLICAN PSALTER, a revision of the Vulgate psalter done by St. Jerome in 346, so called because its use was introduced in the churches of Gaul by St. Gregory of Tours and established by Charlemagne.

GAUDETE SUNDAY, name for the third Sunday of Advent, derived from the first Latin word of the Introit, meaning "rejoice." The liturgy permits rose-colored vestments for this day. The day is one of rejoicing over the closeness of the Redemption.

GEHENNA. Derived from the Greek short form of the Hebrew "Ge-hene-Hinnom," this name was originally applied to a public place south of Jerusalem where trash was being burned. It has been associated with hell (Mt. 5:22). (*Cf.* HELL.)

GENEALOGY OF CHRIST, the record of Christ's descent, tracing the fact that He was of Israelite stock and in particular of Davidic descent. It is recorded in Mt. 1:1–17, giving the ancestry of Joseph and evidence of the legal fatherhood of Joseph through whom, since Jewish usage ignored descent from the female line, the Davidic descent of Jesus is established juridically. The descent is also recorded in Lk. 3:23–38. Luke traces the descent of Christ back to Adam, thus presenting Him as the universal Savior of mankind. In the genealogy as recorded in Matthew's account there are fourteen generations given. In its conclusion Joseph is given only as the legal husband of Mary and so in the text the fact of Mary's perpetual virginity is maintained.

GENERAL, shortened version of superior general, the title given to the chief in spiritual authority over members of a religious order or congregation of men. The title is conferred by election in a general chapter of the order and may be for a limited number of years or for life.

GENERAL CHAPTER, an assembly of all members or delegates of an entire religious order or congregation. It derives its name from the place where members of a religious community were accustomed to gather daily for a reading of a chapter of the rule of the order; this place was called the chapter-house, and later any assembly was called the chapter. A general chapter is gathered to deal with serious problems of policy and matters which effect the religious order as a whole.

GENERAL CONFESSION, sacramental confession in which, despite previous confessions, sins and particularly grave sins, committed in one's life or over a lengthy period of time are again confessed. It may be required where serious doubt exists concerning previous confessions or where willful omissions made previous confessions incomplete. Such confessions are not to be made unless by counsel of one's confessor.

GENESIS, the first book of the Bible. In Greek, its title means "beginning." It was written largely by Moses and

GENESIS—The six days of Creation.

traces the descent of the ancestors of the people of Israel from the beginning of the world down to the twelve sons of Jacob and his family's residence in Egypt (ch. 46) closing with the death of his son Joseph. The doctrine of Genesis presents (a) a noble concept of God as Creator and Master of the world; (b) God's omnipotence (18:14); (c) the fact that God gave a law and that man's obedience to God's law must be free (2:17); (d) the fact that transgression of God's law brings punishment. In this first writing, the Messianic promise is originally given (3:15), and the promises made to Abraham.

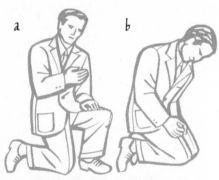

a   b

GENUFLECTION—Both types.

GENUFLECTION also **GENUFLEXION,** an act of reverence made either singly, by touching the right knee to the ground, or doubly, by kneeling on both knees and bowing the head slightly. A single or simple genuflection is the proper act of veneration accorded Christ in the Blessed Sacrament within the tabernacle; a double or solemn genuflection is the proper act of reverence before the Blessed Sacrament exposed. This act of reverence may be made during ceremonies, e.g., before and after the Elevation of the host during Mass. The simple genuflection is also an act of homage made to certain dignitaries of the Church, e.g., the pope, cardinal, or a bishop in his diocese. It is also customary when one kisses a bishop's ring to make a simple genuflection.

GETHSEMANI. In the time of our Lord, this was a garden area situated at the foot of the western slope of Mt. Olivet. The name means "oil-press," in particular a device for extracting the oil of olives. It is the place chosen by Christ for His preparatory meditation prior to His apprehension by the Jews and Roman soldiers and, thus, the scene of the agony in the garden, Christ's betrayal by Judas, and His arrest (Mt. 26:36–46).

GIFT OF TONGUES, one of the charismata, whereby one is given the miraculous gift to speak one language and be heard and understood by many individuals who ordinarily speak and understand a different native language. This is called the "miracle of Pentecost" because the first recorded instance is its use by the apostles following the descent of the Holy Spirit (Acts 2:4–13). The miracle had a twofold purpose: that Christ's teaching was to go to all peoples and that many would be able to hear and understand from the beginning of the apostles' teaching. The miracle was one of speaking, not of hearing.

GIFTS OF THE HOLY SPIRIT, THE SEVEN. Wisdom, understanding, knowledge, counsel, piety, fortitude, and fear of the Lord are these special graces granted by the Holy Spirit which, together with habitual grace, make us docile to the influence of the Holy Spirit. They are conferred with the virtues of the Holy Spirit, but are distinct from them, chiefly because of the mode of their action within us, their function being to perfect the exercise of the virtues.

GIFTS, SUPERNATURAL, the gifts which man cannot merit or achieve by nature. They are God's endowments bestowed on the soul of man.

GILDS. *See* GUILDS.

GIRDLE. *See* CINCTURE.

GIROVAGI. *See* GYROVAGI.

GLORIA IN EXCELSIS DEO, the Greater Doxology of the Mass. These words, translated "Glory to God on high," are the beginning of the Angelic Hymn sung by the angels at the birth of Christ. The Greater Doxology is omitted from the Mass during Lent and Advent when the priest wears purple or black vestments. The first part is found in the Gospel of St. Luke (2:13–14). The second part beginning "We praise Thee . . ." was taken from the fathers of the Church. It is recited in the Mass after the *Kyrie.*

GLORIA PATRI, the first words, translated "Glory be to the Father," and the title of the lesser doxology. It is a prayer of praise, recited frequently, e.g., after the Psalms of the Mass and the Divine Office, except during the last three days of Holy Week and the Office of the Dead.

GLORIOUS MYSTERIES. *See* MYSTERIES OF THE ROSARY.

GLORY. 1. Praise, splendor, honor attributed to one because of excellence. **2.** In Scripture the term "glory" is (a) the physical phenomenon resultant from a manifestation of God (Ex. 24:16); (b) the revelation of God found in His creation (Ps. 18:1); (c) the external manifestation of the Incarnation, the Only-Begotten of the Father (Jn. 1:14). **3.** The glory of the blessed is the eternal reward, i.e., the participation in divine glory, the beatific vision and love of God. In this sense it is called the "light of glory." **4.** Perfect glory is an attribute of God, because of the perfect knowledge of His own goodness. Any glory of man or nature is imperfect and is only a reflection of God's glory.

GLOSSATOR, the writer of a "gloss." The first *glossator* was Walafrid Strabo (d. 849).

GLOSSES, SCRIPTURAL, marginal notes, expansions, alternative readings made by the scribe or translator on an original text of Scripture. The word "gloss" may also describe an entire commentary composed of interpretations of passages from the Scripture given in sequence. Technically, today, the term glosses may be likened to "footnotes."

GLOVES, EPISCOPAL. Made of silk in the color corresponding to the liturgical color of the vestment, and ornamented with embroidery, these gloves are worn by a bishop in celebrating a pontifical Mass, up to the Offertory. A bishop, at his consecration, is invested with gloves but they are of ceremonial use rather than essential vesture of his office.

GLUTTONY, a capital sin of a two-fold nature. It is the inordinate longing for or indulgence in food and drink. In the first instance, since hunger is a natural reaction which prompts one to eat, this longing is directed to the desire for food over and above the necessity of bodily requirement. In the second instance, gluttony results from the use of food or drink in such quantity as to be unnatural or unreasonable. This also extends to the quality of food or drink, the overindulging in special dishes or drinks, simply because they are so tasty. Immoderation in eating or drinking is only venially sinful unless there are other reasons which make it more serious, e.g., giving scandal, or injuring one's health by it. Thus, the excess in drinking of alcoholic beverages may be: (a) venially sinful when it results in a partial loss of reason, becoming more seriously sinful because of scandal or injury to one's health; (b) mortally sinful when it results in complete loss of reason brought on without sufficient cause. By such loss of reason is meant failure to be able to distinguish between good and bad acts or, where memory is impaired, the failure to remember what occurred during the time of intoxication. The taking of narcotics, such as morphine, opium, barbiturates, etc., is venially sinful if taken without a sufficient reason, e.g., by prescription of a doctor; the taking of drugs is mortally sinful when loss of reason results.

GNOSTICISM, collective name for a group of vague and false religious philosophies which took many forms. As such they arose in the first century of the Church, and St. John in writing the Apocalypse was aware of this pseudo-religious philosophy. The errors common to this system which arose in Samaria and Syria were: that our Lord's body was unreal, being something like a phantom (Docetism); second to this was the attendant belief that divine Power merely took hold of a "human body" and used it as a tool instead of Christ being a true Person. Also there was the false teaching that all "matter" was bad and that there was an antagonism between soul and body. This latter led to immoralities and fanatical "purgings." For example, one form of Gnosticism, the Aphite, in-

cluded serpent worship. The Gnostics, the "Know-ers," were refuted by many early writers, but claimed special revelations. Each form was condemned by early councils of the Church, and the many early forms of Gnosticism were refuted by the First Council of Nicaea (c. 325).

GOD. God is the sovereign, Supreme Being, who alone is simply "self-dependent," who exists of himself, and who is infinitely perfect (*cf.* TRINITY). In speaking of God as "a spirit infinitely perfect" we are describing the physical essence of God; when we consider that God "exists of Himself," we indicate the metaphysical essence of God. From the metaphysical essence we deduce the attributes of God, which are God's pure perfections. These attributes are according to St. Thomas Aquinas: entitative attributes, which are God's simplicity, omniperfection, goodness, infinity, immensity, unchangeableness, eternity and unicity, invisibility and ineffability. The other perfections of God are called "operative." To name God, the best we can do properly is to take a name from that perfection which distinguishes Him from His creatures, i.e., His *aseity*, of which God Himself spoke when addressing Moses (Ex. 3:14) saying, "*I am who am.*" Describing Him otherwise, we are guided by God's effects, for "He is that infinite reality which is the exemplary and efficient cause of every reality that exists or is possible to exist." Philosophers and theologians, notably St. Thomas Aquinas (a. 3, I, 13) have presented arguments of reason which prove the existence and attributes of God. Briefly, these arguments are: 1. *Causality.* Since every effect must have an adequate or efficient cause, and since the universe is itself an effect and as such could not produce itself, and since the adequate cause of the universe must itself be uncaused and eternal, it follows that the prime cause (efficient and adequate) is God. 2. *Motion.* That is, passage from power to act as potentiality to existence implies a first, unmoved Mover who is both unmoved and unchanged, and such alone is God. 3. *Contingency.* Beings cannot exist of themselves, the universe does not exist of itself, independently. Beings must be produced ultimately by a being, independent and existing of itself. Such a being is God. 4. *Order.* The universe could not exist without order or design, and such order and design demands a plan and a Lawgiver and this in turn demands an intelligence. Such a supreme intelligence is God. 5. *Perfection.* Existing in the universe are many perfections; these can neither produce themselves nor exist, or be understood unless they are produced by a being who possesses all of them in Himself and in whom such perfections can be understood by comparison. This perfect being is God. 6. *Conscience.* Man is aware of moral obligation; moral obligation presupposes a law, and law presupposes a lawgiver. That sovereign lawgiver is God who created nature and implanted His law. 7. *Consent of Mankind.* Universally, in all times and places, both anthropologically and historically, men testify to God's existence.

GODPARENTS. *See* SPONSORS.

GOLDEN BULL, name sometimes attached to exceptionally important papal bulls. Specifically, the bull of 1356 regulating the election of the Holy Roman emperors is so named.

GOLDEN LEGEND, a widely read book of the Middle Ages, originally titled "The Legends of the Saints." This outstanding book of the Italian language was written by Jacopo de Voragine, O.P. (1228–1298) about 1270 and first printed in 1470. It is a collection of stories about the saints and a contribution to the devotional writings on the saints.

GOLDEN MILITIA, the Order of the Golden Spur, one of the oldest of the papal orders of knighthood. It is under the patronage of the Blessed Mother and its membership is limited to 100. The order is conferred for distinguished service in propagating the faith, or for service in writing or other acts giving glory to the Church.

THE GOLDEN ROSE—As being presented to the Grand Duchess of Luxemburg.

GOLDEN ROSE, an ornament in the form of a spray of roses, stem and leaves, and decorated with gems. Blessed by the pope and solemnly conferred on Laetare Sunday, it has been given, as a token of appreciation for services of loyalty, to cities, countries, or sovereigns. In recent times it has been reserved to Catholic queens and sovereigns, being given in 1925 to Queen Elizabeth of Belgium and last, in 1956, to the Grand Duchess of Luxemburg.

GOLGOTHA. *See* CALVARY.

GOOD FRIDAY, the Friday of Holy Week on which the anniversary of the passion and death of Christ is commemorated. It is the only day of the year on which Mass is not said. The liturgy of Good Friday begins around 3 p.m. It consists of four parts: lessons, the prayers of the faithful, adoration of the Cross, and the Communion service.

GOOD SHEPHERD—An early Christian statuette of Christ as shepherd.

GOOD SHEPHERD. 1. A title and symbol of our Lord based upon the Gospel account of the shepherd found in John 10:11. In representation the symbol usually shows Christ bearing a lamb upon His shoulders. Under this traditional title, Christ was portrayed by early Christians as the master of the flock. **2.** The parable of the Good Shepherd. **3.** Good Shepherd Sunday is celebrated on the second Sunday after Easter.

GOSPEL. The word gospel is taken from the Old English and means literally, "good tidings." The Gospels of the New Testament are the first-century writings of the four evangelists, SS. Matthew, Mark, Luke and John, in which we are told of the life, person, and teachings of the Son of God, Jesus Christ, and in which we learn of the founding of His Church. These four Gospels are the only "gospels" accepted by the Church for inclusion in the canon of the Scriptures. The Gospels of Mark, Matthew and Luke are called the "Synoptic Gospels" (q.v.). The word gospel has also been applied to the entirety of Christian teaching, e.g., preaching the gospel and, because of this, it has become an expression of designating the truth, e.g., the gospel truth.

GOSPEL, THE LAST, the prologue of the Gospel of St. John (1:1–14). It is read at the end of the Mass.

GOSPEL, THE LITURGICAL, the portion or selection from the writings of the evangelists which is sung or read after the Gradual of the Mass. It is a part of the Proper of the Mass.

GOTHIC ARCHITECTURE. This style of building design, introduced at the end of the 12th century, has been distinguished by the pointed arch and the system of stone vaulting. It was not limited in use to church building but is considered to have been distinctly Christian. In varieties it has been classified as "decorated," "perpendicular," "early English," but its name has been applied broadly to other arts where its principles were adapted, e.g., Gothic vestments.

GOTHIC RITE. *See* MOZARABIC RITE.

GRACE. There are in the common use of men three acceptances of the word *grace*. (a) It refers to something freely bestowed which is not due. In this sense it is used classically and in biblical writings. (b) Grace also means the very gift itself, e.g., the grace granted as a favor at court. (c) And grace means gratitude for the thing received. In the understanding of grace in its theological meaning, that is in the supernatural significance of the term, we find these three acceptances: first, the love of God through which supernatural life is conferred. This love of God is uncreated grace. Second, grace is the supernatural, free gift of God. This, directing toward and ordained to eternal life, is created grace. As such it is either *exterior* or *interior*. Third, grace is in turn our gratitude to God. This parallel is not exact, but the three aspects of grace must be considered in reasonably understanding this mystery. The word grace is not found in Mt., Mk., nor Jn. except in the Prologue to John's Gospel (1:14). However, in the entire N.T. the idea of "gift" or that something "will be given" is of constant recurrence (Mt. 21:43; Rom. 8:32; etc.). Indeed Christ's love is the *gift* of His life (Mt. 20:28) and of His body in the Eucharist (Mt. 26:26; Lk. 22:19). Further, while this gift idea is present, there also is the idea of "merit,"

arising from grace itself, and "demerit" or the loss of grace (Mt. 6:4). We see then that the entire order of grace is found in the "giving" by God and the "receiving" on the part of man. *By definition*, grace is "a gratuitous gift infused by God into the rational creature with reference to the end: eternal life." By this we mean specifically created grace. We may further speak of this as *external* or *internal*. External grace, for instance, would be the example of Christ; internal grace is that received in the interior of the soul, enabling us to act supernaturally. This internal grace may be: 1. *gratum faciens*, or that which makes one pleasing or that which is given for the recipient himself. Such would be actual, habitual, sanctifying grace, or charisms. 2. *Gratis datae*, or "freely given," which graces are given to one to be used for the benefit of others, e.g., the gift of prophecy. Grace is of many defined kinds according to their creation and effects. They may be studied briefly under their separate listings: sanctifying; actual; habitual; sacramental; efficacious; sufficient.

GRACE AT MEALS, brief prayers asking a blessing on the food to be eaten at a meal, and offering a thanksgiving after the meal. This is of early custom in the Church (Acts 27:35), and was certainly a part of the *agape* (q.v.) practices of early Christians. The prayers may be either spontaneous or follow prescribed forms.

GRADINE, shelves or steps erected in back of an altar, customarily used for storing candlesticks, flowers, etc. However, this is not a liturgical part of the altar and should be clear of the tabernacle and apart from the altar proper. (*Cf.* ALTAR.)

GRADUAL, a short song or antiphon consisting of a brief text taken from the Scriptures, frequently from the Psalms. As part of the Proper of the Mass, the Gradual is said after the Epistle and immediately precedes the Tract in some Masses. In thought, the Gradual repeats the idea expressed in the Epistle and is, as it were, a scriptural bridge between the Epistle and Gospel of the Mass. The Gradual is sometimes referred to as the Responsory.

GRADUALE ROMANUM, a book containing the liturgical chants of the Mass, both the Proper and Ordinary throughout the year.

GRADUAL PSALMS, the Psalms 119–133. They were also called pilgrimage Psalms, or "songs of ascent," because they were sung by the pilgrims going up to Jerusalem for the major festivals.

GRAFFITO. The plural form of this term, *graffiti*, has been applied to the many crude inscriptions and pictures scratched or drawn upon ancient monuments, the walls of tombs, or catacombs. While they were frequently erroneous and in no manner official, *graffiti* offer to archaeologists and historians valuable records of early customs or practices. For example, the early graffito of the Palatine depicting the use of a loincloth in the crucifixion of Christ, contrary to the pagan custom of nakedness in executions, has served as a guide to artists in all ages.

GRAIL, THE. 1. An organized movement begun in 1921 in Holland by Rev. J. van Ginneken, S.J. (d. 1945). It has for its objective the lay apostolate of women. In a training period of three years, women are instructed to become cultural and apostolic leaders for missionary and catechetical work. The Grail movement was established (1944) in the United States in the diocese of Cincinnati at Loveland, Ohio. It is, as an instruction center, affiliated with the Catholic University as a community college. **2.** An obsolete English word for the Gradual.

GRAIL, THE HOLY, the legendary vessel, either a chalice or shallow dish, used by Christ at the Last Supper at the institution of the Holy Eucharist. While the Holy Grail has figured in story and verse from medieval times to the present, no such authentic relic has been found among the objects of Christian antiquity.

GREATER DOUBLE. *See* FEASTS OF THE CHURCH.

GRECA, name given to the black overcoat frequently worn as semi-official dress by the clergy of Rome.

GREEK CHURCH, the church of the Greek people, being subject to the Archbishop of Athens and All Greece. The term has been erroneously applied to the entire Orthodox Eastern Church. (*Cf.* EASTERN CHURCHES.)

GREEK CHURCH, UNITED, a term often applied erroneously to all Catholics of the Byzantine rite. (*Cf.* EASTERN CHURCHES.)

GREEK FATHERS, collective term for all those patristic writers who were of the early Eastern Church and wrote or taught in Greek. (*Cf.* FATHERS OF THE CHURCH.)

1.

K Y -ri- e * e-   lé- i-son.

GREGORIAN MUSIC—A sample of Gregorian notation.

GREGORIAN MUSIC, the plain chant which is now the liturgical music of the Church. It derives its name from Pope Gregory the Great (d. 604), who gave impulse to chant in church singing (*cf.* CHANT). Pope St. Pius X, by his *Motu Proprio* (1903), restored the Gregorian as the official chant of the Roman Church.

GREGORIAN SACRAMENTARY, a book, originally issued in the 8th century, containing the Ordinaries and Propers of the Mass and the prayers for ordination. It has undergone many revisions and changes, but when first introduced it was a basic source of the Roman rite.

GREGORIAN WATER. Sometimes called the "water of consecration," this is the holy water blessed and used by the bishop at the consecration of a church. In the blessing, small amounts of wine, salt, and ashes are mingled with the water.

GREMIAL also **GREMIALE,** an oblong veil, usually of silk and decorated with embroidery, which is laid on the bishop's knees when he sits during a pontifical Mass. Its practical purpose is to serve as an apron to keep ashes, drops of oils and candle wax from falling on the vestments. It corresponds in color to that of the vestments. A linen gremial is used when Holy Orders are conferred. It is not strictly a pontifical vestment, having been used at all high Masses; a similar lap-cloth, the

mappula, is still used by the Dominicans and the celebrant in Carthusian and calced Carmelite orders.

GRILLE. 1. A wooden or metal grating separating the enclosure of cloistered nuns from the visiting rooms of the public. Frequently the grille has an opening where offerings are passed to the members of the community. It also may be covered by a thin veil. **2.** The partition, usually a grating, which, though separating a penitent from the confessor, does not obstruct the sound of the voice.

GRILLE (1)

GUADALUPE, OUR LADY OF.

This title has been given to our Blessed Mother because of her apparitions to the Mexican convert, Juan Diego, in 1531. At the time, to confirm the apparitions, there was caused to be imprinted on the serape or mantle of Juan an image of the Immaculate Conception. It showed the Virgin Mary with the sun, moon, and stars, and with an angel beneath the crescent. Under this title the Blessed Mother is the declared patroness of Mexico. The feast, celebrated on Dec. 12, is a holyday of obligation in Mexico.

GUARDIAN, the title of an elected superior of a Franciscan friary, usually referred to as "Father Guardian."

GUARDIAN ANGEL. *See* ANGEL, GUARDIAN.

GUILDS. In England formerly spelled "gilds," these were voluntary associations or societies of the Middle Ages, organized for the promotion of individual initiative, special skills, social standing, and the religious life of their members. Chiefly these were of three classes: the merchant guilds, formed by the tradesmen; the craft guilds, incorporating three groups, namely, the learners or apprentices, the more proficient called journeymen, and the masters or employers; the religious guilds, made up of all classes of people who directed themselves to social work, collective alms-giving, and instruction. The guilds had patron saints and chaplains, and their members celebrated religious feasts by attending Mass and receiving Holy Communion in a body. In a distinct manner the guilds were the forerunners of labor unions and of groups later organized for Catholic Action.

GYNAECEUM, a portion of the church set apart for women in the Byzantine and other Eastern Churches.

GYROVAGI. This name was given by St. Benedict (d. 543) to the so-called "tramp monks" who wandered about the various countries but never were attached to any monasteries. They became laws to themselves and their behavior brought about Church regulation to do away with such "aimless" religious life.

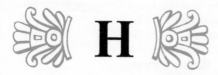

H

HABACUC, BOOK OF, a prophetical book of the Bible written by an unknown prophet of the same name. It was written before the invasion of Palestine by the Chaldaeans (Babylonians) sometime probably between the years 605 and 602 B.C. The book is divided into three distinct parts: the first, a dramatic dialogue between the prophet and God; the second, the "Woes of the Wicked"; and the third, a canticle (ch. 3). The message takes up the problem of injustice on earth, God's reassurance that man's faithfulness will be rewarded, and the petition that God come and bring consolation.

HABIT, RELIGIOUS, the official and distinctive external garment worn by members of a religious order. In color these are generally variations of black, brown or white, but grey and blue are also used. In general, except for some societies who use a variation of the cassock, the habit of male religious is comprised of a tunic, belt or girdle, a scapular and a hood. Among women's orders, the garments are generally a veil, guimpe, full dress and a scapular. The ceremony marking the reception into the religious life is called the "clothing" and sets a member apart as a prospective or professed member of the religious order.

HABITUAL GRACE, the supernatural gift of God infused into the very essence of the soul as a habit. This grace is also called *sanctifying* grace or *justifying* grace, more because it is included in both than to make a distinction. Habitual grace also includes the virtues and gifts of the Holy Spirit. This grace is spoken of by St. Paul as the essential and constant possession of the soul of man, the created, internal gift of God (Rom. 5:5; 1 Tim. 4:14). The Council of Trent (Sess. VI, c. 11) declares the teaching: "If anyone should say that men are justified either by the imputation of Christ's justice alone or by the remission of sins alone, exclusive of grace and charity, which are diffused in their hearts by the Holy Ghost, and that it inheres in them, or even that grace, by which we are justified, is only a favor from God: let him be anathema." Habitual grace is both operative and co-operative. (*Cf.* GRACE; SANCTIFYING GRACE.)

HAGIA, in the Byzantine rite the name of the consecrated elements.

HAGIOGRAPHY, writings not only on the lives and works, but also on the sanctity of saints, thus being more than biography. Whereas biography narrates the life of a person in a chronological or topical manner, hagiography includes an evaluation of a saint in the light of the principles of ascetical and mystical theology. It also includes, at least implicitly, the spiritual lessons to be learned from the saint whereby the reader may be directed toward emulation or imitation of the virtues exemplified by the saint's life. As a literary form, hagiography requires research into the life of the saint, knowledge of theology, and a critical sense in regard to spiritual happenings. In Scripture, the term "Hagiographa" is used to refer to those O.T. writings which treat of neither law nor the prophets.

HAIL MARY. Translated from the Latin *Ave Maria*, these are the first words and the title of the prayer "The Angelical Salutation." The prayer is composed of the words of annunciation addressed to the Blessed Virgin by the angel and by Elizabeth (Lk. 1:28–42) with a supplication added by the Church. Its present form dates back to 1568. While the prayer is not used in the liturgy, it is said in reciting the Divine Office, the Little Office of the B.V.M., and in numerous devotions, notably the Rosary.

HALO, the representation in Christian art of a circle of gold or light surrounding the head of a saint. It is a device of portraying holiness or the "light of grace" in a saint. The halo is distinct from the aureole or nimbus.

HARMONY, BIBLICAL, the study of the four Gospels wherein (a) differences in text are explained; (b) the Gospels are integrated into a single narrative; or (c) an arrangement of verses of the Gospels is made according to the historical order. (*Cf.* SYNOPTIC GOSPELS.)

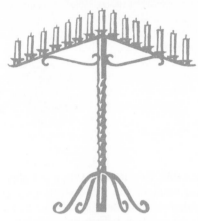

HEARSE

HEARSE, candleholder in the form of a triangle with 15 candlesticks, one of them being placed at its apex and seven each on its left and right sides. It is made of wood or iron and usually mounted on a standard. The hearse is also called the Tenebrae candleholder since it is used during Holy Week when the office of Tenebrae is sung. (*Cf.* TENEBRAE.)

HEART OF JESUS. *See* SACRED HEART OF JESUS.

HEART OF MARY IMMACULATE. Specifically, this is the devotion to the Blessed Mother of God and to the person of Mary as God's Mother. The word "heart" in Hebrew, and as used in the Scriptures, often stands for the higher part of the soul, the intellect and will (Eccu. 23:2). In portraying the heart of Mary and in directing our devotion thereto, we honor her interior fullness of grace, the perfections of her soul. When the heart of Mary is shown pierced by swords, we are directed to the sorrows she experienced in her motherhood of God; when it is represented surrounded with roses, we recall her virtues; when it is shown surrounded with thorns, we are reminded of her sorrow at man's ingratitude toward her divine Son. The devotion has been greatly increased since the Immaculate Heart of Mary was a prominent feature of the apparitions at Fatima in 1917. August 22 has been designated by Pope Pius XII in 1945 as the date for the celebration of this feast.

HEAVEN, the state of perfect happiness which exists in no restricted place. It is where God's special manifestation will be made to all. Heaven is mentioned frequently in Scripture under a wide variety of names: "Kingdom of Heaven" (Mt. 5:3); the "Father's house" (Jn. 14:2); the "crown of glory" (1 Pet. 5:4), etc. St. Paul speaks quite fully of heaven, the requisite justification for attainment (Romans, 8), and he speaks of the judgment which will declare the reward (2 Cor. 2:40). Heaven is the reward and the manifestation of God, through Christ, and is the result of the love of God for mankind and man's love of God in return (1 Cor. 2:9). The happiness of heaven will consist primarily of an infusion or submersion in God's love or the participation through love of the beatific vision, the knowledge of God as He is in His being. The degree to which each one will participate will be dependent upon the merit of each. Joined to this essential and fundamental supernatural beatitude, there will be the enjoyment of contemplating Christ's humanity, companionship of the angels and saints, the perfection of natural endowments, and the satisfactions of peace without struggle and the continued enjoyment without end, or for all eternity. (*Cf.* BEATIFIC VISION; GLORY.)

HEBDOMADARIUS. In monasteries, this is the title of the one appointed each week to be the leader in chanting the canonical hours, etc.

HELL, the place and state of everlasting punishment prepared for Satan and the rebellious angels and to which the souls and bodies of those who die with grave and unrepented sins will be consigned after the last judgment (Mt. 25:31–46). The nature of this supernatural suffering is not known. However, theologians declare that essentially it consists of two facts: first, being deprived of the vision and love of God as known in the beatific vision which is called the pain of loss; second, the actual physical suffering which will result from an outside agent, notably fire, which will be supernatural in character and nonconsuming. The suffering will be in degree according to the guilt of each and will last forever. The reasonable deductions concerning the nature of hell are not the result of speculation but are derived from recognition of the goodness, justice, and glory of God.

HENOTICON, a formula of unity of doctrine proposed by the Acacians to effect a compromise between the Catholics and the heretical Monophysites in 482. It was rejected by Pope Felix III in 484.

HEORTOLOGY, the study of origin, meaning and development of the Church's feasts.

HERESY, the denial or doubt by error of judgment, publicly or privately, by a baptized, professed person of any truth revealed by God and proposed for belief by the Catholic Church (*cf.* APOSTASY; SCHISM). It differs from apostasy and schism, and incurs excommunication by the very fact, which censure is reserved to the Holy See. It must be: deliberate, i.e., with a sufficient knowledge of the true teaching; and obstinate, i.e.; continue in the error of judgment without seeking further to learn the truth. Heresy is of two kinds: *formal*, which is the deliberate and obstinate denial of a truth and the neglect of inquiry into the truth; *material*, when the denial is the result of ignorance and is not accompanied by obstinacy. This latter does not incur canonical censures. Certain persons, as liberals, socialists or communists, are heretics according to the extent to which they ascribe to principles of their party in opposition to the revealed truth and defined teachings.

HERETIC, a baptized and professed person who denies or doubts a truth revealed by God or proposed for belief by the Catholic Church. The title is usually reserved for one who is guilty of formal heresy.

HERMENEUTICS, the science of interpreting the meaning and true sense of the books and texts of Scripture in accord with the principles of exegesis as set forth. (*Cf.* EXEGESIS; INTERPRETATION, SCRIPTURAL.)

HERMESIANISM, title applied to the erroneous teachings concerning reason and faith propounded by Rev. G. Hermes (d. 1831). These teachings were condemned by the Holy See in 1835 and by the Vatican Council.

HERMIT, one who lives alone and apart from the society of others for the purpose of devoting himself to prayer and the cultivation of a personal spiritual life. The practice arose early in the Church, following the persecution of the 3rd and 4th centuries. Hermits were the pioneer monks and gave rise to the religious life. (*Cf.* STYLITE; MONK.)

HEROIC ACT OF CHARITY, the most unselfish act of love in which a living person once and for all offers to God in behalf of the souls in purgatory all acts of merit which he performs during his lifetime and all suffrages to be offered for him after death, i.e., Masses, indulgenced prayers, etc. The act is not made as a vow and is revocable at will. However, it is advisable that the person wishing to make the act consult his or her spiritual director.

HEROIC VIRTUE, the practice of the cardinal and theological virtues in such manner and to such degree as to be extraordinary both in motive and perseverance. It is essential to prove heroic virtue on the part of one who is to be beatified and canonized. (*Cf.* VIRTUE.)

HESPERINOS, the Vesper service in the Byzantine rite.

HESYCHASM, an Eastern Church system of mysticism, first practiced by the monks of Athos in the 14th century. Drawn from Platonist philosophy and borrowing from Asiatic Yoga practices, it is a form of rationalist asceticism which opposes contemplation in its true sense. (*Cf.* QUIETISM.)

HESYCHASTS, name sometimes applied to monks of the Orthodox Eastern Church who lead a life of contemplation.

HEXAEMERON also **HEXAHEMERON,** the title taken from the Greek for the narration of the six days or periods of creation of the physical world as recorded in the first chapter of Genesis.

HEXAPLA, the monumental compilation by Origen, giving the text of the Scriptures, made about 240 A.D. Origen's aim was to give what was actually contained in the Hebrew text and to provide the Church with a uniform text by eliminating the variations found in the codices. The book, of about 12,000 pages, is so named from the six corresponding columns into which it was divided. It contained both Hebrew and Greek texts. An edition containing only the four Greek versions was called *Tetrapla*.

HEXATEUCH, collective name for the first six books of the Bible considered as a unit because of the literary similarity. They are: Genesis, Exodus, Leviticus, Numbers, Deuteronomy, Josue. However, the inclusion of Josue is being abandoned among critical scholars because it is considered to have a markedly different literary style of its own.

HIERARCHY. 1. Celestial hierarchy includes the nine choirs of angels (*cf.* ANGELS). **2.** The hierarchy of the Church has two distinctions: First, by reason of holy orders, the hierarchy is composed of bishops, priests and deacons. Second, by reason of jurisdiction, the hierarchy is made up of the pope and the bishops under his authority. The jurisdiction of the second group may, by delegation, be shared in part by clerics of the first group (c's. 108–144). Thus the hierarchy of the Church includes all grades or ranks of the clergy. (*Cf.* BISHOP; JURISDICTION.)

HIEROMONK, a monk of the Eastern Church who has been ordained a priest.

HIERURGIA, a liturgical rite, e.g., the Mass.

HIGH MASS. *See* MASS.

HINDERING IMPEDIMENTS, conditions which make it unlawful to contract marriage but do not affect the validity of the contract. (*Cf.* IMPEDIMENTS OF MARRIAGE; VALIDATION OF MARRIAGE.)

HISTORY, CHURCH, the study and account of the story, facts, and personages from its beginning to the present of the imperishable society known as the Church. It shows this society at work in the progression of chronology, giving the record of Christ's revelation and its extension among men during succeeding ages. It thus narrates the spread of the Church, its efforts to teach divine truths, and gives an account of the persons who aided or obstructed that spread of truth. Church history is always presented together with secular history since the Church as a society lives and exercises her authority and official organization among the nations of men. (*Cf.* CHURCH HISTORY.)

HOLINESS. 1. In regard to material things, holiness means their dedication or consecration to God's service. In regard to persons, holiness means a degree of union with God through sanctifying grace and the performance of morally good acts. **2.** A title of honor conferred on the pope and used in addressing him, e.g., His Holiness, Pope ————.

HOLINESS, MARK OF THE CHURCH. *See* MARKS OF THE CHURCH.

HOLOCAUST

HOLOCAUST, the first kind of sacrifice, the whole burnt-offering as used in the Hebrew law (Lev. 1, 3).

HOLY ALLIANCE, the treaty between Russia, Prussia, and Austria signed in 1815. It was a non-aggression pact but religious in character since it introduced, after years of political pragmatism, Christian morality into politics. Unfortunately, it was later replaced by expedient alliances, but served to point the way for future democratic negotiations.

HOLY COAT, name of the seamless tunic worn by Christ (Jn. 19:23) just prior to His crucifixion. There are claims to two such garments, one held at the Cathedral of Trier, Germany, and the other at Argenteuil, France. No determination of authenticity has been made by the Church. Both relics have been honored. That of Trier is alleged to have been given by St. Helena, based on the testimony of a 6th century tablet; the coat of

Argenteuil is recorded in a document of the 11th century. Claims are made that the coat at Trier is the outer garment and not the seamless one.

HOLY COMMUNION. *See* COMMUNION.

HOLYDAYS. Known as holydays of obligation, these are the days on which it is required that members of the Catholic faith who have attained the age of reason rest from servile work and attend Holy Mass. The Apostolic See alone can declare, transfer or abolish holydays of obligation for the universal Church (c's. 1244, 1247). Those established now are: all Sundays, the feasts of Christmas, Circumcision, Epiphany, Ascension, Corpus Christi, the Immaculate Conception, Assumption of the B.V.M., St. Joseph, SS. Peter and Paul, and All Saints. By a special decree of the Sacred Congregation of Propaganda, Nov. 25, 1885, the feasts observed as holydays of obligation in the United States, besides Sundays are: the Immaculate Conception (Dec. 8); Christmas (Dec. 25); Circumcision (Jan. 1); Ascension (May 19); Assumption of the B.V.M. (Aug. 15); All Saints (Nov. 1).

HOLY FAMILY, Jesus, the Son of God, the Blessed Virgin Mary, His Mother, and St. Joseph, His foster father. The feast is celebrated on the Sunday within the octave of Epiphany. In art it is customary to portray the Holy Family with Jesus as a baby or child, based upon the fact that St. Joseph died while Jesus was young.

HOLY FATHER, title of reverence accorded the pope as spiritual father of the universal Church.

HOLY GHOST. *See* HOLY SPIRIT; TRINITY.

HOLY HOUR, devotion for one hour's duration consisting of exposition of the Blessed Sacrament, meditation, and vocal prayers, followed by Benediction. Custom and purpose determine the prayers to be recited as well as whether or not a sermon is to be preached. In March 1933, the pope, by decree of the Sacred Penitentiary, granted a plenary indulgence to all who assist at the Holy Hour, with the usual requirements of confession, reception of Holy Communion and prayer for the intention of the Holy Father (S. P., Mar. 21, 1933). A partial indulgence of ten years is granted to those who attend the Holy Hour with contrite hearts.

HOLY NAME OF JESUS. 1. The name "Jesus" is the Latin spelling of the Greek which derives from the Hebrew Yēšûaʻ, the word meaning "Yahweh is Salvation." The name was given by God and declares the redemptive act of love, the salvation of man from sin through Jesus (Lk. 1:31). **2.** The name of Jesus has been honored from apostolic times (Phil. 2:9–10). Celebration of a Feast of the Holy Name arose in the 15th century and was extended to the universal Church in 1721. It is celebrated on the Sunday following Jan. 1, when a Sunday occurs before Jan. 6; otherwise it is on Jan. 2.

HOLY NAME SOCIETY, an association of Catholic laymen founded by the Dominican preacher, Bl. John of Vercelli (d. 1283) at the command of Pope Gregory X, to combat the blasphemies and profanities rampant at the time. The society remains under the direction of the Dominicans. It is an archconfraternity of the Church, endowed richly with spiritual benefits. It is widely established throughout the United States, being erected in dioceses and parishes for the purpose of promoting reverence for the name of Jesus and the spiritual progress of laymen by encouraging frequent reception of Communion, the attendance at retreats, etc.

HOLY OFFICE, CONGREGATION OF THE. Being the most eminent of the Roman Congregations, the Holy Office is entrusted with complete competence (c. 247) regarding all matters of faith and morals, the Pauline privilege, mixed marriages, the examination and condemnation of books or teachings contrary to faith or morals. It is also the tribunal for crimes brought to it for judgment, as apostasy, heresy, schism, profanation of the Holy Eucharist, and certain cases of immorality. It functions under the greatest degree of secrecy because of the nature of its proceedings. The members of the Holy Office are: a cardinal secretary assisted by five other cardinals, an assessor, a Dominican serving under the title of commissary who is assisted by two others. It is likewise assisted by twenty consultors, besides numerous specialists in theology, canon law, etc., notaries, and secretaries.

HOLY OILS, three sacramentals blessed by a bishop. They are: oil of catechumens, holy chrism, and oil of the sick. The first and last are pure olive oil while chrism is olive oil mixed with a small quantity of balsam. The blessing takes place on Holy Thursday in the cathedral of the diocese. (*Cf.* OIL STOCK.)

HOLY ORDERS. *See* ORDERS, HOLY, SACRAMENT OF.

HOLY PLACES, THE, sites in Palestine (Israel) which are connected with the life of Christ, notably the Holy Sepulcher, Calvary, the Upper Room, the Way to Calvary, Gethsemani, and the place where the Temple of Jerusalem stood. Since the 13th century these have been in the care of the Friars Minor.

HOLY ROMAN EMPIRE, a union begun by the German ruler Otto I (d. 973) to bring imperialism and feudalism together. It did not succeed in this intent, but later effected a tie between Church and state. At its foundation it was not called "Holy Roman Empire," the word "holy" being used for the first time during the reign of Frederick I (d. 1190). Substantially an extension of the empire established earlier by Charlemagne in the West, it was an intended bond between rulers whereby the states involved through concerted action could serve as temporal protectors of the Church. As such it failed, bringing frequent clashes between the Church and sovereigns. The imperial crown was conferred on one of the member rulers by election, thus making the emperor nominal head of the others. The Holy Roman Empire was abolished by Napoleon I in 1806.

HOLY SATURDAY, the Saturday of Holy Week.

HOLY SEE, the composite of authority, jurisdiction, and sovereignty vested in and exercised by the pope and his governing groups in the spiritual and temporal governance and guidance of the universal Church. It is located in Rome, chiefly in the Vatican State. The pope as the sovereign pontiff is the visible head of the Church which is the mystical body of Christ. He is the infallible guide of the spiritual welfare of the Church, and in him is recognized, by the clergy and faithful, the fullness of jurisdiction in governing the body of the Church. He governs with the authority and power of Peter, the leader of the apostles. The nature and extent of the governmental functions of the Church demand that the pope have aides and assisting groups. Thus under the direction of the pope the various functions are carried out by the eleven Sacred Congregations, three tribunals, five offices, six commissions (c's. 242–244). From the pope and these varied groups there is a transmission of either jurisdiction or orders to the bishops, vicars and prefects apostolic, mission superiors, and superiors of religious communities, and through these to diocesan synods and provincial and plenary councils, and then to the clergy and faithful. Also serving, not as intermediaries but as convenient representatives, are a number of nuncios and apostolic delegates. Also called the Apostolic See. (*Cf.* PAPACY; VATICAN.)

HOLY SEPULCHER, KNIGHTS OF THE, a papal order of knights, first approved in 1113. There are three classes of the order with varying insignia: Grand Cross Knights, Commanders, and Knights. The insignia may be conferred on women, who wear it on the left side and whose titles are Dames or Matrons of the Holy Sepulcher.

HOLY SOULS, the souls of the dead who died in the grace of God but are detained in purgatory to make satisfaction for temporal punishment due to sins. Their release into heaven may be obtained by prayer and works of suffrage on the part of the living faithful, and such prayers are a work of charity. The feast of All Souls is celebrated on Nov. 2, except when that date falls on a Sunday, in which event it is Nov. 3. (*Cf.* PURGATORY.)

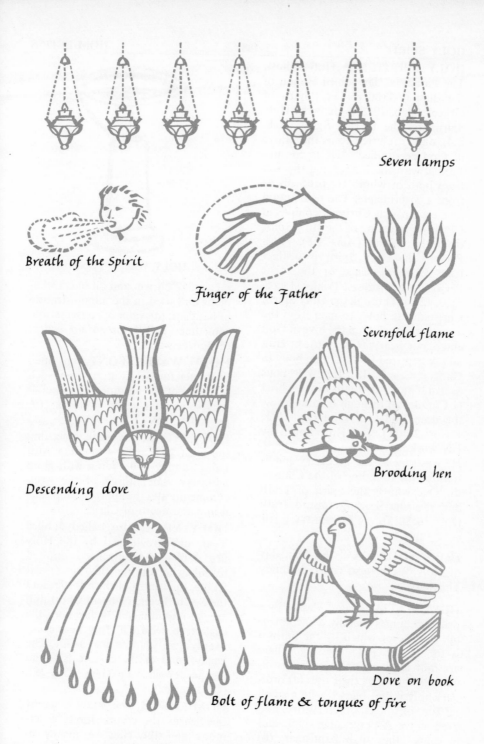

Seven lamps

Breath of the Spirit

Finger of the Father

Sevenfold flame

Descending dove

Brooding hen

Bolt of flame & tongues of fire

Dove on book

HOLY SPIRIT—Some of the symbols used in Church art.

HOLY SPIRIT. The Holy Ghost. The Paraclete. The Third Person of the Blessed Trinity. The "Spirit of Grace" (Heb. 10:29). He is the Holy Spirit and the Eternal Spirit (Heb. 2:4), and is referred to as the "Love of God personified." He is consubstantial with the Father and the Son from both of whom He proceeds as from a co-principle. The redemption of men through Christ is completed by Christ's sending of the Holy Spirit from the Father (Acts 1:8). As a Person, the Holy Spirit is distinct from Divine Essence or the other Persons of the Blessed Trinity (1 Cor. 2:10; 12:4). Through the Holy Spirit, Christian life flows to men from the Trinity, through Him the love of God enters our hearts (Gal. 4:6); in Him all are baptized to make one body in Christ (1 Cor. 12:13); He dwells in us as in a temple, giving us life in Christ (1 Cor. 3:16); through Him we know the deep things of God (Jn. 16:3; 1 Cor. 2:40ff). The Holy Spirit, by His work, gives life to the Church. He was sent as the necessary condition for the founding of the Church, the One who is the Spirit of Truth and the One leading toward truth (Jn. 16:5–15). (*Cf.* TRINITY, THE MOST HOLY.)

HOLY THURSDAY, the Thursday of Holy Week, also called Maundy Thursday.

HOLY WATER. Water, blessed by a priest, becomes thereby a sacramental, the use of which by the faithful is to invoke God's blessing. There are four kinds of holy water, distinguished chiefly by their use: (a) ordinary holy water, blessed with a small mixture of salt as a preservative, and used at the Asperges, blessings, and in fonts other than baptismal; (b) baptismal water, blessed with a slight

HOLY WATER FONT

mixture of chrism and oil of catechumens and used in the administration of baptism; (c) water of consecration, sometimes called Gregorian water; (d) Easter water.

HOLY WATER FONT, an open container for holy water. When such is placed at the entrance of a church it is sometimes called a stoup. (*Cf.* BAPTISMAL FONT.)

HOLY WEEK, the week preceding the feast of Easter, beginning with Palm Sunday and ending with Holy Saturday. The liturgy of the week commemorates the apprehension, suffering and death of Christ.

HOLY YEAR, also called Jubilee Year, one proclaimed by the Holy See. A plenary indulgence is granted to all who during this time visit Rome, the tombs of the apostles and the See of Peter, or to all who fulfill special requirements. It has been the custom to declare a Holy Year every twenty-five years since 1475. The background of the custom is found in the Jewish Law (Lev. 25:8–19). (*Cf.* JUBILEE.)

HOMILETICS, the study whereby one learns the composition of sermons and the effective means of preaching them.

HOMILY, a more or less brief, instructive discourse on a passage of Scripture wherein the spiritual lesson of the scriptural text is made clear. It is generally to be instructive, informal, and intelligent, being a basic form of the preaching art.

HOMOEANS. *See* ACACIANISM.

HOMOOUSIAN, term derived from the Greek, accepted by the Council of Nicaea in 325 and incorporated into the Nicene creed. Literally "consubstantial," it expresses the substantial unity of the Son and the Father. The term was given as the definitive answer to the Arian and semi-Arian heresies by the teaching authority of the Church based on the tradition of essential unity. (*Cf.* CONSUBSTANTIAL.)

HOOD

HOOD, the cone-shaped headdress which is attached to a religious habit at the back of the neck. A remnant of the hood as a liturgical and clerical headdress is found in that small cowl-shaped cloth attached to the mozzetta of a bishop.

HOPE, one of the three theological virtues. It is a supernatural, infused virtue which moves the will to trust in eternal happiness and the all-good God and gives the assurance that the necessary graces to merit eternal life will be ours. Hope is necessary for salvation since, joined to faith—our knowledge and belief in God—and charity—our love of God—it supplies the inducement to exercise our faith and love. It is a positive exercise toward salvation and a negative one in the sense that we fear the loss of heaven. Hope is infused in the soul with sanctifying grace and is a longing given by the Spirit of Grace, the Holy Spirit, for His indwelling within us. From the Holy Spirit comes the encouragement to prevent even the thought of possible loss from weakening us in our exercise of hope (Rom. 8:1–39). The sins against the virtue are, first, those of omission where we fail to make acts of hope at times when we need to overcome temptations against loss of virtue; second, acts of commission, as those which cause us to turn from God or to place our desire in something other than God, acts of despair which are a lack of trust in God, and acts of presumption, as when the mind prompts the will to seek means other than those provided by Christ for attaining heaven. (*Cf.* THEOLOGICAL VIRTUES.)

HOROLOGION, a liturgical book of the Byzantine rite. It contains the prayers of their divine office, hymns and prayers, and their ecclesiastical calendar.

HOSANNA, a word from the Hebrew, meaning "Save, we pray" (Ps. 117:25). The expression came to mean a cry of acclamation and as such it was used in the salutation given Christ when He entered Jerusalem in triumph (Mk. 11:10).

HOSPITALLERS. 1. Name given to religious of either sex who follow the rule of St. Augustine and are devoted to service of the sick. **2.** Women of the Middle Ages who formed an auxiliary group to aid the military orders in caring for the sick. **3.** Hospitallers of St. John of Jerusalem, members of a powerful military order founded in 1092 to care for the poor and strangers in the Holy Land, notably Jerusalem. They fell into decadence in the 16th century.

HOST, the consecrated species of bread as used in the Mass, Benediction of the Blessed Sacrament, and Holy Communion. (*Cf.* ALTAR BREADS.)

HOURS, CANONICAL. *See* CANONICAL HOURS.

HUGUENOTS. This term, derived from the German word for "confederates," became the title for the French Protestants of the 16th and 17th centuries who followed Calvin.

HUMANISM. 1. Any theory or movement in which interest in human welfare is central. **2.** Historically, the term applies to that movement of the 14th to the 16th centuries which sprang from the Renaissance and aimed at placing all learning, literary and scientific, upon a basis of classical antiquity as opposed to learning based on both classical and Christian principles. **3.** Humanism has taken several forms: as an ethical movement beginning with Auguste Comte's work which developed into "humanitarianism;" as a philosophical movement which developed into pragmatism; as a literary cult which rebelled against vocational education; as a sociological endeavor which attempted to make abstract ideals the basis of social action; as a religious movement of the 20th century which sought to subordinate "faith in God" to a social consciousness. This latter was the product of left-wing Unitarians who published in 1933 "The Humanist Manifesto."

HUMANITARIANISM. 1. A social philosophy which mistakenly places the natural good of the human race above the revealed will of God. It may be idealistic, altruistic, or moral and may center on the lesser animals of God's creation. **2.** The so-called positivism of Auguste Comte's philosophy of humanism.

HUMERAL VEIL, a long scarf, about 8 to 9 ft. long and 21 to 36 in. wide. It is worn over the shoulders of the priest at Benediction of the Blessed Sacrament and by the subdeacon at a solemn high Mass. The humeral veil is usually made of silk, and white or golden in color.

HUMILIATI, literally, "the humble ones," members of a pious association who espoused a penitential way of life. The group was wealthy and suffered pride and consequent suppression by Pope Pius V in 1571.

HUMILITY, a supernatural virtue whereby one is enabled to make a true and just estimate of himself, and is inclined to hold in contempt himself and his accomplishments in recognition that all good arises from God alone. It is said to be that "dependence on God that gives wings to prayer" (Eccu. 35:16–21). St. Ignatius terms it a relinquishment of "self-will, self-love, and self-interest." It is positive in not seeking honors and the esteem of others, and self-contemning because man knows evil as his own doing. It is exercised toward God and neighbors; toward God who as the Creator gives man whatever he possesses, and toward one's neighbors by recognizing their worth in the eyes of God. Humility is the opposite of pride, which is the root of all evil, and hence humility is basic to the practice of all the virtues. It is the fundamental of prayer, notably the prayer of simplicity, for Christ rewarded the Syrophoenician woman for her humility (Mk. 7:26–30); it is likewise to be found in Christ's example (Phil. 2:1–11). (*Cf.* PRIDE; VIRTUE.)

HYMN, a poetic composition set to music, having generally a religious theme. Hymns usually, by derivation, are songs honoring God and sung in praise of Him.

HYMNODY. 1. All hymns. **2.** Religious lyric poems. Hymnody in the Church is of two kinds: liturgical or non-liturgical. The former are those hymns which form parts of the Mass, e.g., the *Dies Irae* sung at requiem Masses, or which form portions of the Divine Office. Of these there are some 175, e.g., *Veni Creator; Stabat Mater*. The non-liturgical are those hymns which are sung at devotions or recited in private prayer.

HYPERDULIA, the veneration proper to the Blessed Mother alone, being the highest form of veneration short of adoration. (*Cf.* DULIA; LATRIA.)

HYPOSTASIS, a philosophical term from the Greek, meaning "stand under." It denotes a complete essence, subsistent in itself and not communicable to another being. When this essence is endowed with intelligence it is called a person, and this personality is referred to as an hypostasis.

HYPOSTATIC UNION, theological term introduced at the Council of Ephesus (431) which expresses the union of the human and the divine natures in Christ. An hypostatic union is a personal union by which the Incarnation was brought about; that is, that in Christ there are two complete and distinct natures joined in the one Person of Christ, the Word, who pre-existed from all time. The result of the union is the one Person who is perfect God and perfect Man. While this is a mystery, we know that reasonably Christ because of His Sonship (Heb. 1:1–14) is heir of all things (Gal. 4:7; Mt. 24:18) and is given all power "in heaven and on earth." Being God and Man in the Incarnation, Christ effected our redemption.

HYSSOP

HYSSOP, a caperplant which grows in the Holy Land (3 Kgs. 4:33). Its sprigs were bound into a bunch and used for sprinkling liquids (Ex. 12:22). (*Cf.* ASPERGES.)

I

ICON also **EIKON,** religious image, painted or glazed on flat surfaces and used in Eastern Churches instead of statues. Icons may be large or small, and may be representations on wood or metal. Some of the smaller have a hinged metal cover, usually ornate, which serves as a shield and thus enshrines the icon. The icons play a part in the liturgy of the Eastern Churches, more so than statues of the Roman rite, and an icon representing the saint whose feast is celebrated is hung on the analogion of the church during the celebration.

ICON

ICONOCLASM, from the Greek, meaning "image-breaking," name of a heresy which declared religious veneration of pictures and images unlawful. This heresy, fostered by the Paulicians, Jews and Moslems, arose in the 8th century and, aided by Eastern emperors, developed into a major struggle between Church and state. In 787, at the seventh ecumenical council, the second of Nicaea, the Church defined the distinction between adoration due to God and the veneration paid to saints, and declared that such veneration is an act of homage not to the image but to the person depicted.

ICONOCLASTS, followers of the heresy of iconoclasm.

ICONOSTASIS, in churches of the Byzantine rite, the barrier of more or less solid construction between the sanctuary and the nave which supports one or more rows of icons. An icon depicting our Lord is placed on the right and one with the image of our Blessed Mother on the left side. The iconostasis has three doorways; the one in the center consists of double half-doors which are covered by a curtain. While there is nothing quite like this feature used in churches of the Roman rite, it is paralleled by the rood-screen (q.v.).

IDIOMS, COMMUNICATION OF. Derived from the Latin, *Communicatio idiomatum,* which is the "interchange of divine and human predicates," this theological term means that due to the hypostatic union of the two natures, divine and human, in Christ, the properties or attributes which can be declared of Christ as

God may also be affirmed of Christ as man. The reverse of this is consequently true also, i.e., what is Christ's through His human nature is also possessed by Christ as God. Thus we may say, "God suffered and died." However, there is a limitation in the manner of expressing this communication, e.g., it cannot be said "the Divinity suffered and died." (*Cf.* HYPOSTATIC UNION.)

IDOLATRY, the giving to another person or object that worship which is due to God alone. Idolatry, always a grave sin, is committed: (a) by intending and actually worshiping a creature as God, called formal idolatry; (b) by worshiping God only externally, called material idolatry. Worship is due to God alone not only because of the positive, direct law given in the first commandment, but also because God alone is worthy of worship. No act of worship, however great, could satisfy the worthiness found in God (Is. 42:5–12).

IGNORANCE, the absence of knowledge in one in whom such knowledge could be present. In moral and Church law, ignorance affects the imputability of actions, the validity, or the censures to be incurred. Ignorance can be vincible, that is removable, or invincible, that is irremovable. Invincible ignorance does not incur responsibility and does not alter the validity of an otherwise valid act. Vincible ignorance is either: (a) affected or assumed. This is, for instance, if one wills not to learn in order that he may sin. It never excuses from the responsibility to or the penalty of the law; (b) crass or supine ignorance. Existing in one because he has done nothing to dispel his ignorance, it does not excuse from the penalties of the law which

are incurred by the very fact, unless otherwise qualified in the statement of the law; (c) simply grave ignorance. Present in one who tried to free himself of it but did not go far enough in his efforts, it excuses from penalties that arise from the law itself, e.g., if one learned that there was a law, but did not make himself aware of the conditions or penalties (c's. 16, 2202, 2229).

IHC or **IHS,** the letters, forming the monogram of His holy name and being derived from the Greek six-letter word for Jesus. Thus, the monogram should not be used with periods after the letters. Other interpretations of the characters are only pious fancies.

ILLUMINATIVE WAY, THE, term given to the second degree or stage in the progress of the spiritual life toward perfection. (The first, the purgative; second, illuminative; third, unitive.) It is a secondary step in the sense that one, after having gained, by mortification and meditation, a facility in the practice of virtue, proceeds to the more difficult task of overcoming faults. In the illuminative way the aim is, through the infused gifts of the Holy Spirit, to perceive Christ and follow Him. As expressed in Jn. 8:12, "He who follows Me does not walk in the darkness, but will have the light of life," there is both invitation and assurance declared in the words of our Lord. (*Cf.* CONTEMPLATION; UNION, MYSTICAL.)

IMAGE OF GOD. Man is created in the likeness of God (Gen. 1:26), and this likeness, since man is composed of body and soul, is not of one part only but of man as a whole. Likeness is, however, in the spiritual faculties of man. This likeness is also to be found in man's lordship over created things which are finite and subordinate to man as they are to their Creator. This superiority over other created things exists in man because of man's exclusive possession of intellect and will and, therefore, it is in these faculties of the soul that man's likeness to God rests. Man further improves this image of God he possesses by the practice of supernatural virtues.

IMAGES, representations of sacred things or persons. The primary purpose of images, painted, sculptured, printed, or cast, is to instruct and instill in the viewer inclinations to piety and imitation. The Church, at the second Council of Nicaea, declared that veneration of a relative nature is given to images because of the object they represent or portray, and not because of themselves (Sess. 25).

IMITATION OF CHRIST, title of a devotional book of personal directions for the practice of the virtues found so eminently in the life of Christ. It was first published early in the 14th century and has been attributed to Thomas à Kempis, but it is now held to be the work of Gerard Groote (d. 1384), a native of Deventer in Holland. This book is also titled "The Following of Christ."

IMMACULATE   CONCEPTION OF THE B.V.M. This is the privilege and the singular grace that divine omnipotence bestowed upon the Blessed Virgin Mary to preserve her free from every stain of original sin by receiving into her soul sanctifying grace from the very instant of conception in the womb of her mother, St. Anne. Through this Mary, who was to be the Blessed Mother of the Son of God, was conceived in the

state of holiness and justice. This effect, caused by the act of God, resulted in her being free of the consequences of original sin, as the slavery to the devil, and subjection to concupiscence and darkness of intellect, etc. Further, Mary was not subject to the law of suffering and death which are penalties of the sin of human nature, even though she knew these, experienced them, and endured them for our salvation. The dogma of the Immaculate Conception was defined for the Universal Church's belief by Pius IX, Dec. 8, 1854, as follows: "We declare, announce, and define that the doctrine which states that the Blessed Virgin Mary was preserved, in the first instant of her conception, by a singular grace and privilege of God Omnipotent and because of the merits of Jesus Christ the Savior of the human race, free from all stain of original sin, is revealed by God and must be believed firmly and with constancy by all the faithful." This state proclaimed for Mary is found in Gen. 3:15 where the Blessed Mother is referred to typically, and more directly in the prophetic statement in Is. 7, as well as in the angelic salutation of the angel recorded in Lk. 1:28. It is significant that the declaration of the Church through the Holy Father was made four years before the apparitions to St. Bernadette at Lourdes, France, in 1858, in which the Blessed Mother declared herself to be the Immaculate Conception. Under the Blessed Mother's title of the Immaculate Conception, the United States is dedicated to her patronage. The feast of the Immaculate Conception is celebrated on Dec. 8 and is a holyday of obligation for the universal Church (c. 1244). (*Cf.* MARY, VIRGIN MOTHER OF GOD; VIRGIN BIRTH OF CHRIST.)

IMMANENCE. 1. In scholastic philosophy, a cause is immanent whose effects begin and end in the same agent. **2.** Theologically, divine immanence is that we are in God and God in us. We are in God in that He made us and constantly aids us through grace, and God is in us through the presence of sanctifying grace in our souls. A confusion of this gave rise to modernist ideas that we are emanations from the divine which is contrary to the teaching of the Vatican Council.

IMMENSITY. By this attribute of God we understand that He is not limited to any one place but that He is everywhere, in heaven and on earth and in every place.

IMMORTALITY OF THE SOUL, the attribute by which man's spiritual substance, the soul, is immune from death. That the soul (here we do not consider the body; cf. RESURRECTION OF THE BODY) will continue to exist forever is known both by faith and reason. In Scripture, we read of man being created of body and soul (Gen. 2:7); that a part of this creation, man, continues after death (Ecce. 12:7); and, more specifically that this creature returns to God, for "the souls of the just are in the hand of God, and the torment of death shall not touch them" (Wisd. 3:1). The teaching of Christ not only confirms the O.T. truth, but He fulfilled in Himself and for man the hope of an existence outside of time, and satisfied with assurance the longing of man for security and the purpose of life in following Christ. This truth we learn not only in the Beatitudes (Mt. 5:1–12), but in the "formula" of eternal life as presented by St.

John (Jn. 16:33; 17:3; 10:10; 12:32) in a sequence which culminates in the necessity of Christ's death on the cross. There are also ample arguments from reason which demonstrate this truth of the immortality of the soul. To present only a few: (a) man universally believes in a future life and this belief, arising from his rational nature, cannot be in error; (b) man can know truth which is eternal, but he could not know truth unless in him there was a part capable of such knowledge, a receiver for that which is received, and this must be the soul; (c) man, in doing good and avoiding evil, does so for a sanction or reward, and as God's justice demands such a reward for obeying His law, yet there is no such reward in this life, it must, therefore, be reserved for the soul. (*Cf.* JUDGMENT, GENERAL.)

IMMOVABLE FEASTS, feasts given fixed days in the calendar which are not determined by the date of Easter. Such a feast may be supplanted by a feast of higher rank falling on the same day.

IMMUNITY. 1. An exemption from military service, civil office, etc., extended to the clergy (c. 121). **2.** Diplomatic immunity is the protection from physical harm granted to both persons and properties outside their own nation.

IMMUTABILITY, an attribute of God alone, since He alone is unchangeable not only in His essence but in the perfection of all His attributes. Since change implies an imperfection in the sense that something new could be added to the principal, there could be no change in God who is infinitely perfect.

IMPEDIMENTS OF MARRIAGE.

An impediment of marriage is either an external fact or circumstance which forbids marriage, sacramental or legal, and makes it invalid or unlawful. Impediments arise from the natural or divine law; from ecclesiastical law; from civil law. As such they may be divided according to their effect into: 1. Prohibitive or diriment, these making marriage either unlawful, or unlawful and invalid. 2. Absolute or relative, these forbidding marriage absolutely or between certain persons. 3. Public or occult, known or proven by legal action or not. 4. Temporary or perpetual, i.e., that they may cease or continue. 5. Of degree, or according to the defect of testimony. 6. Of divine or human right. Canon law treats all of these, but makes a division into two chief groups. The first is prohibitory, making marriage unlawful but not invalid: (a) a simple vow of virginity, a vow of perfect chastity, a vow not to marry, a vow to receive holy orders or enter religious life (c. 1058); (b) legal relationship, e.g., adoption, if it is an impediment in civil law (c. 1059); (c) mixed religion, the law forbidding a marriage between a Catholic and a baptized non-Catholic or a member of an heretical sect (c. 1060). The second group are known as diriment impediments. (*Cf.* DIRIMENT IMPEDIMENTS.)

IMPOSITION OF HANDS.

At the administration of the sacraments of baptism, confirmation, and holy orders, this is the act whereby the priest places his hands on the head or touches in a solemn manner the body of the recipient. (*Cf.* ORDERS, HOLY.)

IMPRECATORY PSALMS,

collective term for those Psalms in which there are passages which seem to invoke curses or revengeful punishment on an enemy. Psalms 17, 34, 51, 58, 68, 108, 136.

IMPRIMATUR,

the Latin word, literally "Let it be printed," used by Church authorities to extend permission for the printing of writings, prayers, pictures, etc. The word is generally followed by the name of the ordinary of the diocese in which the printing or publishing was done, or where the author lives. (*Cf.* CENSOR.)

IMPROPERIA,

that portion of the office of Good Friday recited or sung during the veneration of the cross. It consists of the "reproach" addressed to all by Christ, speaking to the Jews, notably from Micheas 6. The term sometimes is applied to the musical notation for singing this portion.

INCARDINATION,

the formal act whereby a cleric is subordinated to a superior of a diocese, a vicariate, or becomes a member in some religious community (c's. 111–118). Incardination is a necessity, for without it one cannot be ordained. Incardination may take place in several ways: 1. By reception of first tonsure, i.e., a bishop can confer tonsure on a layman who is his subject, being in the diocese of the bishop's jurisdiction by domicile. 2. By formal letters of (a) excardination followed immediately by (b) formal letters of incardination (c. 112). 3. Rarely, by reception, with written permission of his superior, of a residential benefice on the part of a cleric in a diocese other than his own. (*Cf.* EXCARDINATION.)

INCARNATION,

the assumption of human nature, including human body, human soul and will, and all human characteristics except sin, by God the

Son. Thus, there was united in one Person two natures, the divine and human. This union is known as the hypostatic union. This assumption of a human nature by the Second Person of the Blessed Trinity is foretold in the promise of a redeemer, notably in the "Emmanuel prophecy" recorded in Isaias (7:14): "Behold a virgin shall conceive, and bear a son, and His name shall be called Emmanuel." The accomplishment of this fact is stated in the Gospels (Mt. 1:23–25). St. John states it simply and forcibly: "And the Word was made flesh and dwelt among us." The purpose of the Incarnation is set forth by St. Paul (Rom. 1:16) who speaks of the Gospel as a "power of God unto salvation," for it was this "salvation" of men which was the mission of Christ on earth. St. Paul further declares (Tit. 3:4f.) that we have been saved through the Incarnation. The benefits of the Incarnation are God's goodness and grace, and these benefits are intended to be shared by all. This is declared by St. Paul (Tit. 2:11–15) in the Epistle read at the first Mass on Christmas day. (*Cf.* REDEMPTION.)

INCENSE, the hardened resins of various plants or trees which, when burned, give off an aromatic smoke. Incense may be in the form of powder or small grains. Burned in the thurible, it is used in the liturgy of the Church to offer honor to the eucharistic God, symbolizing virtue and the ascent of prayer and man's good works to the throne of God. Also used in the liturgy are unburnt grains of incense, e.g., grains are placed together with the relics in the sepulchers of altars and affixed, in the form of a cross, to the side of the paschal candle.

INDEX OF FORBIDDEN BOOKS, an official list, published by the authority of the Holy Office, condemning books or writings which have been judged by competent Church authority to be contrary to faith or morals, or discreditable to the Church. A member of the faithful may not read a writing included in this list without permission of his ordinary. In certain cases, excommunication is involved. The natural law alone forbids the reading of books which are, in prudent judgment, considered to be gravely dangerous to one's faith or morals. Thus it is not necessary that a book be listed in the Index to be forbidden. There are twelve classes of publications which are forbidden by general law (c. 1399). In brief, these are: 1. Editions of the original text and the ancient Catholic versions of the Scriptures published by non-Catholics or translations of the Scriptures made or published by non-Catholics. 2. Books which, by argument, defend heresy or schism, or which tend to undermine religion. 3. Books containing attacks on religion, good morals, divine worship and purity. 4. Books by non-Catholics treating of religion or religious discipline unless approved by authority. 5. Books which, presenting commentaries to or versions of Scripture, are published without approbation; also works on visions, etc., published without approval. 6. Books which attack Catholic dogma or the hierarchy, or which defend errors condemned by the Holy See. 7. Books which teach or encourage sorcery, magic, etc. 8. Books defending forbidden acts, as suicide, dueling, divorce, etc. 9. Books treating of or narrating obscene things, or which arouse the passions. 10. Non-official editions of liturgical books. 11. Books propagating false indulgences. 12. Printed images of our Lord, the Blessed Virgin, the angels, saints, or other servants of God which are not in keeping with the teachings of the Church.

INDICTION, a method of reckoning the years, based upon a cycle of fifteen years, beginning with the year 313.

INDIFFERENTISM. 1. Denial of the worship of God, arising from a willful failure to recognize the duty of man in matters of religion. **2.** The turning away from religious practices, patterned on the early Gnostics, out of the mistaken consideration that all religions are "relatively" true.

INDULGENCE, the remission of the temporal punishment due for sins and, hence, the satisfaction due to God for one's sins. The Church grants such indulgences after the guilt of sin and its eternal punishment have been remitted by sacramental absolution or by perfect contrition (c. 911). Indulgences are *plenary* or *partial.* Plenary, when they remit all of the temporal punishment due to sin; partial, when a part of this punishment is remitted. Should one seek to gain a plenary indulgence but, because of some unforgiven venial sin, not all of the temporal punishment is taken away, that person gains a partial indulgence at least (d. 926). As granted by the Church in terms of time (years, days, and quarantines), a partial indulgence remits as much of the temporal punishment as would be expiated by the performance of a canonical (imposed) penance in the early Church for that length of time or for the penances of a fasting season (quarantine). Indulgences as granted by the Church may be gained for oneself, or by the living for the holy souls, unless otherwise declared, but no one can gain an indulgence for another living person (c. 930).

The granting of indulgences is founded upon three doctrines of Catholic faith: the communion of saints, the treasury of the merits of Christ, and the Blessed Virgin and the saints. Determination of the extent of an indulgence and the necessary terms for its gaining are given by the authority of the Church through the Congregation of the Sacred Penitentiary. The conditions required for the gaining of an indulgence are: one must be baptized, a subject of the Church, free of excommunication, and in the state of grace and, if seeking it personally, i.e., for oneself, one must have the intention of gaining it and perform the work for which the indulgence is granted. Plenary indulgences demand that one be free from every venial sin. Indulgences officially granted by the Church are listed in the Raccolta, published by the Congregation of the Holy Office, and translated and published for use of the faithful by authorized publishers. Indulgences are strictly interpreted by the Church and governed by canon law (c's 911–936). (*Cf.* RACCOLTA.)

INDULT, the grant of a special faculty, made by the Holy See to bishops or others in authority, to do something not otherwise permitted by the general law of the Church. It is similar to the issuance of a license to perform sacred functions over and above the ordinary rules. It differs from a dispensation. (*Cf.* DISPENSATION.)

INDWELLING OF THE HOLY SPIRIT. The presence of God in the body and soul of a human person is attributed in a singular manner, both in Sacred Scripture and the writings of the fathers, to the Holy Spirit. Although God, that is the three divine Persons, are present in all places by His power, a loving indwelling takes place in a special manner in those persons of grace and sanctity, in different degree, who accept this divine familiarity by their extent of love. Thus the indwelling is the more or less perfect extension of charity, or the love of God. As expressed by Christ: "If anyone love Me, he will keep My word, and My Father will love him, and We will come to him and make Our abode with him" (Jn. 14:23). And the evangelist further explains: "If we love one another, God abides in us and His love is perfected in us. In this we know that we abide in Him and He in us, because He has given us of His Spirit" (1 Jn. 4:12–13). (*Cf.* LOVE OF GOD.)

INFALLIBILITY. In its Catholic, doctrinal meaning, infallibility is the end result of divine assistance given the Church whereby she is preserved from the possibility and liability to error in teachings on matters of faith and morals. That infallibility was always present in the Church, even from apostolic times, is frequently affirmed by actions and declarations of the apostles (Gal. 1:9) and spoken of by the fathers of the Church as the "charisma of truth" (St. Irenaeus). The doctrine of infallibility was defined by the Vatican Council (Sess. III, cap. 4) and promulgated on July 18, 1870, the day before war broke out between Germany and France, which war led indirectly to formal suspension of the Council three months later. The doctrine defines that infallibility is: 1. In the pope personally and solely as the successor of St. Peter. 2. In an ecumenical council subject to confirmation by the pope. 3. In the bishops of the Universal Church teaching definitively in union with the pope (*cf.* MAGISTERIUM). As such, infallibility does not extend to pronouncements on discipline and Church policy, and by no means includes impeccability or inerrancy of the pope in his private opinions. It is, briefly, the assured, guarantee of the unfolding of the apostolic deposit of faith by authority of the Church whereby Christ's doctrine must and will be handed on by an infallible Church guided by the Holy Spirit. It is distinguished from both biblical inspiration and revelation. (*Cf.* INSPIRATION, BIBLICAL; REVELATION.)

INFAMY, the serious loss of good name. This may be: **1.** "Infamy of fact." As arising from a known and open crime, it is canonically also called "irregularity from crime" (c. 895). **2.** "Infamy of law." This is brought about by a vindictive penalty imposed on one, or a condemnatory sentence imposed for certain crimes (c's 2314, 2320, 2328, 2343, 2351, 2356, 2357). Infamy of law ceases only by dispensation of the Holy See since it arises from common law and is perpetual. Infamy of fact ceases when by good life and a probationary period of time the good name is restored; in canon law the ordinary may declare when this restoration has taken place (c. 2295).

INFIDEL, an unbaptized person, or one not knowing or believing the divine origin of religion.

INFINITE, that which is without limits. In the negative sense, it is said of that which has no termination; in the positive, of a reality which extends without end. When referred to God, infinite is the attribute declaring that there is no limit to the perfection of God and that He has the complete fullness of every perfection, in Himself and through Himself, above all things existing or possible of existing by His creation.

INFULAE. This Latin plural word is the term applied to the two lappets which hang down from the back of a mitre. They usually have fringed ends.

INFULAE

INFUSED VIRTUES. These virtues are not acquired by the repetition of good acts prompted by grace, but gained by a direct "pouring in" by God. Thus they are more accurately called supernatural virtues or principles of action placed by God as a special gift into our souls. They are higher than acquired moral virtues, and they grow with the increase and exercise of habitual grace. (*Cf.* VIRTUE.)

IN PETTO. Literally "in the breast," this term is applied to the procedure whereby the Holy Father sometimes decides to elevate one or more to the rank of cardinal but, for various reasons, wishes to withhold the publication of his decision for a period of time. Thus the cardinal is created "in petto."

INQUISITION. 1. Historically, a legal court of the Church, sometimes operated in co-operation with the civil authority, for the investigation and sentencing of persons professing or accused of formal heresy. As such, the inquisitions were first begun in 1233 by Pope Gregory IX, based on the "Inquisitorial plan" originated by Pope Lucius III. In 1227–1299, French councils had already decreed that an "inquisition" or court consisting of one priest and two laymen should be set up in each parish to check and prevent heresy. Especially in view of the fact that barbarism was not entirely expelled by the Christian impact, this led to abuses which to some degree were in the very structure and, as seen by the authorities, in the crude application of too zealous a form of justice. Some of these abuses were: refusal of legal advisers, acceptance of testimony of heretics and excommunicates, the use of torture, and the denial of natural rights to the accused. **2.** Canonical inquisition is the inquiry made in accord with canon law prior to being summoned before an ecclesiastical court.

INQUISITION, THE SPANISH. Established as a separate and distinct use of the tribunal inquiry, the Spanish Inquisition was set up by the Catholic sovereigns, King Ferdinand and Queen Isabella, by special authorization from the Holy See in 1476. Its purpose was primarily to (a) protect the *Conversos*, the Jewish converts, from retaliation of their fellowmen and from relapse; (b) to seek out the lapsed Jewish converts, the Maranos; (c) to prevent the relapse of the *Moriscos*, the Moorish converts, and to keep them from forming harmful alliances with various heretical groups. Thus it became a semi-political machine, a mixture of ecclesiastical and state effort to protect Christian Spain when the nation faced unusual conditions. It was, however, only six years after its institution that protest was made to Rome because of cruel and illegal practices, and Pope Sixtus IV issued brief threatening penalties for abuses of canonical procedures. Torquemada, appointed Grand Inquisitor in 1486, attempted to make the Inquisition effective and, while working under the commonly accepted criminal code and procedure of his day, introduced the law of 1492 whereby the Jews were given a choice of becoming Christians or exiles. This caused great hardships to Jews, and led to open persecution and widespread abuses. It worked to the detriment of Spain, and, while the number of its victims has been exaggerated historically, the Inquisition was a ruthless tool of both zealots and political self-seekers. It continued, with vastly changed and controlled procedures, in Spain until the early 19th century.

I.N.R.I., the first letters of the Latin inscription which, by Pilate's order, was placed on the cross of Christ's crucifixion (Jn. 19:19). The words "Jesus of Nazareth, King of the Jews" were taken from Pilate's sentence. It was written in Latin, the language of administration in Judaea, and also in Hebrew (Aramaic) and Greek. That this inscription stood as written,

against the protest of the Jews who wished to disclaim Christ's kingship (Jn. 19:21), was due to the irrevocability of a Roman sentence and thus it has become the lasting testimony of the kingship of Jesus.

INSPIRATION OF SCRIPTURE. Foremost in the Catholic teaching concerning the Sacred Scriptures is this precept of inspiration by which is understood: that God is the author of the Sacred Books, that God used the agency of men to produce what He wished to be written, and that He placed in the Scriptures the contents which He wished men to have. First, we may state that the Jews accepted the fact of inspiration as is demonstrated by the record of King David when he declares: "The spirit of the Lord hath spoken by me, and His word by my tongue" (2 Kgs. 23:2). Also, Moses is recorded as having written his canticle at the dictation of God (Deut. 31:19). St. Paul, speaking to the Jews at Rome (Acts 28:25), appeals to their acceptance of inspiration as an argument, stating, "Well did the Holy Spirit speak through Isaias the prophet to our fathers ..." Second, while it is evident, it is not necessary to depend upon this argument from Scripture itself to arrive at a conviction concerning inspiration. St. Clement of Rome, the 4th pope (d. 97), in an epistle to the Corinthians affirms the inspiration of St. Paul who previously wrote to them (1 Clem. 47, 3). Likewise, St. Justin (d. 166) wrote of the prophets "being filled with the Holy Spirit." Third, the Councils of Florence, Trent, and the Vatican declare for the truth of inspiration. Fourth, Pope Leo XIII defines inspiration "as a supernatural influence whereby God so moved and impelled the sacred writers to write, and so assisted them when writing, that the things He ordered, and those only, they, first rightly understood, then willed faithfully to write down, and finally expressed in apt words and with infallible truth" (*Prov. Deus. EB.* 110). This sums up the affirmations of Catholic philosophers and theologians. (For the distinction between revelation and inspiration, *cf.* REVELATION.)

INSTALLATION, canonical term for the procedure by which one can validly take possession of an ecclesiastical office or benefice (c. 147).

INSTITUTE, RELIGIOUS. As defined by canon law, a religious institute is a community of men or women who live in accord with special rules, practicing the observance of the vows, taken simply or solemnly, of poverty, chastity and obedience (c. 487).

INTENTION. 1. The free prompting whereby the will chooses the end for which one acts and tends to use the means for undertaking the action. **2.** Sacramental intention is the disposition and purpose necessary on the part of the administering person as well as on the part of the one receiving the sacrament. The one who seeks to administer a sacrament validly and with a right intention must be aware of the intention when the sacrament is given, that is, have an *actual intention*, but a virtual intention does not invalidate. This intention must be to do the action required by the sacrament, to affect a specific person or definite matter through the sacrament. The intention necessary for the one who receives a sacrament should be at least an implicit habitual intention for valid reception; however, an explicit habitual

intention is required for reception of ordination, and a virtual intention (i.e., an intention placed consciously before the act even if at the moment of reception or during the ceremony one is distracted) is necessary for matrimony.

INTERCESSION. In general, intercession is one's praying or acting in behalf of another, usually at the request of the one to be benefited. The term is used in the Church in regard to the commendation of oneself to the saints. The Council of Trent declared in the decree to the bishops concerning instruction that they teach the faithful, "the saints, ruling together with Christ, offer their prayers for men to God, and that it is good and useful to invoke them suppliantly and to have recourse to their prayers and to their powerful help in obtaining benefits from God through Jesus Christ . . ." (Sess. 25, DB, 984). The saints follow Christ in interceding for us with God the Father (Heb. 7:25); also the act of *dulia* is performed not to obtain *from* the saints but *through* them (*cf.* DULIA). The saints, knowing of man's needs, knowing that Christ knows these also and as Mediator bestows all favors of grace through Mary, His Mother, unite theirs with the prayers of Mary, direct them to Christ, and aid us as intermediaries.

INTERDICT, a censure which deprives the faithful, either lay or cleric, of certain spiritual benefits but permits them to remain in the communion of the Church (c. 2268). An interdict may be either *personal* or *local*. The first affects a person immediately, while a local interdict may affect members of the faithful indirectly by being imposed upon a definite territory. It is said to be *general* when it includes the entire territory, and *particular* when it extends only to a part of the territory, e.g., a church. A local interdict does not forbid the administration of the sacraments to the dying if regulations are observed, but it does forbid, with several exceptions, the celebration of any divine services in the territory. A personal interdict forbids one to take part in any divine service or attendance at them, with the exception of hearing sermons (c. 2275). Anyone who causes a place to be put under interdict is personally interdicted (c. 2338). An interdict is imposed sometimes as a punishment on an entire parish for some scandal against religion or the clergy. (*Cf.* CENSURE.)

INTERIM, the historical name given to three temporary settlements between Charles V of Germany and the Lutherans: Ratisbon in 1541, Augsburg in 1548, and Leipzig in 1548. They were each attempts at restoration of religious unity. Also referred to as "Interim Religion."

INTERNAL FORUM. Forum means a place of judging and the one who judges, as well as the power of judging. In its canonical sense, the term is either *Internal forum* or *External forum.* The first one is the tribunal or the power used in matters of sacramental confession or things committed to a confessor outside the sacrament. The second, External forum, refers to that jurisdiction which is exercised for the public or social good, e.g., a dispensation granted privately and recorded in the diocesan archives or parish records.

INTERNUNCIO, a legate of the pope, a lesser representative than a nuncio. His duty is to foster friendly relations between a government and the Holy See or transact certain dealings of a more personal nature. Also called "apostolic internuncio."

INTERPRETATION, SCRIPTURAL (BIBLICAL). Also called hermeneutics, this is the science or study which determines the rules for finding and explaining the true sense of Sacred Scripture. There are two chief senses of Scripture: the *literal* and the *spiritual* (also known as typological, mystical, or real). The literal sense is that concerned with what is expressed directly by the words, that is, the meaning the writer intended to convey. The spiritual sense is the meaning expressed immediately through a person, an event or a thing by means of words, or the meaning arising directly, not from the words, but from what is signified by the words. In the spiritual sense, there are different kinds of expression: *metaphorical, allegorical,* or *anagogical.* Metaphorical, e.g., would be when in Psalm 117:22 the Israelites are described as the cornerstone; allegorical, when Christ is called the "Paschal Lamb"; anagogical, when St. Paul calls Jerusalem the heavenly city. There are certain rules or principles under which interpretation proceeds. The *general* rules are those which examine the background, e.g., history and culture of the people of the Bible; the *writer;* the *book* or literary character; and the *vocabulary* or the meaning of the words as symbols of thought expressed. *Special* principles are those which consider inerrancy, the Church authority regarding Scripture, the faith as contained in the Bible and committed to the Church, and the harmony between the two Testaments, the Old and the New. (*Cf.* EXEGESIS; INSPIRATION.)

INTERSTICES. Canon law determines the periods of time which must elapse between the reception of the several minor and major orders before ordination to the priesthood. The interval between tonsure and the different minor orders is to be determined by the bishop. The legal time between the final minor order and subdeaconship is at least one year; between subdeaconship and deaconship at least three months; and the same between deaconship and priesthood. Under certain conditions, these interstices can be lessened by the bishop (c's 974 and 978). (*Cf.* ORDERS, HOLY, SACRAMENT OF.)

INTINCTION, term for a method of giving Holy Communion, now used by some Churches of the Byzantine rite and the Melkites. Before being given to the communicant, the consecrated bread is dipped into the consecrated wine.

INTOXICATION. *See* GLUTTONY.

INTRODUCTION, BIBLICAL, the formal study in theology in which immediate preparation is given for the more advanced studies of the Scriptures. Under this title the general and special principles which govern the interpretation and defense of Scriptures are presented. It may be called biblical criticism or be included under the broader course of study embraced by the term exegesis. (*Cf.* CRITICISM, BIBLICAL; EXEGESIS; INTERPRETATION, SCRIPTURAL.)

INTROIT, the short passage of Scripture, usually from the Psalms or prophets, together with an antiphon, which forms the first words of the Mass proper. They are read when the celebrant first goes to the right side of the altar after he has said the prayers at the foot of the altar. The word is taken from the Latin word *introitus,* meaning an "entering" (*cf.* MASS). The Introit was added to the Mass in 1570 in a new missal published during the pontificate of Pius V.

INVESTITURE, term given to that practice of the early Middle Ages which was an important feature of the feudal system. In this, it was the lord's or sovereign's right to appoint to Church offices, thus subjecting churchmen, as bishops, abbots and priests, to the control of a lay person. It resulted in the historic evils of the succeeding years because no concern was paid to the qualifications necessary for assuming these responsible positions. Holy orders were conferred on ignorant, unworthy people; ambitious men chose the clerical state to attain preferment and advancement and, in this case, it sometimes led these Church opportunists to claim the right to marry. In turn, this gave rise to the custom known as "lay investiture," or the conferring by the overlord of a ring and crosier on a prelate, as signs of the right to hold office and collect revenue. As the basic cause of many evils, lay investiture was cast aside in widespread reforms, beginning with the Concordat of Worms signed in 1122 between Henry V and Pope Callistus II.

INVITATORY also **INVITATORI-UM,** the opening prayer of the Divine Office recited before Matins on each day. It consists of Psalm 94 and an antiphon that differs according to the day and season. It is omitted only on the feast of Epiphany and the last three days of Holy Week.

INVOCATION OF THE SAINTS.
See SAINTS, INTERCESSION OF.

IRREGULARITY FROM CRIME,
a canonical impediment arising from mortal, external, i.e., publicly known or occult sin. Designated to protect the dignity of the sacrament and withhold the reception from unworthy individuals, it renders it unlawful for a person to receive ordination, and indirectly forbids the exercise of orders which have been received. Irregular because of crime are: 1. Apostates, heretics, schismatics. 2. One who, except in extreme necessity, has permitted himself to be baptized by a non-Catholic. 3. Those who attempt marriage or go through a civil ceremony while bound by a valid marriage, sacred orders, etc. 4. Voluntary murderers. 5. Those who have mutilated themselves or attempted suicide. 6. Clerics who practice medicine or surgery without an apostolic indult, provided that death resulted from this practice. 7. Those who abuse sacred orders by performing acts reserved only to one in orders or to a higher order, or by those who have been forbidden to exercise their office by canonical penalty (c. 985). (*Cf.* DEFECT, IRREGULARITY OF.)

IRREMOVABILITY OF PASTORS.
This is the right granted by canon law whereby, in certain instances, the priest has stability in his assignment as pastor since he cannot be replaced without due process, voluntary retirement, or by personal request (c's. 2147–2156). (*Cf.* PARISH PRIEST.)

ITALA VETUS,
a name used in reference to the old Latin version of the Bible before the 4th century. The translation of the Vulgate was largely made by St. Jerome (d. 420) from that old Latin version at the insistence of Pope Damasus I.

ITINERARY also ITINERARIUM,
a prayer consisting of the canticle Benedictus, an antiphon, the Our Father, versicles and four collects. It has been provided as a "blessing" and prayer to be said by clerics when about to undertake a journey. It appears, for convenience, at the end of the Breviary.

J

JACIST, name of a particular branch of the Jocist movement, the Young Christian Farmer (*Jeunesse Agricole Chrétienne*). Its membership is made up of young farm workers and it is dedicated to promote the spiritual welfare of its members through the ideal of Catholic Action (cf. JOCIST).

JACOBINS. 1. The name applied to members of a political group of the French Revolution. This group, founded in 1789 at Versailles, France, assumed a religious guise by accepting for membership persons from religious orders. **2.** Name, more or less popular, applied to early French Dominicans. The name was derived from the first Dominican house in Paris on the Rue St. Jacques. **3.** Name given to liberals or those holding radical views on matters of religion or politics. As such, it is derived from the French revolutionary group who later became radical extremists.

JACOBITE CHRISTIANS, a group of heretical monophysites of the 6th century. The name derived from the group's founder, *Jacobus* Baradai, Bishop of Edessa.

JAMES, LITURGY OF ST. This early form of the liturgy was developed in Jerusalem from the Antiochene liturgy, and later supplanted by the liturgy of Constantinople. It appears now only in remnant form in the liturgies of some Eastern Churches.

JANSENISM. This movement had its origin in the book, *Augustinus*, published in 1640, two years after the death of the author Cornelius Jansen, Bishop of Ypres. It developed a system whose principal teachings centered in the denial of man's ability to resist temptation and the rejection of the doctrine that Christ died for all men. These teachings were vigorously attacked by theologians. Later, in the 17th century, the followers of Jansenism practiced austerities and claimed that only persons with perfect contrition could receive the sacraments of penance and Holy Eucharist. It was a harsh, unyielding teaching which declared that men could not keep some of the commandments. Its influence was extensive for many years and led to a particularly un-Catholic attitude toward moral issues which is still evident in rigoristic moral teachings. Jansenism was condemned as early as 1654 by a decree of Pope Innocent X (d. 1655).

JANUARIUS, MIRACLE OF ST., the name applied to a famed liquefaction of a phial of solidified blood, said to be blood of the martyr St. Januarius (d. 305). The change of this blood from solid to liquid form takes place 18 times during the year on major feast days. The phial is kept in the Cathedral of Naples.

JEHOVAH, a hybrid form of the Hebrew name of God which is *Yahweh*. Also called the Tetragrammaton, meaning "four letters," namely JHWH which is read Yahweh.

JERONYMITES. Also called *Hieronymitae* or Hieronymites, these were several groups of religious hermits in Spain and Italy who followed the way of life of St. Jerome. They flourished for a time in the late 14th and early 15th century.

JERUSALEM, the principal city of the Holy Land. Its name is taken from the Hebrew, meaning "city of peace." As a city, Jerusalem was written of as early as 2000 B.C., under the name Ursalim, in Egyptian texts. A strategic site midway between the northern and southern tribes of the Israelites, it was selected by King David (d. 972 B.C.) as his capital. His choice was made to establish the best site from a political, military and religious point of view. It was the city in which the passion, death, and resurrection of Christ took place, and is thus honored among Christians. The Jerusalem that Christ knew was destroyed in 70 A.D. by the Roman general, Titus. It is situated 15 miles west of the Jordan River on a range of mountains running north and south, lengthwise of Palestine. As a name, it is celebrated as a symbol of the lot of the people of Israel, and it is borrowed as a symbol of reward or heaven (Apoc. 21:2 and 18ff).

JERUSALEM, PATRIARCHATE OF. Established in the administration of the Church, the see of Jerusalem became a patriarchate in 451 by declaration of the Council of Chalcedon. It was led into schism in 1453, partly because of political ill-feeling and continued resentment dating back to the time when Constantinople was given importance and recognition in the 5th and 6th centuries. It remains a unit of the Orthodox Eastern Church with its patriarch in authority.

JESSE-WINDOW—From the Cathedral of Chartres, 12th century.

JESSE-WINDOW, a stained-glass representation of the genealogy of Christ, in the form of a multibranched tree. It took its name from Jesse, the father of King David, who was the root of the line of descent.

JESUATS, a popular name applied to the members of the congregation of the Apostolic Clerics of St. Jerome. They were suppressed in 1668 by Clement IX because of abuses of their rule. They are not to be confused with "Jesuits."

JESUIT REDUCTIONS, mission settlements founded by the Jesuits in South America. As a consequence of false accusations concerning the Jesuits' political ambition, their settlements were destroyed in the early 18th century.

JESUIT RELATIONS, collections of letters written by Jesuit missioners from their missions, particularly those of North America. The "Relations" include personal letters, letters of an instructive nature to fellow religious, and most notably those documents intended for publication. They are a basic source of information on early life among the natives, on topography and conditions such as weather, natural resources, etc.

JESUIT RINGS. In the latter half of the 17th Century, the Jesuit missionaries used to award rings to converts in New York State territory. The rings were made of brass or bronze and showed religious representations.

JESUITS, the name of members of the Society of Jesus. Originally this was a group of clerks regular, called "Company of Jesus," founded by St. Ignatius of Loyola in 1534. The Jesuits engage in teaching, missionary and parish work, and conducting retreats.

JESUS. *See* HOLY NAME OF JESUS; CHRIST.

JEWS, THE. Their name is derived from the Hebrew for Judah, name of one of the twelve Hebrew tribes and of one of the two kingdoms. The Jews are an ancient people whose ancestors were nomads and whose original home was Arabia from where they migrated to near-by regions. Their history as a nation begins with the call of Abraham to the worship of the one true God. From that time also dates the destiny of the Israelites as the Chosen People (Gen. 12:1ff). Their history comes up through the ages, with little unity achieved until King David (1012–972 B.C.) founded the first real monarchy. But, following a revolt of the ten tribes which was a divine punishment for Solomon's (d. 931 B.C.) worship of false gods, a division took place, resulting in the foundation of two kingdoms, Judah and Israel. With the last of the Machabees, Simon, in 134 B.C., the rule of Israel first passed on to the Hasmonean leaders and then to the Herodians, 40 B.C. Domination by the Romans followed and continued through the time of Christ. In the years 66–70 A.D., the Jews revolted but suffered bitter defeat resulting in the destruction of the temple in Jerusalem, that symbol of the religion identified with the Hebrew nation. This was the break between the new, rising Christianity and Judaism. Then followed the *diaspora*, the scattering of communities of Jews throughout the world. From ancient time to the present, the Jews have suffered persecution, most frequently because of their refusal to accept the burden of responsibility as the chosen people, or because of their religious and nationalistic feeling. The Nazi and Soviet persecutions of the 20th century and even the callous anti-Semitic feeling of the republican peoples, are types of this historic pattern. The Jewish religion, of external observance and deep interior piety, has maintained a singular nationalistic pattern, but in more recent times there has been a growing division in their formality of legal observances, namely, the distinction between the orthodox and the reformed. In many respects, the Jewish historians have been more fair in the treatment of their persecutors and the peoples among whom they reside than has been the record of history concerning them. Following the second world war, the Israeli nation, under the influence of their widespread recognition and united effort, has again achieved a single land and center, though it still is a divided unit. While this begins a new phase of their history, it remains to be determined by future developments what this new nation will attain.

JOB, BOOK OF, the twentieth book of the O.T., most probably written by Moses about the 7th century B.C. It records the life and problems of a God-fearing man, Job, who lived in the land of Hus which bordered Arabia. The theme of this prose-poem concerns wisdom and seeks to teach, presenting the problem of and answer to whether a man may be innocent and yet suffer the ills of nature and life. The answer to its problem remains that the suffering of the innocent still rests in the inscrutable will of God. It also teaches the justice of God (31:3), the duties of man (Ch. 31), that before God no man is innocent (4:17), and that man will survive after death (14:15).

JOCIST, the J.O.C. movement, taken from the French title *Jeunesse Ouvriere Chrétienne* (Young Christian Workers). This was an organized movement of specialized Catholic Action founded in Belgium by Canon Joseph Cardijn in the early twenties. Its objective is multiple, but centers on the union of effort by men to make, with the grace of God, all work and all pursuits an apostolate. It aims to (1) form the wage earner, the professional man, the farmer, and the student along the Christian pattern with Christ as the ideal; (2) to transform all these pursuits, the individuals, and their social life by Christlike ideals, and by example to effect the spread of religion; (3) to form groups which will encourage and aid individuals along these ideals. Its pattern of effective method is to "observe, judge and act," or size up a situation, to see how best to apply Christian principles, and then take steps to change the situation along Christian lines. This Catholic Action movement was introduced into the United States at Manchester, N. H., in 1935, under the name "Young Christian Workers."

JOEL, a prophetic book of the O.T., named after its author Joel (Jahweh is God), the son of Pethuel, who lived and prophesied probably during the reign of Joas (836–797 B.C.). The book tells of a plague and the penance of the people, and the outpouring of the Spirit and salvation.

JOHN, GOSPEL OF ST. The Fourth Gospel of the N.T. It is not classed as synoptic but is regarded as the culmination of the revelation of Christ. Traditionally, it is said to have been written by St. John, the evangelist and "beloved disciple," in the year 100 A.D. It is regarded as a historical book of great dogmatic value, for the author, by recording certain events in the life of Christ and by special selections from His words, points out the revealed glory of Christ. In the words of St. John (20:31), the book was written "that you may believe that Jesus is the Christ, the Son of God, and that believing you may have life in His name." Its principal doctrines are: that Jesus of Nazareth is the Israelite

Messias and truly God, the Second Person of the Trinity (3:16–18); that Christ is the Savior; that the work of Christ continues through the Holy Spirit both for individuals and the Church (16:5–15); the role of the Church; the interior working of grace; and the precept of charity.

JONAS, BOOK OF. This brief prophetical book of the O.T., also called Book of Jonah, was probably written by Jonas himself in the reign of Jeroboam II (782–753). Its central theme is the world-wide love and providence of God.

JOSEPH, ST., the foster father of Jesus Christ, the betrothed (i.e., in Jewish law, the husband) of the Blessed Mother (Mt. 1:19). St. Joseph is characterized as a "just" man, and this is evidenced by his "just" treatment of Mary in not seeking publicity for her when she was known to "be with child." It is through Joseph that Christ has "legal" descent from David. St. Joseph is honored in the Church as her universal patron and this patronage is celebrated on March 19. Another feast is that of St. Joseph the Workingman, celebrated on May 1.

JOSUE, BOOK OF, a prophetic-historic book of the O.T. of unknown authorship. It is also called Book of Joshua. Its principal religious teaching is the fidelity of God to His promise, for it narrates the promise made to Abraham that his descendants would come to possess the land of Canaan. From the name Josue comes the Greek form of the name: Jesus.

JOYFUL MYSTERIES. See MYS-TERIES OF THE ROSARY.

JUBILATE SUNDAY, name given to the third Sunday after Easter.

JUBILEE. 1. In Church use, a time of prayer and penance, announced by the Holy Father. The Church proclaims special indulgences, notably a plenary indulgence, for the occasion. The word is probably derived from the Hebrew "Jabel," meaning "ram's horn used as a cornet." In Jewish history, the 7th year was the sabbatical year or a year of rest, and the 50th year was celebrated as a year of rest and restitution, particularly a fallow year, the reverting of property to former owners, emancipation of slaves, and the remission or suspension of debts (Lev. 25:1–55). Both events in Jewish Law were begun by the blowing of a ram's horn trumpet. In the Church, the first Jubilee was celebrated in 1300 by Pope Boniface VIII. Since 1470, the custom has been to announce an "Ordinary Jubilee" every 25 years. The pope may, however, proclaim an "Extraordinary Jubilee" in the event of any special centennial or unusual time, e.g., a golden anniversary of a pope's ordination. Each jubilee proclamation is accompanied by a document which sets forth the requirements for gaining the indulgences and the special faculties granted to ordinaries and confessors. **2.** The so-named "Book of Jubilees" is an apocryphal writing, narrating the O.T. and probably written in the late 1st or 2nd century A.D.

JUDGES, BOOK OF. The 7th book of the O.T. is so named because of the national heroes whose deeds form its main theme. The word "judge" here does not mean *ruler*, but one who distributes justice to the people and maintains the rights of the downtrodden and, thus, "judge" is used here as the equivalent of "deliverer." As an historical book, Judges contains the religious history of Israel from the time of Josue to Samuel. It covers a period of about 150 years (1200–1050 B.C.), and the time of the six great judges is arranged in chronological order. In particular, the book teaches the religious interpretation of the history of the chosen people, the wisdom of God, His justice and holiness, His mercy and His punishment of sin, especially grave sin, e.g., idolatry.

JUDGES, SYNODAL. These judges of ecclesiastical courts are chosen in the diocesan synod; those selected outside of a synod are called pro-synodal. Such judges must be priests and should be skilled in canon law (c. 1574). (*Cf.* SYNOD.)

JUDGMENT, GENERAL. The act of God, sometimes called the "Day of Jahweh," prophesied to follow the end of the world as we know it, or the cosmic ruin of the earth and its inhabitants (Joel 2:28ff.; Acts 2:17ff.) It was to follow the second coming of Christ (1 Cor. 1:8). This time will be when, through the Second Coming, the spiritual kingdom of God will be restored. It is called the Parousia and it was foretold by Christ (Mk. 13:24). The event of the Parousia will be followed by the Judgment and the Renewal at the end. At this time, the former corporeal condition of man will be spiritualized, i.e., men will arise in some transformation (1 Cor. 15:35–57). Then will all be judged and their eternal reward or punishment fixed (Jn. 5:28, 29).

JUDGMENT OF GOD. An early method of trial, practiced in the time before legal procedures were established, whereby it was contended that the innocence of a person would be established by the direct, perhaps even miraculous, intervention of God if the conditions were fair for such a conclusion. It was a superstitious practice.

JUDGMENT, PARTICULAR, the judgment of the soul of one who has died, immediately after death, and wherein the salvation or damnation of the person for all eternity is determined. This is not an intermediate step between the death of an individual and the final or general judgment of all mankind. It is the immediate satisfaction of hope for the individual in accord with his merit and degree of service and love as well as a judgment concerning guilt (Rom. 8:28–34). (*Cf.* PURGATORY.)

JUDICA PSALM, the name applied to Psalm 42. Preceded and followed by the versicle "I will go unto the altar of God," this Psalm is recited before all Masses except requiems and Masses said during Passiontide. It forms the first portion of the prayers recited by the celebrant and acolyte at the foot of the altar.

JUDITH, BOOK OF. This historical book of the O.T. was most probably written in Hebrew by an unknown author, but undoubtedly later than the date of the events which it records, namely, the reign of Nabuchodonosor (605–562 B.C.). Its doctrinal teaching is the merciful help of God and His justice.

JURISDICTION. This power belonging to the Church as a perfect society, whereby the Church effects a rule to the spiritual good of its members, has been defined as: "the public power granted by Christ or by

His Church through canonical mission, of governing the baptized in matters referring to salvation." It thus refers to the power to make or pass laws, and to enact and pass sentences and to punish. Jurisdiction is *ordinary* when it is attached to an office of the Church, e.g., the power of diocesan bishops to govern in their dioceses. It is *delegated* when it is given by one having the right to another, e.g., the faculty for hearing confession given to an assistant priest. Only the pope has universal jurisdiction, i.e., it extends to all baptized persons everywhere, independently of any civil authority, in all that concerns the proper object of the Church's mission or the salvation of souls (c. 218).

JUSTICE. 1. The cardinal and moral virtue by which one, having due regard for both law and duty, gives to everyone his due, i.e., what is owed to him as a human being, be it due in actual goods or those things which are his because of dignity. Therefore this extends certainly to God, to one's neighbor, as well as to oneself. It is exercised in respect to the rights of others, while at the same time subjectively, with charity, it governs man's relationship to others. It is the prime cardinal virtue and includes many subordinate virtues. As an imperative virtue, justice implies obedience, truthfulness, gratitude and religion, as applied in regard to God, one's neighbor, or oneself. **2.** The

state of *original justice* is that condition possessed by Adam and Eve before they sinned, or that condition under which they possessed everything that was their "due" as created by God for His glory. **3.** *Social justice* is that which regards the rights of the common good or the relations of the individual to society. **4.** Justice also may take various subdivisions which in turn are only aspects of the application of the virtue. These may be for example: *commutative* justice, or the virtue regulating the actions or rights existing between single individuals; *distributive* justice, or that between superiors and subjects; *legal* justice, or that which is concerned with the individual and the society to which the person belongs as a subject.

JUSTIFICATION, primarily and simply the possession of sanctifying grace. However, before this possession can be accomplished there must be baptism and this is, in order of sequence, preceded by faith, the virtue of acknowledgment of God, and acceptance of the consequences of that belief. Thus the Council of Trent (Sess. III, Ch. 8) declared "Faith is the beginning of man's salvation, the foundation and root of all justification; without which (i.e., faith) it is impossible to please God and to obtain fellowship with his sons." Faith is man's assent to revealed truth (Council of Trent, Sess. III, Ch. 3). It is thus the basis of justification (Rom. 1:16–17).

K

KALEMAUKION

KALEMAUKION, the black, cylinder-shaped head-covering, with a flat brim at the top, worn commonly and for liturgical functions by clerics of the Byzantine rite. Bishops and monks wear it with a veil that covers it and falls down to the shoulders.

KENOSIS, a broad term derived from the Greek word for "empty," applied to the "kenotic theories" or certain heretical theories which have been advanced by Protestant theologians concerning the Incarnation. In one way or another they attempt to advance the idea that Christ "gave up," "divested himself," of certain divine attributes in becoming man, basing their idea on a mistaken interpretation of the passage of St. Paul's letter to the Philippians, 2:6–9. Its proper meaning is not that Christ "emptied" Himself of a part or all of His divinity, but concealed or did not permit His Godhead to be evident.

KEYS, POWER OF. *See* POWER OF THE KEYS.

KINGDOM OF GOD. In the O.T., this was the governing of the people of Israel by God. Later, the Israelites came to look forward to a "new" kingdom. In the N.T., there are numerous references to the "kingdom of God," and parables which speak in a less direct manner of this kingdom having come through Christ. Most emphatically has the knowledge of this kingdom and the knowledge of the mystery of the Incarnation been given to the disciples of Christ. It is a declaration of the divinity of Christ (Lk. 10;2–23), the knowledge of which the disciples will bring to others that they may attain to their salvation—participation in God's love in heaven.

KING JAMES VERSION OF THE BIBLE. This translation of the Bible, known as the "Authorized Version," was undertaken in 1607 at the order of King James I. It is a revision of the earlier and faulty version, called the Bishop's Bible (1568). The King James Version became the official Bible of the Church of England, but it is now largely displaced by other versions. Catholics are forbidden to use it.

KINGS, BOOK OF, the collective name given to four distinct historical books of the O.T. The first and second, known as First and Second Books of

213

Samuel, are a continuation of the history of Israel, following that of the Book of Judges, covering the period of Samuel and the two kings whom he anointed, Saul and David. These books were written by an unknown author probably before the end of the exile, i.e., the 6th century B.C. They proclaim the religious history of Israel and the national faith, and bring insight into the reign of that king from whose great line of descendants there would arise Christ, the King of kings. The Third and the Fourth Book of Kings are also known as First and Second Books of Kings when the preceding books are named the First and the Second Book of Samuel. These Books cover a span of some 400 years, recounting the last days of King David, the reign of Solomon, the division of the kingdoms, the destruction of the temple, and the exile. The last two Books were written before 530 B.C. The authorship is, but doubtfully, attributed to Jeremias.

KINGSHIP OF CHRIST. Based upon scriptural declarations (Lk. 1:33) and the traditional teaching of the Church, Christ is King (1) by birthright as the Son of God; (2) by right as the Redeemer; (3) by the power which is His as legislator, judge and executor (Acts 10:42). In 1925, Pope Pius XI in his encyclical, *Quas Primas*, formally set forth the doctrine of the Kingship of Christ and declared the last Sunday in October the date for celebration of the liturgical feast of Christ the King.

KISS, LITURGICAL USE OF. The kiss as a mark of honor and reverence is frequently used in the liturgy of the Church, e.g., kissing of the altar by the celebrant during Mass. As a more formal salute and a mark of brotherly affection of Christians, the *Pax* or "Kiss of Peace" is given at solemn Mass after the *Agnus Dei*. After kissing the altar, the celebrant places his arms over the arms of the deacon and, while they bow to each other, the celebrant says *Pax tecum* (Peace be to you) to which the deacon responds with *Et cum spiritu tuo* (And with your spirit). The *Pax* is then passed on similarly to the subdeacon and other clerics present.

KNIGHTS OF COLUMBUS, a fraternal organization of Catholic men founded in New Haven, Conn., in 1882, to develop and promote genuine Catholicity among its members. It is devoted to works for promotion of charity and education, furtherance of historical study, and provision of benefits to members and survivors in the families of deceased members. It is organized to function under an executive board, a supreme council and sub-councils which are either state or subordinate councils.

KNIGHTS, ORDERS OF. The 12th century saw the rise of several orders of knighthood which were actually religious orders while at the same time they were military in character. As such, the knights took the three vows of poverty, chastity, and obedience, and shared the immunities of monks; they were directly under the Holy See. These orders were: Knights of Hospitallers of St. John, founded in 1113; Knights Templars, organized in 1118; the Teutonic Order of Knights, begun in 1190.

KNIGHTS, PAPAL, honorary titles conferred by the papal court on laymen for outstanding services rendered to the welfare of society, and to the Church and its welfare. In rank, the titles range from prince to baron, inclusive. According to their importance these are: 1. Supreme Order of Christ; 2. Order of Pius IX; 3. Order of St. Gregory the Great; 4. Order of St. Sylvester; 5. Order of the Golden Militia or Golden Spur; 6. Order of the Holy Sepulcher.

KNOW-NOTHINGISM. This political movement began in 1852 in the United States as a residue of the defunct Native American Party. Its object was to seize political power to carry out its program of marked hostility to foreigners and Catholics. The members of this secret society were bound by oath to answer all questions concerning their activities with the reply "I don't know." The movement gained some power in several eastern states to put through several anti-Catholic statutes but, not being endorsed by either of the major political parties, it faded rapidly after 1857 and disappeared entirely.

KNOX VERSION, the translation of the Bible, from the Vulgate, by Msgr. Ronald A. Knox. Begun in 1939, it was published in 1949. The task was undertaken at the request of the hierarchy of England and Wales. This work is marked by a greater use of prose form, and a choice of words which are based upon the most recent research, and thus are more compatible with modern spoken English.

KU-KLUX-KLAN, a variously-formed society, begun in the post-Civil War years at Pulaski, Tenn. It was a secret group organized against Catholics, Jews, Negroes and the foreign-born. Its history, with its various changes and reorganizations, is most ignoble. In 1928, its title was changed to "Knights of the Green Forest," and just prior to World War II it took on a Fascist-Nazi character. It is defunct, local bad-boy antics notwithstanding, and has been rejected by all right-thinking people.

KYRIALE, a book of chant. It contains the words and musical notation for the Ordinary of the Mass, i.e., the Kyrie, Gloria, Credo, Sanctus, Agnus Dei, and the antiphons Asperges and Vidi Aquam.

KYRIE ELEISON, the invocation of the Trinity said in the Mass before the *Gloria*. It consists of: the invocation of God the Father by saying three times the Greek words *Kyrie Eleison* (Lord, have mercy!), the invocation of God the Son by reciting three times the words *Christe Eleison* (Christ, have mercy!), and the invocation of the Holy Spirit by repeating three times *Kyrie Eleison*.

LABARUM

L

LABARUM. The military standard, first used by Constantine in 312 as a sign of his conversion to Christianity, consisted of a staff with a loosely fastened, short cross-arm from which the banner streamed. In the Church, it is sometimes seen in symbols, e.g., a sheep holding the staff.

LADY CHAPEL. Small chapels, dedicated to the Blessed Mother, are so named.

LADY DAY, a name applied in some places to the Feast of the Assumption, Aug. 15.

LAETARE MEDAL, a gold medal presented annually by the University of Notre Dame on Laetare Sunday. It is awarded to Catholic laymen of the U. S. who have served their country and their Church in a distinguished manner. A citation setting forth the reasons for the award accompanies the medal.

LAETARE SUNDAY, the title of the 4th Sunday of Lent, taken from the first Latin word of the *Introit* which means "Rejoice." This Sunday is distinguished in the liturgy as one of the occasions in the Roman rite when rose-colored vestments may be worn. It also is the day on which a traditional award of the Church, the Golden Rose, is blessed.

LAICISM, the erroneous concept that the administration of the Church can and should be in the hands of the laity. More recently, those advancing this thought of a break between Church and state maintain that all affairs of human society, as education, hospitals, government and labor, should be conducted without regard to religion. These attempts are classed under the term secularism. Historically there have been many forerunners of laicism such as Gallicanism, Febronianism, etc. Laicism was condemned by Pope Pius IX, Dec. 8, 1864, in the encyclical *Quanta Cura*, called the "Syllabus of Errors." (*Cf.* SECULARISM.)

LAMB OF GOD. 1. In Jewish sacrifices, especially at the Passover, a lamb was often the victim. As such, in Scripture, the lamb prefigured the Messias. As a title, it was applied directly to Christ by St. John the Baptist (Jn. 1:29-34) when he pointed his finger at Christ and declared

216

"Behold the Lamb of God." In this sense, the lamb, a symbol of innocence, is Christ and He is designated as one sent by God to be offered up as God wishes. Further recognition is given to this understanding of Christ as the Lamb of God at the Last Supper when Christ and his disciples gather to eat the Pasch and the two sacrifices, of the feast of the Pasch and of the New Law which is there instituted, are paralleled (Lk. 22:7–23). **2.** The lamb as a symbol in Christian art refers to Christ. It is often seen bearing a *labarum*, or as reclining on a book with seven seals as described by St. John (Apoc. 5:1–6). **3.** The title of a prayerful appeal, the *Agnus Dei*, recited three times in the Mass.

LAMENTATIONS, a book of the O.T. consisting of poetic elegies, attributed to the prophet Jeremias. It contains laments over the destruction of Jerusalem in 586 B.C. by the Neo-Babylonians and, since this and the accompanying sufferings followed upon frequent transgressions of God's law, also a number of confessions of guilt and appeals for mercy. The book emphasizes the power of God and the necessity to seek His mercy. The Lamentations are recited in the Office of the Tenebrae during Holy Week.

LAMMAS DAY, an old and seldom used name for the feast of St. Peter-in-Chains, celebrated August 1.

LAMPS. First introduced into the Church out of necessity, lamps became later symbols of honor. In the early Middle Ages they were hung before reliquaries and the tabernacle. From the 13th century onward, the lamp has been used to honor continually the Divine Presence. It is now called the sanctuary lamp, and

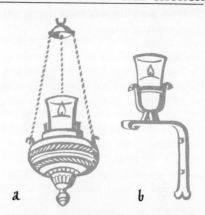

LAMPS—Sanctuary lamps (a) suspended by chains; (b) bracket type.

it is required that at least one lamp should burn continually before the Blessed Sacrament. If more than one lamp is used, the number should be uneven. It also is required that this lamp burn olive oil, beeswax, or vegetable oils, and be suspended or rise at least 7 ft. off the floor.

LANCE, THE HOLY. 1. The spear used to pierce the side of Christ during the crucifixion. Several portions are claimed as relics, but none are authenticated. One portion, allegedly found by St. Helena at Jerusalem, is preserved in St. Peter's in Rome. **2.** A liturgical instrument called the *lance* is a small, usually golden, two-edged knife, used in Byzantine liturgies to cut portions of the bread to be consecrated. **3.** A symbol in the form of a spear, of several saints, notably SS. Matthew, Thomas, and Longinus.

LANGUAGE OF THE CHURCH. In the Roman rite, the language used in the liturgy is Latin. Latin is also used for the official pronouncements, the definition of doctrine, the legal documents and canon law of the Church. It is used for historical reasons, and for accuracy from the standpoint of stability. By an apostolic indult of 1954, the Holy Office has granted to the English speaking Catholics of the United States and Canada the use of English in the ceremonies of matrimony, baptism, and extreme unction, with the exception of the words of the form and the exorcisms. This grant also permits the use of English in the giving of twenty-six blessings and the blessings for burial of adults and infants.

LAPPET. See INFULAE.

LAPSED, a term, from the Latin word *lapsi,* applied from the 3rd century to Christian converts who had abandoned the practice and faith of Catholics and returned to pagan practices and beliefs. There were three classifications, those who offered incense at pagan ceremonies, who partook in pagan sacrifices and those who obtained, false or true, legal documents saying they had conformed to pagan requirements. More recently, the term "lapsed Catholic" has been, not too accurately, applied to one who has become either a heretic, apostate, schismatic or who has failed to comply with the requirement of making his Easter duty.

LAST DAY. See JUDGMENT, GENERAL.

LAST SUPPER. At this momentous event of the gathering of the apostles and Christ in the Upper Room for the eating of the Pasch, Christ instituted the sacrament of the Holy Eucharist, Christ's gift of Himself. This fact of the redeeming mission of Christ foreshadowed the sacrificial act which took place the following day: the crucifixion (Lk. 22:14–22). Christ's redeeming mission was to be repeated by the apostles, and St. Paul

(1 Cor. 11:24) recalls this twenty-five years later (*cf.* EUCHARIST, HOLY). It was also at the Last Supper that Christ spoke of His relationship to God the Father (Jn. 16:22–33) and the love of God which marks His followers (Jn. 14:23).

LAST THINGS. See ESCHATOLOGY.

LATAE SENTENTIAE. This expression refers to a penalty which is incurred by the very fact of transgréssion (*ipso facto*), i.e., deliberate action. The wording of the law must indicate that the penalty, e.g., excommunication, is incurred by committing a forbidden act. (*Cf.* FERENDAE SENTENTIAE.)

LATERAN CHURCH. Officially, the Church of our Most Holy Savior, called St. John Lateran, is the Cathedral of the bishop of Rome, the pope. The basilica, part of a donation of the Laterani family, was presented to the Church in 311.

LATERAN COUNCILS. Of those councils of the Church held at Rome, the first, in 313, decided against the Donatists; the second, in 649, condemned the false teaching of "one will" in Christ as advanced by the Monothelite heresy; the third, in 769, repudiated Iconoclasm; the fourth, in 1059, laid down the procedure for the election of popes; the fifth, called the First Lateran, was the ninth of the ecumenical councils and the first general council in the West, held in 1123 (*cf.* ECUMENICAL COUNCILS); the sixth, called the Second Lateran, (tenth ecumenical), was convened in 1139 to settle the schism of the antipope, Anacletus; the seventh, called the Third Lateran (eleventh ecumenical), held in 1179, condemned the Albigenses and enacted clerical reforms; the eighth, called the "Great Council" (Fourth Lateran), met in 1215. Presided over by Pope Innocent III, it established Easter Communion and set up the four years' truce of all Christian nations. The ninth, called the Fifth Lateran, of 1512, established a censorship of books among other actions. (*Cf.* COUNCILS.)

LATERAN TREATY. By this treaty between the Holy See and the Italian government, signed Feb. 11, 1929, Vatican City became an independent state; Catholicism was declared the official religion of Italy and religion was made a part of public school courses; the Holy See renounced all claim to the historic papal states; canon law of the Church was accepted as valid throughout the Italian countries. (*Cf.* VATICAN STATE, CITY OF.)

LATIN. Now called a "dead" language, Latin originated in Latium, the mid-province of Italy, and became the dominant language of the Roman empire. It was the commonly spoken language of all peoples of the Western world, the legal language of Rome and the means of transmitting the culture of Rome. (*Cf.* LANGUAGE OF THE CHURCH.)

LATIN RITE, the Roman Church liturgy. (*Cf.* ROMAN RITE.)

LATRIA, that worship which is reserved to God alone. The word is derived from the Greek term for "to serve" and thus, by extension, has come to mean adoration. Distinctive of this form of worship, due to God because of His infinite excellence and the homage owed to Him by man as a created being, is sacrifice; the one and only sacrifice of the New Law is the most holy sacrifice of the Mass. (*Cf.* CULT; DULIA; HYPERDULIA.)

LATROCINIUM. *See* EPHESUS, ROBBER SYNOD OF.

LATTEN. *See* BRASSES.

LAUDS. Literally "praises," this is the name given to the second hour of the Divine Office. It is composed of four Psalms, a canticle together with antiphons, a little chapter, hymn and versicle, the Benedictus and orations, the collect of the day and commemorations. (*Cf.* DIVINE OFFICE.)

LAURA, term applied to a series of streets or an area about which there are arranged small hermitages of monks, attached to or supported by a monastery. While the monks live a quasi-hermit life along or within the *laura*, they participate in some of the community life and in the religious duties of the monastery.

LAVABO, the ceremony of purification during the celebration of the Mass. It takes place on the epistle side of the altar and consists of the physical washing of his hands by the celebrant. The title comes from the first word ("I will wash . . .") of the portion of Psalm 25 which the celebrant recites while washing his thumbs and forefingers. The *Lavabo* follows the Offertory and is an act in preparation for the Consecration. Besides the evident use of the act, it is symbolical of the washing of the apostles' feet by Christ which, in turn, was a symbolical act of spiritual cleanliness (Jn. 13:8–10).

LAW. Basically, law is a reasonable, intellectual rule which one who holds authority imposes upon many for the common good. Law can only be reasonable when the one in authority can see the consequences of what he imposes, and knows and seeks the general good. Imposition of the law is by promulgation, i.e., making it known to those it binds. It is applied to many rather than to one because it is to affect the group, e.g., society. Law also is applied to a body or system of rules, e.g., canon law.

Law may be divided into many cumulative groups of rules, as common law, civil law, etc. However, law as applied to human beings, called human law, is divided broadly into: *eternal, natural, positive*. Eternal law, also called *divine* law, is the divine wisdom that directs all created to their true end. A natural law is the eternal law as seen in all creation and by which all things are inclined to their natural acts and ends. Such natural laws may be *physical*, e.g., the law of gravitation, or *metaphysical*, e.g., the unchangeableness of the essence of a thing. A positive law is one which is made known as the will of the lawgiver, e.g., a moral law as "You shall not kill," or a jurisdictional law such as an article of the Bill of Rights. (*Cf.* CANON LAW.)

LAXISM, a moral system whereby one who seeks a right or at least an informed conscience, is permitted to follow the opinion or evidence which favors or inclines toward liberty, i.e., to evade the acceptance of an obligation, even though the opinion is open to doubt and question. Laxism was condemned in 1679 by Pope Innocent XI because it leads to the judging of sinful practices as lawful.

LAY BAPTISM, the administration of the sacrament of baptism by a lay person or by one who is not designated as an ordinary minister. Lay persons may only lawfully baptize when there is danger of death and only then when no priest is present (c. 742). Also, should the one lawfully baptized by a lay person survive,

those ceremonies omitted in the baptism must be supplemented in church as soon as possible (c. 759). (*Cf.* BAPTISM.)

LAY BROTHERS AND SISTERS. These men and women who are members of a religious order or community, but are not in holy orders and are not choir monks or nuns, or brothers or sisters, devote themselves to the secular affairs of monasteries or convents. They do, however, participate in some prescribed religious duties, as daily attendance at Mass, prayers, etc.

LAY INVESTITURE. *See* INVESTITURE.

LAYMEN AND LAYWOMEN, in general, the laity; but also the men and women who are not members of a religious order (except tertiaries) or have not received holy orders. As members of the Church, lay persons form the greater portion of the faithful. They have certain duties, common to all members. The laity has also certain rights, e.g., to receive the necessary spiritual goods from the clergy, in accord, of course, with Church discipline (c. 682).

LAY ORGANIZATIONS. *See* NATIONAL CATHOLIC WELFARE CONFERENCE.

LEAGUE OF THE CROSS, the name of the total abstinence society for English Catholics. The League was founded in 1873 by Cardinal Manning (d. 1892).

LECTERN, a reading stand, movable or permanent, used in church. It is sometimes covered by a cloth corresponding in color to the liturgical color of the day.

LECTION. *See* LESSON.

LECTERN

LECTIONARY, a book of lessons, but chiefly the one which contains the scriptural readings chanted by the deacon or subdeacon during solemn Mass. Also a book containing the lessons for Matins.

LECTOR, literally, a "reader." Specifically: **1.** The cleric who has received the second of the minor orders in the Roman rite (*cf.* ORDERS HOLY). **2.** The first scholastic theological degree conferred in Dominican schools of theology, for example, Lector of Sacred Theology, abbreviated S.T.L.

LEGATE, an officially appointed representative of the pope. A legate is called a nuncio when he is assigned as a permanent representative before a civil government, or an apostolic delegate when representing the pope in the affairs of the Church. (Cf. APOSTOLIC DELEGATE.)

LEGATE A LATERE, the title of a special, confidential representative of the pope. Usually, he is entrusted with particular powers to enable him to carry out his mission.

LEGEND, GOLDEN. *See* GOLDEN LEGEND.

LEGITIMATION. A child is legitimate if conceived in or born of a valid marriage, unless the parents were under a solemn vow of chastity. A child, not legitimate because of some impediment or condition, is afforded legitimation by (a) the subsequent marriage of the parents, provided they could have validly married before the conception or birth of the child. (If an impediment existed, it suffices that the impediment cease before the birth of the child.) (b) By dispensation when the dispensation is given by one who has ordinary power, or by a general indult.

LENT, the period of six and one half weeks from Ash Wednesday to the date of Easter Sunday. During Lent, for forty days, excluding Sundays, there is imposed fasting for all Catholics according to the laws of fast. This fasting is reminiscent of the forty days of our Lord's unbroken fast (Mt. 4:3-4). The entire period of Lent is also a time of spiritual preparation for the passion, death and resurrection of Christ. It is observed as a time of penitence, other than fasting, and as a time of prayer. The liturgy of the Church reflects the spirit and significance of this period of spiritual preparation: each day has a special Mass assigned to it; those Masses date back to the 7th and 8th centuries; there are no feasts observed on Sundays; private votive Masses are forbidden; no requiems are permitted, except at funerals, and on the first free (vacant) day of each week; purple vestments are the daily color (except Laetare Sunday); the organ is silent; the Gloria and Alleluia are omitted and a special Preface of the season is said; the solemnization of marriage is forbidden. Special rules, regulations and recommendations may be made by the ordinaries. (*Cf.* ABSTINENCE; FASTING.)

LEOPOLDINE ASSOCIATION, an historic mission-aid group founded in Austria in 1829 to give help, both financial and spiritual, to the Catholic Church in America. It was named after Leopoldine, the daughter of Francis I of Austria, who was the empress of Brazil. Many churches and dioceses in the United States owe their early growth to the aid of this group.

LEPER WINDOW, a low window in the chancel wall of some medieval churches, usually with bars and shutters, through which lepers could observe and attend Mass.

LESSON, name of the Epistle and Gospel read during the celebration of Mass. In general, a lesson is a selection from the Scriptures, from the fathers of the Church, or other writers of the Church. These extracts are appointed to be read at religious ceremonies or as portions of the Divine Office. Also called a "lection." (*Cf.* LECTIONARY.)

LEVITICUS, title of the 3rd book of the O.T. This title is certainly pre-Christian in origin and appropriate since the book deals chiefly with the duties of the Levites (hereditary ministers) regarding sacrificial worship. It was the liturgical book of the Israelites. The book also presents a number of moral teachings, notably the importance of liturgical service, the sanctity of priesthood, and the imitation of God's holiness.

LIBERALS, CATHOLIC. In so far as Catholics profess the views and principles of the "Liberal," Socialist or Communist parties, they may be classified as heretics. Thus, on degree of participation, for example, if one were to profess the liberal idea that the Church is subject to the state, he is a heretic. However, the term Catholic Liberals applies particularly to those Catholics who through their affiliation with liberalism sought to reject or limit the authority of the Holy See. Liberalism, the political system opposed to absolutism, is not condemned as such by the Church, but that aspect of it which seeks to obtain freedom or emancipation from moral restrictions is not to be accepted by Catholics and is condemned by the *Syllabus* of Pius IX. There must, of course, be a distinction made concerning the transposing of the words. Catholic Liberals are one group. They are not to be confused with "Liberal Catholics." The latter are not political in the broad sense of the word "liberalism." Rather they are individuals "qualified" by the term "liberal" and are variously engaged in promoting views which seek to inject Catholic thought into social and economic life in an effort to elevate the moral character of these activities. While some of their views may be looked on as more "free" than is consistent with sound Catholic teaching, the "Liberal Catholic" is an individual rather than a party affiliate. (*Cf.* MODERNISM; SECULARISM.)

LIBER PONTIFICALIS, title of a collection of the lives of the popes, particularly one containing the biographies of the popes from St. Peter to Stephen V (d. 891).

LIBER USUALIS, the book containing the Proper of the Masses for all Sundays and for the feasts which supplant the Sunday, together with the hours of the Office except Matins and Lauds, and the accompanying chants.

LICENTIATE, an academic degree awarded for proficiency in theology, philosophy, canon law, Scripture. It cannot be awarded in theology until the end of the fourth year of the theological course. The degree in theology is abbreviated S.T.L.

LIE, any word, sign or action through which one expresses the opposite as he knows it or wills it. This is usually done with the motive of deceiving others. It is also a lie if one says what is true but believes it to be false. It is not a lie to say what is false if one believes what he says to be true. Actions which are lies are classified as hypocrisy. Lies may be *malicious*, i.e., injurious of another; *officious*, i.e., those told for one's own or another's advantage; *jocose*, i.e., a lie told for amusement. To lie is never permitted, because a lie is intrinsically evil, and while in itself it is only venially sinful, it becomes mortally sinful as soon as it violates another virtue, e.g., charity toward one's neighbor.

LIGAMEN, the bond of an existing valid marriage whereby both parties are forbidden to contract another marriage before the death of one of them.

LIGHTS. *See* CANDLES; LAMPS.

LILY, an often used symbol of chastity. It is used in regard to the Blessed Mother, St. Joseph and other saints.

LIMBO. This is considered, from the meaning of the word "fringe" or "edge," to be "outside of heaven."

There is a distinction as to the purpose: 1. "Limbo of the fathers" meant that state or reserve in which the souls of the just as Abraham, Isaac, Jacob, etc., were detained until the complete redemption by Christ through which heaven was opened to them. This was the "paradise" spoken of by Christ in addressing the good thief at the crucifixion (Lk. 23:40–44). It was the limbo of the just to which Christ's soul descended. 2. The "limbo of children" is that state wherein the souls of unbaptized children and adults, who die without committing grievous actual sin, enjoy perfect natural happiness. Here they are excluded from the supernatural excellence of heaven, namely, the vision of God, but they do know God and love Him with their perfected natural faculties.

LINTEUM also **LINTHEUM,** an ancient veil used to cover the chalice and paten in the early days of the Church. It is replaced today with the chalice veil.

LITANY, a prayer in the form of short invocations, said alternately or as petitions with responses. Originally this term was applied to any prayer of supplication repeated often; later it was introduced into the liturgy with the clergy leading and the people responding. The use of litanies was introduced into processions and into certain ceremonies. We have an example, in shortened form, in the Kyrie of the Mass. While there are many litanies, only five have been sanctioned for public devotions. These are: the Litany of Loreto (Litany of the Blessed Virgin), Litany of the Saints, Litany of the Holy Name, Litany of the Sacred Heart, and Litany of St. Joseph.

LITERAL SENSE OF SCRIPTURE,

the interpretation of the Sacred Scriptures in which is sought the actual meaning that the writer intended to convey. Frequently, a word has several meanings, but in context or its use with other words it is given but one meaning by the writer. There are distinguishing marks of literal sense. It may be *explicit*, i.e., the actual statement conveyed by the words. *Implicit* sense may also be present, for the use of one word rather than another indicates that the writer wished to imply more than what the words actually mean. Every part of Scripture has, of course, a literal sense, for the author must have so intended. While this is true, there may be texts which have several possible meanings. What is attempted by seeking the genuine literal sense is to determine whether a Scripture text may have more than one inspired and certain literal meaning. (*Cf.* INTERPRETATION, SCRIPTURAL; INSPIRATION OF SCRIPTURE.)

LITTLE OFFICE OF THE B.V.M.

In honor of the Blessed Mother, prayers containing the same elements as the Divine Office have been arranged in a shorter form. The "Little Office" was introduced in the 11th century, attributed to St. Peter Damian. In content, it is made up of lessons, Psalms, the Lord's Prayer, canticles, hymns, antiphons, collects, commemorations, and the Ave Maria. It is the daily office recited in common, or privately, by some groups of sisters, lay-brothers, and is obligatory for some tertiaries. The prayer as a devotion has grown in popularity with lay people and often is recommended to members of sodalities of the Blessed Mother.

LITURGICAL BOOKS, official publications which govern the liturgical functions of the Church. In the Roman rite there are six major liturgical books: 1. The Roman Missal, official book of the Propers and Ordinaries of the Mass, arranged for the sequence of feasts throughout the liturgical year, together with the attendant ceremonies. 2. The Roman Breviary, containing the Divine Office (*cf.* BREVIARY). 3. The Roman Martyrology. 4. The Roman Ritual, containing the ceremonies of the sacraments and blessings for priests. 5. The Roman Pontifical. 6. The *Caeremoniale Episcoporum*, the book of sacraments, blessings, and ceremonies for bishops. In addition to these, but rather as abbreviations of the above official six, there are: The *Memoriale Rituum*, containing the Holy Week ceremonies for small parish churches; the *Clementine Instruction* which governs the Forty Hours' Devotion; the *Officium Majoris Hebdomadae*, containing the music, psalms, and lessons, etc., for Holy Week; three singing books: the antiphonary; the *Graduale;* the *Kyriale*. The Holy See, through the Sacred Congregation of Rites, alone can authorize changes in the liturgy. No bishop can authorize a change without an apostolic indult. The Sacred Congregation of Rites publishes authentic decrees governing all liturgy. Translation is regulated by Church law. The printing of these books must be authorized and the publishers must be approved.

LITURGICAL MOVEMENT. The basic intention of this movement is to put the liturgy into the life of moderns, more consciously and more effectively, and to teach them how to participate fully in the corporate worship of the Church. It is an effort to revitalize Catholicism and to encourage the members of the mystical body to realize the daily living of the life of Christ, through the Mass, the Divine Office, the sacraments, sacramentals, and attendant circumstances of art and practice. The modern movement began in 1840 under the urging of Dom Prosper Gueranger of Solesmes. However, the greatest impetus came in 1903 when Pope St. Pius X published his *Motu Proprio* and gave official approval to the movement.

LITURGY. This word itself means public service or duty. The sacred liturgy is the public worship which Christ, as divine Head of the Church, gives to God the Father, and that which the faithful of Christ give to Christ and through Him to God, the Father. It is thus the public worship by the mystical body. Its purpose is the greater glory of God and the sanctification of all men. The liturgical worship of the Church is made up of the sacrifice of the Mass, the sacraments, the Divine Office, and the sacramentals. The liturgy is defined as "the worship of God by His Church." 1. The eucharistic sacrifice of the Mass is the center of the religion of the Church established by Christ, for through this unbloody immolation, the Church renews what Christ accomplished on the cross by offering Himself to God the Father. In Eastern Churches the Mass is called "The Holy Liturgy" or "The Offering." As such, private devotions which prompt the faithful to participate in liturgical functions, as retreats, meditation, the Rosary, etc., are not liturgical. An analysis and understanding of the sacred liturgy was set forth in the encyclical,

Mediator Dei, of Pope Pius XII. 2. The Divine Office is the official, universal prayer of the mystical body of Christ. 3. The sacraments and sacramentals are means of grace for the sanctification of members of the mystical body.

While sometimes considered as a part of the liturgy, such adjuncts as music, church art, vestments, etc., are only properly "liturgical appurtenances" which serve to make liturgy visible, effective, and pleasing. (*Cf.* MASS; SACRAMENTS; DIVINE OFFICE.)

LOCI THEOLOGICI. These "theological sources" were first introduced in a writing by Melchior Cano (d. 1560) and were listed as seven *prime* or proper bases: Scripture, Tradition, the magisterium of the Church, the councils, the decisions of the popes, the fathers of the Church, and theologians; and three *secondary* or improper bases: human reason, philosophy, and history.

LOGIC, that science or art which teaches the method of acquiring knowledge through the study of reason and acquiring the means of discovering the truth. It is introductory or preparatory to the study of philosophy. It is applied through inductive and deductive procedures; actually, sound reasoning.

LOGOS. Literally, "The Word," this term is exclusive with St. John (Jn. 1:1–18). Jesus, the Messias, the divine Son of God is presented by St. John as the *Logos*, the second divine Person of the Blessed Trinity (*cf.* TRINITY). In the Prologue of St. John's Gospel, the *Logos* is presented as eternal, distinct from God the Father, yet truly God who became man, the God-Man, Jesus of Nazareth. Perhaps the use of the term by St.

John was due to his recognition of the term among Greek philosophers, but his choice was more one of inspiration, which by its very force would satisfy the minds of men as does the "Word Incarnate." The term is interchangeable with the word "wisdom" as used by St. Paul (1 Cor. 1:24), thus the *Logos* is the wisdom of God made manifest in the Son. (*Cf.* INCARNATION.)

LOLLARDS, name of followers of the native heresy of medieval England, supported by John of Gaunt and the theologian John Wyclif. The movement, called Lollardy, was anticlerical and defied Church authority and, toward the end of the 14th century it sought, by individual interpretation, to emphasize the authority of the Bible. By the end of the 15th century, the movement had almost disappeared.

LONGANIMITY, a virtue referred to hope, and one of the fruits of the Holy Spirit. It is both longsuffering and forbearance, and teaches one to consider the future good, to wait with patience and constancy, that is, continuing over an extended period of time to practice virtues and seek sanctification.

LORD'S PRAYER. The *Pater Noster*, that is, the "Our Father" prayer, has been taught by our Lord to the apostles (Mt. 6:9–13). Essentially, it consists of three prayers for the glory of God (hallowed be Thy name, Thy kingdom come, Thy will be done) and an expression of the extent of that glory (on earth as it is in heaven), followed by three requests (for food, forgiveness, and freedom from temptation) and a final plea for deliverance from evil, i.e., moral evil.

LORD'S SUPPER. The Last Supper is sometimes referred to by this name. It is also a little used term for Holy Thursday.

LORETO, LITANY OF. *See* LITANY.

LOS-VON-ROM MOVEMENT. German title, literally "away from Rome," of the political and religious move started in Germany in 1897 whereby its leaders, by exploiting the racial feeling of Germans in Bohemia, sought to draw them away from allegiance with Catholic Austria and link them to Protestant Prussia.

LOURDES, APPARITIONS OF. A series of 18 apparitions which began Feb. 11 and ended on July 16, 1858. During this time, the Blessed Virgin Mary appeared to fourteen-year-old Bernadette Soubirous in the rock cave of Massabielle along the river Gave near Lourdes in France. At the last apparition the Blessed Mother declared her identity, saying, "I am the Immaculate Conception." Four years before (1854) the Church had defined as a dogma the truth of the Immaculate Conception of the Blessed Mother. After the apparitions at Lourdes, a flowing spring of water, whose properties are not unusual, has been the apparent means of effecting miraculous cures through the patronage of the Blessed Mother. Also there was constructed, in accord with the Virgin's request, a chapel which has become one of the great churches of southern France, and people from all over the world go on pilgrimage to Lourdes in honor of the Blessed Virgin Mary. A feast in the Roman rite is celebrated in commemoration of these apparitions on Feb. 11.

LOVE FEAST. *See* AGAPE.

LOVE OF GOD, the greatest of the virtues, both in practice and accomplishment. Embracing all other virtues, it is called the "essence of perfection." St. Thomas declares this theological virtue of charity thus: "Essentially, the perfection of the Christian life consists in charity, first and foremost in the *love of God*, then in the love of neighbor." In the Church, this love is by *command*, by the direct *teaching of Christ*, and by tradition and teaching. We find this by *command* (Deut. 6:5) which is both the directive to adore God and give Him an absorbing love: "Thou shalt love Yahweh thy God with thy whole heart, and with thy whole soul, and with thy whole strength." As a religious precept, it is the center of the O.T. teaching and the center of the New Law which Christ established. Christ's teaching was direct and positive. He calls this the greatest commandment (Mk. 12:29–31) and demonstrates the manner of its practice: "If anyone love Me, he will keep My word . . ." (Jn. 14:23ff.), assuring all that the Spirit of love will further teach them (Jn. 15:26), and finally Christ declares the degree and extent of this love, using Himself as the example: "as I have loved you" (Jn. 15:12). The basic source of love of God is found in our dependence on God, for, as St. Thomas states, the love that God has for us "infuses and creates the goodness which is present in all things." God loves because He creates; we love because we are created. There is no brief statement which would serve to demonstrate how to practice this love of God. It may be put as: giving one's self to God, avoiding sin, praying and meditating, practicing self-denial and conforming to the will of God. Being progressive and capable of extension, each of these is thus a continuous work of perfection of self. (*Cf.* CHARITY.)

LOW MASS. *See* MASS.

LOW SUNDAY, the first Sunday after Easter, also called "Sunday in white" (*Dominica in albis*), or *Quasimodo* from the first word of the Introit. It has been designated as "low" not because of degree of the feast, but simply because it follows the great feast of Easter.

LUKE, GOSPEL OF ST. The third of the synoptic Gospels written by the apostle, St. Luke, the physician, definitely between the years 60 and 63 A.D. In content this writing has been described as "the announcement of good tidings." It has six parts: 1. the narrative of the infancy of Christ; 2. the Messianic office of Christ; 3. the manifestation of this office in Galilee by Christ; 4. the preaching of Christ; 5. the Passion of Christ; 6. the culmination, the Resurrection and Ascension of Christ. The Gospel is a genuine history of the origin of the Christian faith (its history of development is presented in Acts of the Apostles, also written by St. Luke). It is marked for its historic and literary qualities, its emphasis upon the joy of its author's message, its recognition of the necessity for prayer, and the place it gives to the Blessed Mother. It points to Jesus as the Son of God and the Son of Man, and the reign of God's will through the established Church of Christ.

LUNA also **LUNETTE,** a small crescent-shaped clip or a circlet, made of gold, which holds the consecrated host. It is slid into the monstrance along a groove or track for exposition of the Blessed Sacrament.

LUST, the inordinate desire for or satisfaction of the appetite for sexual and carnal pleasure. Here is not included the natural and legitimate purposes of sex in which pleasure exists as a part of both the stimulus and the function. It is only inordinate when sought in a way not in keeping with the natural purpose of the appetite, or in the legitimate exercise of the appetite to an excessive degree. Lust is one of the capital or deadly sins. It may also be applied to the other human appetites, e.g., tasting, but generally these are inordinately exercised, and classed as concupiscence. The virtues opposed to lust, and aiding in its control, are: chastity, and its subordinates, continence and modesty.

LUTHERANISM, the religious belief practiced collectively by Lutherans. It had its rise in the teachings made up and taught by Martin Luther (d. 1546) in Erfurt and Wittenberg in Germany. As a teaching, it finds its center in a justification by faith alone. (Based on Luther's translation of Rom. 3:28.) There is a confusion of original sin with concupiscence, since Luther held that original justice was connatural to Adam and Eve, and original sin so corrupted human nature that man could no longer do good, for his reason had degenerated and his free will had been taken from him. This resulted in man's domination by concupiscence which in itself was looked on as evil. With man so fallen and so dominated, Christ's redemption was entirely done for us and, taking Christ's merits as one's own, there was no need for further effort on man's part, either in imitation of Christ or personal merit. Man could ignore or cover up sin. There follows that habitual grace is non-existent; actual grace is God working in us and man, therefore, only needs faith in or abandonment to God and His mercy. Thus Luther did away with the sacraments, keeping baptism, penance (as only a declaration followed automatically by remission), and a non-consecrated eucharist wherein Christ is only present by faith of the believer. There follows no need for an established priesthood since truth comes from the Bible which is freely interpreted. Luther also denied purgatory, indulgences, prayers for the dead, and the intercession of the saints.

LYONS, COUNCILS OF. The first council convoked at Lyons, in France, in 1245, by Pope Innocent IV was the 13th ecumenical council. The second, in 1274, was convened by Pope Gregory X, and is the 14th ecumenical council. Both councils were concerned with national and international affairs and moral reform. (*Cf.* ECUMENICAL COUNCILS.)

M

**MACHABEES, FIRST AND SEC-
OND BOOK OF.** These are two
books of history, presenting the story
of the successful resistance of the
Jews to foreign dominance. Their
authors are unknown, but the first
book was written not later than 103
B.C. and the second possibly about
125 B.C. The title is derived from
Machabeus, the assumed name of
Judas, the third son of Mathathias,
taken from the Hebrew name meaning "hammer." Being books of history and accounts of action, their
doctrinal content is slight, centered
chiefly around survival after death,
the resurrection of the body and the
eternal punishment of sin.

MACEDONIANISM, the heresy
which, begun in 360 by some Arian
bishops, taking its name from one of
them, Bishop Macedonius of Constantinople, taught that the Second
Person of the Trinity was inferior to
the First Person, and the Holy Spirit
inferior to the First and Second. It
was condemned at the 2nd ecumenical council.

MADONNA, name applied to representations of the Blessed Mother in
either painting or sculpture. Properly
speaking, such representation is designated as a Madonna only when the
central figure is that of the Virgin,
even when the Christ child or others
are depicted.

MAGDALEN, a descriptive title conferred upon a penitent prostitute who
has been placed or voluntarily seeks
reform in a religious community. The
name is derived from the place of
residence of St. Mary Magdalen, i.e.,
Magdala.

**MAGISTERIUM OF THE
CHURCH,** the power given by
Christ to the Church which He
founded together with infallibility by
which the Church teaches authoritatively the revealed truth of the Scripture and holds forth the truth of
Tradition for the salvation of men.
This fact is contained in the nature
and extent of the mission given to the
Church (Mt. 28:19), and the recognized acceptance of that mission as
recorded in the Acts of the Apostles.
Thus the Church, taking the deposit
of faith and gathering the orally
transmitted and written truth (Tradition), formally declares, through
councils and infallible definitions, her
magisterium. (*Cf.* INFALLIBILITY;
TRADITION; APOSTOLICITY.)

MAGI, THE. Originally the Magi,
"wise men," were a priestly tribe of
soothsayers of Media who served
under their Persian conquerors. The
name was used by Matthew (2:1–12)
to indicate "sages" who came to
adore Christ. While they are declared
to come from "the East," their home-
land was probably the land beyond

the Jordan River and east of the Dead Sea. They probably visited Christ after the purification (Lk. 2: 22–38) which took place forty days after birth. The gifts they brought to present to the newborn Christ were products of their native land, Arabian in character, and were such as would be presented to a king. While their names are not known, medieval legend calls them Gaspar, Melchior and Balthasar.

MAGNANIMITY, that quality of soul which prompts a person to undertake great things for God and one's neighbor. It is the disposition to act selflessly with genuine motives. In this there is no feeling of ambition to direct or control others by wielding power over them, or any lesser motive such as money, recognition, glory. It is combined with unselfish thought, high ideals or high-mindedness. It arises from a free practice of all virtues, notably charity and justice, in many diverse actions. Its opposite, actually a defect, is pusillanimity which causes one, through a "smallness of soul," to refrain from acting for others out of fear of failure or out of a feeling that "there is not enough in it for me."

MAGNIFICAT, THE. This title has been given to the canticle spoken by the Blessed Mother on the occasion of her visit to her cousin, Elizabeth, as recorded in Luke (1:46–56). The Magnificat is an expression of genuine humility, which is drawn largely from O.T. thought, especially the Psalms (Ps. 23:8; 30:8; 33:4; 70:18; etc.). It acknowledges the goodness of God, that God is her Savior, and that God is to be served. The title comes from the first word of the Latin version. (*Cf.* VISITATION.)

MAJOR ORDERS. *See* ORDERS, HOLY.

MALABAR RITE. Properly called the Syro-Malabar rite, this is the liturgy used by the Eastern Catholics of Malabar of southwest India. The Syriac language and much of the Syriac liturgy are used, but many of the physical appurtenances of the Roman Church and even some of its prescribed ritual, e.g., Communion under one species, have been introduced.

MANICHAEISM, a heresy introduced in Persia by Mani, about 242. It taught a religious dualism, with a constant struggle going on in man's nature between two deities, God and Satan.

MANIFESTATION OF CONSCIENCE, the disclosing of one's spiritual condition outside of the sacrament of penance, usually done for the purpose of obtaining guidance. Religious superiors are forbidden (c. 530) to require a manifestation of conscience from their subjects.

MANIPLE, a vestment worn over the left forearm of the celebrant at Mass. Originally, this was merely a napkin of cloth which served a practical purpose; then, rather than being worn, it was carried in the left hand. After the 12th century, this has become more and more ornamental, to be now but a reminder of the former "hand cloth" in the present-day vestigial maniple. This is of the same color as the vestments for the day, should be of cloth, 2 ft. in length at least, and should hang loosely.

MANNA, the food which was continuously and miraculously supplied to the Israelites during the entire years of wandering in the desert as recorded in Exodus (16:1–36). This bread from heaven was a true type of the sacrament of the Eucharist, our spiritual food.

MANTELLETTA, an outer, sleeveless garment, which fastens at the neck, is open in front and reaches to the knees. It has slits through which the arms are put. The mantelletta, worn by cardinals, bishops, abbots and certain prelates, is red, purple, or black in accord with the dignitary who wears it. It is the outer garment of a bishop, other than the ordinary, on entering a church to pontificate.

MANTUM. Much like the cope, but with a short train, this garment is only worn by the pope. It is either white or red.

MANUTERGE, a small linen towel used by the celebrant of Mass at the Lavabo to dry his fingers.

MAPPULA, a name, infrequently used, for the gremial veil.

MARCIONISM. Begun in 144 by Marcion, this was the heresy which held that the God of the Jews was not the God of the Christians nor the Father of Christ. It imposed a rigoristic asceticism on its followers. It continued for about four centuries and was then condemned with Manichaeism.

MARIOLOGY, the study, as a part of theology, which treats of the life, role, and virtues of the Blessed Mother of God. It demonstrates the prerogatives, the eminent fullness of grace which was hers, and her position as Co-Redemptrix and Mediatrix of all graces. (*Cf.* MARY, VIRGIN MOTHER OF GOD.)

MARK, GOSPEL OF ST., the second of the synoptic Gospels, written by St. Mark in the period between 53–63 A.D. St. Mark was a close acquaintance of St. Peter, St. Paul and Barnabas, and wrote his Gospel chiefly to furnish the Christians of Rome with a record of doctrine, notably the preaching of St. Peter. It centers upon the ministry of Christ while on earth, with a strong affirmation of the divinity of Christ, declaring Christ the Incarnate Son of God.

MARKS OF THE CHURCH. As declared by the Council of Trent (1545–1563), the marks of the Church are four: oneness, holiness, catholicity and apostolicity. These are distinctive characteristics, evident in the oneness of doctrine; holiness, because it dispenses the means of sanctification; catholic, because of its extension to all through its mission to the world; and apostolic, because of its succession of ministry from St. Peter and the apostles. (*Cf.* APOSTOLICITY; CATHOLIC; HOLINESS.)

MARONITES, name of the members of the Eastern Catholic Church, Arabic-speaking Syrians, who inhabit Lebanon. The Maronites are in communion with Rome, and have a college for the education of their clergy in Rome.

MARRIAGE. The sacrament of matrimony is the marriage contract between baptized persons which was raised by Christ to the dignity of a sacrament (c. 1012). The marriage contract is that made by two persons of the opposite sex by which each acquires the exclusive and irrevocable right over their bodies, until the death of one of the parties, for the procreation and education of children. While this last is the primary end of marriage, there are secondary purposes, notably the mutual aid, both material and spiritual, and the overcoming of sexual concupiscence in a legitimate manner. Its essential properties are: *unity*, i.e., one spouse; and *indissolu-*

bility, i.e., a contract for life. While the contract is that of the two parties, God is the author of marriage. The love of husband and wife, their mutual self-giving in a natural vocation for life, is called a gift (charisma) by St. Paul (1 Cor. 7:7). Marriage is symbolized in and modeled on the love of Christ for the Church, His bride (Apoc. 19:7). (*Cf.* IMPEDIMENTS OF MARRIAGE.) Marriage is regulated by the divine law, church law (c's. 1021–1141), and by civil law.

MARTYR, one who suffers death for a cause. In the Christian tradition a martyr was one who, rather than apostasize, gave up his life (Heb. 10:26–31). There were martyrs of the O.T., but, as St. Peter declares, they only are considered heroes of the faith in the Christian age (Heb. 10: 39). St. Ignatius of Antioch urged the early Christians to make the sacrifice of their lives for Christ, and there is ample evidence that many did die during persecutions. The term has also been applied in the Church to those who died natural deaths, but whose lives were living testaments of the faith. In this latter sense, it is no longer recognized as a title; but it is in this sense, and because of her "living" sufferings that the Blessed Mother can be called the "Queen of Martyrs" as well as being their Queen in heaven.

MARTYROLOGY. 1. A list of the early martyrs of the Church whose lives and holy deaths were witness to the faith, together with a brief note on the lives of many of them. **2.** A listing by day throughout the year of the saints who are commemorated in the Church calendar. **3.** The Roman Martyrology, a liturgical book, is the listing with readings of the saints honored in the Church and to it the names of newly canonized saints are added. It first was published in 1584, and now numbers more than five thousand entries. **4.** The American Martyrology is a list of 136 martyrs and confessors of the Church (not all died a violent death) whose death occurred within the present territory of the United States.

MARY, FEASTS OF, days set aside to worship God with special commemoration of events referring to Mary, the Mother of God. These are seventeen in number, but there are many other days when votive Masses of the Blessed Virgin are read and when commemorations of Mary are made during other Masses. In the order throughout the liturgical year the feasts of Mary are: Immaculate Conception of the Blessed Virgin Mary, Dec. 8; the Purification, Feb. 2; Apparition of the B.V.M. at Lourdes, Feb. 11; the Annunciation, Mar. 25; Mary, Queen, May 31; the Visitation, July 2; Our Lady of Mount Carmel, July 16; Our Lady of the Snow, Aug. 5; the Assumption, Aug. 15; Immaculate Heart of Mary, Aug. 22; the Nativity of Our Lady, Sept. 8; Most Holy Name of Mary, Sept. 12; Seven Sorrows of the Blessed Virgin Mary, Sept. 15 (also on the Friday after Passion Sunday); Our Lady of Mercy, Sept. 24; the Most Holy Rosary of the Blessed Virgin Mary, Oct. 7; the Motherhood of the Blessed Virgin Mary, Oct. 11; the Presentation of Our Lady, Nov. 11.

MARYMAS, name used in medieval times to refer to any day on which the Blessed Mother was celebrated with a feast.

MARY, SATURDAY OFFICE OF. The proper office (*in Sabbato*) of the Divine Office is said in honor of Our

Lady on all Saturdays of the year except those of Advent, Lent, Ember days, vigils and feasts above those of the rank of simple; however, the occurring simple feast is commemorated at Matins and Lauds.

MARY, VIRGIN MOTHER OF GOD. The central point of the theology of Mary is that she is the Mother of God. It is because of the fact that Mary has been foreordained by God from the beginning to her divine motherhood that she was conceived "full of grace" and thus placed in the singular position of being the most perfect human being that an omnipotent God could create. She was immaculately conceived, as God's Mother she co-operated in our redemption, she was our Lord's most intimate associate while He was on earth, and upon her death she was assumed bodily into heaven where she is queen, reigning over heaven and earth.

For our knowledge of Mary we depend upon the Scriptures and dogmatic Tradition. From the Scriptures we attain our basic understanding of her as the Mother of God. In the O.T., in a text called the *Protoevangelium* (Gen. 3:15), we find the first significant reference to Mary. There mention is made of the "Second Eve," through whom will be effected the redeemed restoration of all mankind. The seed is Christ (Gal. 3:16), and Mary, being the Mother of Christ and the mother of all in the spiritual order (Rom. 9:7f.), is the woman who is designated to crush the dominion of the devil over men. Later, Isaias (7:14–17) tells us of the Virgin who will conceive and bear a son and we find the fulfillment of this prophecy in the Gospel (Mt. 1:23). Another prophet, Micheas, in speaking of the

motherhood names the place (Bethlehem) where it will take place (Mic. 5:2–3). Also in the O.T., we read of Mary as queen (Ps. 44) and the place on the right hand of the Messianic King—a place of recognized and reserved honor.

In the N.T., the Gospels of Matthew and Mark narrate events concerning the life of the Blessed Mother, but in the Gospel of St. Luke we find the fullest treatment. He records the annunciation, and from his declaration of Mary as "full of grace," and other sources, the Church declared Mary's Immaculate Conception. (Papal bull, *Ineffabilis Deus*, Pius IX, 1854.) St. Luke records the first miracle brought about by Mary: the sanctification of St. John the Baptist in the womb of Elizabeth at the Visitation. On that same occasion (Lk. 1:43), Elizabeth greets Mary as the "Mother of my Lord." From Mary, God the Son took His human nature, and He will forever remain the son of Mary and she will be forever the Mother of God. Finally we read of the place of Mary in heaven at the throne of God (Apoc. 12), and we see her in glory as no other.

The Church, studying, searching, and interpreting both the Scriptures and Tradition, has defined those doctrines concerning Mary about which the Scriptures are not specific. From extra-scriptural sources we know Mary was the daughter of Joachim and Anne. These two saints are celebrated with a feast in the Church calendar. On Nov. 1, 1950, Pope Pius XII declared the doctrine of Our Lady's Assumption. Toward the close of the Marian Year (1954), on Dec. 8, the pope declared the doctrine of the Universal Queenship of Mary and established a feast, that of "Mary, Queen," to be celebrated on May 31.

From apostolic times, Tradition, the Church, and the faithful have accorded to Mary, the Mother of God, the second highest degree of honor, hyperdulia. She has been celebrated in feasts, throughout the year, in the Divine Office, in devotions as the Rosary, litany, her Immaculate Heart, etc., and by title she has been hailed the patroness of many countries, and has been honored in hymns, songs, poetry, sculpture, painting and literature as no other creature. It is under her title of the Immaculate Conception that Mary was declared the Patroness of the United States, with the patronal feast day celebrated on Dec. 8. The name of Mary, because she is the Mother of God, is honored with multiple titles: she is the Blessed Virgin Mary, the Co-Redemptrix; the Mediatrix of all Graces; the Blessed Mother, etc. (*Cf.* VIRGIN MARY.)

MASONRY also **FREEMASONRY.** The Masonic brotherhood was begun in 1717 in London, England. It was originally a secret political society, but later, retaining its secrecy, it borrowed the naturalistic philosophy of French thinkers. It was condemned in April 28, 1738, by Pope Clement XII because of its philosophy, its secret plotting against the Church and some governments, and the danger to the faith of Catholics who might join it. Also many lodges, or branches, proved to be anticlerical, anti-Catholic, and anti-Christian. It was claimed, at the International Masonic Congress in Paris, 1899, that the organization had taken a leading part in all the revolutionary movements of the 19th century. Thus, according to canon law (c. 2335) anyone joining the Masons, or any group plotting against Church or state, is by the very fact (*ipso facto*) excommunicated, reserved simply to the Holy See. Before absolution, the penitent must sever all relations with the organization. This law and its application also holds for affiliated female societies. (*Cf.* SECRET SOCIETIES.)

MASS. 1. The Sacrifice of the Mass; the Sacrifice of the Most Holy Eucharist. Bl. Peter Canisius, S.J., in his *Catechism* defined the Mass as: "The Sacrifice of the Mass is really the holy and living representation and at the same time the unbloody and efficacious oblation of the Lord's Passion and that blood-stained sacrifice which was offered for us on the cross." We may establish that the Eucharist is a true sacrifice and a representation of our Lord's sacrifice. The real presence is affirmed by the words of Christ in instituting the Holy Eucharist, His supreme gift of Himself. He said: "This is My body"—"this is My blood" (Lk. 22: 19–20), and asked that this act be repeated in "remembrance" of Him. That this was so understood and was repeated to proclaim the death of the Lord was declared by St. Paul (1 Cor. 11:24–26), and that this was a sacrifice is seen in his statement of this being performed on the table (altar) (10:21). This is again affirmed by St. Paul (Heb. 13:10).

The true nature of a sacrifice is realized in the Mass. By declaration of the Council of Trent, Christ is recognized as the offering Priest, the Victim offered, and the immolation in the sacramental order. These essentials of the sacrifice are present in the three main actions of the Mass: the Offertory, the Consecration, and the Communion.

In apostolic times, the Mass was celebrated in the evening with the people partaking of a meal (1 Cor. 11:17–34) called "the charity" (*cf.* AGAPE). Thereafter the Eucharist was celebrated without a fast before Communion. However, toward the end of the first century the time shifted to the morning (*cf.* CATECHUMENS). The name "Mass" is probably derived from the Latin word *missio*, meaning a "dismissal," that is the bidding of farewell to those who had gathered (usually at some home). The development of the liturgy, here meaning the sequence of parts and the prayers, was gradual over the first seven centuries; there was no essential change, but the adoption rather, of symbolical associations, as the vestments used. The parts of the Mass as we have it today are (those marked with an asterisk change each day according to the feast): Introit*, Kyrie Eleison, Gloria (except when not permitted), Collects*, Epistle*, Gradual*, Gospel*, the Creed (except when not called for), Offertory*, Lavabo, Prayer to the Trinity, Secret*, Preface*, Sanctus; the Canon with the Consecration, the Our Father, the Breaking of the Host, Agnus Dei, and the preparatory prayers of the Communion; the Communion of the priest and faithful, the ablution, Communion*, Postcommunion*, the *Ite* or Dismissal, the Blessing, and a final Gospel. (*Cf.* LITURGY.)

There are four types of the Mass, each being the same sacrifice, distinguished by its solemnity in the execution of the liturgy: pontifical Mass, solemn or high Mass, sung Mass (*Missa cantata*), and low Mass. There are several other titles to distinguish a Mass depending on where it is celebrated or on what occasion it is said: A "conventual Mass" is celebrated daily in choir, in cathedral or chapter churches; a parochial Mass is said for the people of a parish; a votive Mass is said according to the wish of the celebrant, but not according to the feast of the calendar; the requiem Mass is said at a funeral or for a deceased person; *Missa recitata*, is a Mass in which those attending respond to the prayers, etc. (The parts of the Mass are explained under their separate entries.)

2. Sometimes the term "Mass" is used as designating the musical score to which the sung portions of the Mass are set, e.g., a Bach Mass.

MASS OF THE CATECHUMENS. This name is given to the portion of the Mass from its beginning to the Offertory, at which it was permitted that catechumens could be present. (*Cf.* CATECHUMEN; ENERGUMEN; DISCIPLINE OF THE SECRET.)

MASTER OF CEREMONIES. In Church terminology, this is a male person, usually a senior acolyte or one in holy orders, who directs and assists at liturgical ceremonies, guiding the celebrant and assistants in the performance of the ritual.

MASTER OF NOVICES, in a religious community, the person chosen to direct the formation and spiritually guide the new, unprofessed members of the community. He or she (mistress of novices) should be 35 years of age, and be professed for at least 10 years. The master should be eminently prudent and learned and he has full authority over the novices, subject to the superiors (c's 559–565).

MASTER OF THE SACRED PALACE, the priest, usually an eminent theologian and canonist, who personally attends the pope. This office is always awarded to a Dominican. His duties are to live in the Vatican, supervise the preaching before the Holy Father, and handle some secretarial affairs.

MASTER OF THE SENTENCES, the title awarded to Peter Lombard (d. 1160) for authorship. (*Cf.* SENTENCES, THE BOOK OF.)

MATERIALISM. Originally, this was the philosophy of Greek thinkers of Asia Minor of the 6th century B.C. who attempted to explain the beginning of the world in terms of matter, without reference to a creating, divine power. It gave rise to a development of materialistic monism which declared that the real was the only substance (Spinoza), and then led to a form of idealism wherein the idea or the ego is the "forever becoming." More recently it has advanced the proposition that material goods, such as wealth, or sensuous pleasures, are the only values for man. With Karl Marx there was developed a dialectic materialism which maintains that material forces, economic and social, determine the development of society. This led to communism. The Church has opposed and condemned this philosophy of dialectics. Pope Leo XIII (*Rerum Novarum*, 1891) showed its evils, and Pius XI denounced Communism in an encyclical ("On Atheistic Communism," 1937). The bishops of the United States declared that "Materialism excites greed" (Joint statement on Peace and War, Nov. 1939), and accused it as a false philosophy, of being the cause of economic depression. (Statement on the Present Crisis, April 25, 1933). (*Cf.* COMMUNISM.)

MATINS, name of the first and chief hour of the Divine Office. (*Cf.* DIVINE OFFICE; BREVIARY.)

MATRIMONIAL COURT. Chiefly, this is a diocesan tribunal whose duty it is to investigate and determine the validity of a marriage bond and handle appeals against the bond of marriage.

MATRIMONY. *See* MARRIAGE.

MATTER, SACRAMENTAL. The term is applied to the outward sign in the administration of the sacraments, that is, to material which can be perceived by the senses or action which can be observed. This matter must be joined to the form (*cf.* FORM) of the sacraments, and both must be valid. The matter of a sacrament may be (a) *remote*, which is the material used, e.g., water in baptism; (b) *proximate*, which is the application of the remote matter, e.g., the pouring of the water in baptism.

MATTHEW, GOSPEL OF ST., the first of the synoptic Gospels written by the apostle, St. Matthew. It was the first of the Gospels, originally written in the Aramaic language between 40 and 50 A.D. and translated into the Greek sometime before 70 A.D. The characteristic of Matthew's writing was his orderly arrangement, with five major portions presenting narrative accounts followed by a like number of discourses, either sermons or inspirational judgments. The central theme is so phrased that the Gospel has been called the "Gospel of Fulfillment" or the "Gospel of the Kingdom," the latter name being favored because of one particular verse on the kingdom found only in this account (21:43).

MAUNDY THURSDAY, name given to the Thursday of Holy Week, derived but corrupted from *Mandatum*, the first word of the rite of washing of feet. This act, retained in the liturgy of Holy Thursday, is one of humble example, for it was a lesson in humility that Christ performed this service (Jn. 13:1–17). It is also an act symbolizing purification.

MAURISTS, popular name for members of the French Benedictines, founded by St. Maur in 1618 and disbanded in 1700 at the time of the French Revolution.

MEDALS, RELIGIOUS, flat, mostly round, discs made of metal, wood, or plastic with a religious representation on one side, or both, and/or an inscription or ejaculation on the reverse side. Shaped usually like a coin, they can be retained on a person, pinned on, or worn about the neck by means of a connecting ring and chain or string. They are blessed and are sacramentals. Intended as "portable" miniatures, their use in the Church is very ancient, probably derived from the eastern icons. In the Middle Ages, medals were regarded as amulets; it also was customary to give them to pilgrims to demonstrate that they had gone on pilgrimage. The subjects depicted on medals may be of our Lord, the Blessed Mother, the saints, or as commemorative pieces of special religious events, e.g., a year of jubilee.

MEDIATOR. Only Christ is so named, because: 1. He brought about the reconciliation of God and man; 2. He effected our salvation by reparation; 3. He made it possible for us, through Him, to act and share in the divine life and love and thus, through the co-operation with grace, merit our own salvation (Jn. 15:10–17). This work of Christ as Mediator is effective because He was sent by God, and at the same time is man's representative: "For there is one God, and one Mediator between God and men, Himself man, Jesus Christ" (1 Tim. 2:5).

MEDIATRIX OF ALL GRACES. The Blessed Virgin Mary, as mediatrix of all graces, depends completely on the merits of her Son, Jesus, as the Universal Mediator. The teaching of the Church is that all the same graces which are necessary for man and which were merited for all mankind by her Son through His redemption, are merited by Mary too, but *de congruo*, that is, founded on charity (love) and friendship with God; also that Mary pleads now in heaven for man for the application of graces and distributes them to men. The Church, by decree of Jan. 21, 1921, approved a proper Mass and Office of Mary, Mediatrix of all Graces. In 1954, May 31 was designated for the Feast of Mary, Queen.

MEDITATION. Composed of acts of the intellect and will, this "thought prayer" includes reasoning as to the purpose of one's prayer (direction), the analysis of concepts (picturing what one thinks about in relation to God), comparison (comparing one's thought with what is pictured in the mind), affections (the desire in the mind), resolution (the resolve to accept and follow the thought of God and His love), and culminates in a communion or inner joy with God and His saints. This prayer is mental discourse, the mind's "daydream" on some concept or proposition of God. Its object may be any mystery of our faith, the life of Christ, the history of the Church, the liturgy, or the saints. Its purpose is twofold: 1. To make one understand one's faith more deeply and apply its truths to oneself. 2. To love and hope in God and to will to do those things which serve God better. Meditation has several forms: thought and longing concerning the truths of faith; examination and "contemplation" on the life of Christ; thoughtful reading of a spiritual text; and thoughtful colloquies or little "conversations" (discoursive prayer) with Christ or the saints. Mental prayer is defined as "a silent elevation and application of our mind and heart to God in order to offer Him our homage and to promote His glory by our advancement in virtue." (*Cf.* CONTEMPLATION.)

MEEKNESS, a virtue related to the virtue of temperance. Meekness moderates anger by controlling the passion of anger and by not permitting one's anger to be aroused over trivial things. Meekness is not to be confused with indifference or spinelessness. As used in the Beatitudes (Mt. 5:4) it is the virtue of "manly resignation" to adversity.

MELETIAN SCHISM. Headed by Meletius, bishop of Lycopolis in the year 306, this schismatic movement sought to supplant Peter, the bishop of Alexandria. Its followers, after the censorship of Meletius by the Council of Nicaea, turned to Arianism.

MELKITE RITE, the Byzantine rite as used by the Melkites. It is in Arabic, but certain parts, for example, the lessons, are retained in Greek. The Melkites are Arabian-speaking Catholics of Syria, Palestine and Egypt. There are a number in the United States whose clergy are subject to the ordinaries of the Roman rite.

MEMENTO, a prayer for a specific intention. There are three mementos in the Canon of the Mass. The first, the prayer for the living, beginning with the word *Memento* ("Be mindful"), is said right after the beginning of the Canon. This is followed by the second, the *Communicantes*, a commemoration of the Church triumph-

ant. The third, the memento for the dead, is said as the second prayer after the consecration; it begins with the words *Memento etiam* ("Be mindful also").

MEMORIA. 1. Literally, a commemoration, the lowest ranking feast of the Benedictine and Dominican calendars. **2.** Name of a reliquary; also a chapel built to enshrine the body of a saint.

MENAION, the name applied to any one of a set of 12 liturgical books which contain the offices of the movable feasts of the Byzantine rite.

MENOLOGY also **MENOLOGIUM. 1.** A collection of lives of the saints, arranged in sequence according to their feast days, month by month. **2.** A calendar of the liturgical feasts, with readings from the lessons of each feast, arranged for each day and listing the feasts of the saints on these days.

MENSA, literally, a table. In liturgical language, the mensa is: **1.** the flat table-top of a fixed altar; **2.** the altar stone of a portable altar. (*Cf.* ALTAR; ALTAR STONE.)

MENSAL FUND, a fixed amount contributed from Church revenues to support a bishopric, usually that of a cathedral. Also the amount subscribed each year for the support of a resident priest. The term is not commonly used.

MENTAL RESERVATION or **MENTAL RESTRICTION,** the practice of putting into words a meaning which is different from that which the words ordinarily have. It is not to be considered merely an equivocation, nor is it dissembling. Mental reservation is either *strict*, i.e., when the actual truth cannot be had from the words expressed; or *broad*, i.e., when the truth can be readily determined from the words although it is not actually contained in them. Strict mental reservation (e.g., the lie) is always forbidden. Broad mental reservation may be considered permissible if there is justifiable reason for it; or on basis of the conviction that the questioner has no right to exact the truth. (*Cf.* LIE.)

MERCY, SPIRITUAL AND CORPORAL WORKS OF, acts of the virtue of charity done to the benefit of others. The corporal works of mercy are: feed the hungry; give drink to the thirsty; clothe the naked; shelter the homeless; visit the sick and imprisoned; ransom the captive; and bury the dead. The spiritual, directed to the spiritual rather than the physical want, are: instruct the ignorant; advise the doubtful; correct sinners; be patient with those in error or who do wrong; forgive offenses; comfort the afflicted; and pray for the living and the dead.

MERIT. 1. A good work performed for another which entitles one to a reward. **2.** In the theology of the Church, merit is the effect or recompense of sanctifying or co-operative grace; it is the "fruit of grace." That there is a correspondence between merit and reward, that the merciful shall obtain mercy and the humble will be exalted, is evident from the Sermon on the Mount (Lk. 6:27–39). In fact, Christ, through the redemption, has merited all for men. Man himself, strictly speaking, cannot merit anything from God, for we can never repay adequately; we can do nothing to give profit to God who has all, and so God owes us no reward; God is not a debtor of man, but man is indebted to God. But, as St. Augustine says, our merits are "the gift of God" as they proceed from His grace, and in this sense we may merit for a good and supernatural work: first, in justice (*de condigno*) since we share, through the Church and sacraments, in the merits of Christ, and a reward has been promised. Second, because of friendship (*de congruo*) and mercy; being in the state of grace, we are deserving of a "friendly reward" and by the mercy of God we are assured of the possibility of reward (Rom. 8:28–30).

MESSIAS (MESSIAH). "The desired of all nations" (Agge. 2:8) who was Jesus Christ, the one who was to come and save the people of Israel (*cf.* CHRIST; PROTOEVANGELIUM). The identity of Jesus Christ, the Good Shepherd, with the type as described in the O.T. (Zac. 11:12; 12–13) is demonstrated in the N.T. (Mt. 26:15; 27:9).

METAPHYSICS. This part of the science of philosophy abstracts the nature of reality, or the essence or nature of things. It penetrates and analyzes being and the principles that are true of all beings. It is divided into: 1. General, called ontology, which treats of being, substances, accidents, etc. 2. Special, which in turn is divided into (a) cosmology, the study of the world (from the universe to the atom as they exist in reality); (b) psychology, the study of the soul; (c) theodicy, the study of the reality of God.

METROPOLITAN, title of an archbishop who is the head of an ecclesiastical province or territory, in which one or more suffragan bishops may be ruling over dioceses or portions of the province. The metropolitan is always an archbishop and has the jurisdiction over his own diocese (usually that of the chief city of the territory), and has certain rights and duties regarding his suffragan bishops. (*Cf.* BISHOPS.)

MILITARY ORDER. *See* KNIGHTS.

MILLENIUM. There has been extended speculation from the early Jews to the present about this period. It was considered to be 1000 years of bliss when the just will reign. This was to be before the Second Coming of Christ (the general judgment), and also was heretically held to be a like period after the final judgment. But according to interpretation of Apoc. 20:1–10, millenium means an age of grace wherein the faithful are living, whether on earth or in heaven.

MINISTER, in the ecclesiastical sense, (a) an ordained cleric or (b) one who has the authority to administer to others, e.g., to confirm. Sometimes also a title of a superior of a religious community. It is more proper to say "celebrant" of the Mass rather than "minister," since there may be other clerics assisting the celebrant, e.g., deacon, subdeacon, who are referred to as ministers.

MINOR ORDERS. *See* ORDERS, HOLY.

MIRACLE, a phenomenon in nature which can be seen by the senses and which is outside of the ordinary law of nature and brought about by some power outside the law of nature, that is, by special activity of the First Cause, the source of all law, God. We have first to consider the miracles related in Scripture. Miracles were used to prove revelation. The Church, as set forth in the third chapter of the Vatican Council, teaches: "In order that the service of our faith should be agreeable to reason, God has willed to join to the internal helps of the Holy Spirit some external proofs of His revelation, namely, divine deeds, especially miracles and prophecies, which, inasmuch as they plainly show forth the omnipotence and infinite knowledge of God, are most certain signs of revelation and are suited to the intelligence of all. Wherefore, both Moses and the prophets, and above all Christ the Lord Himself, performed many and most manifest miracles and uttered prophecies; and we read of the apostles that 'they, going forth, preached everywhere, the Lord working withal and confirming the word with signs that followed'." And from the same Council, we have the following canon of faith: "If anyone shall say that divine revelation cannot be made credible by external signs, but that men must be moved to believe solely by the internal experience or private inspiration of each one, let him be anathema."

In the process of canonization of a saint, the Church demands that proof of two miracles be presented and authenticated before beatification (except in a case of true martyrdom) and that two more miracles be proven to have taken place through the intercession of the beatified before the person is canonized and declared to be a saint (c. 1999–2141). (*Cf.* CANONIZATION.)

MIRACLE OF GRACE. This name is given to the remarkable change in the soul whereby one is turned from a life of sin or converted to the faith.

MIRACLE PLAYS also **MYSTERY PLAYS.** Early form of drama which, beginning in the Middle Ages (13th–15th centuries), presented the lives of saints, a religious historic event, a Scripture story, or some teaching of the faith. Primarily, they were teaching aids, but later on action was introduced into these plays to serve the purpose of genuine drama. They were usually presented out-of-doors, frequently in the courtyard or square before a cathedral by touring troups of players. Miracle plays preceded the Mystery plays; the latter were distinguished by centering primarily on events of the O.T. or N.T. and lives of the saints. Many of them, following the pattern of the early Greek theater, introduced verse which became for centuries the form of the later drama.

MIRACULOUS MEDAL, a medal struck after the apparitions to St. Catherine Laboure in 1830. It shows on one side a representation of the Blessed Mother together with the words "O Mary conceived without sin, pray for us who have recourse to thee." On the opposite side it bears the letter M with a cross and twelve stars beneath which are representations of the Sacred Heart and the Immaculate Heart of the Blessed Virgin.

MISERERE, the first word of its Latin version and title of Psalm 50. It is the fourth penitential Psalm and the most widely used Psalm of penance.

MISSA, the Latin word for Mass. (*Cf.* MASS.)

MISSAL, the liturgical book of the Roman rite, the *Missale Romanum*. It contains the formulas and rites for the celebration of Mass together with the text of the Ordinary (portion said at every Mass) and the Proper (portion which changes with each feast) of the feasts throughout the year. It also contains the Masses for special occasions, prayers for the preparation before and thanksgiving after Mass, and various blessings. The missal began to take its present form under a law of 802 and its form was almost set as we now have it (except for the addition of new feasts, etc.) with the official publication ordered by Pope Pius V in 1570. It was not until the 20th

MIRACULOUS MEDAL—Back and front.

century, with the decrees of St. Pius X regarding frequent Communion, that the use of the missal by the laity assisting at Mass became widespread. The missal appears today in a variety of complete or incomplete translations for the use of the laity, either as "Sunday Missals" with the content limited to the feasts of Sundays, or the "Daily Missal" containing all feastdays of the liturgical year.

MISSION. This word has a variety of meanings as used by the Church, all of which stem from the apostolic commission given to the apostles by Christ (Mk. 6:7–13), and are concerned with the teaching role of the Church in its mission to all men. **1.** Mission is the smallest or simplest territorial organization of the Church. It may be attached to another parish, and is administered by the parish resident priest. **2.** Mission is a title of ordination to Holy Orders (c's. 979–981). **3.** A mission is a territory administered by a priest appointed by the Congregation of Propaganda. Some of these territories have been assigned to the administration of religious orders who appoint superiors over them. As soon as such a district develops, it is made into a prefecture apostolic. **4.** Foreign Missions are the work of the Church in pagan lands under the Sacred Congregation of the Propaganda. **5.** So-called popular missions are series of instructions, sermons, and devotions conducted in a parish for the spiritual welfare of the people. They usually last for several days and may be conducted annually. **6.** Mission Sunday is the second last Sunday in October. Those who make their confession, receive Holy Communion on that day and pray for the conversion of unbelievers gain a plenary indulgence (S.R.C.

Apr. 14, 1926). **7.** Divine Mission is the procession of one Divine Person from another, proceeding by being sent, and producing a new effect in the one sent, e.g., the Son from the Father. (*Cf.* TRINITY.)

MITRE, a folding hat, made up of two equal, cone-shaped parts which rise to a divided peak at the top, the two parts being joined at the base by a cap of soft material to allow flat folding. Attached to the rim in the back are two lappets (*infulae*) which hang down and are usually fringed. The mitre is worn by cardinals, bishops, abbots and certain dignitaries, e.g., prothonotaries apostolic, outside of Rome, and on certain occasions. There are three types or grades of the mitre, the use of each determined by the rubrics: (a) the *precious* mitre, made of cloth or silk of gold, and highly ornamented with embroidery and gems; (b) the *gold* mitre, made of cloth of gold; (c) the *simple* mitre, made of white silk or linen with red-fringed lappets. The mitre has evolved to its present form, but its use as a headdress goes back to the Jewish priestly vestment (Ex. 39:26).

MIXED MARRIAGE. A marriage between a Catholic and a non-Catholic is forbidden by Church law, but a dispensation may be obtained. Such dispensation can only be obtained and the marriage be valid if promises (*cautiones*) are made. These are formal and serious promises made by both parties. The non-Catholic promises to cause no danger to the faith or to lead the Catholic into immoral practices. Both parties must promise to raise the children, present or prospective, in the Catholic faith alone. These promises should be made in writing. In the case of a mixed marriage, the banns are not announced, and there is no nuptial Mass; however, the ordinary may permit some ceremony. In those instances where the non-Catholic is baptized it is called a marriage of *mixed religion*, and the marriage is unlawful but not invalid. Where the non-Catholic is not baptized, the dispensation is classified as one of Disparity of Worship and such a marriage is both unlawful and invalid. (*Cf.* IMPEDIMENTS OF MARRIAGE.)

MODERNISM. Called the "synthesis of all heresies," this was a result of subjectivist thinking which sprang up at the beginning of the 20th century. Among others it took hold of the younger clergy, who found it impossible to reconcile teachings of the faith and the Church with the beliefs of modern science. While containing a wide variety of teachings, all argued for the bringing into harmony with science the doctrines of the Church by means of a radical innovation of reinterpretation. Modernism attacked the most fundamental teachings, as Revelation, faith, Scripture, authority of the Church, etc. All its teachings also centered on Kant's philosophy of agnosticism and, with the destruction or refusal to accept even the scientific proofs for religion, the adherents set about to introduce a "spontaneous" religion. This took the form of establishing man's inner experience, "religious feeling," as the core of this religion, making it quite simply naturalistic. The Church, through Pope St. Pius X, issued two documents condemning modernism: the Decree of the Holy Office, *Lamentabili*, of July 3, 1907, and the encyclical, *Pascendi*, of Sept. 8, 1907. The decree lists 65 condemned propositions of modernism and the encyclical offers an analysis of the propositions of modernism in the light of philosophy, theology, and the teaching of the Church. According to a declaration of the Holy Office of March 22, 1918, those confessors and preachers who make a profession of faith before receiving their faculties in accord with c. 1406, must take an oath against modernism.

MODESTY, that accompanying virtue of the virtue of temperance, which enables one to moderate the external manner, e.g., in dress, in deportment, in conversation. This virtue of modesty is an index of the restraint of thought that marks a person's actions. Its opposite is insolence, boorishness, and all actions which are unbecoming.

MOLINISM, a theory proposed by the Jesuit theologian Louis de Molina (d. 1600) on the relation between grace and free will. It was denounced by theologians of the Thomistic and Augustinian schools because Molina placed too much value on human cooperation at the cost of the efficacy of grace. It was thus the proposition of Molina that grace, either sufficient or efficacious, does not differ before we give our consent. Dominican scholars reject all forms of Molinism. (*Cf.* GRACE.)

MONARCHIANISM, a heresy which sprang from Adoptionism. It was condemned at the councils of Antioch (268 A.D.).

MONASTERY, the community residence of a group of religious who live in seclusion, lead a life of contemplation, and recite the Divine Office in common. This term is used of both male and female religious. The physical property of a monastery differs, but in general each is composed of a church, chapter house, cloister, refectory, work area and individual cells, all usually forming a quadrangle. Over and above the requirements of the particular religious group, a monastery, to be set up, must be canonically erected, i.e., permission in writing must have been obtained from the ordinary; and there must be sufficient means to support the community (c. 496).

MONASTICISM. This mode of life developed very early in the history of the Church. It basically is characterized by asceticism and a life of self-denial which is followed by a group of religious who wish to live in common, under a specific rule, to perfect themselves in the love of God. It arose from the wish of some who sought to be hermits because of individual problems, and banded together for a specific purpose. As early as 451 A.D. at the Council of Chalcedon it was necessary, however, to place such groups under the authority of the bishops. The rule of St. Benedict of Nursia, drawn up in the 6th century, brought about the spread of monasticism in the west. Monastèries were the centers of education through the 12th century, but then were eclipsed by the universities and cathedral schools.

MONITA SECRETA, title given to a spurious, fabricated code by a Polish Jesuit, Jerome Zahorowski, who was discharged from the Society in 1611. It alleged that the fifth general of the Jesuit order had given secret orders to expand the influence and power of the Society.

MONK. Originally, the term referred to a hermit, or a member of a community of men who lived apart from the world under religious vows of poverty, chastity and obedience in accord with a specific religious rule. More popularly, a monk is one who lives in a monastery, or one distinguished from other orders of clerks regular, congregations or societies. Such as are now called monks in the Roman Church are: Benedictines, Cistercians, Trappists, Carthusians, Premonstratensians, and Camaldolese.

MONOPHYSISM also **MONOPHYSITISM,** a heresy begun by Eutyches (d. 454) and condemned by the Council of Chalcedon in 451. It held that there was but one composite nature in Christ.

MONOTHELISM also **MONOTHELITISM.** In the 7th century, when the emperor and the patriarch of Constantinople sought to bring the eastern factions together, the heretical teaching was advanced that Christ had only one will, both human and divine, thus denying the humanity of Christ. This heresy was condemned by the 6th ecumenical council of Constantinople in 680.

MONSIGNOR, title of minor prelates of the Roman court, both active and honorary, but who, as prelates, have no jurisdiction. There are various classes of honorary prelates ranging in degree of rank: **1.** Prothonotaries Apostolic of which there are four grades: (a) participating (7 in Rome); (b) supernumerary; (c) prothonotaries *ad instar;* (d) honorary or black monsignors. **2.** Auditors of the Rota. **3.** Domestic prelates. **4.** Privy chamberlains. **5.** Honorary chamberlains. **6.** Papal chamberlains. The first four grades are addressed "Right Reverend Monsignor." The plural term is "Monsignori." They are permitted to wear violet, with the cassock and vesture for religious ceremonies varying according to the grade. (*Cf.* ROCHET; MANTELLETTA.)

MONS PIETATIS. "Pawnshops for the poor," i.e., funds to provide financial aid to the poor as loans or as direct aid, were set up in the early 16th century through the Fifth Lateran Council (1511), and operated throughout Italy, France, Spain and the Low Countries. They no longer operate as Church institutes.

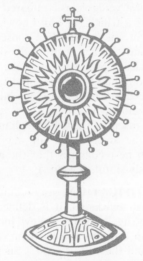

MONSTRANCE

MONSTRANCE. Also called *ostensorium*, this is the special vessel for presenting the Eucharistic Host for adoration by the faithful. It is the shrine wherein the Blessed Sacrament is placed at the ceremony of exposition. The monstrance may be made of any metal, but mostly it is of gold or silver. Since the 16th century, when it came to be shaped like the sun, surrounded by rays, the monstrance has evolved to a degree that it may be of any suitable shape or size. However, it is by dignity that it

should be of high art in design and decoration. It is obligatory that there be a small cross on the top of the monstrance (S.R.C. 2957), and it is proper that it should not be ornamented with small statues or representations of saints. It is into the monstrance that the lunette, bearing the host, is placed.

MONTANA CASE. So named because it was submitted to the Congregation of the Holy Office by the bishop of Helena, Montana, this marriage case concerned a non-baptized man validly married to a woman baptized in the Anglican Church. After divorce, the man wished to become a Catholic, be baptized, and marry a Catholic. The decision of the pope through the Holy Office was to dissolve the previous non-sacramental marriage in favor of the faith, thus permitting a licit and valid marriage to the Catholic party. (Decision of Nov. 6, 1924.)

MONTANISM. The heresy, begun by Montanus of Phrygia (circa 156) and flourishing for a short time, was based upon an unhappy and austere code of conduct, and denied the forgiveness of sins. Tertullian became an apostate by becoming a Montanist in 207.

MONTH'S MIND, non-official name for the anniversary requiem Mass said a month after the death or burial of a person.

MORALITY PLAY, term applied to any religious drama which points out the struggle between virtue and vice, e.g., *Everyman.* (*Cf.* MIRACLE PLAYS.)

MORAL THEOLOGY. Properly, this is part rather than a division of the science of theology. In its more restricted sense, moral theology deals with God's laws, specifically with the determination whether acts are right or wrong in the light of God's laws. It provides the scientific exposition of human conduct as directed by reason and faith to the attainment of our supernatural end. It gives us the fundamental rules by which we must regulate our actions, and discusses the application of these rules in innumerable variety of circumstances, covering the whole of life. Moral theology is divided into three major parts: first principles; the commandments; and the sacraments. (*Cf.* THEOLOGY.)

MORGANATIC MARRIAGE, a licit and valid marriage between a man of noble rank and a woman of inferior rank. It is usually subject to the condition that succession of the family title will not descend to the children. It does not differ in any way, in so far as Church law is concerned, from any other marriage, and carries no special favors outside of the law.

MORSE

MORSE, the clasp which fastens and holds a cope about the shoulders. The morse may be of metal, consisting of a hook and eye or chain and hook arrangement, or it may be of cloth. Metal clasps are not used in Rome. The morse may be jeweled but only for copes of prelates.

MORTAL SIN, the transgression, with full knowledge and free consent of the will, of a divine law (every just law is derived from the divine law, either natural or positive) in a serious matter. Sin is mortal because of: (a) Matter. This means when the nature of sin is such that it can never be venial (e.g., unbelief, lewd actions), or when the matter is important as compared to a light matter (e.g., theft of a valuable as compared with stealing a trifle). (b) Full knowledge, which means the absolute consciousness that the act is mortally sinful. This clear awareness may be had when one makes up his mind to act and need not be a conscious advertence while performing the act. (c) Free consent of the will, which means that one freely wills an act even though he recognizes that the act is seriously sinful. (*Cf.* SIN.)

MORTIFICATION, any conscious form of self-denial. It is defined as: "The struggle against our evil inclinations in order to subject them to the will, and the will of God." Such ascetical practices are necessary to the perfection of the Christian: "If any man will come after Me, let him deny himself" (Lk. 9:23). It is obvious that a closer union with God can only be attained by detaching oneself from love of material things (*cf.* DETACHMENT). However, mortification should be effective, that is, it should be directed by a pure motive, e.g., to give up sweets in order to lose weight is essentially different from mortifying one's love for sweets out of love of God. While mortification involves the entire make-up of the pleasure urge of one's body, mind, and soul, it must be performed with discretion. At the same time, there is a broad basis for application, e.g., all the senses may be subject to self-denial, thus custody of the eyes, to avoid looking at or seeing pleasurable subjects, may be practiced in many ways. (*Cf.* ASCETICISM.)

MOTHER OF GOD. *See* MARY, VIRGIN MOTHER OF GOD.

MOTIVE, SPIRITUAL, the reason or purpose for action which imparts an added moral goodness to a good act. (*Cf.* LOVE OF GOD.)

MOTU PROPRIO. Literally, from the Latin, "by one's own accord," this term refers to papal documents, containing the words, *Motu proprio et certa scientia.* These documents are written on the personal initiative of the pope and are either administrative or confer personal favors of the pontiff. The most famous of recent years and the one which is quoted as the "Motu Proprio" by title is that issued by Pope St. Pius X (Nov. 22, 1903) on Church music. It restored the use of Gregorian chant, instructed on the type of music proper to Church ceremony, the choir, etc.

MOVABLE FEASTS. Because the Church calendar is determined upon a luni-solar cycle, there are some feasts which occur earlier or later in the civil calendar. These feasts are set as to date by their place in regard to the feast of Easter. The feast of Easter is always the first Sunday following the first full moon after the vernal equinox, March 21. Easter, therefore, may come as early as March 22, or as late as April 25. The movable feasts, established in each year in relation to the date of Easter, are: Ascension Day, Pentecost, Trinity Sunday, and the feast of Corpus Christi. There are also other feasts which may be considered as movable from the standpoint that they do not fall on the same date but are determined by the calendar adjustment, e.g., the Feast of Christ the King occurs on the last Sunday of October. (*Cf.* CALENDAR, ECCLESIASTICAL; FEASTS OF THE CHURCH.)

MOZARABIC RITE. Also called the Rite of Toledo or the Visigothic rite, or Isidorian rite, this derived from the Gallican rite and was used throughout Spain and what is now Portugal up to the 11th century. It is used now only in a chapel of the Cathedral of Toledo, chiefly as a memorial. The rite differs from the Roman in many aspects, e.g., the bread and wine are prepared before the Introit, the Gospel is sung, and it has multiple prefaces.

MOZZETTA, a non-liturgical vestment. It is a short cape of silk or wool reaching to the elbows, open in front and only fastened at the throat although it has a row of buttons for fastening. To the collar in the back is

MOZZETTA

affixed a small hood which, however, is not used but is rather a vestige of a vestment of earlier times. The mozzetta is worn over the rochet, is a mark of jurisdiction, and is permitted to be worn by cardinals, archbishops and bishops in their own dioceses and by abbots in their abbeys.

MUNDATORY. The linen towel used as a purificator in the Mass is sometimes referred to by this name.

MURATORIAN FRAGMENT. This partial manuscript, written before 200 A.D., contains a list of books (canon of Scripture) which were recognized as authoritative at Rome at the end of the 2nd century. The fragment was discovered by Muratori in the Ambrosian Library of Milan in 1740 and named after him. It includes the four Gospels, the Epistles of St. Paul (except Heb.), two Epistles of John and Jude and the Apocalypse.

MUSIC, CHURCH. Music for the Church must be in accord with the spirit of the liturgy (c. 1264). Forbidden for use in Church are: Masses by Mozart, Haydn, Farmer, Lambillotte, Schubert, Wiegand, etc., also music based upon profane operas. Likewise, the use of percussion instruments, e.g., the drum, and the piano, is not permitted. (*Cf.* CHANT; GREGORIAN MUSIC.)

MYSTERIES OF THE ROSARY. Those events in the lives of Jesus and His Mother, Mary, upon which one reciting the prayers of the Rosary, either privately or publicly, is to meditate are called the mysteries of the Rosary. There are fifteen mysteries, one each to be meditative material for the fifteen decades of the full Rosary. Each subject should be spoken or thought of before beginning a decade and, according to the practice

of meditation, kept in mind during the reciting of the prayers. For convenience, and in sequence, the mysteries are divided into three groups of five. The *Joyful Mysteries* are the Annunciation, Visitation, Nativity, the Presentation, and the Finding of the Child Jesus in the Temple. The *Sorrowful Mysteries* are the Agony in the Garden, the Scourging, the Crowning with Thorns, the Carrying of the Cross, and the Crucifixion. The *Glorious Mysteries* are the Resurrection, the Ascension, the Descent of the Holy Spirit, the Assumption of the Blessed Virgin into Heaven, and the Coronation of the Blessed Virgin as Queen of Heaven. It is also recommended that a cycle of these mysteries be observed when saying the Rosary daily, that is, a Rosary of five decades. Thus, Monday the joyful mysteries are meditated on, Tuesday the sorrowful and Wednesday the glorious. On Thursday, the cycle begins again. The Sunday cycle is this: during Advent and until Septuagesima Sunday, the joyful mysteries; from Septuagesima until Easter Sunday, the sorrowful mysteries; on Easter Sunday and continuing through to the first Sunday of Advent, the glorious mysteries are to be meditated upon. (*Cf.* ROSARY.)

MYSTERY. The supernatural truths which the Church teaches and which cannot be known without revelation, are not contrary to reason, but rather above reason. They are of such a profound nature that they cannot be understood by man even after revelation and must, therefore, be accepted on faith in revelation and the authority of the Church. St. Paul speaks of the "Mystery" as being that of the redemption, a composite of all the other mysteries: "We speak of the wisdom of God, mysterious, hidden, which God foreordained before the world unto our glory . . . to us God has revealed them through His Spirit" (1 Cor. 2:7–10). To St. Paul, the greatest proof of God's love for us was our redemption in Christ (Eph. 1:7–12). Mysteries must be considered as ideas or works of God which are beyond the reach of man's natural knowledge. Such mysteries, while they are innumerable in man's experience, are part of his belief in the Church, as, the Redemption, the Incarnation, the Trinity, the Eucharist, etc.

MYSTICAL BODY OF CHRIST. The truth of faith, embracing the Scriptural teaching of Christ as the Head and the members of the Church as the "body" of Christ. Pope Pius XII in his encyclical, *Mystici Corporis Christi* ("The Mystical Body of Christ," 1943) writes: "If we would define and describe this true Church of Jesus Christ—which is the One, Holy, Catholic, Apostolic, Roman Church—we shall find no expression more noble, more sublime or more divine than the phrase which calls it 'the Mystical Body of Jesus Christ.' This title is derived from and is, as it were, the fair flower of the repeated teaching of Sacred Scripture and the Holy Fathers." Pius XII then goes on to state who are members of the body: "Only those are really to be included as members of the Church who have been baptized and profess the true faith and who have not unhappily withdrawn from body-unity or for grave faults been excluded by legitimate authority." The term has been in use in the Church since the 9th century, but its basis in Scripture is most secure. St. Paul spoke of the "Head of the Body" (Col. 1:18) and

while the Head is distinct from the body, it is united (Col. 1:24) with the body and is the cause of the supernatural growth of all the members. This is the teaching of the early Church, for all were "in Christ" and each was to grow into the likeness of Him, an image of the invisible God, and subserving the good of the whole, a unity based on charity.

MYSTICAL SENSE OF SCRIPTURE. Besides the literal sense (*cf.* LITERAL SENSE OF SCRIPTURE), there is another, the mystical sense of Scripture. It is also called spiritual or typological. Through this there is found a meaning authoritatively revealed by God to man, though not the exact meaning of the words. St. Thomas states: "The things signified by the words (literal sense) may also signify other things (spiritual sense)." Thus the spiritual sense is founded upon the literal sense, with the spiritual sense brought out upon the solid findings of interpretation. There can be no exact limit as to the ways in which the spiritual sense is derived, but there are certain guides: (1) We can make a derived understanding from the manner of expression, e.g., if the literal sense is expressed in a metaphor then the spiritual sense is in the metaphor, e.g., Christ referring to Peter as the "rock", the spiritual sense being that in this person is the "foundation" stone of the Church. (2) We may gather, since the O.T. as a whole prefigures the N.T., that there are types of the O.T. which prefigure the Church on earth, and this is the allegorical sense, which is a kind of spiritual sense as is the anagogical sense. (*cf.* ALLEGORICAL SENSE; ANAGOGICAL.) The spiritual sense of Scripture, because of the difficulty in interpretation, should be used sparingly and be founded upon sound exegesis.

MYSTICAL THEOLOGY. This portion of the science of theology is the furthest development of moral and ascetical theology. It considers not the ordinary ways of perfection, but the extraordinary ways. As such it deals with infused contemplation, special supernatural gifts, and all supernatural experiences and phenomena related to contemplation. (*Cf.* THEOLOGY.)

MYSTICISM, the subject matter proper to mystical theology, i.e., the study of the mystic states. In regard to the mystic, the word refers to those supernatural acts or states which our own industry is not able to produce, even in a low degree, or for a short, momentary time. St. Teresa of Avila reduces these to degrees of mystical contemplation, naming four: (a) the prayer of quiet, wherein the spirit rests without distraction; (b) full union, in which the presence of God is dominant; (c) ecstasy, in which the senses are not used; (d) transforming union, or the presence of God and the sharing of the divine life of Christ. This is one system, but there may be others in the sequence of perfection. Mysticism is the approach and investigation, and even participation, in the supernatural life.

N

NAHUM, BOOK OF, a prophetical book of the O.T. written by Nahum, whose name means "comfort." Little is known of the author except that he was an Elcesite of the tribe of Simeon. The book was written probably between 622 and 612 B.C. The writing is very poetic and the main theme is the fate of Nineveh, the oppressor of the people.

NAME, CHRISTIAN, the name given to a child in baptism. It should be the name of a saint or a name abbreviated or derived from a saint's name and this name is to be entered on the baptismal record. If the parents have not chosen a saint's name, the pastor is to supply one and this name together with that chosen by the parents is to be entered on the baptismal record (c. 761).

NAME-DAY, the day on which the feast of the saint whose name one bears is celebrated. In some countries, rather than the birthday anniversary, the name-day is observed.

NAME OF MARY. First mention of this name is made in Genesis. It was the given name of the sister of Moses. (*Cf.* MARY, VIRGIN MOTHER OF GOD.)

NAMES OF OUR LORD. Jesus Christ as the Second Person of the Blessed Trinity has been given a variety of names descriptive of His accomplishment of the redemption of man. Many of these are derived from O.T., from the descriptive names given to Christ by the apostles, and many are names of honor given to our Lord by Christian writers or found in the liturgy. Examples from O.T.: Emmanuel (Is. 7:14); Holy One (Ps. 15:10); Prince of Peace (Is. 9:6). From the N.T.: Beginning and end (Apoc. 1:8); Lamb of God (Jn. 1:29); Wisdom of God (1 Cor. 1:24). From the liturgy: Captain of our salvation (Matins of Epiphany); Peaceful (Vespers I of Christmas Day).

NARCOTICS. *See* GLUTTONY.

NATIONAL CATHOLIC WELFARE CONFERENCE. As a successor to the National Catholic War Council (1918–1919), this national organization of the Catholic bishops of the United States was called into being on February 20, 1919, its title being abbreviated N.C.W.C. Its first meeting was held on Sept. 24, 1919. The conference has advisory powers only, not jurisdictional, and as such is not looked upon as a formal council. Thus, when not in formal Council, the bishops merely deliberate, suggest and recommend to all bishops their resolutions for universal adoption throughout the country. Yearly the conference prepares and publicizes a joint statement expressive of the common viewpoint of the assembled bishops. The conference is organized to direct its attention to a wide variety of national problems concerning the Church and to procedures which, while friendly recommendations, bear the dignity of the teaching sphere of the Church. In organization there is first an administrative board, which meets annually in the spring at Washington, D.C. This board is headed by a chairman elected by the board members for a term of one year, and he is assisted by a vice-chairman, secretary and treasurer. It is the work of this board to supervise through the heads of departments as based upon the Papal Brief, *Communes*, of Pope Benedict XV, April 10, 1919. These departments are: Executive Department, Department of Education, Legal Department, Press Department, Department of Catholic Action Study, Department of Lay Organizations, Department of Social Action (Social Work and Hospitals), and the Department of Youth. Besides these standing departments there are a number of episcopal committees, each concerned with a special work of current or permanent importance. In general these committees are: American Board of Catholic Missions, Committee on the Propagation of the Faith, on the Confraternity of Christian Doctrine, on Seminaries, for Polish Relief, for the Spanish speaking, on Motion Pictures, on War Emergency and Relief, for the Montezuma Seminary, to complete the Shrine of the Immaculate Conception, on the National Organization for Decent Literature, on the Mexican Seminary, for the North American College at Rome, and the Special Committee to Promote the Pope's Peace Plan. Their joint work, the annual statement of the assembly, and the periodic statements of the committees are a catalogue of Catholic Action in the United States.

NATIONAL COUNCILS OF CATHOLIC MEN AND WOMEN. These are organizations which comprise the N.C.W.C. Department of Lay Organizations, and unify Catholic activity of more than three thousand national, state, diocesan and local organizations of the laity.

NATIONAL SYNOD. *See* SYNOD.

NATIVITY OF CHRIST. *See* CHRISTMAS; INCARNATION.

NATIVITY OF THE BLESSED VIRGIN. While the exact date of the birth of the Blessed Mother is not known, her genealogy is given in Mt. 1:1–16, and a feast celebrated on Sept. 8 commemorates the event.

NATURALISM, a rationalistic system of philosophy and theology which denies the supernatural and centers on nature alone. Its arguments are of two lines: rejection of God through a pantheistic concept that deifies nature, and rejection of revelation.

NATURAL THEOLOGY. Also called theodicy, this is the highest branch of the study of philosophy which investigates and demonstrates what human reason, unaided by revelation, can know about God.

NAVE, the main or central space of a church, comprised of the area between the entry and the sanctuary. Formerly this included the transepts, if there were any, but now a distinction is made. It is in this area that pews for the faithful are placed.

NEMOURS, EDICT OF.

Demanded by the Catholic League of France and signed by Henry III of France (d. 1589), this edict outlawed Calvinism in France.

NEO-SCHOLASTICISM.

This movement, also called Neo-Thomism, was begun in the late 19th century, notably at the University of Louvain. Neo-Scholasticism was effective in bringing Thomistic thought back into favor. Pope Leo XIII aided it by making scholasticism official in the Roman colleges and universities and introduced it into all Catholic schools with the publication of his encyclical, *Aeterni Patris* (1879). The movement attained wide influence and transformed the intellectual position of Catholic philosophy throughout the world. It continues with widespread teaching and publication of numerous journals of philosophy and new translations of the works of St. Thomas Aquinas.

NESTORIANISM,

a heresy begun by Nestorius, a priest of Antioch, after he became patriarch of Constantinople in 428. He declared that the Blessed Virgin was mother only of Christ's human nature and he banned the term "Theotokos" (Mother of God); he also taught that only Christ as man died on the cross. This heresy was condemned by the ecumenical council of Ephesus in 431, but persists to this day in an isolated group of Syria who have a Nestorian diocese in Malabar.

NEW TESTAMENT. *See* BIBLE.

NICAEA (NICE) COUNCILS OF.

The first ecumenical council was convoked at Nicaea by Constantine the Great in 325. It was called to settle the dispute over the relationship between the First and Second Persons of the Blessed Trinity, and it also condemned the heretical teaching of Arius (Arianism). The Second Council of Nicaea (7th ecumenical council) was held in 787 and defined the Catholic teaching regarding the veneration of images and condemned the heresy of adoptionism.

NICENE CREED.

The formal and orderly presentation of the chief doctrines of the Catholic faith was formulated at the first ecumenical council of Nicaea (325 A.D.). It established in an authoritative and true expression of belief the divinity of the Second Person of the Trinity by pronouncing that the Son is "consubstantial with the Father." It was at the beginning of the 11th century that this Nicene Creed, already incorporated in the liturgy of the Mass in some places, was officially made a part of the Roman rite of the Mass by Pope Benedict VIII, and it remains so today.

NIGHT, DARK, OF THE SOUL.

The term refers to a phase of the spiritual progress to perfection as outlined by St. John of the Cross in the first part of his writings. It is also called the "passive night of the senses" and as such is considered as a passive purification of the senses of the soul, which is to say it is concerned with a purification of internal trials positively willed by God or at least permitted by Him, as periods of aridity (a lack of will to pray), desolation, doubts in and temptations to despair of prayer, and other internal trials. St. John of the Cross teaches that souls are led into the passive night of the senses when God raises them from the state of beginners in contemplation to the more advanced state of proficients, that is, when they begin to partake of the first gifts of infused contemplation. It precedes the second purging, the passive night of the soul, which period occurs before the soul is raised to the transforming union with God (in so far as this is possible in life) and which can only take place when the soul is purged of every least inclination to self-love.

NIMBUS, a radiance of light used in art which may surround the head of a saint to depict his sanctity. It differs from the halo in that it is less defined. (*Cf.* AUREOLE.)

NOBLE GUARDS. Chosen from the Roman nobility, their members form the highest rank in the corps of the papal military service. They appear with the pope on state occasions of solemnity.

NOCTURN. 1. Originally the title of the entire night office as said between midnight and 4 a.m., consisting of Matins and Lauds of the Divine Office. **2.** Now the name of a division of Matins, of which there are three, each consisting of a group of three Psalms, their antiphons, versicles and responses, the Our Father, an absolution, a blessing, and three lessons. On simple feasts and ferias there is read but one Nocturn made up of nine Psalms and three lessons.

NOMOCANON, a collection, in alphabetical arrangement, of Church and civil law in use in the Eastern Church.

NONE, the name of the 9th hour of the Divine Office. This part of the breviary is constructed like the other lesser hours. (*Cf.* DIVINE OFFICE.)

NORTH AMERICAN COLLEGE. Founded at Rome in 1859 by Pope Pius IX, the enrollment in this educational institution for the training of men for the priesthood is made up chiefly of students from the United States.

NOVATIANISM, a schism and heresy, organized by Novatian who established himself as the first anti-pope in 251. It taught among other things that those who had fallen away from the faith could never be reconciled with the Church. Novatian was condemned by Pope St. Cornelius and a Roman council. The schism lasted until about 350.

NOVENA, a cycle of prayers spanning nine days. It consists of prescribed prayers and devotions, and usually includes the reception of the sacraments of penance and Holy Eucharist. A novena may be made in common in church or in private. The *Raccolta* lists 36 novenas that are indulgenced by the Church. The practice is commemorative of the "Novena of the Apostles," i.e., the days spent in prayer by them in the Cenacle between the Ascension and Pentecost (Acts 1:13–14), and the only novena which must be observed in parochial churches is that preceding the feast of Pentecost.

NOVICE. A novice is one who, having been confirmed in his or her religious vocation by a period of postulancy, enters a further time of preparation known as the novitiate. Usually the period of the novitiate is not less than one year and at its conclusion, upon recommendation of the superiors, the novice is permitted to be professed as a religious. Reception into the novitiate is governed by canon law (c's. 542, 544).

NUMBERS, BOOK OF, title of the fourth book of the O.T. It gives historical narratives and accounts on legislation, telling the history of the wanderings of the Israelites in the wilderness from the Sinaitic region to the plains of Moab, describing the ecclesiastical hierarchy of the Jewish priesthood, and emphasizing the justice of God and the power of intercession.

NUN, a member of a religious congregation of women. In canon law, nuns are classed as "moniales," i.e., women religious in solemn vows.

NUNC DIMITTIS, the title of the song of Simeon (Lk. 2:29–32). It is taken from the first words of the song's Latin version.

NUNCIO, title of a representative of the Holy See. A nuncio serves in a permanent diplomatic capacity, with the rank of ambassador. (*Cf.* LEGATE.)

NUPTIAL MASS AND BLESSING. In the Roman rite there is a special Mass assigned to be read at a marriage. The blessing to the married couple is read by the priest immediately after the *Pater Noster*. The blessing, however, is never given without the Mass being celebrated. The solemn blessing with the Nuptial Mass is forbidden during Lent and on Easter Sunday, and during Advent and on Christmas Day. The ordinary may grant permission for the solemnity of marriage within this period. A simple marriage ceremony may take place at any time of the year.

O

O ANTIPHONS. So called because each begins with the letter O, these are the "great" antiphons recited from December 17 to 23 inclusive at the Magnificat in Vespers.

OATH. An oath is an invocation of God as witness to the truth of a statement or to the honesty and fidelity of a promise. It is thus made either as an assertion of the truth or as a promise to perform some action. To be valid and lawful, it is necessary that the one making the assertion is absolutely convinced of the truth, or that the one making the promise has firmly resolved to keep it. It also is necessary for validity that the oath be made according to formula, direct or indirect, and that there be an intention, at least virtual, so to swear. (*Cf.* PERJURY.) We are advised against taking oaths lightly or using them too frequently by St. James in his Epistle, 5:12.

OATH AGAINST MODERNISM. *See* MODERNISM.

OBEDIENCE. 1. The moral virtue by which one is enabled to submit to the will or law of one in authority or one delegated by him who is his representative. Through this virtue one is enabled to recognize the authority and follow the law without hesitancy. The application of this virtue may be called for by (a) a contract, (b) by a vow, (c) by piety, (d) by the office of one in authority. **2.** The counsel of obedience is the denial of self to combat pride, and to submit one's independence of mind and will for a greater ideal (Lk. 9:23; Phil. 2:8). **3.** The vow taken by a religious obliges him to obey his superior in all things which are commanded in virtue of obedience. This is an explicit obligation when given "in virtue of obedience," whereas it may be only adherence to the counsel when some regulation is concerned. **4.** Obedience in marriage: the wife has the obligation to obey the husband. This is not a formal vow, but arises out of the effects of the marriage contract.

OBLATION, literally, an offering. In the Mass, it is that act in which the celebrant places the unconsecrated bread on the paten and raises it up before the consecration.

OBLIGATION, DAYS OF. *See* HOLYDAYS.

OBREPTION. In canon law, the term refers to a statement made in writing which declares something as false in a petition or a rescript. (*Cf.* SUBREPTION.)

OBSESSION, the state of being molested though not actually possessed by the evil spirits.

OCCASION OF SIN. This is not to be confused with the danger of sinning. An occasion of sin may be a person, place or thing which offers one the opportunity, inducement or enticement to sin. Occasion also involves the internal or subjective inclination to sin. The occasion may be proximate, i.e., when it is such that it almost always results in sin. This proximate occasion may be (a) free, i.e., easily avoidable, or (b) necessary, i.e., avoidable only with difficulty, if at all.

OCTAVE. The total of eight days made up of a feast day and the seven following days is so called. The feasts of Christmas, Easter, and Pentecost, e.g., have octaves. The name also applies to the last, the eighth, day of such Church feasts.

OCTAVE PSALMS, the name applied to Psalms 6 and 11.

OFFERTORY. In the Mass, that essential action which follows the Gospel, or the Creed if it is said, wherein the celebrant reads the prayer of the proper called "Offertory verse" and then, after taking the veil from the chalice, offers first the bread to be consecrated on the paten, then the chalice containing wine and water. In the law of the Israelites there were three kinds of offerings: thank-offerings or "sacrifices of praise" (Ps. 49:14); vow-offerings made in fulfillment of a vow (Ps. 60:9); and free-will offerings (Ps. 53:8). All are contained in the offering of the Mass. In the Sacrifice of the Mass, Christ offers Himself; bread and wine become the body and blood of Christ; Christ is the Priest and offers Himself for the whole world. Thus the Mass is a true, unbloody sacrifice. The offertory is the first essential act of the sacrificial rite.

OFFICE. 1. The Divine Office, the official prayer of the Church (*cf.* BREVIARY). **2.** Any portion of the Divine Office is often referred to simply as the "Office," e.g., the Office of a particular feast. **3.** The liturgy of the Church, including both the Divine Office for the day together with the Mass. (*Cf.* LITURGY.)

OFFICE OF THE DEAD, the title of the Divine Office as recited on November 2, All Souls' Day. The prayers are for the repose of the souls of the dead, and a form consisting of 1st Vespers, Matins, and Lauds, is often chanted before a funeral Mass.

OILS, HOLY. *See* HOLY OILS.

OIL STOCK

OIL STOCK, a cylindrical metal case, usually made with three separate compartments, each for one of the Holy Oils and so marked with the initials of the oils. The method of keeping the oil in the stocks is to saturate a piece of cotton or wool. The oil stock is to be retained in a proper, safe place in the church or baptistry. (*Cf.* AMBRY.)

OLD CATHOLICS. Catholics who refused to accept the decree of papal infallibility as defined by the Vatican Council in 1870 were given this name.

OLD TESTAMENT. *See* BIBLE.

OMBRELLINO, from the Italian, literally, a "little umbrella." The ombrellino has a flat top made of white silk and ornamented with gold fringe and is supported by a longer staff than the ordinary umbrella. It is used as a canopy when the Blessed Sacrament is carried from one place to another in church in another than a solemn procession. (*Cf.* BALDAQUIN.)

OMBRELLINO

OMNIPOTENCE, an attribute of God, recognized in the ability of the Creator to do all things that are possible. Knowledge (wisdom), will, and power are one in God. It is also the distinct mark of sovereignty as those sovereign powers claimed by Christ in sending forth His disciples: "All power in heaven and on earth has been given to Me" (Mt. 28:18). It is by this power that the world-wide kingdom, which the Resurrection inaugurated, will be established.

OMNISCIENCE. This is God's attribute of knowing all things simply and absolutely. The doctrine of Providence implies omniscience, for God, in ruling and directing all things to His own glory, must know all things, even the most secret, and He must know them now rather than as a sequence. (*Cf.* ATTRIBUTES OF GOD.)

OMOPHORION, a vestment worn by bishops of the Byzantine rite. It consists of a ten-inch wide band of silk or velvet which is wrapped loosely around the neck so that one end hangs over the left shoulder in front and the other over the left shoulder to the back, the ends reaching almost to the ground. It corresponds to the pallium of the Roman rite.

ONTOLOGISM. The principle tenet of this philosophic system which was first advanced by Malebranche (d. 1715) and was developed in the early 19th century, is that the human intellect may in this life possess the immediate knowledge of God. In its extreme form, it was condemned by the Holy See under seven propositions (Decree of the Holy Office, 1861) and later in 1887. It is in error because it eliminates the supernatural character of intuitive vision and leads to pantheism.

OPUS OPERATUM. *See* EX OPERE OPERATO.

ORANGE, COUNCILS OF. The first of these councils, held in 441 at Orange (Aransio) in Southern France, pronounced on the administration of the sacraments and ecclesiastical jurisdiction. The second was called in 529 and condemned semi-Pelagianism.

ORARION, the stole worn by the deacon in the Byzantine rite. It is made up of a narrow band of silk, four yards long, and embroidered on it three times is the word "Holy" in Greek.

ORATORY, a place set aside for divine worship, but not primarily for the public, thus differing from a church (c's. 1188–1196). There are three types of oratories: (a) public i.e., one erected for the use of a community, such as religious, but to which, for convenience or other reason, the public has access for divine services; (b) semi-public, one which is intended for the use of some particular group (of some size), e.g., a chapel in a seminary, and to which the public does not have access; (c) private, i.e., an oratory for the particular use of a family or person, usually within the house or manorial building. It requires an apostolic indult before such an oratory can be established.

ORDERS, HOLY, SACRAMENT OF. The sacrament of the New Law, instituted by Christ, by which spiritual power is given together with the grace to exercise properly the respective office. The sacrament gives a permanent character, meaning that it cannot be repeated, and that it ordains one for all eternity. The sacrament is conferred through a series of ceremonials, each distinctive in its effect since each gives additional power and grace to the one receiving. Preliminary to the reception of holy orders, but not a part of the sacrament, is the conferring of tonsure by which one acquires the clerical state (c. 108). In the course of events leading up to the reception of holy orders, following tonsure, there are four preparatory steps which are not properly sacramental but are necessary: these are called the four *minor orders*, namely, porter, lector, exorcist and acolyte (c. 949). After the acceptance of these four minor orders there follows the first major order which is the subdiaconate, which in itself is not a sacrament but because of its essential character and its traditional importance is considered the first of the major orders. The effects produced and signified by the sacrament of holy orders through the administration of ordination to the diaconate, the priesthood, and the episcopacy, are the *power* of orders and the *grace* of the Holy Spirit, which are found to be sufficiently signified by the imposition of hands and the words which determine it. In the ordination to the diaconate, the *matter* of the sacrament is the one imposition of the hands of the ordaining bishop; the *form* consists of the words of the Preface, essentially these which begin: "Send down on him, we beseech Thee, O Lord, the Holy Spirit . . ." The next major order is ordination to the simple priesthood, which confers the power to consecrate the body and blood of Christ, to forgive sins and administer extreme unction. "In the ordination to the priesthood, the matter is the first imposition of hands of the bishop which is done in silence, but not the continuation of the same imposition through the extension of the right hand, nor the last imposition to which are attached the words: 'Receive the Holy Spirit: whose sins you shall forgive' . . . etc. The form consists of the words of the Preface which begin: 'Give we beseech Thee, Almighty Father . . .' " Finally, the full reception of the sacrament of holy orders is the episcopal ordination or consecration which is a receiving of the fullness or complete power, conferring the power to confirm and to ordain. The matter of episcopal ordination is the imposition of hands which is done by the bishop consecrator; the form consists of the words of the Preface which begin: "Complete in your priest the fullness of your ministry . . ." etc. (Apostolic Constitution, Pius XII, Nov. 30, 1947.) The ordinary minister of the sacrament of holy orders is a consecrated bishop (c. 951), and the extraordinary minister is one who has faculties to confer certain orders, by common law or indult of the Holy See (c. 951). For the administration of the episcopate, the consecrating bishop must be one who has received a special mandate from the Holy See (c. 953). All the degrees of holy orders are morally one sacrament. The sacrament as seen in the record of Scripture is specific in that the laying on of hands is used, not only to give the Holy Spirit, but to confer authority and spiritual powers (2 Tim. 1:6). Through the sacrament of holy orders there is conferred on God's ministers the threefold power of teaching, ministering and governing (Mt. 28:19–20).

ORDERS, RELIGIOUS, a title loosely applied to all religious groups of men or women. According to canon law (c. 488), the following distinctions are made: (a) an order is a religious community, men or women, in which solemn vows are taken; (b) a congregation is one in which only simple vows are made, and these may be temporary or perpetual; (c) exempt religious are those belonging to a religious institute which is withdrawn from the jurisdiction of the local ordinary; (d) a clerical community is one in which the majority

of its members are priests; (e) a lay institute of religious is one wherein the majority are not ordained, e.g., Christian Brothers.

ORDINARY. 1. In Church law, this term designates one who exercises ordinary jurisdiction in the external forum (as well as in the internal forum), which jurisdiction is attached to an office by law. Thus it includes, besides the Roman pontiff, residential bishops as of a diocese, abbots, prelates nullius, vicars-general, administrators apostolic, vicars and prefects apostolic and their successors in office, the administrator assigned to a vacant diocese, and the major superiors of exempt clerical communities (major superiors being: abbots, superior general, and provincial). Local ordinaries include the above except the major superiors. **2.** The Ordinary of the Mass is the constant (with slight exceptions) part of the prayers of the Mass (*cf.* MASS). **3.** That portion, called Ordinary, of the Breviary which other than in the Psalms does not change.

ORDINATION. *See* ORDERS, HOLY, SACRAMENT OF.

ORDO, the usual title which is also the first Latin word of the book "The Order for the Recitation of the Divine Office and the Celebration of Mass." The book contains, in sequence throughout the year, brief directions for the Mass and the Divine Office to be said every day of the properly approved calendar of the Church. Each diocese, religious order, and congregation has its own Ordo. It is a necessary book for the priest and, while written in Latin, it is printed with a great number of abbreviations.

ORIENTAL CHURCH, SACRED CONGREGATION FOR THE. This Roman Congregation of the Holy See exercises, according to canon law (c. 257), jurisdiction over the dioceses, bishops, clergy, religious and faithful of the Oriental (Eastern) rites. The Orientals are bound by the Code of Canon Law by all canons containing dogmatic definitions, and those dealing with faith and morals. In the United States, with headquarters in New York City, the "Catholic Near East Welfare Association" serves as an adjunct to this Sacred Congregation for the purpose of collecting alms for the faithful of the Oriental rites. (*Cf.* SACRED ROMAN CONGREGATIONS.)

ORIGINAL JUSTICE. *See* JUSTICE.

ORIGINAL SIN. The consequence of the fall of man's first parents, Adam and Eve (Gen. 3:1–24), who sinned against the all-loving God and thus lost divine grace, is for their descendants called original sin or stain. As a result of this first sin and as its consequences there follow death, concupiscence or the rebellion of man's lower appetites against reason and will, and a darkening of the intellect. By the redemption of man by Christ, everyone was restored to the friendship of God and given the grace, beyond our natural powers, to attain the everlasting love of God in heaven.

The nature of the sin committed by Adam and Eve is mixed and grave. Because of its nature it affected all their descendants. It was a sin of pride in all its elements (Eccu. 10:15). It was also a sin of gravest disobedience and ingratitude. Its effects were overcome by the redemption, as St. Paul declares (Rom. 8:14–23). By baptism we receive the grace of incorporation in the body of Christ, and this life, guided by the Spirit, aided by the sacraments and the Church, leads to final triumph over concupiscence and death by bodily resurrection with Christ on the day of His final coming. St. Thomas declares: "Original sin is concupiscence, materially, but privation of original justice, formally" (I–II, qu. 82, Art. 3), and "original sin is called concupiscence rather than ignorance, although ignorance is comprised among the material defects of original sin" (Ibid.).

ORLEANS, COUNCIL OF. Held at Orleans, in France, in 511, under the patronage of the Frankish King Clovis, this national council enacted important Church legislation.

ORTHODOX CHURCH. The word "orthodox" was originally used to distinguish those Churches which accepted the Council of Chalcedon and its rulings from the heretics who rejected it. After the schism of 1054 resulting from the age-old differences between the Greek Church and the Holy See, the term was used to distinguish those same Eastern Churches from Rome. The Orthodox Eastern Church was formed of a group of these Churches, united more or less under the patriarchate of Constantinople. (The Byzantine Greeks in Italy and the Maronites of Syria retained communion with Rome.) At the capture of Constantinople by the Turks, in 1453, the authority of the patriarch of that city was lessened. Thereafter the Orthodox Eastern Church broke up into the more or less autonomous national Churches of Cyprus, Georgia, Sinai, Russia, Greece, Bulgaria, Rumania, Yugoslavia, Albania, Czechoslovakia, Estonia, Finland, Poland, Latvia, Lithuania, and the previous patriarchates of Alexandria, Antioch and Jerusalem. Some of their national status has largely been lost through the dominance of Russia over some of these countries. (*Cf.* EASTERN CHURCHES.)

ORTHODOXY, FEAST OF. Observed in the Byzantine rite on the first Sunday of Lent, this feast celebrates the restoration of the icons to the churches, the defeat of iconoclasm, and the triumph of orthodoxy (true doctrine).

OSCULATORIUM. The "Kiss of Peace" is known also by this Latin name.

OSTENSORIUM. *See* MONSTRANCE.

OSTIARIUS, the Latin title for the lowest of Minor Orders. (*Cf.* DOORKEEPER; ORDERS, HOLY, SACRAMENT OF.)

OUR FATHER. *See* LORD'S PRAYER.

OUR LADY. This familiar and endearing title of the Blessed Virgin Mary is a prefatory to many fuller titles given to the Blessed Mother for her favors to the Church, e.g., Our Lady of Mount Carmel; Our Lady of Ransom; Our Lady of Hope; Our Lady of Fatima; Our Lady of Beauraing; etc.

OXFORD MOVEMENT. Initiated in 1833 by Dr. Keble of Oxford, this movement sought, and with a considerable record of success, to return the Church of England to apostolic Christianity. In its wider scope it vindicated the supernatural character of Christianity. It was aided by such men as Cardinals Newman and Manning, and Hurrell Froude, Faber, W. G. Ward and Isaac Williams. Its work was carried on through closely reasoned publications called "Tracts of the Times." Through the conversion of some of the leaders, notably Newman and Ward, and its work, the movement affected the entire Catholic Church of England.

P

PAIN BÉNIT, the French term for "blessed bread." The ordinary bread blessed after the celebration of Sunday Mass and given to the people, is a sacramental and is not consecrated, nor made like the unleavened bread used in the celebration of the Eucharist, but is of pious custom, recommended to be eaten for the good of body and soul. The practice dates back to the 4th century. (*Cf.* ANTIDORON.)

PALATINE. 1. Persons having some lesser official standing at the Vatican. **2.** Palatine library: the original name of the Vatican library, but now only used of a particular donation of books at the Vatican, made by Maximilian of Bavaria in 1622.

PALL. 1. A piece of linen, about 5 or 6 inches square, folded two or three times and highly starched, which is placed on top of the chalice (over the paten when carrying it to the altar), and over which the chalice veil is draped. Today the practice is to make the pall by forming a pocket, sewn at two sides, and placing a piece of cardboard into this pocket to stiffen it, but this is not authorized. Because of its intimate use in the sacrifice of the Mass, the pall should be washed by a cleric in major orders before being handled by a lay person in a more thorough cleaning (c. 1306). **2.** The funeral pall or, as it is sometimes called, the hearse-cloth, is a black cloth of sufficient size, decorated simply, which is draped over the coffin during a funeral requiem Mass, or over the catafalque during a requiem when the body is not present.

PALLIUM

PALLIUM, a narrow circular band made of white wool with two pendants about twelve inches long which hang down in front and back when the pallium is worn. It is ornamented with six small black crosses, one on each pendant and four on the quadrants of the circular portion. The pallium is worn around the neck and shoulders and over the chasuble by the pope and archbishops. Each metropolitan, within three months after his consecration, must petition the pope for the pallium. He wears it in solemn pontifical Mass, on certain

263

days, and only within his province, and it is buried with him. Its use by archbishops dates back to the 8th century.

PALMS, BLESSED. Leaves of the trees of the palm family are blessed on Palm Sunday and distributed to the people as sacramentals. They also may be the leaves and branches of the olive tree or of local trees or shrubs. This action is done to commemorate the triumphal entry of Jesus into Jerusalem when the people paved His path with olive branches as a sign of victory and of reverential honor (Mt. 21:8–10; Lk. 19:29–40).

PALM SUNDAY, the title of the Sunday feast before Easter. On this Sunday, palm leaves are blessed and carried in a procession which follows the blessing ceremony. The liturgy recalls the entry of Christ into Jerusalem, but the Mass recalls the Passion of Christ. The Gospel is the account of the Passion by Matthew (Chs. 26–27).

PAPABILE. This popular, colloquial Italian term is applied to the one who, after the death of a pope, is considered most likely to be elected because of his record, etc.

PAPACY. 1. A term which signifies: (a) the office of the supreme head of the Church as the Vicar of Christ and the successor of the apostle St. Peter; (b) the historic political and temporal power of the Church as it has been and is residing in Rome, and its influence on the national and international aspects of history in ages past and present. **2.** The collective listing of the successive popes since St. Peter. **3.** The length of reign of any one pope.

PAPAL BLESSINGS. The blessing bestowed by the Holy Father. The papal blessing may be given by bish-

ops in their dioceses on Easter Sunday and on two other feasts they may choose. Its form is prescribed by the ritual. This blessing carries a plenary indulgence (A.A.S. 1942).

PAPAL CHAMBERLAIN. *See* MON-SIGNOR.

PAPAL FLAG, the official flag of the Vatican. It consists of two equal fields of yellow and white, divided vertically, and bears on the white portion the seal of the Vatican which is formed of the tiara, the crossed keys, and the inscription in Italian "State of the City of the Vatican."

PAPAL LETTERS. These are of six kinds, each having its specific use and each bearing some official pronouncement. They emit either from the pope personally or through him from one of the official congregations or commissions of the Holy See. They are, in the order of their importance: bulls, briefs, autographs (written by the pope's own hand and comparatively rare), the *motu proprio*, encyclicals, and *epistolae* (ordinary letters signed by the Holy Father).

PAPAL STATE. Vatican city, and as such an independent state, is comprised of approximately 104 acres of land entirely contained within the limits of the city of Rome (*cf.* LATERAN TREATY). This Papal State is governed by a special commission, with several functions performed by the Apostolic Signature. Before 1870, the papal states were the temporal land holdings of the papacy.

PARABLE, a fictitious but lifelike story, told to illustrate a fact or truth (*cf.* ALLEGORY). A great part of our Lord's teaching as presented in Scripture was told in parables and He is the recognized master of this art of offering doctrine by means of happy illustrations from life. The word parable means "a placing of one thing beside another" for the purpose of comparison. It is a concrete method of teaching. There are more than thirty-two parables recorded in the Gospels, with a large proportion telling in indirect manner of the "kingdom of God" (Mt. 13:24ff; Mk. 4:26, etc.). The power of the parables resides, over and above their exposition and their vividness, in the affinity which exists between the natural and the spiritual orders.

PARACLETE. From the Greek, meaning "advocate," the word is now used of the Holy Spirit. (*Cf.* ADVOCATE; HOLY SPIRIT.)

PARADISE. The word as used in Genesis (2:9) is derived through the Greek from its Persian origin, and means literally an "enclosed park." By adaptation, it has come to be a synonym for heaven. However, it is also used in Scripture for the state of bliss, lacking the vision of God, or limbo, as spoken by Christ to the penitent thief on the cross (Lk. 23:43).

PARALIPOMENON, 1 AND 2. The title of these books of the O.T., as chiefly used by Catholics, is derived from the Greek meaning "the book of what was omitted." The books are also called Chronicles. The work, consisting of two parts, was written by unknown authors (probably Levite) about the middle of the 4th century B.C. The history presented is a running account beginning with Adam (the first portion largely genealogies) and ending with the decree of Cyrus permitting the captive Israelites to return from Babylon. Its central teaching is the universal presence of God as the omnipotent ruler of the world.

PARALLELISM. A characteristic of the poetic form as found in the Scriptures, it unites the lines by an equal distribution of thought in such a way that the individual lines correspond with each other. Parallelism is of three kinds: (a) *Synonymous*, when the second line merely echoes the first, e.g., "He who dwells in heaven laughs at them, the Lord derides them" (Ps. 2:4). (b) *Antithetic*, when the second line is in direct contrast to the preceeding, e.g., "They have given way and fallen down, but we stand secure and abide" (Ps. 19:9). (c) *Progressive*, when the idea expressed in the first line is developed or completed in the following lines, e.g., "The law of the Lord is perfect, refreshing the soul; the command of the Lord is firm, instructing the ignorant" (Ps. 18:8).

PARASCEVE, literally, a preparation, but as used by St. John (19:14), it meant the preparation for the celebration of the Pasch, and thus is used in the liturgical name of Good Friday: Sixth feria in parasceve.

PARENTS, DUTIES OF. Arising out of the office of parent and binding upon both, not by equal share, but in fullness upon each, unless some physical reason prohibits, these duties are: to love the children and to show no preference between them; to provide for their upkeep and health, to set a good example, to protect them from occasions of sin, and to secure their education and instruction in Christian doctrine. The neglect of these duties is seriously sinful in the degree of responsibility.

PARISH. In general, a parish is a territorial division of a diocese. A quasi-parish is a division of a vicariate or prefecture apostolic. According to canon law a parish is established as canonical when it has: (a) definite boundaries which have been determined by the local ordinary or by recognized custom; (b) a sufficient means of support from some source which need not be an endowment. This support, of course, means the financial means necessary to maintain the required buildings and support, at least in major part, the assigned priest or priests. Stole-fees may be a portion of the pastor's support; (c) a parish priest with the ordinary powers of that office. These are by virtue of the order of priesthood and official assignment of the bishop. There are other qualified distinctions: 1. A *national* parish is one based primarily on the language spoken, but is only canonical in the above sense, even though it includes people who live in the territories of other parishes. 2. A *religious* parish is one authorized but which has as habitual pastor a priest of a religious community or order. Such parishes are obliged to the same reports to the ordinary as those operated by diocesan clergy.

PARISHIONER, a Catholic who by the fact of domicile or quasi-domicile lives within the territorial boundaries of a parish. Thus one does not become a parishioner by paying pew rent or dues in another parish whose territory does not include his home. The parishioners are to be admonished to attend their own parish church, the exception being for those who attend national parishes.

PARISH PRIEST, by designation (c. 451ff), the pastor of a parish. A parish priest has ordinary power and is not simply a delegate of the ordinary. As such he rules the parish in his own name, but under the delegated authority of the bishop. Being fully qualified, the parish priest has a degree of stability in his office. As a pastor the parish priest may be *irremovable*, i.e., given the pastorship of a parish so constituted and the character of which cannot be changed without apostolic indult (c. 454). Or the parish priest may be *removable*, i.e., the parish priest may be reassigned to another parish. Particular laws govern the assignment, transfer, and removal of parish priests. In the strict sense, no parish priest is considered irremovable since under the law and for sufficient reason the ordinary can transfer or reassign all priests.

The parish priest has, besides rights, certain parochial duties. Before taking possession of the parish he must take the anti-modernist oath, and make the profession of faith. He also must not be absent from the parish without permission for any extended time; he must offer Mass for the people of the parish about 87 times a year (c. 466) on the proper days unless authorized by the bishop to say the Mass on another day. The sacraments must be given to the people upon reasonable request; he should know his parishioners by periodic visitation, train the young, bring back the lapsed, have care of the sick and dying and encourage works of charity in the parish, and augment faith and piety (through establishment of associations or otherwise). He, of course, must keep the parish books (finances), and make account of his personal effects. Broadly, these are the functions of administration; there are many other duties which arise out of pastoral cares.

PAROCHIAL MASS. 1. The Masses which are prescribed by law to be said for the people of a parish by the pastor. **2.** The principal Mass of the parish read on Sundays or holydays, usually a sung or high Mass.

PAROCHIAL SCHOOL, a school of any grade, erected by the right of the Church to so establish means of education, and built by the parishioners to serve the children of their parish. Catholic people should send their children, whenever possible, to parochial schools or Catholic schools of higher learning. Parents need the permission of the ordinary to send their children to schools which are not Catholic, and even then it is mandatory to provide religious training for the children. Under specific conditions, absolution may be refused to parents who send their children to non-Catholic schools.

PAROUSIA. *See* JUDGMENT, GENERAL; ESCHATOLOGY.

PASCH. The feast of the Passover was originally the first great feast of the Jewish liturgical year, which later began with the month called Nisan (March–April). The feast commemorates the salvation of the Israelites when the avenging angel passed by their homes and struck down only the first-born of the Egyptians (Ex. 11: 1–10). The Pasch was celebrated at "eventide," i.e., in the evening at sunset (Deut. 16:6), on the evening of the 15th of the month, the first day of the Azymes (agricultural feast of seven days), and consisted of the sacrificing of a lamb, roasting it, and eating it with bitter herbs and unleavened bread. The Pasch as a sacrifice was a type of the sacrifice of Christ on the cross and His eucharistic sacrifice.

PASCHAL CANDLE, the large candle which is blessed at the solemn service on Holy Saturday. Inserted into the candle are, in the form of a cross, five grains, or particles, of incense. The candle should be of beeswax for the greater part, about 75 per cent, or according to the percentage determined by the ordinary. The paschal candle is to be lighted at the solemn Mass or the parochial Mass and at Vespers on Easter Sunday, Monday and Tuesday; on Saturday after Easter and on all Sundays, until the Gospel of the Mass on Ascension Day. It may also be lighted on the major feasts of the Easter time. The paschal candle is used at the ceremony of blessing baptismal water when it, or part of it, is immersed in the water.

PASCHAL CANDLE

PASCHAL PRECEPT. *See* EASTER DUTY.

PASSION OF CHRIST. The suffering and sacrificial death of Jesus Christ on the cross, as it was foretold by Isaias (42:13–43:12), and is recorded by all the evangelists (Mt. 26 and 27; Mk. 14 and 15; Lk. 22 and 23; Jn. 18 through 20). The word "passion" alone usually refers to one of these Gospel accounts, read in the liturgy of the Mass of Palm Sunday, and Tuesday, Wednesday, or Friday of Holy Week.

PASSION OF THE MARTYRS, a name usually applied to the written account of the sufferings and death of a martyr.

PASSION SUNDAY. The fifth Sunday of Lent, two weeks before Easter, is so named because it begins the liturgical season of Passiontide. It is distinguished in that the attention of the liturgy is directed to the Passion of our Lord, and the universal sorrow indicated by the veiling of all images in the church.

PASSIONTIDE. *See* PASSION SUNDAY.

PASSION WEEK, the week between Passion Sunday and Palm Sunday.

PASSOVER. *See* PASCH.

PASTOR. *See* PARISH PRIEST.

PASTORAL EPISTLES. The Epistles of St. Paul (1 and 2 Timothy and Titus) have been given this collective name since, owing to the character of their contents, they were addressed to Timothy and Titus as individual pastors rather than to a church or a group.

PASTORAL LETTERS. Written by a bishop and addressed to all the faithful, both clergy and laity, under his care as members of his diocese, these are documents directed to the administration of the diocese. They may have emanated from the bishop directly or from a synod he has convened. The term has been applied incorrectly to the annual statement made by the bishops of the United States. (*Cf.* NATIONAL CATHOLIC WELFARE CONFERENCE.)

PASTORAL STAFF. *See* CROSIER.

PASTORAL THEOLOGY. This branch of theology is not a distinct unit but rather a formal presentation of the application of other theological studies to the care of souls and the regulations concerning the administration of the sacraments on a practical as well as an ideal basis. Thus, pastoral theology takes dogmatic teaching, moral theology, ascetical theology, and canon law and synthesizes them into the procedures of practical ministry. It directs the cleric in the knowledge of applying the office of teaching, ministering and directing (governing) which is his by commission through the successors of the apostles. (*Cf.* THEOLOGY.)

PATEN, one of the sacred vessels used in the celebration of the Mass. It is a shallow, concave, circular dish, slightly larger than the circumference of the top of the chalice, with thin edges. The paten must be made of gold or silver, with the inner or upper surface at least gold plated; it may be engraved on the lower or bottom side, but the top should be smooth. The paten is consecrated by a bishop or one authorized by him; it is used in the Mass to hold the host, to gather up particles of the broken host from the surface of the corporal (hence the thin edges), and during a solemn high Mass it is held, hidden in the humeral veil, by the subdeacon, from the Offertory to the Pater Noster.

PATER NOSTER, THE. *See* LORD'S PRAYER; THE MASS.

PATIENCE, an integral and potential part of the virtue of fortitude. Patience moderates one's inclination to sadness or rebellion at the endurance of evils or sufferings. It is reasonable control, and in practice makes one withstand with reserve of soul, out of the motive of love of God and in union with Christ, all physical and moral sufferings. Its opposite vices are impatience and insensibility but not indifference.

PATRIARCHS (PATRIARCHATE). In older times, a patriarch was one who held jurisdiction over primates and metropolitans. In the Roman Church, patriarch is largely an honorary title. Today the extent of jurisdiction and the title are present in the patriarchates and attached to their patriarchs. These are: (a) Rome, the pope, by title Patriarch of the West, with actual jurisdiction over all of the Catholic Eastern Churches, and the Church of the Roman rite; (b) the Coptic Patriarch of Alexandria and the Melkite, Syrian, and Maronite Patriarchs of Antioch, the Armenian Patriarch of Cilicia, and the Chaldean Patriarch of Babylon. These are patriarchs by title and have supreme jurisdiction, subject to that of the Supreme Pontiff of Rome. Since the schism of the east and west, there are patriarchs of the non-Catholic eastern churches who hold varying degrees of authority but are each supreme in their patriarchates. These are: (a) Orthodox: Constantinople, Alexandria, Antioch, Moscow, Serbia, Roumania. (b) Coptic: Alexandria. (c) Syrian Jacobite: Antioch. (d) Nestorian: Iraq. (e) Armenian: the Armenians in the U.S.S.R., Constantinople, Sis, Jerusalem. These have no allegiance to Rome under jurisdiction.

PATRIARCHS, SCRIPTURAL. The ancient heads of the tribes of the Israelites or the notable leaders of families who lived in Jerusalem (1 Par. 8f.) are so named. In all there were 19 patriarchs. Especially honored are Abraham, Isaac, and Jacob, and the period during which they reigned is known as the Age of the Patriarchs. The title patriarch as used concerning David (Acts 2:29) was one of honor.

PATRIMONY. Referring to one of the conditions under which a cleric is permitted to receive holy orders, patrimony actually is "sufficient means of their own" so that they need not depend upon others for their support (c. 979–981).

PATRIOTISM, CHRISTIAN. As outlined by St. Paul (Tit. 3:1–3), the nation is derived from God. Faith in Christ, therefore, guarantees Christian patriotism, i.e., that man fulfill his duties to society.

PATRIPASSIANISM. An eastern form of the Sabellian heresy of the early 3rd century is so named because its adherents believed that God the Father suffered on the cross.

PATROLOGY. This branch of theology studies and investigates the life, writings and doctrines of the orthodox writers of Christian antiquity (*cf.* FATHERS OF THE CHURCH). Patrology cannot concern itself with every writer on a Christian subject but only with those who can be quoted with authority, whose writings have been approved by the Church, and, strictly speaking, whose lives have been deserving. The study may be limited to periods of time in the history of the Church or be confined to one or more ages. The period of patrology may, for example, be one or more of the following: (a) Christian antiquity, i.e., the first eight centuries of the Church; (b) the Middle Ages, or shortly after the death of Charlemagne (d. 814) until about the Reformation; (c) the modern period, from the Reformation to the present. Patrology gives a history of dogmatic teaching, a composite picture of the doctrines of the Church, and is a background of theological culture and a source of apologetics and persuasive reasoning. This study is also sometimes called patristics.

PATRON. 1. One who erects and provides the physical necessities of a benefice. **2.** The saint, assigned by name, under whose intercessory protection a person, place or thing is placed. Thus, a person's patron saint is the one after whom one is named. Since 1630 the patrons of cities, dioceses, countries, special work, religious orders, etc., must be approved by the Holy See (c. 1278). The titular saint of a parish church is selected by the bishop, and on the feast of the saint, parish priests must offer Mass "for the people" of the parish. **3.** A saint who by popular devotion is selected as the patron, for veneration and intercessory affection, by groups, e.g., St. Francis de Sales, patron of the Catholic press. A saint so selected may be confirmed by the Holy See as the official patron.

PAULINE PRIVILEGE. This is not the dissolution of sacramental marriage, but applies only in the instance of the marriage of unbaptized persons. Those unbaptized cannot receive a sacrament, other than baptism itself. The Pauline Privilege is based upon the teaching of St. Paul presented in 1 Cor. 7:12–15, and is treated in canon law (c. 1120–1127).

Its application is this: If in a valid marriage, contracted by two unbaptized persons, one of the parties later receives valid baptism and the unbaptized party refuses to live with the baptized spouse without causing the latter grave sin, the unbaptized person must be questioned as to whether he or she will be baptized or live in peace without causing sin to the baptized (called "giving interpellations"). These interpellations may be dispensed with for good reason. It follows then, that, if the answers are negative, the baptized party is free to contract marriage with a Catholic, provided he or she gave no cause of dissatisfaction to the unbaptized party after having been baptized. Thus, upon entry into the second marriage, the bond of the first is dissolved by force of the Pauline Privilege which is given in accord to the will of Christ in favor of conversion to the Christian faith. (*Cf.* MARRIAGE; MONTANA CASE.)

PAX, Latin word, meaning peace. **1.** The kiss of peace (*cf.* KISS OF PEACE). **2.** *Pax dei*, the immunity from the consequences of private feuds granted to clerics and others and extended to some places as confirmed by Pope John XIX in 1030 (*cf.* TRUCE OF GOD). **3.** The Pax or *osculatorium*, a carved tablet or disc with a handle used in medieval times to convey the kiss of peace from the celebrant to the people present. Also called *pax-brede* in England. **4.** *Pax Romana*, title of a confederation of Catholic University students whose objective is the promotion of international peace. **5.** *Pax vobis*, the greeting which the bishop gives to those present at his Mass, instead of the *Dominus vobiscum*, after the *Gloria*.

PECTORAL CROSS. As an official ornament of office, this cross has come to be used only since the 17th century. It is worn on the breast, suspended from a chain or cord about the neck, by the pope, cardinals, abbots, abbesses, and certain other prelates. The pectoral cross should be made of gold and may be decorated with gems; that of a bishop usually contains relics of a martyr.

PECTORAL CROSS

PELAGIANISM, a heresy, begun shortly after 400 A.D. by a British monk, Pelagius. Its teaching rejected the doctrine of original sin, emphasized the natural over the supernatural to the extent that it was impossible to attain salvation without grace. Its teaching was ably refuted by St. Augustine. Pelagianism was condemned by the Councils of Carthage (411) and Milevis (416). It died out after the condemnation given by the Council of Ephesus in 431. (*Cf.* SEMI-PELAGIANISM.)

PENANCE, SACRAMENT OF. In this sacrament, the sins of a repentant sinner committed after baptism are forgiven by the absolution of a duly ordained priest. The *matter* of the sacrament is twofold: *remote*, all sins committed after baptism; *necessary*, all mortal sins which have not been forgiven. The *form* of the sacrament is: the words of absolution together with the prayers, *Misereatur . . . In-*

dulgentiam . . . and *Passio . . .* spoken by the administrator. These prayers may be omitted for just cause (c. 885). The *effects* of the sacrament are: forgiveness of sin through the infusion of sanctifying grace; the remission of the punishment due to sin, i.e., all of the eternal punishment and at least part of the temporal punishment; the pouring in of sacramental graces; the re-enlivening of merits lost by mortal sin. By Church law, annual confession is obligatory (c. 906). This sacrament is administered through the power of Christ (Mk. 2:3-12) and given to the apostles (Mt. 16:18ff; 18:15-18), and commissioned to the apostles and their successors (Lk. 24:47ff). It was practiced by the apostles (Ac. 5:11; 3 Jn. 9ff). (*Cf.* CONFESSION.)

PENITENTIAL PSALMS. Psalms 6, 31, 37, 50, 101, 129, 142 have been given this collective name because of their expression of sorrow for sins and of repentance.

PENITENTIARY, SACRED APOSTOLIC. The first in rank of the tribunals of the Holy See, but only in the sense that it is an extension of the tribunal of penance, the Sacred Penitentiary exercises jurisdiction in the sacramental "internal forum." Its deliberations are most secret; it acts to grant absolution from reserved cases, to issue instructions to confessors, and it handles secret cases, such as dispensations from secret matrimonial impediments or private vows. The Sacred Penitentiary came into existence as an aid, directly under the pope, in the pontificate of Pope St. Gregory (d. 604). Since 1917, the Sacred Penitentiary studies the dogmatic content of prayers and grants indulgences upon them after approval of the content.

PENSION. According to canon law, the local ordinary may impose upon a parish the obligation of a pension (fund for sustenance) for a pastor or priest who has resigned or been disabled. Such a pension continues only during the lifetime of one pensioned (c. 1429, sec. 2).

PENTATEUCH. Literally, from the Greek, "five books," this is the collective name for the five O.T. books (the name signifies a "book of five rolls") written by Moses. Consisting of Genesis, Exodus, Leviticus, Numbers, and Deuteronomy, the Pentateuch gives the religious history of mankind from the creation of the world and the first man, particularly that of the Chosen People, to the death of Moses. It also records the laws of the theocratic system of the Jews. The Pentateuch is referred to in the N.T. as "the book of the Law" (Gal. 3:10) and simply "the Law" (Rom. 3:21).

PENTECOST. Originally, this was the second feast in rank of the Jews, the celebration of thanksgiving for the harvest and the ending of Passover time. Later it was a celebration of the giving of the law to Moses at Sinai. In Christian recognition, Pentecost is the feast celebrated 50 days after Easter or ten days after the Feast of the Ascension. It commemorates the descent of the Holy Spirit on the apostles (Acts 2:1–42) as foretold by Christ (Jn. 16:7). It marks the beginning of the active apostolic work, and is hailed as the birthday of the Church, for it was through the coming of the Holy Spirit that the Church began to form the members of the new kingdom.

PERFECTION. For Christians, the word perfection has always had a moral and religious sense. It was so used by Christ (Mt. 5:48) as the fullness of the application of the new law and the attainment of the fullness of Christian life. Perfection is, so far as man's life here on earth is concerned, only relative, for his full perfection can only be attained after the resurrection of the body and the possession of the intuitive vision of God in heaven. It is thus the tending toward that ultimate which is the perfection spoken of here. This is accomplished by the observance of the law, the practice of virtues, the use of sacraments, and the meriting of grace. Perfection is judged primarily in the Christian life by the norm of charity, that is, according to the love of God and love of neighbor for the love of God. It also is judged by the two other theological virtues, faith and hope. There is one ultimate to the attainment of perfection and that is union with God. Even on earth such union is possible, first, through the Eucharist, second, through the various stages of prayer and contemplation. In this latter there are three groups of those seeking perfection: the beginners, those who live a spiritual life but have made no progress; the proficients, those who have tamed their passions and achieved a marked degree of fervor in prayer; the perfect, those who have attained stability in acting in a relatively perfect manner, or a total dominance of charity.

PERFECTION, COUNSELS OF. *See* EVANGELICAL COUNSELS.

PERJURY, lying or withholding truth under oath. (*Cf.* LIE.)

PERPETUAL ADORATION, the worship of God, especially at the altar where the Blessed Sacrament is exposed. It is continuously carried on by one or more persons, day and night.

PERSECUTION, the enacting of rule whereby it is demanded under penalty that one conform to a specific religious pattern. The Church has suffered a number of persecutions throughout the ages, ranging from those of the Romans to those of the 20th century in Mexico and Russia and in places dominated by Russia. The objectives of persecution may be twofold: the supplanting of one religion with another, or the attempt to destroy all religious belief.

PERSEVERANCE, FINAL. *See* FINAL PERSEVERANCE.

PERSON, philosophically, the complete individual substance of a rational or intelligent nature which subsists of itself and is incommunicable to every other being. Thus, the human person is neither body nor soul, but the rational being arising out of both. (*Cf.* TRINITY, BLESSED.)

PESCHITTO. The word means "simple" and, as applied to a version of the Bible, refers to a simple text or one not marked with critical notations. It first appeared in the 10th century, being applied as a title to a Syriac version of the O.T. made from the Hebrew.

PETER'S CHAINS, FEAST OF. Celebrated in the Church liturgy on August 1, the feast commemorates the dedication of the basilica of St. Peter-in-Chains, recalling the captivity of St. Peter in 44 A.D., as recorded in Acts (12:1–25).

PETER'S CHAIR, FEAST OF. Commemorating the establishment of his episcopacy in Rome, the feast is celebrated on January 18; that of St. Peter's residence in Antioch is celebrated on February 22.

PETER'S PENCE, the name of an annual collection, of a voluntary amount, taken up among all Catholics for the maintenance of the Holy Father. It was begun in the 8th century, and originally consisted of a tax of a penny on each household, hence the name. The amounts now collected are sent to Rome by the bishops.

PHILOSOPHY. 1. The science of natural reason which consists of the criticism and organization of all knowledge, be it drawn from empirical science, rational learning, experience, or other sources. Philosophy as a study includes logic, or the principles of thought and knowledge; metaphysics, or the reality of being and the order which exists among things; ethics, or the natural principles of good action; aesthetics, or the knowledge of beauty and its order. Philosophy, especially scholastic philosophy, must be studied for two years by students for the priesthood (c. 1365, 1366). **2.** Philosophy of religion: a critical analysis of the reasonable nature and value of religion and its relation to revelation, ethics, etc. In this sense, it is general rather than applied to a particular religious belief. (*Cf.* THEOLOGY.)

PIETY, the virtue of the conscious sense of duty and the willingness to respond. It is a gift of the Holy Spirit through which the great virtue of charity is applied in a special manner, as a loving duty. Piety is not to be considered as the emotional response to things religious, nor is it to be an assumed attitude whereby the spirit is saddened by what might or ought to be done, often posed by cast-down eyes and folded hands.

PILGRIM, the name given to one who goes on a pilgrimage, i.e., who travels to a holy place, such as a shrine, with the intention of benefiting spiritually. The purpose may be to venerate, to do penance, to offer thanksgiving, or to plead for graces. It does not imply that the journey be made solely as a penitential undertaking with the attendant discomfort, real or contrived, as a necessary condition. The *Raccolta* (q.v.) lists the pilgrimages which have been indulgenced by the Church, e.g., the faithful who visit the more important sanctuaries of the Holy City (Rome) may gain a plenary indulgence on the day of their departure, if they confess their sins, receive Holy Communion, and pray for the intentions of the pope (S.P. Ap., April 4, 1932).

PISA, COUNCILS OF. Properly, these were not councils, for both were convened without authority. The first, in 1409, was called by a group of cardinals to depose two popes, Gregory XII and Benedict XIII, but it only served to make a bad situation worse. The second, in 1411, was definitely schismatical and was denounced by the Fifth Lateran Council which met the following year.

PISCINA also **SACRARIUM,** in churches, the basin with a pipe leading directly to the ground into which sacred water which remains after use at a ceremony is poured. This may be baptismal water, the water used for the first rinsing of corporals, etc. The *piscina* is often built into the side wall of the sanctuary, on the epistle side of the altar, with a shelf which serves as a credence table. Today, the practice generally is to have the basin built into the sacristy wall.

PISTOIA, SYNOD OF. The synod, an attempt by Grand Duke Leopold of Tuscany, and the Jansenist, Scipio Ricci, to gain control of religious affairs to dominate politically, was called without recognition by the Church in 1786. Ricci was condemned by Pope Pius VI and submitted to the judgment of the Church.

PLAIN CHANT. *See* CHANT.

PLANETA, Latin name, rarely used, for the Roman chasuble.

PLENARY INDULGENCE. *See* INDULGENCES.

PLUMBATOR. The duty of this lesser official in the apostolic chancery is to affix the lead seal of the Holy See to the documents of apostolic bulls.

PLUVIALE. *See* COPE.

PNEUMATOMACHI, a group of the Macedonian heresy. Its members were so named because they were recognized as "enemies of the spirit." They were condemned at the second ecumenical council.

POLYGLOT BIBLES, editions of the Bible in which the text, translated into several languages, is printed in parallel columns. Such editions have a critical rather than practical value, e.g., the Vatican edition of Sixtus V, published in Rome in 1587. (*Cf.* HEXAPLA.)

PONTIFICALE. *See* LITURGICAL BOOKS.

PONTIFICAL MASS. 1. Solemn Mass celebrated by the pope. **2.** The solemn Mass, celebrated by a bishop with the ceremonies as prescribed by the *Pontificale;* it is usually so called when a bishop celebrates Mass at the throne (from the Introit to the Offertory) of his own cathedral. A bishop must have the permission of the local ordinary to pontificate outside of his own diocese.

PONTIFICALS. In addition to the regular vestments, these are the ceremonial vestments and adjuncts proper to a bishop, worn or used by him when celebrating a pontifical Mass and consisting of buskins, sandals, pectoral cross, tunicle, dalmatic, mitre, gloves, and ring. If the bishop pontificates in his own diocese, the crosier is included. Also considered pontificals are the gremial veil, the throne, the mozzetta and the cappa magna which two latter are worn by the ordinary when entering the church.

POPE, the Roman Pontiff who, by divine law, has supreme jurisdiction over the universal Church (c. 218–221). He is the supreme superior of all religious (c. 499). The pope may act alone or with a council in defining doctrine for the universal Church or in making laws (*cf.* INFALLIBILITY). He is addressed as: His Holiness the Pope. By title and right he is: Bishop of Rome, Vicar of Jesus Christ, Successor of St. Peter, the Prince of the Apostles, Supreme Pontiff, Patriarch of the West, Primate of Italy, Archbishop and Metropolitan of the Roman province, and Sovereign of the State of Vatican City. (*Cf.* APOSTOLIC SUCCESSION.)

PORTABLE ALTAR. *See* ALTAR.

PORTER. *See* DOORKEEPER; OSTIARIUS.

PORTIUNCULA. Literally, "little portion," this name is given to the small chapel within the basilica of St. Mary of the Angels, located near Assisi in Italy. More widely known is the *Portiuncula Indulgence*, originally attached to the chapel which was dedicated on August 2nd and thus the indulgence may be gained on that day. Since July 10, 1924, by decree of the Holy See, the Portiuncula Indulgence may be gained as a plenary indulgence (*toties quoties*) as often as the conditions are fulfilled. These conditions are: confession, reception of Holy Communion, and a visit to a church which enjoys the privilege, together with the saying, six times each, the Our Father, Hail Mary, and Glory be to the Father. The indulgence may be gained from midday of August 1st to midnight of August 2nd (c. 923) and is applicable to the poor souls. Should the 2nd of August occur on a weekday, the indulgence may be transferred to the following Sunday. It may be gained in all churches or public oratories of the Friars Minor, of the Capuchins, and of the Conventuals. Members of the Third Order Secular may gain it in any church or public oratory where the Third Order is canonically erected or, if none exists in the place, then in any church. Since May 1, 1939, any pastor may, with his bishop's permission, apply to the Sacred Penitentiary for the privilege of having the Portiuncula Indulgence in his parish.

POSSESSION, DEMONIACAL, the domination of a person's body by one or more evil spirits, that is, devils. The Church has always recognized this possibility (Christ drove out devils, Mk. 5:1–20) and also has recognized the power of Christ over the demons as was demonstrated, as well as the power commissioned by Christ to her. Thus, the Church instituted the order of exorcist and permits her priests, upon authority of the bishop, to perform exorcism. (*Cf.* EXORCISM; EXORCIST.)

POSTCOMMUNION. Said on the epistle side of the altar, this final prayer of the Mass is a short prayer of thanksgiving and petition. Often supplementary prayers, corresponding with the number of collects, follow. On ferias during Lent the "prayer over the people" is said.

POSTULANT. A person preparing to ask for admission to a religious novitiate is so called. In religious communities where perpetual vows are to be taken, both men and women must spend at least six months as postulants (c. 539–541).

POVERELLO, IL. Meaning "the little poor one," this is an Italian title of endearment for St. Francis of Assisi.

POVERTY, one of the three evangelical counsels. It embraces, as an ascetical practice, the voluntary renunciation of the right of ownership while implying the reasonable use of material goods. Taken as a vow, poverty covers all things which have a value in money; the simple vow forbids the use of all such things without consent of one's superior; the solemn vow deprives the religious of all right of ownership and makes invalid all acts contrary to the vow. (*Cf.* EVANGELICAL COUNSELS.)

POWER OF THE KEYS. The grant of authority whereby Christ, through the metaphor of "keys," passed on to St. Peter and his successors the supreme jurisdiction over the Church on earth. The fact is recorded in Matthew (16:18–20) and is recognized as the transmission of authority and a definition of St. Peter's powers. These powers, consisting of a "binding" and a "loosing" in the spiritual order on earth, i.e., all powers necessary to the well-being of the kingdom, were recognized by the apostles from the rabbinical terms for "binding," that is, of granting or forbidding, as contained in the Jewish law. (*Cf.* AUTHORITY OF THE CHURCH.)

PRAGMATISM. First formally presented by C. S. Peirce and William James, this false philosophical system judges truth by its useful results, and interprets ideas in terms of their consequences. It states that the meaning of an intellectual conception should be considered on the practical consequences which might result and constitute the entire meaning of the conception. Pragmatism arose toward the end of the 19th century and was largely worked out at Harvard University in the United States. It served to instill vague and uncertain thought as to the existence of God, the freedom of the will, and immortality.

PRAYER—The *Orante* figure of early Christian art shows the classical attitude of prayer: raising the mind and soul to God lifts up the hands in a work of adoration and praise; the hands are opened to offer thanks and speak for the heart, and also to receive divine gifts.

PRAYER. The active expression of the virtue of religion which can be practiced by all is prayer. It differs from sacrifice which requires a minister. Prayer, by simple definition, is the raising of the mind and soul to God. Classified by its purpose, there are four types of prayer, that of adoration, of praise, of thanksgiving, and of petition. Prayer also is distinguished by the manner of expression. *Vocal* prayer is the recitation of prayer according to a set form, e.g., the Lord's Prayer, or the Rosary. *Mental* prayer is the direction and control of thought toward God or a truth of religion (*cf.* MEDITATION). Prayer may be *private*, i.e., said alone, or *public*, that is, said in a group or in the name of society together. Prayer is necessary for salvation, for it is seeking and expressing the "power of God unto salvation," the soul's communion with God. Christ Himself is the example of man in prayer. He prayed to the Father at all the moments of His life, and man prays in His name (Jn. 14:13–14). (*Cf.* INTERCESSION; MASS; LITURGY.)

PRAYER, APOSTLESHIP OF. *See* APOSTLESHIP OF PRAYER.

PREACHING. *See* HOMILETICS.

PRECENTOR, the title, only of honor, of the singer who intones the antiphons. It may also be applied to the person who prepares the music for divine services.

PRECEPTS OF THE CHURCH. *See* COMMANDMENTS OF THE CHURCH.

PRECIOUS BLOOD, FEAST OF THE. This feast, commemorating the death of Christ, our redemption, and the Sacrifice of Calvary, is celebrated on July 1 in the Roman Church.

PRECONIZATION, the formal and public proclamation by the pope in the consistory of the appointment of a new bishop. The appointment may already have taken place, but preconization is necessary since precedence among bishops depends upon this announcement.

PREDELLA. Also called footpace, this is the platform on which the priest stands when saying Mass. It should be at least 3 ft. 9 in. deep to permit genuflections to be made without difficulty. It is often inappropriately referred to as the top of the altar steps.

PREDESTINATION, the determination, beforehand, of one's actions. The idea that God is selective, that He pre-determines the eternal status of the soul of some individuals was an early heresy of the Church which was condemned by the Council of Mainz in 848. In a wide sense, predestination may be taken as the divine providence of God whereby He rules the world, knowing by His infallible prescience the events of the future even as they will occur in time. In its strict sense, it means God's supernatural providence and His promotion through grace of the eternal education of all rational creatures. It is thus that predestination means both the glory intended by God for all men and the means He has guaranteed for attaining that glory (1 Tim. 2:4–5, 2 Pet. 1:11–18).

PREFACE. Preceding the Canon of the Mass, the Preface is a solemn prayer offered by the priest in the name of all, opening with the dialogue prayer which exhorts all to lift up their minds to God in thanks. There are 15 different forms of the Preface in the Roman Missal, one of which is assigned to the feast being celebrated, or to the season. (*Cf.* MASS.)

PREFECT APOSTOLIC also **VICAR APOSTOLIC.** These titles are conferred upon priests who by assignment and under the direct authority of the Holy See, whether they have episcopal consecration or not, govern a missionary district where the hierarchy has not been established. Their rights and faculties are governed by canon law (c. 293ff).

PRELATE. There are two groups of prelates: 1. Ecclesiastics, having ordinary jurisdiction in the external form as bishops, vicars general, prefects apostolic, etc. 2. Honorary prelates, who have no jurisdiction in the external forum, e.g., a titular bishop. Besides these two groups, there are minor prelates whose dignity and honor are conferred by title and rank. These are: prothonotaries apostolic (four grades of rank or dignity); auditors of the Rota; domestic prelates; privy chamberlains; honorary chamberlains; papal chaplains; papal chamberlains. (*Cf.* MONSIGNOR.)

PRESANCTIFIED, MASS OF THE. In this Mass, celebrated on Good Friday of Holy Week, there is no consecration and the priest receives in Communion a host consecrated previously. It is not strictly speaking a Mass, but rather a Communion for the priest. No Communion is given to the laity.

PRESBYTER. In the early days of the Church, a presbyter was a member of the group who served and advised the bishop. The group was more or less of a governing body, and each presbyter could be commissioned by the bishop to perform certain official duties, e.g., baptize, preach, etc. (1 Tim. 3:8–10).

PRESBYTERY. 1. The governing council of a church in the early days of the Church. Of this group the bishop (*episcopos*) was a special presbyter, i.e., one presiding (Acts 20:28; 1 Tim. 3:4–5). **2.** The little-used name for the residence of a parish priest.

PRESCRIPTION. In canon law, as in civil law, this term is applied to the legal method by which one obtains title to goods or frees himself from certain obligations (c. 1508–1512).

PRESENCE, REAL. *See* EUCHARIST, HOLY.

PRESENTATION OF THE BLESSED VIRGIN MARY. Celebrated on November 21, this feast commemorates the presentation of the Blessed Mother as a child in the temple where she served and was trained. This fact is not mentioned in the Gospels but is spoken of in apocryphal writings and the Church only recognizes the fact and not the details of narration.

PRESUMPTION. This sin is committed by one who either trusts too much in his own strength or who, in order to attain salvation, expects of God that He do something which He would not will to do. Thus, one who expects to attain salvation by his own efforts alone or thinks he will attain it on account of the merits of Christ, without applying these merits or seeking them, sins by presumption. It is a sin opposed to the theological virtue of hope.

PRIDE, the chief of the capital sins. It is a sin which prompts and is partially present in all other sins. In itself it is the inordinate desire for honor, recognition, distinction. Pride arises from self-love. It is mortally sinful when it is such that it causes one to refuse to be subordinate even to God; it is less sinful if, in being submissive, one still seeks inordinately for honor. Thus to be submissive to an inferior, or to flatter one who does not deserve it, for the sole purpose that he will recognize you and esteem you, is sinful.

PRIEST, he on whom the priesthood has been conferred, who offers sacrifice, and who has the threefold power of teaching, ministering, and governing. (*Cf.* ORDERS, HOLY, SACRAMENT OF.)

PRIMACY. *See* PRIMATE.

PRIMATE. Formerly, this was the title of a bishop who had jurisdiction over all bishops and metropolitans of a large area or nation, but was himself subject directly only to the Holy See. The title now may be honorary, e.g., the Primate of All Ireland. As a position, primate is no longer recognized by canon law.

PRIME, one of the hours of the Divine Office. (*Cf.* BREVIARY; DIVINE OFFICE.)

PRIOR, a superior of a monastic order who is an assistant of the abbot. In a monastery which has no abbot, the prior is in full authority. The office is usually selective and the one chosen serves only for a definite term. The title may be applied to the superior of a school founded and staffed by religious.

PRIORESS, the superior of a religious order of women. Her rank corresponds to that of a prior.

PRIORY, an institution or monastery, governed by a prior.

PRISCILLIANISM, a form of the Manichaean heresy. Introduced into Spain from Egypt in the 4th century, it was condemned at Bordeaux in 384, and died out after again being condemned at the Synod of Braga in 561.

PRIVATE MASS. This term covers a variety of meanings. It may signify, according to its application, (a) a Mass said in a private place; (b) a low Mass; (c) a non-conventual Mass; (d) a Mass which is not public; (e) a Mass which is said detached from the full liturgy of the day; (f) a low requiem Mass.

PRIVATION. Also called *Privatio Officii,* this is the ecclesiastical penalty imposed upon a cleric, depriving him of his position or right without special procedure. The cause may arise out of the law or out of the actions of the cleric (c. 188).

PRIVILEGE. In canon law, "a privilege is the concession of a special right made by the proper superior" (c. 63–79).

PRIVILEGED ALTAR. A priest can gain a plenary indulgence for a departed soul for whom he celebrates Mass on an altar so designated (c. 535).

PROBABILIORISM. In this moral system, the lawfulness of a doubtful action is interpreted by maintaining that one is free to act against the law if the reasons for his opinion are more probable than those which favor the law.

PROBABILISM. This system of moral interpretation, which is more commonly followed by Catholic moralists, declares that one may follow the opinion that favors liberty to act against the law as long as there is certainty that the opinion is well-founded, even though the contrary opinion may be more probable. This cannot be used in regard to the sacraments.

PRO-CATHEDRAL. A church is so called when it is being used by a bishop as a temporary cathedral.

PROCESSIONS, parades by the clergy and the faithful, either within the church or from one place to another. Processions may be either liturgical in nature, i.e., part of the prescribed ceremony of a feast, or they may be simply devotional. They are undertaken as supplication, as a rejoicing, or as an act of piety. Liturgical processions are held on Candlemas day when candles are carried; on Palm Sunday when the newly blessed palms are carried; on Rogation days; and on Corpus Christi day when the Blessed Sacrament is carried in the procession. The Roman Ritual prescribes the order to be followed and the attendant ceremony. In a procession of the Blessed Sacrament, the bishop or priest who carries the monstrance must walk. A plenary indulgence is gained by those who take part in a eucharistic procession, with confession, reception of Communion, and prayer for the intention of the pope (S.P., September 5, 1933).

PROCURATOR, title of the agent or representative acting in behalf of a religious group. A procurator may be assigned permanently. The most general office of procurator is that of one whose charge it is to supply the material goods of an institution, such as food, clothing, etc., in which matters he serves as an agent of management and purchase.

PROFANITY. The disrespectful use of the name of God, either in anger or thoughtlessly, is venially sinful. Profanity is seriously sinful if the anger or thoughtless use is directed against God or if it has added seriousness such as scandal, denouncement of religion, or lack of charity.

PROFESSION OF FAITH. Such profession (declaration of firmness of one's belief) may be demanded by divine law or Church law. By divine law, one is obliged to profess his faith publicly, if not doing so would imply or give the impression of de-

nial, contempt for religion, insult to God, or scandal to those near. When the request arises from proper authority, one must profess his faith even at the risk of one's life. By Church law, one is demanded to make a public profession of faith upon occasion: every adult about to be baptized, every convert from heresy before at least two witnesses. Church law also demands (c. 1406) that all administrators of vacant dioceses, diocesan consultors, vicar generals, parish priests, rectors and professors of seminaries, censors of books, confessors, preachers and students before receiving the subdiaconate, must make the profession of faith found at the beginning of the Code of Canon Law. The usual form under which a profession of faith is made is the Creed of Pius IV with whatever additions are required.

PROFESSION, RELIGIOUS, the contract made by taking the public vows in a religious institute when one enters the religious state. It may be perpetual or temporary. It must be made according to the laws, e.g., for valid profession one must be 16 years old before taking temporary profession, and 21 years, complete, before perpetual profession (c. 572ff).

PROMOTER OF JUSTICE. Usually trained in canon law, the Promoter of Justice is appointed in each diocese to serve in accord with canon law somewhat as a "district attorney" of the diocese. When serving in regard to marriage cases, he defends the "bond" of marriage and his role is governed by canon law, chiefly by canons 1971–1973.

PROMOTER OF THE FAITH, the cleric who serves in a Church court, or represents the side of the Church in a case. His function is to examine and formulate objections as a defense of the Church's position. In cases of beatification and canonization of saints, the title is usually "Advocate of God." (*Cf.* CANONIZATION.)

PROPAGANDA, CONGREGATION OF. *See* PROPAGATION OF THE FAITH, SACRED CONGREGATION OF.

PROPAGATION OF THE FAITH, SACRED CONGREGATION OF. The task of this branch of the governmental organization of the Church is to care for the administration and expansion of the mission fields in the world. It exercises jurisdiction over all missionary territory, that is, all parts of the world where the hierarchy has not been established. It appoints prefects and vicars apostolic, and supervises the clergy and faithful in these territories. It also maintains at Rome the Pontifical College of Propaganda Fide, known as the "Urban College" from its founder Pope Urban VII, who established the school in 1627. (*Cf.* CONGREGATIONS, PAPAL.)

PROPAGATION OF THE FAITH, SOCIETY FOR. International association, founded May 3, 1822, at Lyons, France, to aid by prayers and alms the missionaries and missions of the Church throughout the world.

PROPER. 1. The two major divisions of the Breviary: (a) the Proper of the season, i.e., the liturgical passages appointed to be recited on days of the year which have a special Mass and office; (b) the Proper of Saints, i.e., the liturgical passages appointed for feasts of saints throughout the year. **2.** The Proper of the Mass is comprised of those parts of the prayers of the Mass which vary according to the feast being celebrated on each day. These are: Introit, Collects, Epistle, Gradual, and Alleluia; or the substitutes for them, the Gospel, Offertory, Secret, Communion, and Postcommunion. There may also be a proper Preface and sometimes a Sequence. (*Cf.* MASS.)

PROPHECY, a message of truth which, received from God and transmitted by a prophet who serves as the intermediary between God and the people (Jer. 1:9), tells of future events that could not otherwise be known.

PROPHETICAL LITERATURE OF THE BIBLE. Classed under this title are the writings of the four major and twelve minor prophets of the O.T., together with the Books of Baruch and Lamentations, the latter being appendices of the Book of Jeremias. The major prophets are Isaias, Jeremias, Ezechiel, Daniel; the minor are Osee, Joel, Amos, Abdias, Jonas, Micheas, Nahum, Habacuc, Sophonias, Aggeus, Zacharias, Malachias.

PROPOSITIONS, CONDEMNED, the title of the 80 propositions condemned by Pius IX in the syllabus attached to the papal bull, *Quanta Cura* (1864). They are under ten sections treating of Pantheism, Naturalism, Absolute Rationalism, Moderate Rationalism, Indifferentism, Latitudinarianism, Socialism, Bible Societies, Liberalism, and errors about the Church and her rights.

PROSE, the name for a sequence that is not written in verse form.

PROTESTANT. Strictly speaking, the name is applied to any follower or adherent of a religious group or sect which separated from the Church at the time of the Reformation. It also includes those members who belong to one of the many offshoots of these original bodies. The term was first used when, following the Diet of

Speyer in 1529, Frederick of Saxony and others "protested" against the Diet's degree permitting Catholic worship.

PROTESTANTISM. Excluding traditional Christianity based upon Church authority, this religious system adheres broadly to three predominant principles: the supremacy of the Scriptures as the sole source and means of doctrine; the reasoning that justification is by faith alone; and the role of priesthood belonging to all believers. Among the various sects there are vast differences of interpretation of these principles with equally great innovations of dogmatic understanding. As a system, this new type of religion arose in the 16th century with the intervention of political forces, personal and administrative abuses within the Church, and the individualistic rebellion of men against the established form of Christianity. This latter was expressed by such leaders as Luther in Germany in 1521, by Zwingli in Switzerland a few years later, and in England by Henry VIII and Wolsey in 1527. The position of the Catholic Church was set forth in the twenty-five sessions of the Council of Trent (1545–1563) and this supplies a definite statement of Catholic doctrines denied by Protestants.

PROTHONOTARY APOSTOLIC. *See* MONSIGNOR.

PROTOCANONICAL BOOKS OF SCRIPTURE, the title applied to all books of the Scriptures which were found in the Hebrew Bible. The term protocanonical was first used by Sixtus of Siena in 1566 for denoting those books whose inspired character had always been accepted. (*Cf.* DEUTEROCANONICAL.)

PROTOEVANGELIUM, THE. Literally the "first gospel," this is the title of that portion of the book of Genesis (3:15) wherein God gives the prediction to fallen man of the promise of his redemption.

PROTOPRESBYTER, title of the first in rank among presbyters. (*Cf.* PRESBYTER.)

PROVERBS, BOOK OF. Called by the fathers of the Church the "Wisdom of Solomon," this Book of the O.T. was written by several authors who are listed in the text, but the principal writer was Solomon, who supplied two collections of proverbs, numbering about 510. The subject matter of this book is the art of right living, with some points being more emphasized than others, e.g., parents and children, the relations between God and men. Its central theme is wholesome teaching about true wisdom, taking special interest in the practical life which it aims to direct. The proverbs were written over many years, some as early as 800 B.C., the last being added about 400 B.C.

PROVIDENCE OF GOD. The order and care of all things, both natural and supernatural, which God exercises to bring these to their prescribed end, is manifested in the natural and positive divine laws and especially in the grace and help given to a person. Thus the Church is the provision made by God's goodness and mercy to work for the salvation of men through His providential care. The providence of God is not limited (Wisd. 8:1), it extends to even the least (Mt. 6:24–30), and it frees man of anxiety. It does not mean that man is free from effort, but that he should calmly pursue his labor, and God's provision will be evident. Likewise, it does not mean that man's life is free of difficulties because providence allows these that there may be proportion, according to the necessity of man to keep his thoughts occupied with the objective God prepared for him, eternal salvation.

PROVINCE. 1. Territory, consisting of two or more dioceses, over which an archbishop is head; the territory governed by a metropolitan in accord with canon 274. The archbishop is the ordinary of an archdiocese but he has certain privileges and control over the other dioceses of his suffragan bishops according to law. **2.** The extent of a religious community, that is, the district within which all properties and members comprise one unit, usually under the special management of a provincial.

PROVINCIAL, the head of a province of a religious community. He is either elected or appointed, his office is administrative, and he is subject to his superior general.

PROVISION, CANONICAL, the conferring and valid obtaining of an ecclesiastical office (c. 147).

PROVISORS, STATUTE OF. Issued by King Edward III of England in 1351, this decree nullified papal appointments made without consent of the king.

PROVOST GENERAL, title of the head of certain religious orders or congregations, e.g., Jesuits, Discalced Carmelites, etc.

PRUDENCE, one of the four cardinal virtues. It is that which in practice enables one to judge rightly about an act of virtue and so is basic to the performance of all virtuous actions. Prudence is a virtue of practical reason and in application is directed particularly at the proper exercise of the moral virtues. All formal sin is opposed to the virtue of prudence.

PSALMS, BOOK OF. Also named the Psalter, this book of religious poems has been called "the inspired hymnal of the O.T." In the Catholic version of the Bible, which follows the Vulgate and the Hebrew versions, there are 150 Psalms, or one less than in the Protestant versions, and therefore there is a discrepancy in the numbering sequence. David, both a poet and musician, was the author of many of the Psalms, certainly of numbers 2 and 15, 31, 68 and 109, because of references in the N.T. attributing these to him. He was the recognized national poet of the Hebrews and the promoter of liturgical chant, but many of the Psalms were written before his reign (1012–972 B.C.). The dominant theme of the Psalms is the greatness of the one and only God, the Creator, Ruler, and King of Kings. Added to this are God's attributes, particularly His right to worship and His justice. Besides this theme, the Psalms record again the history from creation up to the Babylonian captivity.

PSEUDO-ISIDORE, term applied to writings judged to be apocryphal and attributed to Isidore Mercator (d. 850).

PSYCHOANALYSIS, the searching for and investigation of motives for action which ordinarily are not in the consciousness. As based upon the approach developed by Freud, it is unacceptable because his system is founded upon materialism, determinism and hedonism, and it denies freedom and responsibility. Apart from this, the study of personality and the treatment of disorders has a place in the psychotherapeutic portion of medicine under the moral limits which protect the individual.

PSYCHOLOGY. This branch of philosophy which studies the science of the mind, its functions, structure, and effects, is divided according to the type of problem studied, e.g., abnormal, which treats of cases which depart from the "normal;" social psychology, which treats of group behavior, thought, etc.

PULPIT, term derived from the Latin word *pulpitum*, meaning a "stage" or "scaffold." Historically, it was first erected as a place from which one could address those in church and it replaced the *ambones*,

PULPIT

being erected on one side of the nave. No regulations are established for the construction of the pulpit from a liturgical standpoint, but it is assumed that it be practical as well as decorative. Today with public address systems, the pulpit is generally simplified in structure since it is not necessary to consider its acoustical advantages as to place, etc. It is simply a raised platform with a railing.

PURGATORY. The souls of those who have died in the state of grace suffer for a time a purging which prepares the soul to enter heaven and appear in the presence of the beatific vision. The purpose of purgatory is to cleanse one of imperfections, venial sins and faults, and to remit or do away with the temporal punishment due to mortal sins which have been forgiven in the sacrament of penance. It is an intermediate state in which the departed good can atone for unforgiven sins before receiving their final reward. (For an account of one making propitiation for the dead refer to 2 Mac. 12:39–46.) This state is not described in the teaching of the Church but its existence is a truth of faith defined by the Council of Trent (Sess. 25). Purgatory will last only until the general judgment. (*Cf.* HOLY SOULS.)

PURIFICATION OF THE B.V.M. In commemoration of the Blessed Mother having submitted to the Jewish law of ritual cleansing after childbirth (Lev. 12:1–8), a feast, called Candlemas, is celebrated on Feb. 2.

PURIFICATOR, a small linen cloth used during the Mass to dry and clean the chalice. It is usually from 12 to 18 in. long and from 9 to 10 in. wide and is kept folded.

PUTATIVE MARRIAGE. Invalid because of a diriment impediment or lack of consent, such marriage, however, was contracted while at least one of the contracting parties was in good faith as to the validity. (*Cf.* DIRIMENT IMPEDIMENTS.)

PYX. 1. A small, round container, usually made of silver or gold, about 1½ to 2 inches in diameter and less than 1 inch deep, in which the Blessed Sacrament is carried to the sick. This is usually enclosed in a small silk-lined bag or pouch and suspended from the neck of the priest by a silk cord. **2.** In the Middle Ages, a pyx was a form of tabernacle suspended above the altar from a chain. These were usually highly decorated.

Q

QUADRAGESIMA. From the Latin, meaning the "fortieth," the term has become the collective title for the entire period of Lent.

QUADRIVIUM, parts of the seven liberal arts studied in the Roman curriculum of studies and borrowed by 9th century teachers. The quadrivium consisted of arithmetic, geometry, astronomy, and music. The other three, called "Trivium," were grammar, rhetoric, and logic.

QUAESTOR. This title was applied to one who went about preaching that alms might be collected.

QUARANTINE. In the ancient Church, this was a period of forty days of rigorous fasting, penance and prayer. The quantity of indulgence guaranteed under the name quarantine is the amount of temporal punishment due to sin which would be remitted by this forty-day period of penance.

QUARTER TENSES. *See* EMBER DAYS.

QUEEN, MARY, FEAST OF THE BLESSED MOTHER. By proclamation of Pope Pius XII on November 1, 1954, this feast is to be celebrated yearly on May 31. The queenship of Mary extends to the universal Church, for she is by divine prerogative Queen of heaven and earth. Her queenship is to be venerated "as something extraordinary, wondrous, eminently holy" (*Ineffabilis Deus*).

The queenship of Mary has been declared formally by Pope Pius XII, thus: "Mary is queen by grace, by divine relationship, by right of conquest and by singular election" (AAS, 38, 1946, 266).

QUIETISM. Originating in the teaching of Miguel de Molinos (d. 1696), this system represented as the Christian spiritual ideal of perfection the complete passivity of the soul. Molinos' motto was: "Let God act." His error was that a continuous act of love being made or attained does away with other acts of virtue, even with the resistance to temptations. Quietism was condemned as heretical by Pope Innocent XI in 1687.

QUIET, PRAYER OF. St. Teresa of Avila gave this name (Life, Ch. 14) to that degree of contemplative prayer wherein the union of the soul is, by infused grace, characterized by a cessation of reason where contemplation is yet imperfect and where the intellect can still be distracted.

QUINISEXTUM COUNCIL. The Synod held in Trullo in 692 is sometimes referred to by this name which, literally, means the "fifth-sixth" council. Its proceedings remained unsigned by the pope, Sergius I (d. 701).

QUINQUAGESIMA, the title of the first Sunday before Lent.

QUIRE, a little used name for the place where choir singers stand in the church; more simply called the choir.

R

RABAT

RABAT. This French word is the name of a small piece of black, blue or white cloth which is divided in the middle and which, attached to a rudimentary collar and resting upon the upper chest, is worn by some of the French clergy but is not generally in use. In white, it is worn by the Brothers of Christian Doctrine.

RABBI

RABBI, the cloth which is attached to the front of a Roman collar and largely serves the purpose of holding the collar down. The name is derived from the French *rabat*.

RACCOLTA, THE. Containing the prayers, devotions, and aspirations which the Church has enriched with indulgences, this book is periodically published in Latin under the title *Enchiridion Indulgentiarum* and its translation is permitted by authorization of the Holy See. The conditions for gaining an indulgence and the amount of the indulgence as well as the date of grant made by the Sacred Congregation of the Penitentiary are listed with each prayer or devotion.

RASHNESS. Characteristic of this is the tendency to assent, without sufficient reason or basis for one's rash judgment, to the existence of a moral defect in another. It is a sin against justice and opposed to the virtue of prudence.

RATIONALISM, THEOLOGICAL. This doctrine, originated in Germany by Christian Wulff (d. 1754), held that reason is the ultimate judge of truth. It made observance of the moral law the equivalent of religion and it denied revelation. The term is also applied to the theory that the mind of man can and should assent only to those truths which are proved by reason, and as such it is developed in the Protestant principle of private judgment. As a repudiation of supernatural faith, rationalism is allied to deism, pantheism and materialism and has been condemned by the Holy See. (*Cf.* PROPOSITIONS, CONDEMNED.)

RATIO STUDIORUM, the abbreviated and usual title of the system of pedagogy as first published by the Society of Jesus in 1599. The full title is *Ratio atque Institutio Studiorum Societatis Iesu.* In its broad scope and method, it set up the orderly system and subjects which would serve to train the minds of students while at the same time giving basic knowledge in the arts, particularly of grammar and rhetoric.

RECIDIVIST. One who, in spite of repeated confessions, relapses into the commission of the same sins with the result that little effort is made toward improvement, or the inclination to improve is lost, is called a recidivist. The degree of sincerity on the part of the penitent determines the pastoral care necessary so that the penitent can make spiritual progress.

RECOLLECTION. In leading a spiritual life, recollection means the awareness of the presence of God in one's soul. Because of this awareness, excesses in actions and pleasures are curbed, distractions by the details of ordinary living are avoided. In practice, spiritual life is accompanied with a moderation in speech and the use of all senses (Ecce. 5:1–6).

RECONVENTIO, term applied to the counter claim made by a defendant in an ecclesiastical court.

RECTOR. 1. A term which is used as synonymous with the pastor of a church (c. 216). **2.** The head of a church which is neither a parish church nor a capitular one or one used by a religious community for divine services, e.g., a church dedicated for worship by pilgrims. **3.** The cleric who is in charge of a seminary or college chapel and by authority is the director of the institution, being responsible for the buildings, the worship, and those in attendance.

REDEMPTION OF MAN. This was the purpose for which Christ, the Second Person of the Blessed Trinity, came into the world as Man and God, that is, to save sinners (1 Tim. 1:15). In the O.T., we see the record of God the Father's merciful preparation and design to save the world, i.e., man, through his Son. This was accomplished by the sacrifice of Christ who offered Himself on the cross to God as a victim, and whose obedience ("to the death of the cross") was more meritorious than all of the sacrifices offered before by the Jews. Christ's act was prepared for, His arrival announced (Mt. 3:1–12), and when He came He declared: "The time is fulfilled, and the kingdom of God is at hand. Repent and believe in the gospel" (Mk. 1:15). Through Christ's act of propitiation the kingdom (man's reinstatement in the friendship of God and in his right to heaven and the means) is made known to the apostles (Mt. 13:11) and it is given to all (Mt. 21:43), and given through love which is the true source of all giving: the Father gives His Son (Jn. 3:16); the Son, Christ, gives Himself, His life (Mt. 20:28) on the cross and in the Eucharist (Mt. 26:26); and the Holy Ghost is given to confirm this opening of the kingdom by means of the Church and grace (Acts 2:38). The redemption of man accomplished by Jesus Christ is the regaining of the kingdom of heaven.

REDUCTIONS. *See* JESUIT REDUC-
TIONS.

REFORMATION, THE. *See* PROT-
ESTANTISM.

REFRESHMENT SUNDAY. The
Laetare Sunday, i.e., the 4th Sunday
of Lent, is sometimes referred to by
this name.

RELATIONS. *See* JESUIT RELATIONS.

RELICS, SACRED. Any part of the
bodily remains of a saint is so designated. Such relics if they are notable
in size should not be kept in private
houses without the bishop's permission. The relics of saints (martyrs generally) are enclosed in the sepulcher
of an altar or altar stone (portable
altar) (*cf.* ALTAR). It is forbidden to
sell sacred relics. Sacred relics are to
be authenticated, that is, declared by
sworn statement to be genuine. It is
the common practice to classify lesser
relics such as those items which have
been intimately connected with the
life of a saint, e.g., pieces of clothing,
etc., as second class, and those objects which have been touched to the
body of a saint, as third class. However, these are more the distinctions
borrowed from the practice than the
recognition of the Church. The cult
of sacred relics, that is, honor given
to the remains of a saint or any part,
is lawful but these relics may not be
exposed for public veneration without the approval of the ordinary.
Relics which are considered sacred
but are not portions of a saint's body,
are such things as relics of the true
cross. These must also be authenticated and are subject to the above
rules. Other relics, not authenticated,
but honored for ages may be retained,
but the Church does not vouch for
their genuineness.

RELIGION. St. Thomas defines this
as "a virtue by which men give due
worship and reverence to God."
While being variously defined, and
recognized under natural religion as
the relationship between God and
man without revelation, religion is,
in the ultimate sense, the recognition
by an intelligent creature of his origin
and his ordered progress in attaining
to God.

RELIGIOUS LIFE. That life under
a fixed mode with simple or solemn
vows in which the ones who have
chosen it keep the common precepts
of Christian conduct and bind themselves to observance of the three public vows of poverty, chastity and
obedience. It is a life conducive to attaining a higher degree of perfection
through the living of the counsels.
There are several distinctions which
arise from the type of vow or condition under which the members live:
(a) an *order* is a religious community
wherein solemn vows are taken; (b)
a *congregation* is one with simple
vows, temporary or perpetual; (c) a
monastic congregation is a union of
independent monasteries under the
same superior; (d) an *exempt religious institute* is one withdrawn from
the jurisdiction of the ordinary; (e) a
clerical community is one wherein
most of the members are priests; (f)
a *lay institute* is one whose members
are not priests (*cf.* NUNS; SISTERS).
The term *religious* is applied to members of a religious institute. Also
called *regulars.*

RELIQUARY, a container in which
a relic or relics are kept. In former
times, the Latin term *theca* (plural,
thecae) was sometimes used for reliquary.

RENAISSANCE. Beginning in the
14th century in Italy and continuing
at its height through the 15th and
16th centuries, the Renaissance was

a period of radical changes in the intellectual, artistic, political, social, and even geographical structure of Christian civilization. It had its origin in a realization of the Greek culture and Greek scholarship which succeeded the fall of Constantinople, and was centered on interest in classical culture. It was augmented by the introduction and widespread use of the printing press. It marked the trend toward humanism and laid the groundwork for the Reformation.

REQUIEM, a Mass for the dead. It is offered on All Souls' Day, on the day of death, on the day of burial (funeral Mass), on the 3rd, 7th, or 30th day after death, or on any day when the rubrics permit and the intention to pray for the dead is had by the celebrant. The Roman Missal lists four requiems: those for All Souls' Day, being three Masses; for the day of death; for the anniversary of death; and the ordinary Mass for the dead.

REREDOS

REREDOS, a carved, decorated screen at the back of the altar and rising above it. It is sometimes built against the altar, but should be entirely separate. Rules demand that it not interfere with the ciborium above the altar, that it leave the tabernacle free on all sides, that it be far enough

behind the tabernacle to give space for the crucifix and, when permitted, the seventh candlestick.

RERUM NOVARUM, Latin title of the encyclical "On the Condition of Labor" by Pope Leo XIII, published May 15, 1891. It presents the Church's position on social morality and the principles of justice and charity which should regulate the relationship of capital and labor. On the 40th anniversary of its publication, Pope Pius XI published the encyclical entitled *Quadragesimo Anno* (May 15, 1931) which treated of the same subject.

RESCRIPT, the written reply of a religious superior to a request, report or question (c. 36–62). In make-up, it repeats the request and its facts together with the reasons, and then offers the answer with the conditions. It is the usual form through which dispensations are granted or denied.

RESERVATION OF THE BLESSED SACRAMENT, the retaining of a consecrated host or hosts in the tabernacle. Also the removal of the Blessed Sacrament, reserved in the ciborium, from the main tabernacle on Holy Thursday to a place of proper reverence. This place may be an adjoining altar, called the "Repository Altar."

RESERVED CENSURE. *See* CEN-SURE.

RESIDENCE. In canon law, this term applies to the rule that a parish priest may not be absent from his place of assignment for an extended time without permission of his ordinary (c. 143).

RESPONSORY, a series of versicles and responses, sung or recited together with the *Gloria Patri* after each lesson of the Divine Office.

RESTITUTION. 1. The act of returning or replacing the goods which a person has found or stolen because of a violation of commutative justice. The obligation is grave in degree with the real or supposed value of the goods, and the obligation can arise out of wrongful possession or unjust damage, as to one's reputation. **2.** The duty to compensate a person for his labor.

RESURRECTION OF CHRIST. The physical rising from death by Christ on Easter as recorded in the Gospels (Mt. 28:1–20; Lk. 24:1–9; cf. Jn. 20:1–18) was accomplished through the power that was His as the Son of God as He promised (Mt. 17:22). And through the subsequent coming of the Holy Spirit the certitude of the Resurrection is brought home to the disciples (Jn. 16:13ff).

RESURRECTION OF THE BODY. That the body will be reanimated is a doctrine of revealed truth and an article of the Catholic faith. St. Paul, in speaking of the resurrection of the body (1 Cor. 15:1–58), bases his statement on (1) the Resurrection of Christ as the verification of the atoning power of Christ's Passion (15:14); (2) the hope of Christians (15:30); (3) the fact that it is not contrary to reason; (4) the parallels formed in nature (15:35–41). He concludes with a description of the excellence of the risen body (15:44f). (*Cf.* JUDGMENT, GENERAL.)

RETABLE, a modified reredos (q.v.). It is a low panel erected behind an altar, chiefly for decoration, but it may have a practical purpose, e.g., to support lights, etc.

RETREAT. 1. Name of a period of time varying in length from several days to a month during which the faithful, cleric and lay, may undertake prayer, meditation, devotions and spiritual exercises for the purpose of advancing in spiritual living or amendment of life. **2.** The place, frequently called a "retreat house," may be any suitable place of quiet.

There are several systems or set procedures for retreats, e.g., the Spiritual Exercises of St. Ignatius. However, the basic requirements are solitude with the keeping of vocal silence, a schedule of prayer, and a series of spiritual conferences or talks given by a priest-director who is usually titled "the retreat master."

REVELATION, the means by which man knows divine truths; the written font of truth such as the Scriptures and unwritten Tradition which have come down to us from practices and the attendant argument of history. In the Church which is, through Christ, the living teaching authority, there is a twofold revelation. As defined by the Council of Trent, this revelation is "contained in written books and in traditions without writing—traditions which were received from the mouth of Christ Himself and from the apostles under dictation of the Holy Spirit and have come down to us, delivered, as it were, from hand to hand" (Sess. IV, EB 46). Revelation as the Church possesses it and exercises it is by the Holy Spirit, inspiring the Scripture, and aiding the Church (1 Cor. 2:7–8). (*Cf.* INSPIRATION OF SCRIPTURE.)

RHEIMS-DOUAY VERSION. *See* BIBLE.

RIDDEL, medieval English term for curtains which were hung at either side of an altar.

RIGORISM, a condemned moral system. It declares that the law must be followed unless the contrary opinion is certain, which binds one at all times. (*Cf.* PROBABILISM.)

RING, a circular band of precious metal, sometimes bearing a precious gem. Rings used in the Church are: (a) the wedding ring; it is blessed at the marriage ceremony and is worn on the fourth finger of the left hand as a sign of fidelity; (b) the pontifical ring of bishops, abbots, and prothonotaries; (c) the plain gold ring presented to nuns and sisters at their profession in religion to remind them of their espousal to Christ.

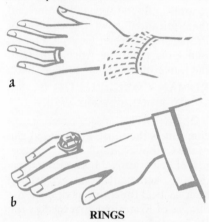

RINGS

RING OF THE FISHERMAN. *See* FISHERMAN, THE RING OF THE.

RITE. 1. The collection or system of language, forms, ceremonies, prayers, together with the accompanying rules, vestments, and other objects or implements, used in carrying out the public worship, the administration of sacraments and church functions of a church or group of churches. There are nine such rites in the Catholic Church: The Latin or Roman, Byzantine, Armenian, Chaldean, Coptic, Ethiopian, Malabar, Maronite, and Syrian. As such, the word rite is often considered synonymous with "liturgy" (*cf.* LITURGY). **2.** A single religious function with its prescribed form, as the rite of baptism. **3.** A group of ceremonies, forms and prayers which are joined in solemnity of an occasion or an event, e.g., the rite of consecration, the rite of Holy Thursday, etc. **4.** A variation of ceremony permitted by Church law in which a particular group, because of custom, performs functions in accord with a special rule or ritual, e.g., the Dominican rite, as a slight variant of the Roman.

Rites are historically local in origin, arising in ancient times in a particular place, e.g., Antioch, and slowly spreading to other areas of adoption. They likewise are developments, with additions and changes being introduced. At the present time the rite is governed by law, with prescribed rules of execution carried out to the last detail. Also a member of a Church group becomes identified with the rite of that group, and under canon law it is forbidden for one belonging to the Roman rite to pass over to an Eastern rite, or vice versa, or to make a change back to the original rite, without permission of the Holy See (c. 98). Membership in a rite is by being born into it, that is, children belong to the rite of the father; or membership can be by conversion into a particular rite.

RITES, SACRED CONGREGATION OF. In the administrative bodies of the Holy See, this is the unit whose mark is the regulation and control of liturgical worship, the veneration of relics, and the beatification and canonization of saints. It was not set up as an organized unit until 1588 when Pope Sixtus V consolidated previous recommendations and established the congregation. Today, according to canon 253, this congregation has jurisdiction of rites and ceremonies of the Latin Church, i.e., all rites recognized in the West. It also governs the ceremonies for the celebration of Mass, the administration of the sacraments, and other aspects of divine worship.

RITUAL. Of this liturgical book, the *Rituale Romanum*, which contains the instructions, prayers and ceremonies to be used in the administration of the sacraments, blessings, devotions, etc., an official, authorized publication is brought out from time to time with any changes which the Holy See has authorized (*cf.* LITURGICAL BOOKS). It is the official source of rubrics. There may be portions of this published for convenience, e.g., that for music, Psalms and lessons of Holy Week, called the *Officium Majoris Hebdomadae.*

ROBBER SYNOD. *See* LATROCINIUM.

ROCHET, a shorter adaptation of the alb with tight-fitting sleeves. It is worn by the pope, cardinals, bishops, abbots, prelates, and canons. The rochet is adorned with lace on the cuffs and lower edge, the length of the lace depending upon the dignity of the wearer.

ROGATION DAYS, the Monday, Tuesday and Wednesday before the feast of Ascension; also called the Lesser Litanies. They are marked by a procession, the object of which, together with the prayers, is to ask God's mercy and blessing upon mankind and his work. The Litany of the Saints is chanted during the procession. It is the Christian substitute for the ancient Roman feast called *robigalia* which was marked by a procession on April 25 to obtain a good harvest.

ROMAN CATHOLIC. The designation of one belonging to the Roman rite merely makes a distinction according to the rite followed. Ritually,

the name of the Church founded by Christ and of its members is *Catholic.* The term Roman Catholic has come to be the accepted designation of the one true Church and is recognized officially for legal documents, etc. (*Cf.* CATHOLIC; MARKS OF THE CHURCH.)

ROMAN COLLEGE. Usually, this name is applied to the Gregorian University in Rome. It may, however, be used as a collective title of all the schools and seminaries of Rome and the Vatican, thus of the College of Propaganda, Urban College, Gregorian University, the Angelicum, and the numerous national colleges, etc.

ROMAN CONGREGATIONS. *See* SACRED ROMAN CONGREGATIONS.

ROMAN RITE. Also called Latin rite, this is the most widely used rite of the Catholic Church. It is the manner of celebrating Mass, administering the sacraments, and performing ecclesiastical functions as done in the diocese of Rome and governed by the Roman Ritual. (*Cf.* RITE.)

ROME. The capital city of today's Italy, the seat of the government and principal city of the ancient Roman Empire, was inhabited as early as the 8th century B.C. After having spent some time in Jerusalem and Antioch, St. Peter journeyed to Rome in 42 A.D. and established the Church, making numerous converts and enduring the first-century persecutions. It is within the city of Rome, called the city of seven hills, that the entire area of Vatican State proper now is confined. By treaty with the Italian government certain other properties apart from the Vatican State are considered as territorial parts of the state of Vatican City. Since the founding of the Church there by St. Peter, the city of Rome has been the center of

Christendom. The city itself is the diocese of the pope as bishop of Rome.

ROOD-SCREEN, a more or less open screen of wood or stone which separated the sanctuary transept from the nave in churches of the Middle Ages. It was usually as high as the middle of the arch and was highly ornamental. The name is derived from the large crucifix (called "rood" in old English) which surmounted the screen, often with the figures of St. John and the Blessed Mother on either side of it.

ROSARY, the name of both a devotion and the chain of beads used for counting the prayers. As a devotion, the Rosary arose in the 15th century and became very popular. It was begun by a Dominican preacher, Alan de Rupe (d. 1475) in northern France and Flanders. Belief that the devotion was revealed to St. Dominic was chiefly due to a report of a vision of de Rupe which became current. The devotion is directed to the Blessed Mother and has been highly indulgenced by the Church. The Rosary as a devotion is of three parts. It consists of an initial prayer, the Apostles' Creed, followed by the Our Father and three Hail Marys and a Gloria Patri, which are said beginning on the crucifix and continue on the pendant portion of the chain of beads. There follow fifteen decades or groups of ten beads separated by a single bead. Each decade consists of the recitation of the Our Father, ten Hail Marys, and concludes with one Gloria Patri. The devotion is for private or public use and, while saying the prayers of each decade, the person praying is to meditate on the mysteries of the Rosary, fifteen in all (*cf.* MYSTERIES OF THE ROSARY). The implement, or the popularly called "beads," may be a chain with pendant and all fifteen decades, sometimes called a "full" rosary, or it may be only a pendant with five decades of beads, this latter being the more familiar. Blessed and with the permitted indulgences attached, the rosary implement is a sacramental. A feast honoring the Blessed Mother and commemorating the Rosary is celebrated on October 7. Among the many indulgences attached to the devotion is: The faithful who recite the Rosary together in a family group, besides the partial indulgence of 10 years, are granted a plenary indulgence twice a month, if they perform this recitation daily for a month, go to confession, receive Holy Communion, and visit some church or public oratory. (S.P.M. March 18, 1932 and July 26, 1946.)

ROSE, GOLDEN *See* GOLDEN ROSE.

ROSE WINDOW

ROSE WINDOW, a circular, stained glass window, with tracery radiating from the center. Such windows are used frequently in churches of Gothic architecture and may be placed at the ends of transepts or in the facade of the nave.

ROTA, SACRED ROMAN, the most renowned tribunal of the Holy See. It was founded as a court early in the 13th century. At present, fourteen judges serve the court. All cases handled by the Rota are decided by a panel of three judges called *turnus,* all of whom must sign the verdict. As a rule, all pleading before the Rota is in writing. The Rota has care of marriage cases, matters of ecclesiastical law, and handles cases after they have been presented before the first court and a court of appeal. Cases are handled gratuitously or with a minimum payment of expenses. There are two classes of lawyers, all versed in canon law and usually in civil law: Consistorial lawyers, who are entitled to plead causes of beatification and canonization in consistories; and Procurators of the Sacred Apostolic Palaces, whose office permits them to plead before the Rota although their title is largely honorary.

RUBRICS, the term for the rules of ceremony and form which govern a liturgical function or rite.

RULE, RELIGIOUS. Regulating the order of life, the discipline, practice and observance as laid down in the constitution of a religious order or congregation, the rule is usually directed to the particular work for which the order or congregation was founded. Many such are derived from the early formulation of rules laid down by SS. Basil, Augustine, Benedict, Francis, Dominic. The rule binds each member under obedience.

RURAL DEANS. *See* DEAN.

RUSSIAN CHURCH. *See* ORTHODOX CHURCH.

RUTH, BOOK OF, an historical book of the O.T., probably written by a contemporary of King David. It narrates the history of the age of Judges and the ancestry of David. In content, the writing is deeply religious, mirrors divine Providence, and forecasts the calling of the Gentiles.

RUTHENIAN CATHOLICS, inhabitants of southwest Russia, Catholics of the Byzantine rite, now completely under the U.S.S.R. The Ruthenians have two bishops in the United States. (*Cf.* EASTERN CHURCHES.)

S

SABAOTH. Meaning, literally, "of hosts" or "of armies," this has been attached as a title of majesty to the name of God, signifying His command over all earthly and heavenly forces.

SABBATH, the seventh day of the week in Jewish religious law. It has been supplanted under Christian tradition with Sunday, the Lord's Day. In Latin, *sabbatum* is the name of Saturday in liturgical writings.

SABELLIANISM, another name for the Monarchian heresy as propounded by Sabellius (circa 220).

SACRAMENTAL. Any object or action which the Church places within the reach of a person and by which a person receives certain spiritual favors from God through his own action, is so designated. Sacramentals differ vastly from sacraments since they produce effects through the Church's prayer to God and only certain sacramentals require a particular disposition on the part of the person using it, e.g., blessed ashes on Ash Wednesday. The Holy See alone can constitute new sacramentals, abolish, change or interpret those already in use. Examples of sacramentals are: Holy water, the sign of the cross, vestments, candles, rosary, blessings, etc.

SACRAMENTS, THE SEVEN, 1. It is necessary to set forth the essential elements of a sacrament. These are: (a) a sensible sign instituted by God which gives sanctifying grace; (b) both matter and form are present with each sacrament, the matter being the material used, the form the accompanying words and/or action; (c) each demands a minister, someone authorized to give the sacrament with the intention of doing what the Church intends. 2. It is well to know that the sacraments produce grace. Since grace is a gift of God, the sacrament must come from and depend upon God. Sanctifying grace is given by reason of the rite itself (*ex opere operato*), and grace is not given if the sacrament is not received with the necessary moral disposition. In addition, each sacrament confers a special grace, called sacramental grace. It is the teaching of the Catholic Church that every one of the sacraments of the New Law was instituted by Christ as defined by the Council of Trent. These are: baptism (Mt. 28:18ff); the Holy Eucharist (Mt. 26:26); penance (Jn. 20:21ff); matrimony (Mt. 22:2ff); extreme unction (James 5:14–15); confirmation (Acts 2:42; 8:15; 19:6); holy orders (Jn. 20:21–22). (See also entries under individual titles of each sacrament.)

SACRED COLLEGE OF CARDINALS. The members of the Sacred College are those cardinals who ac-

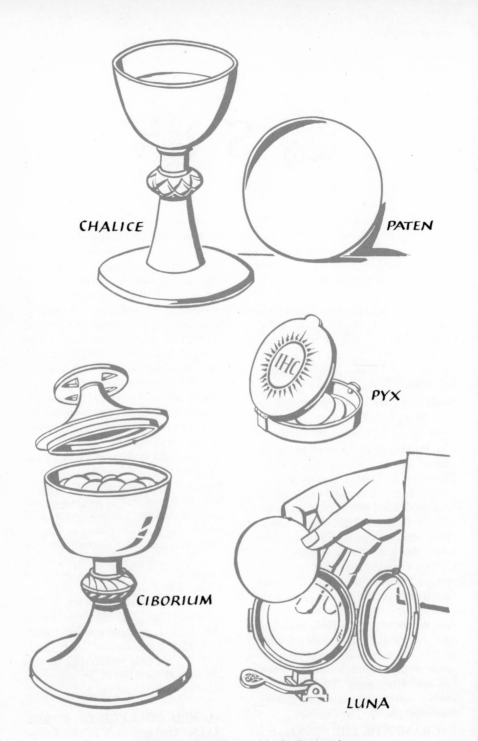

CHALICE

PATEN

PYX

CIBORIUM

LUNA

SACRED VESSELS—Used in the Roman rite.

cording to canon law (230) have a particular place in the Church: "The cardinals of the Holy Roman Church constitute the senate of the Roman Pontiff and aid him as chief counselors and collaborators in the government of the Church." Among many privileges granted to them is the very important function of electing a successor to a deceased pope.

SACRED HEART OF JESUS. 1. Devotion to Jesus Christ, consisting of worship of Him through His heart as representing His love shown in the Incarnation, His Passion and death, the institution of the Eucharist. The devotion further is centered on reparation to Christ for man's ingratitude, manifested particularly by indifference to the Holy Eucharist. The worship is not directed to the Heart alone, but to the Person of Jesus Christ. The Church forbids public cult of the Heart separated from the rest of the body, but allows private veneration, as in the case of Sacred Heart badges. The devotion is based upon the doctrine or dogma "God is love" as found in Scripture (1 Jn. 4:8). **2.** A feast, requested by our Lord Himself, commemorates the unrequited love of the Sacred Heart in the Eucharist, and is celebrated on the Friday after the feast of Corpus Christi. **3.** Representation of the Sacred Heart of Jesus may be in picture, statue, medal, or the familiar "badge." **4.** Enthronement of the Sacred Heart in the home is the acknowledgment of the sovereignty of Christ over the family. It is expressed through solemn installation by the head of the house of a representation of the Sacred Heart in a place of honor, together with an act of consecration, in the presence of the entire family. Further indulgenced practices for individuals or families are to spend an hour in reparation before the Blessed Sacrament, or before an image of the Sacred Heart in the home between the hours of 9 p.m. and 6 a.m.

SACRED ROMAN CONGREGATIONS. These chief organs of aid, employed by the supreme pontiff in the government of the Church, are administrative groups. "Each of the Congregations is in charge of a Cardinal Prefect, or, if the Roman Pontiff himself is the Prefect, the Congregation is governed by a Cardinal Secretary" (c. 246). In session throughout the business year of the Curia and holding their meetings in the Vatican, these congregations are: Congregation of the Holy Office; Sacred Consistorial; for the Oriental Church; of the Sacraments; of the Council; of Religious; of the Propagation of the Faith; of Rite; of the Ceremonial; for Extraordinary Ecclesiastical Affairs; of Seminaries and Universities; for St. Peter's Basilica.

SACRED VESSELS. These are the chalice, paten, ciborium, pyx, and lunette. They are used during the celebration of the Mass or as containers of the Blessed Sacrament. Less sacred are those closely associated with divine worship, the monstrance and the communion plate.

SACRIFICE. The supreme act of worship consists essentially in (a) an offering of a worthy victim to God; (b) the offering made by a proper person, as a priest; (c) the destruction of the victim; (d) offering for the purpose of obtaining pardon for sin or a favor (Lev. 8:1–36). In the Christian Law, the supreme sacrifice is that of the Mass, the unbloody repetition of the Sacrifice of Christ on Calvary. (*Cf.* MASS.)

SACRILEGE. This term refers to the unbecoming treatment of a person, place, or thing which has been consecrated or dedicated to God. It is personàl when directed against a person, e.g., injury to a cleric; it is local when directed against a place, e.g., murder done in a church; it is real when committed through the dishonoring of sacred things, e.g., unworthy reception, administration, or profanation of a sacrament or sacred vessels. Thus, simony is also a sacrilege since it is irreverent misuse of a spiritual thing. (*Cf.* SIMONY.)

SACRISTAN. This title is given to the person assigned to care for the sacristy and its contents, to prepare for the celebration of Mass, i.e., arrange the vestments, etc. He may be a priest, religious, or lay person.

SACRISTY, a room adjoining the sanctuary, with a door into the sanctuary and usually one connection with the body of the church, where vestments, linens, and other articles used in divine service are kept. It is recommended that this room be not too small, be well lighted, and protected by barred windows because of the nature of the equipment retained there. St. Charles Borromeo (d. 1584) wrote extensive instructions for the fitting of the sacristy, many of which indicate the necessity for efficiency and convenience.

SAINT PETER'S BASILICA. St. Peter's, the largest church in the world, adjoining the Vatican palace, the home of the pope, is built above the circus of Nero, the place where St. Peter, the first pope, suffered martyrdom. The building was first erected by Constantine, but the present structure dates from its completion in 1626. Many artists and craftsmen contributed to its singular beauty, the vast dome being the design of Michelangelo. Recent archaeological findings, excavated from beneath the church, attest to the history of the early Christian life and tradition. The church is kept in constant repair by skilled workmen, called *sampietrini*, and is served by a chapter of thirty canons. It is provided for by a Sacred Congregation whose members direct and govern the occasions and solemnity of celebrations, e.g., jubilees, when the church is the place of ceremonies of world-wide importance.

SAINTS. To those members of the mystical body of Christ who have lived and died, whose lives were notable for holiness and virtues practiced, and who have been officially declared saints by the Church through the process of beatification and canonization, the faithful may render veneration (*dulia*) and prayers of intercession. The saints are for the faithful, first, examples of the virtuous life, and secondly, as members of the Church triumphant, representatives of the living members of the mystical body and the suffering souls. There are several classifications of saints recognized by the Church which are not due to their occupation in life but rather to the quality of their sanctity; e.g., martyrs, virgins, confessors, doctors, bishops, etc.

SAINTS, INTERCESSION AND VENERATION OF. The Church has always recognized the intercessory power of saints. Arising from O.T. Jewish belief in the "merits of the fathers" (Jer. 15:1; Ez. 14:14), the Church recognized that all members unite in worship before the throne of God (Apoc. 6:9–11). This uniting with the saints is not only through seeking their intercession, but also through the veneration that the Church gives to the saints, called *dulia*, which is adoration of God through the saints. That all the faithful have a close association with the saints is attested by St. Paul who addresses the living faithful by the term "saints" (Col. 1:2). (*Cf.* INTERCESSION.)

SALT, LITURGICAL USE OF.
1. As a symbol of wisdom and friendship with God (Mk. 9:48), a few grains of common salt, which has been exorcized and blessed, are placed on the tongue of the one being baptized. **2.** Water to be blessed is mixed with a little salt.

SANCTIFYING GRACE. Infused into the very essence of the soul, sanctifying grace is a certain supernatural quality granted by God, without which we are not sanctified or assured justification and salvation. It is "God abiding in the soul" (Jn. 14:23) and the Council of Trent declares: "It is called our justice because by its inherence in us we are justified." (Denz. No. 809.) Sanctifying grace is lost through mortal sin; it is increased through good acts done for and through God, and particularly through the reception of the sacraments. It is also called habitual grace, but this is a broader term. (*Cf.* GRACE.)

SANCTUARY, in modern church buildings that portion of the church wherein the high altar is located, extending to the communion rail. Besides the altar it should be furnished with a bench for the ministers, stools or benches for the acolytes, and a credence table. It also may have choir-stalls, an episcopal throne, and an aumbry.

SANCTUS, THE. Following the Preface of the Mass, this short prayer is accompanied with the ringing of the bell three times, and is a welcome and a hymn of praise heralding the opening of the Canon of the Mass. It recalls two events in the life of Christ, the welcome of the angels at the Nativity (Lk. 2:14), and the praise offered to Christ at His entry into Jerusalem (Mk. 11:1–10). It demonstrates in human terms the praise which the angels give before the throne of God in heaven (Apoc. 4:18).

SANDALS, low shoes, with leather soles and the upper part of silk or velvet, usually embroidered, worn by bishops when celebrating pontifical Mass. In color they correspond to that of the vestments worn. Sandals are not worn at requiem Masses or on Good Friday.

SAPIENTAL BOOKS. The biblical books of Wisdom, Proverbs, Ecclesiastes, the Canticle of Canticles, and Ecclesiasticus are known under this collective title.

SARDICA, COUNCIL OF. Held in 343 at Sardica (now Sofia in Bulgaria), this meeting of Eastern and Western bishops was an attempt to settle the dispute over the approval or condemnation of Athanasius at various local councils.

SARUM USE, a form of the Latin rite as formulated by St. Osmund (d. 1099). First used in the diocese of Salisbury, it was later introduced into Scotland and Ireland and replaced the ancient Celtic ritual. Up to the Reformation, it was commonly used in England and Scotland. It resembles the Dominican rite as used today.

SATAN, Lucifer, the devil, the chief tempter and head of the evil spirits. The name Satan first appears in Job (1:6) and means "the opponent."

SATISFACTION. 1. The ancient legal meaning of this term was the compensation for a debt or offense. St. Anselm applied it to the redemptive act of Christ wherein the justification of man was established. Christ's death on the cross was the satisfaction for the sins of the whole human race. **2.** Sacramental satisfaction is the voluntary acceptance on the part of a penitent of the sacrifice (penance, alms, etc.) which is necessary to expiate the temporal punishment due to sin. Like Christ, the Christian must die so that he may live in Christ (Gal. 2:19), that he "walks in the Spirit" (Gal. 5:25), and is a member of Christ (Gal. 2:20). **3.** A term for the penance imposed by a superior in a religious institute.

SCALA SANCTA. Literally, "the holy stairs," this is a flight of 28 steps leading to the papal chapel in the old Lateran palace. While now covered with wood, the original stairs beneath were thought to be the steps leading up to the praetorium of Pilate. They were alleged to have been brought from Jerusalem by St. Helena about 326.

SCAMNUM, Latin name for the bench on the epistle side of the sanctuary where the celebrant, deacon, and subdeacon sit during parts of the high Mass. It is a bench without arms or back. It replaces the *sedilia* (q.v.).

SCANDAL. Giving scandal means to provoke by words or conduct the occasion for the sin of another or to cause another's spiritual ruin.

SCAPULAR. 1. Basically a garment, a part of a religious habit, which consists of a piece of cloth, shoulder wide, which is placed over the head and hangs down, front and back to the prescribed length. **2.** The scapular

SCAPULAR

as a sacramental, in imitation of the larger form, is usually two small pieces of cloth, about 2x3 in., which are joined by strings; it is worn around the neck, under the clothing, and hangs down front and back. There are some 18 kinds of scapular recognized by the Church, each being worn as a badge of some confraternity into which the wearer is enrolled. The most common are: the white (Trinitarians), red (Lazarists), brown (Carmelites), black (Servites), blue (Theatines). The indulgences attached to the white, black, and brown scapulars can only be gained by having the names of those enrolled recorded and sent to a church where the confraternity is established. **3.** The scapular medal, bearing on one side an image of the Sacred Heart and on the other a representation of the Blessed Mother, may be worn in substitution of the small scapular (see 2 above) only after one has been enrolled in the scapular of a confraternity. If it is worn in place of several kinds of scapular, the priest blessing it must make the sign of the cross over the medal—once for each scapular the medal substitutes for—and each new medal must be so blessed. Once enrolled, it is not necessary to be enrolled again and the small scapular, when replaced by a new one, may be worn without obtaining a blessing for the new one.

SCHISM. The crime of one who voluntarily separates himself from the Catholic Church through refusal to submit to the authority of the Church or the pope and forms another sect is punished with excommunication incurred by the very fact of the action. Basically, schism is a breaking away from the Church, but differs from apostasy and heresy.

SCHISM, EASTERN. After a series of minor breaks over Iconoclasm and jurisdictional matters, the ecclesiastical leaders of the East and West split into two factions in the 9th century. One followed the pope of Rome, the other the patriarch of Constantinople. The immediate dispute was over the assumption of power by Photius (d. 897), with the confirmation of the emperor Michael III. Photius was deposed in 896 by the new emperor Leo VI. The breach had been accomplished by a series of political and religious actions which continued for the next seven hundred years. With the fall of Constantinople in 1453, the center of Oriental Christianity fell and, despite the efforts of the Council of Florence (1439) which had effected a brief reconciliation, the Orthodox Church became official under the Russian empire.

SCHISM, THE GREAT. The dispute between allegiances to the claimants of the papacy, Urban VI (d. 1389) and Clement VII (d. 1394), divided the Church along lines of political and international rivalries, for the Latin nations and France supported Clement while the German and English rulers supported Urban. The Great Schism ended in 1417 with the election of Pope Martin V.

SCHOLASTIC. 1. A student of scholastic philosophy. **2.** A member of the Society of Jesus who has completed his novitiate and is studying preparatory to ordination.

SCHOLASTICISM. The name of this method and system of thought, which embraces all the intellectual activities, artistic, philosophical, and theological, carried on in the universities of the Middle Ages, is derived from the term *doctores scholastici* which was the 9th century term for a teacher of the arts. It was the system, taken from the Greek and adapted through recognition of revelation and tradition, which became the philosophy of a Christian society, and which recognized the superiority of theology. As a method it was marked by emphasis upon logic, deduction, system, and the form of syllogistic argumentation; subordination to theology; and the disputation formula whereby a thesis or doctrine is defended by a syllogistic presentation against objections. (*Cf.* NEO-SCHOLASTICISM.)

SCHOOLMEN. The masters of scholasticism in the Middle Ages, e.g., St. Thomas Aquinas, St. Albert the Great, etc., have been recognized by this name.

SCHOOL, PAROCHIAL. *See* PAROCHIAL SCHOOL.

SCOTISM. Developed by the famous Franciscan Schoolman, Duns Scotus (d. 1308), this system distinctly differs from Thomism. Primarily, it holds that immortality of the soul is beyond human reason; that these are two substantial forms in man; that will holds a certain superior position to intellect, this being seen in the contention that ultimate happiness will be the act of loving God (will) rather than intellectual vision.

SCREEN. *See* ROOD-SCREEN.

SCRIPTURE. *See* BIBLE; CANON OF SCRIPTURE; REVELATION.

SCRUPLES. Being a basis of confusion over the morality of actions, scruples arise when a troubled conscience, prompted by imaginary reasons, causes one to constantly dread sin where no sin exists, or to hold a venially sinful action mortally sinful. It is a conscience ruled by fear. The causes may be varied, as disorder of health (physiological), predominance of sentiment over reason, lack of judgment, etc. Remedies are prayer and trust in God, restoration of health (if ill health be the cause), formation of a right conscience, and obedience to a counselor if one is required.

SCRUTINY, in the ecclesiastical sense, the examination of a person as to spiritual fitness before awarding him an office in the Church.

SEAL OF CONFESSION. The most grave obligation of keeping secret whatever has been revealed by a penitent in the sacrament of penance is always binding under mortal sin; no exception is made, not even in order to save one's life. The confessor is bound by the seal (c. 889), even if the confessor were a layman, masquerading. All sins confessed, even public sins, are subject to the seal. The obligation of the seal arises out of the role of judge in which the confessor acts, rather than from the act of absolving. It is founded upon the natural law, the positive divine law, and Church law.

SECOND COMING OF CHRIST. *See* JUDGMENT, GENERAL.

SECRET, DISCIPLINE OF THE. *See* DISCIPLINE OF THE SECRET.

SECRET OF THE MASS. This is the variable part of the Mass which immediately precedes the Preface and which may consist of one or more prayers, said in a low voice by the priest as he bows over the bread and wine. The content of the prayers is to ask God to accept the offerings for the consecration which will follow soon. Thus the Secrets are called *super oblata* prayers, i.e., prayers over the oblations. (*Cf.* MASS.)

SECRET SOCIETIES. Membership in any of such societies is denied Catholics by law of the Church. Besides the Freemasons (*cf.* MASONRY), these societies are Good Templars, Odd Fellows, Sons of Temperance, Knights of Pythias, and any women's auxiliary group of these. These are forbidden under censure. Besides, the Church law states that those belonging to not necessarily secret societies as such but notoriously anti-social societies cannot receive ecclesiastical burial unless they repent (c. 1240) and members of any condemned society cannot be validly received into associations of the faithful (c. 693). Also the Holy Office (Nov. 5, 1920) warned against the dangers to the faith of the young by the activities of the Y.M.C.A. All societies which have religious rites or oaths of blind obedience fall under the general condemnation of the Church.

SECULAR CLERGY. *See* DIOCESAN CLERGY.

SECULARISM. As defined in the statement of the bishops of the United States (Nov. 14, 1947—*Secularism*), this is "a view of life that limits itself not to the material in exclusion of the spiritual, but to the human here and now in exclusion of man's relation to God here and hereafter. Secularism, or the practical exclusion of God from human thinking and living, is at the root of the world's travail today." The bishops conclude: "The fact of God and the fact of the responsibility of men and nations to God for their actions are supreme realities, calling insistently for recognition in a truly realistic ordering of life in the individual, in the family, in the school, in economic activity, and in the international community."

SECULARIZATION. 1. The civil action depriving the Church of use or possession of properties. **2.** The act of separating a professed religious from his duties and obligations as a member of a religious congregation or order, done through papal indult and in accord with canon law.

SEDIA GESTATORIA

SEDIA GESTATORIA. From the Italian, meaning "portable chair," the term is applied to the formal throne-like chair on which the pope sits and is borne on a platform during solemn processions of entry into St. Peter's, etc. Those who carry the platform are dressed in crimson and are called *sediarii.*

SEDILIA, throne-like bench, usually in three partitions and with a back, whereon the celebrant, deacon, and subdeacon sit during parts of a high Mass. Liturgically it has been replaced by the *scamnum.*

SEE, EPISCOPAL. *See* DIOCESE.

SEMI-ARIANISM. This heresy, promoted in the 4th century by Acacius, which taught that Christ the Son was only *like* God the Father, was condemned by the First Council of Constantinople (381).

SEMINARIAN, one who attends an ecclesiastical seminary. Seminarians have certain obligations, arising out of the dignity of their purpose. Those who are incorrigible, seditious, wanting in disposition or health, or who are not able students are to be dismissed according to canon law.

SEMINARY, an ecclesiastical college of higher learning. Its sole purpose is to train young men for the reception of holy orders. It is customary to classify a preparatory school as a "minor seminary" and the more advanced schools "major seminaries." The college school, however, has a six-year course of training, consisting of two years of philosophy (junior and senior years of college proper), and four years of theology. Only those seminaries which are classified as having an apostolic faculty (c. 1378) can confer licentiate and doctoral degrees in theological subjects, canon law, or Scripture.

SEMI-PELAGIANISM, a heresy which arose in the 5th century. Propounded by a group of monks at the

Abbey of St. Victor in Marseilles, it affirmed that grace is merited by man and is made efficacious by the human will. It was condemned by St. Augustine who wrote against it, and by the Second Council of Orange in 529.

SENTENCES, THE BOOK OF. This compilation of theology in four volumes, by Peter Lombard (d. 1160), was the standard textbook of the time until replaced by the *Summa* of St. Thomas Aquinas.

SEPARATION. 1. In marriage, this is the physical parting of man and wife (from bed and board) for due reason (c's. 1128–1132). Thus the innocent marriage partner may separate from the other in case of found adultery. Also, if one of the parties is a grave occasion of sin to the other, the innocent party may separate. This is not a divorce of the Church, though civil divorce may accompany the separation. The Catholic parties to a valid marriage may not remarry after a separation until the other party dies. A Catholic should not seek a civil divorce without consulting the ordinary. **2.** Separation of Church and state: In the United States the spheres of both religion and the state are established by constitutional law and definition. Thus "separation" can only be understood as the guarantee of government that it will not set up an "official" church for the country which would be favored by the government. The bishops of the United States declared: "Authoritative Catholic teaching on the relations between Church and state, as set forth in papal encyclicals and in the treatises of recognized writers on ecclesiastical law, not only states clearly what these relations should normally be under ideal conditions, but also indicates to what extent the Catholic Church can adapt herself to the particular conditions that may obtain in different countries." (Statement, *The Christian in Action*, Nov. 21, 1948.)

SEPTUAGESIMA, the 3rd Sunday before Lent. It begins the preparatory period for that penitential season.

SEPTUAGINT. Translated from the Hebrew into Greek by 70 Jewish scholars and called the Alexandrian version, this Bible text was most widely used in the early Church. It is commonly referred to among scholars as LXX.

SERAPH, the name of the angels of the angelic choir of Seraphim, which is one of the choirs who adore before God. The word comes from the Hebrew "fiery" (Is. 6:1–4).

SERMON ON THE MOUNT. The sermon preached by Christ in the first few months of His ministry sounds the keynote of the new teaching He came to introduce. It is a declaration of the New Law, the guarantee that it will last, and it shows the new spirit in action. Love is to be the center and love can ask more than fear (old law) can command (Mt. 5:1–7:29). (*Cf.* BEATITUDES.)

SERVER. *See* ACOLYTE.

SERVILE WORK, any occupation which is performed by bodily action for material gain. Church law forbids all servile works, court sessions, public markets, etc. on Sundays and holydays of obligation.

SEXAGESIMA, the name of the second Sunday before Lent.

SEXT, the part appointed for the sixth hour of the Divine Office. (*Cf.* BREVIARY; DIVINE OFFICE.)

SHEPHERD, GOOD. Our Lord applied this title to Himself in the parable recorded in the Gospel of St. John (10:11). It is noted in other biblical references (Is. 40: Ez. 34, etc.); Christ, in attributing it to Himself, tells that He will offer Himself in immolation for men (Heb. 13:20).

SHRINE. Erected to encourage private devotion to a saint or Christian mystery, a shrine contains a picture, statue, or some central religious feature capable of inspiring devotion. The term has come to be used broadly to refer also to a special place of pilgrimage, e.g., Lourdes, where intense devotion or veneration is both a part of the religious motivation as well as a feature of the structure. Shrines may be set up in homes, churches, or outdoors. They are to be considered as an aid to devotion rather than a curiosity or distraction.

SHROUD, THE HOLY, the winding sheet used in the burial of Christ in the tomb (Mt. 27:59–61). A famous relic, kept at Turin, is usually referred to as the "Holy Shroud of Turin," and is alleged to be that worn by Christ. Photographic evidence and chemical tests have demonstrated the image of a man which is claimed to be that of Christ. The Church has not pronounced upon this relic's authenticity. The figure is presented on the cloth in the manner current at the time of Christ's burial, that is the sheet was placed lengthwise, the body placed upon it, and then the cloth was brought over the head and face and again brought down the body's length on top before winding was wrapped around it and the body.

SHROVETIDE, collective name of the few days immediately preceding Lent. At this time, it was customary to hold carnivals in anticipation of the long fast of Lent. It was climaxed on Shrove Tuesday, before Ash Wednesday, with a variously named festivity, e.g., Mardi Gras.

SIGNATURE. *See* APOSTOLIC SIGNATURE.

SIGN OF THE CROSS, the most frequently used sacramental of the Church. The sign is a repetition in motion of the symbol of our salvation, the cross on which Christ died. The sign of the cross is made during the Mass, at blessings, and generally at the opening and closing of prayer. The indulgenced sign is made by placing the left hand on the breast and with the right hand touching the forehead (saying: *In the name of the Father . . .*), then moving the right hand down to the breast (saying: *. . . and of the Son . . .*), and moving the right hand to the left shoulder (saying: *. . . and of the Holy . . .*) and then the right shoulder (saying: *. . . Ghost. Amen . . .*). The faithful, as often as they devoutly sign themselves with the sign of the cross, are granted an indulgence of 3 years; whenever they make the same holy sign with blessed water, they may gain an indulgence of 7 years. (S.P. Feb. 10, 1935 and June 14, 1949).

SIMONY. The term is derived from one Simon Magnus who tried to purchase the gift of the Holy Spirit from St. Peter (Acts 8). Simony may be of two kinds: 1. Simony of divine right is the deliberate intent to buy or sell a spiritual thing, or a temporal thing connected with a spiritual thing for a price (c. 727). By spiritual things are meant graces, sacraments, prayers, etc.; a temporal thing connected with a spiritual thing is, e.g., an indulgence. The price may be the money or any other consideration of value, even praise. 2. Simony of a Church right consists in the exchange of things as goods because of the irreverence to a spiritual thing connected with the exchange, e.g., demanding compensation, in addition to the recognized stipend offering, for the expenses connected with divine service, as candles, etc. The penalties are attached by canon law (c. 2392).

SIMPLE FEAST, the lowest rank of feast celebrated in the Church. (*Cf.* FEASTS.)

SIN. The free transgression of a divine law is a sin. Since every law is derived from the divine law, natural or positive, every transgression of a punitive law, i.e., the law of legitimately constituted authority, is a sin. Sin may be *mortal* or *venial.* It is mortal when the transgression is of a divine law in a matter that is serious and when the consent to sin recognizes both the law and the serious matter. A sin is venial when it is either committed out of imperfect knowledge and consent, when one transgresses a law which does not bind seriously, or when a sin is actually grave but, because of an invincibly erroneous conscience, the one committing it is ignorant of its gravity. Sin is also classified as to type: *Internal sins* are those committed through use of the spiritual faculties, e.g., imagination; *actual sin* is any sinful act or omission of a prescribed good act; *habitual sin* is the state of sin of one who has not repented. The sin is *formal* when it is deliberate against a law, even if the law is only supposed to exist; it is *material* when the transgression is against a law, but when knowledge of the transgression's sinfulness is lacking it is actually no real sin because it lacks consent. (*Cf.* COMMANDMENTS OF GOD; PRECEPTS OF THE CHURCH.)

SINS AGAINST THE HOLY SPIRIT. These sins, directed against the operations of the Holy Spirit in the soul, are: despair, presumption, envy, obstinacy in sin, final impenitence, and in particular the deliberate resistance to the known truth.

SISTERS, name of the women members of a religious community or order. Usually there is this distinction: sisters are religious women with simple vows, nuns have taken solemn vows (c. 488). There are many groups of sisters who follow a particular order and whose lives are devoted to special works of charity. Among their manifold tasks are caring for the sick, teaching, perpetual adoration.

SISTINE CHAPEL. Called the "pope's chapel," this is the principal chapel of the Vatican palace. It is here that the consistory of cardinals meets to elect a new pope. The present chapel was begun in 1473 and completed only at the turn of the century. It is most notable for its murals by the painters Michelangelo and Raphael, especially the ceiling frescoes by the former which depict the creation and the religious aspiration of man.

SOCIALISM. The scientific phase of this movement, which sprung from the sources of liberalism, came in with the leaders F. Lassalle (d. 1864), K. Marx (d. 1883) and F. Engels (d. 1895). It was given impetus with the publication of the Communist Manifesto (1848) and the appearance of *Das Kapital* in 1867. Its purpose, basically, was to unite workers into a political party, to end private ownership of the means of production, and to exclude religion from education. It was opposed by the Church, notably by Pope Leo XIII. The American bishops declared in an extended statement for Social Reconstruction (Feb. 12, 1919); "Socialism would mean bureaucracy, political tyranny, the helplessness of the individual as a factor in the ordering of his own life, and in general social inefficiency and decadence." (*Cf.* COMMUNISM.)

SOCIETY, RELIGIOUS, a body of clerics, regular or secular, organized for performing an apostolic work.

SOCINIANISM. Developed by Socinus (d. 1604), this system of the Unitarian sect taught that Christ was only a lesser God who was given assignment by the Supreme God. Its followers were called Socinians or "Polish Brethren."

SOCIOLOGY. The name of this study of society and social relations is derived from a coined word first used by Auguste Comte (d. 1857). As a science, its conception of society is involved and its method is still developing in practice and study.

SODALITY, an association of the faithful for the promotion of piety, charity and public worship. It may be either a pious union or a confraternity (c. 684ff).

SON OF MAN. This title is ascribed to Christ alone who is both God and man. As used by Christ in referring to Himself (Mt. 9:6), it means that our Lord as a man among men claims to exercise the authority of God in heaven, and it is a declaration of the doctrine of the Incarnation.

SORROWS OF THE BLESSED VIRGIN MARY. Sometimes referred to as the Seven Dolors, they are: the prophecy of Simeon (Lk. 2:34), the flight into Egypt (Mt. 2:13), the loss of Christ on the visit to Jerusalem (Lk. 2:46), Christ on the way to Calvary, the crucifixion, the descent from the cross, and the entombment of Christ (Lk. 23:26–56). Two feasts of the Roman calendar commemorate these sorrows of the Blessed Virgin, on the Friday of Passion week and on Sept. 15.

SOTERIOLOGY, in theology, the study of the central thesis of the Christian doctrine, i.e., the salvation and sanctification accomplished by Christ (Rom. 3:23–25).

SOUL. The real spiritual substance which, united to the body, constitutes a man, is created by God (Gen. 2:7); in his soul, man is of the "image of God" (Gen. 1:6, 26); the soul is immortal (Mt. 10:28). The soul is declared by the Council of Vienne the immediate substantial form of the body. (*Cf.* IMMORTALITY OF THE SOUL.)

SOUTANE. *See* CASSOCK.

SPIRIT, HOLY. *See* HOLY SPIRIT.

SPIRITUAL EXERCISES OF ST. IGNATIUS. Written by St. Ignatius Loyola (d. 1556), the practical considerations and meditations contained in this book are directed to the amendment of one's life and the achievement of personal sanctification, and are psychologically penetrating. The first portion is devoted to the consequences of sin, the second to Christ as the exemplar, the third to amendment in imitation of Christ, the fourth to the award of the good.

SPIRITUAL WORKS OF MERCY. Seven in number, these are: to convert sinners, instruct the ignorant, counsel the wayward, comfort the sorrowing, bear adversities patiently, forgive offenses, and pray for the living and the dead.

SPONSORS, the persons who offer and speak for one (a) in baptism, and assume certain spiritual responsibilities; (b) the person who stands for one receiving the sacrament of confirmation. Church law requires that the sponsors for *baptism*, one at least and never more than two, should be fourteen or more years of age, should be baptized, have the use of reason, and intend to undertake the responsibility. A sponsor may not be the father, mother or spouse of the one baptized; he must be named by the parents or guardian; he must in the act of baptism personally, or through a proxy, touch the person baptized. His responsibility is to watch over the religious education of the child. A sponsor contracts a spiritual relationship with the person baptized. In *confirmation* the sponsor must be already confirmed, have the use of reason, and intend to act in this capacity. He must be a Catholic in good standing and may not be a parent or spouse of the one confirmed; he must be chosen by the parents or guardian, unless custom intervenes, and must touch personally or by proxy the one confirmed.

STAFF. *See* CROSIER.

STATE OF GRACE, the condition of the soul, having habitual grace.

STATIONS OF THE CROSS. Also called "The Way of the Cross," this devotion to the Passion of Christ consists of prayers and meditations on fourteen occurrences experienced by Christ on His way to the crucifixion. The devotion is conducted either by the faithful personally, making the way from one cross to another and saying the prayers, or by having the officiating priest move from cross to cross while the faithful make the responses. For the Stations themselves there must be fourteen crosses (pictures alone do not suffice) and they must be blessed by one with authority to erect stations. The devotion is heavily indulgenced.

STATIONS, ROMAN. In early times, those were the churches of Rome and its environs to which the people and clergy went in procession. The church was designated for each day (84 in all) and there the pope or his representative sang Mass. The days were those of Lent, Ember days, Sundays of Advent, and certain feasts.

STIGMATA. From the Greek, meaning "marks," this refers in Church use to the wounds, scars, or skin abrasions which, corresponding to the wounds suffered by Christ in the crucifixion, appear on the flesh of individuals. Stigmata are accompanied with pain. Numerous instances are recorded of this charism having been bestowed on persons of unusual holiness, more than 300 in all.

STIPEND. The voluntary offering now given to a priest is not meant as an equivalent of the Mass, but is representative of the bread and wine formerly given to the clergy by the faithful for use in the Mass. The amount of the stipend may vary in amount but the minimum offering may be established by local law to avoid confusion. The acceptance of a stipend by a priest is a serious obligation to fulfill the intention, and the offering must be definite, e.g., a priest may not say a Mass on one's casual remark and then ask for a stipend from the person. Stipends are either *manual*, i.e., given directly by the person out of devotion; or *quasi-manual*, i.e., offerings from some fund established for that purpose. Stipends are governed as to practice by law of the Church (c's. 824–844).

STOLE. This vestment, being a long, narrow strip of cloth the same color as the other vestments, is worn by the priest as a mark of his priestly office. Whereas the priest wears the stole about the neck, both ends hanging down in front, the deacon wears it across his left shoulder and crossed at the opposite side beneath the arm.

A purple stole is worn by a priest when administering the sacrament of penance, a white when giving Benediction of the Blessed Sacrament or extreme unction, and a stole of the color of the feast (or white) when preaching.

STOLE-FEE. The sum given to the celebrant for performing parochial functions, e.g., administering baptism, assisting at marriage, etc., is so called. The fee may be fixed as a definite amount by the local ordinary (c's. 1234–1237).

STYLITE

STYLITE. The term has been applied to a hermit who had his hermitage atop a pillar.

SUBDEACON. *See* ORDERS, HOLY, SACRAMENT OF.

SUB-DELEGATE. *See* DELEGATION.

SUBREPTION, in canon law, the term for the suppression or distortion of truth in a petition for a favor by rescript.

SUBURBICARIAN DIOCESES. These are the seven dioceses nearest to Rome: Albano, Frascati, Ostia, Palestina, Porto, Santa Rufina, and Velletri. Their bishops are designated cardinal-bishops, and each works in one or more of the Congregations or Commissions of the Vatican. (*Cf.* CARDINAL.)

SUFFRAGAN BISHOP, a bishop of a diocese of a province other than the metropolitan. (*Cf.* BISHOP.)

SUFFRAGES, additional prayers of the Divine Office for particular intentions, e.g., for the Church.

SUNDAY. The first day of the week, also called the "Lord's Day," is set aside for public worship. This was true in the early Church under the apostles who recognized that the Christian mystery supplanted that of the Old Law, the Sabbath (Acts 20: 7). On this day, called *Dominica* in the Latin missal, Catholics by law are obliged to assist at the Sacrifice of the Mass.

SUPPEDANEUM. 1. Another name for the predella of the altar. **2.** The small footrest sometimes pictured beneath the feet of the figure on a crucifix.

SURPLICE. The name of this wide-sleeved garment of white linen which reaches to the knees is derived from the Latin *superpelliciae*, meaning "above the fur clothing." It was used from the 11th century to be put on above the practical, fur-lined tunics worn in the churches.

SUSPENSION, a church censure, affecting only clerics. It forbids them to exercise certain powers which their office holds (c's. 2278–2285).

SWISS GUARDS

SWISS GUARDS. The members of this small force are specially chosen young Catholic men from Switzerland to serve as personal guardians of the pope. They are guards of gates and doors of the Vatican State. Organized in 1505, they have two historic uniforms, one consisting of a blue tunic and breeches, the other, designed by Michelangelo, consists of a tunic, breeches, and stockings with alternate yellow, red, and blue vertical stripes. To this latter is added a helmet and breastplate of steel on state occasions. In all, the Swiss Guards number 110 men and six officers; they are now trained in modern arms but seldom carry other than a sword or halberd.

SYLLABUS. The word, derived from the Greek, means a "collection." As a writing, emanating from the Holy See, a syllabus bears similarity to an encyclical, but is a specific statement of the position of the Church. There are two famous such writings. 1. The Syllabus of Pius IX, published in 1846. Properly, this is the encyclical *Quanta Cura*, which condemned some 80 errors of the day. 2. The Syllabus of Pius X, *Lamentabili Sane Exitu*, published in 1907. It listed and condemned 65 propositions taken from the writings of the modernists, especially those which are heretical, as, denial of the divinity of Christ, divine origin of the sacraments, etc. (*Cf.* MODERNISM.)

SYMBOL, the term for a religious creed in symbol. In Church art, symbols arose as early as the 3rd century and were used to represent persons and mysteries. The cross is a symbol of Christ. The fish, a symbol of Christ, is derived from the Greek letters for the word fish which spell out with its letters the initials of the declaration, "Jesus Christ, Son of God, Savior." These emblems of religious truth may be single and refer to one teaching or person, or mixed, referring to different doctrines, e.g., grapes and wheat. Many of the symbols are multiple, e.g., taken from Scripture, from language, and representative of a teaching such as the symbol Λ–Ω = *Alpha* and *Omega*.

SYMBOLISM. Symbolism is the signifying of something so that it may be more clearly understood. In this meaning, we have the symbols in Scripture (Jer. 1:11–14). The Church also uses symbolism in its liturgy, e.g., the salt in baptism.

SYNAXIS. The Greek verb for "assembling" or "to assemble" has for its noun the word *synaxis*, which is Eucharist. Hence, its meaning in the first days of the Church was a "gathering together to celebrate the Eucharist." In the Byzantine rite, synaxis is as a feast where the people gather to honor the saints whose feast day preceded this celebration.

SYNOD. This term is now applied to a periodic gathering of the clergy of a diocese, called at least every two years by the bishop, at which time administrative matters are settled. The bishop determines what clergy will be present and might include all if the welfare of souls would not suffer. The bishop is the only legislator and the clergy or religious act only in a consultative capacity. The subject matter is recommended by canon law (c's. 356–362).

SYNOPTIC GOSPELS. The Gospels of SS. Matthew, Mark, and Luke which, proceeding along the same general lines of exposition, present a general view of Christ and His teaching and in so doing mutually support each other. SS. Matthew, Mark, and Luke are thus called synoptists.

SYRIAN RITE. The rite is twofold, that of the East being the same as the Chaldean rite, that of the West the liturgy used by Catholic Syrians, Malankarese, and by the Jacobites of Syria and Malabar. The liturgy is developed from that of Antioch of the 4th century, sometimes called the Liturgy of St. James. Distinctive features are: the words of the Consecration are sung aloud; Communion is under both species; the Divine Office has seven hours; baptism is by immersion and a "pouring on" of water. (*Cf.* LITURGY.)

TABERNACLE

TABERNACLE. 1. In the modern church, the place where the Blessed Sacrament is retained. According to canon law, "the most Holy Eucharist is to be preserved in an immovable tabernacle placed in the center of the altar" (c. 1269). It should be of durable material, skillfully constructed and safely locked, and should be damp-proof. It likewise should be dignified, suitably ornamented, and covered completely with a tabernacle veil. Before use, it must be blessed according to the Ritual. In the early days of the Church it was customary to have the Blessed Sacrament kept by lay people or clergy for security. By development, other means were used: a cupboard, a tower, or a suspended pyx. The name is derived from the word "tent." **2.** In Scripture, the word tabernacle was the center of the cult of the Jews. It is described in Exodus (26:1–37).

TAMETSI, the opening word of the law, enacted by the Council of Trent (Sess. 24), on the solemn form of the marriage contract. The law stated that no marriage was valid unless contracted before the pastor or his delegate and two witnesses. The *Tametsi* law gave way to the *Ne Temere Decore* of April 19, 1908, which has been retained substantially in the Code of Canon Law under marriage legislation (c's. 1012–1141).

TEMPERANCE. One of the four cardinal virtues, temperance prompts moderation and self-control in actions and thoughts, and particularly the pleasures of the senses.

TEMPLARS. *See* KNIGHTS, ORDERS OF.

TEMPORAL POWER, the authority wielded by the Supreme Pontiff as a sovereign head of an independent state, the State of Vatican City.

TEMPTATION, literally, "putting to the test." Through original sin, human nature is subject to temptation and it is a truth of divine faith that the devil tempts men to evil (1 Pet. 5:8). Temptation is, then, the action upon the concupiscence which may result in the commission of sin; an enticement to sin. By being watchful in mind and will, men can overcome temptation and gain merit by so doing.

TENEBRAE, literally, from the Latin, "darkness." The name was formerly applied to the public chanting of Matins and Lauds of the Divine Office on the evenings of Wednesday, Thursday and Friday of Holy Week, each being the anticipated office of the following day. The lessons are chiefly from the Lamentations of the prophet Jeremias and the Psalms, and the general intent is penitential. The ceremony is quite simple, consisting of the extinguishing of fourteen candles on a multiple triangular candleholder, called the "hearse," and leaving a fifteenth white candle burning at the apex of the hearse. This final lighted candle is a symbol of the risen Savior.

TERCE or **TIERCE,** the third hour of the Divine Office. (*Cf.* DIVINE OFFICE.)

TERNA. Made up and presented to the Holy See by a chapter of canons, the *terna* was a list giving the three names of those whom the chapter had selected and approved for possible elevation to the episcopacy. Its use has been abolished by a decree of the Sacred Consistorial Congregation of July 25, 1916.

TERTIARIES. These are members of one of the three classes of associations of the laity recognized by the Code of Canon Law (c. 684ff), namely, Third Orders. The associations promote Catholic life and action. They are not religious in the proper sense of the term and, while they may take private vows, they merely submit to following a daily practice of religion in their lives. They may be associated with the following religious orders: Franciscans, Dominicans, Premonstratensians, Carmelites, Benedictines, Augustinians, Servites, Trinitarians.

TEUTONIC KNIGHTS. *See* KNIGHTS, ORDERS OF.

THAUMATURGUS. From the Greek, meaning "wonder worker," this word is sometimes attached as a title to a saint who is noted for miracles, e.g., St. Vincent Ferrer.

THECAE. *See* RELIQUARIES.

THEOLOGIAN. 1. One who is trained in the science of theology. This refers primarily to one who has not only studied theology in general, but who has made special scholarly studies in one or more of the branches of theology and has attained a doctorate or at least a licentiate degree. **2.** A student aspiring to Holy Orders who is taking the last four years of study in a seminary. (*Cf.* THEOLOGY.)

THEOLOGICAL VIRTUES. Faith, hope, and charity are the three theological virtues. *Faith* is the supernatural virtue through which, aided by divine grace, one is enabled to believe firmly in the truth of the authority of God as He has revealed it. Because of God's revelation of this truth, one has the serious obligation to believe; from this evidence there also arises the duty to make an act of faith as soon as His revelation is recognized. It further is one's duty to make repeated acts of faith during one's life by practicing one's religion, as attending Mass, etc. And acts of prayerful faith should be made to effectively resist temptation (*cf.* FAITH). *Hope* is the supernatural, infused virtue through which one is enabled to rely on the omnipotence, goodness, and fidelity of God, and to look forward to eternal salvation to be attained through the means God has established. Acts of hope are necessary after one reaches the age of reason, upon recognition of one's end and purpose in life, as an aid to overcome temptations and as an expression of faith. This also is explicitly done by the external practice of one's religion as a practical Catholic (*cf.* HOPE). *Charity* is the supernatural, infused virtue through which one loves God as the greatest good for God's own sake, and oneself and one's neighbors for the love of God. To make acts of love for God is a necessity, because they are the proper and essential means to attain salvation, e.g., receiving the sacraments. It is of *precept*, upon reaching the age of reason, that one must make acts of loving God, i.e., avoid mortal sin, avoid temptation, etc. (*Cf.* CHARITY; LOVE OF GOD.)

THEOLOGY. The term is derived from the etymology of the word itself. Theology is the science of God and the things which treat of God. It is the study of God in Himself, and of His relations with creatures. As a science, theology is both methodical, i.e., referring to the character of the knowledge, and systematic, i.e., referring to the extent of knowledge, and the integration of the various concepts into a unit. Like all science, it proceeds from certain definite principles, prime or universal principles, which are evident in themselves. We thus come to a knowledge of God through reason and by revelation. Theology, then, is the reasoned methodical and systematic exposition of revealed truths. (*Cf.* REVELATION.)

Theology is a synthesis, a unit term embracing many divisions. Thus one does not become a theologian by studying one phase of theology or by reading one book of theology, but by gaining knowledge systematically, both as to extent and to the full application. The fruit of such study may be said to be the acquisition of the science of God. The divisions of theology are many. As to method, there is first *positive theology*, which is the recording and defending of revealed truth. This in turn is divided into *biblical* theology, i.e., the examination of truth as found in Scripture, and *historical* theology, i.e., the examination of truths of God in both Scripture and Tradition, and the demonstration of the teaching of Christ and the apostles as handed down through the Church. Secondly, *scholastic theology*, which is the explaining, illustrating, and deducing of new truths systematically. Thirdly, the *positive scholastic*, which is the combination of the first two into effective presentation. As to system, as objective, theology embraces *dogmatic* and *moral* theology. Dogmatic theology is the demonstration of faith and reason, dealing with God's laws; this has two lesser branches called *ascetical* theology or the methods of perfection, and *mystical* theology or the extraordinary methods and gifts of perfection. Moral theology is the science of the laws which regulate the duties of man to God. Besides the above and growing from them are a series of the practical applications of theology, dependent upon the above, yet making necessary distinct studies for the trained theologian. These are: *liturgy*, or the manner of theology applied; *apologetics*, or the reasoning of theology applied; *pastoral* theology, or the demonstration of theology applied. This latter in turn comprises the study of canon law, the rules of the Church in applying theology; *homiletics*, the preaching of the truths of theology; *catechetics*, the teaching of the truths of theology; and *rubrics*, the application of the truths of theology. (See also entries under individual titles.)

THEOPHANY. The term, applied to the direct or hidden appearances of God in the Scriptures, is derived from the Greek, meaning literally "God in brightness." God appearing on Mt. Sinai (Ex. 19:1–25), in storm; in the cloud (Ex. 24:15–16), and in divinity at the transfiguration (Mt. 17:1–9) are examples.

THEOTOKOS. Literally, "God-bearing," this title was given to the Blessed Mother in the 4th century and it founded the widespread devotion to the Blessed Virgin which continues to the present day in both the Eastern and Western Churches. The term was one of dispute beginning in the early 5th century when the Nestorian heresy denied the divine maternity of the Blessed Virgin. The doctrine was confirmed and the Nestorians condemned by the third ecumenical council of Ephesus in 431.

THIRD ORDERS. *See* TERTIARIES.

THOMISM, the system of scholastic thought developed by St. Thomas Aquinas (d. 1274). Basically, the work of St. Thomas was a systematic critique and elimination of Platonism in metaphysics, psychology, and epistomology, advancing along Aristotelian lines beyond St. Augustine. He developed a harmony of faith and reason, establishing man as an efficacious cause in the doctrine of creation, and presented this in his monumental work *Summa Theologica.* Thomism as a system is recognized and imposed by Church law (c. 1366). (*Cf.* SCHOLASTICISM.)

THRONE. 1. The platform with a canopy, necessary unless built into or above the altar, on which the monstrance is placed at Exposition of the Blessed Sacrament. A small throne is sometimes called a *thabor.* A throne is required for solemm Exposition.

Sometimes the throne is built into the tabernacle itself. **2.** The name is applied to the episcopal throne, the *cathedra,* which is placed on the gospel side of a sanctuary. It is usually erected on three steps and is permanent in a cathedral.

THRONES. *See* ANGELS.

THURIBLE. *See* CENSER.

THURIFER, title of the acolyte who is charged with the care and supply of the thurible.

TIARA, the diadem which the pope wears at his coronation and at other solemn non-liturgical ceremonies. This headpiece, consisting of a cloth-of-silver lining, rising about 15 in., is circled by three ornamented crowns or coronets of gold, one set above the other. Pendants (*infulae*) are attached to the rim in the back, in a similar way as on the mitre. The origin of the tiara is not known, though it is fashioned after the Persian royal headpiece. Its symbolism is not known, but it is said to be representative of the threefold authority of the pope in the magisterium of the Church.

TITHES, a law of the Israelites (Lev. 27:30). It required the offering of the tenth part of all produce, animals and plants (*cf.* Mt. 23:23–24) for the support of religion. Today, canon law permits the law and custom of each locality to prevail in the support given to the Church.

TITULAR BISHOP. *See* BISHOP.

TITULUS. The term is referred to the superscription placed on the cross on which Christ was crucified, declaring Him "Jesus of Nazareth, King of the Jews." (*Cf.* CRUCIFIXION.)

TOBIAS, BOOK OF. Generally considered to be historical, this book of the O.T. was written by an unknown author probably about the year 220 B.C. It tells of the highly edifying life-stories of one Tobias and his son of the same name. The general theme is the presentation of the truth that the most important thing in this life is to put full confidence in God. The writing teaches by both word and example of the perfection of God, of the sanctity of marriage (8:5), and of good works and prayer.

TONSURE—Both types.

TONSURE, the introductory ceremony by which a layman becomes a cleric. It is not a part of the sacrament of holy orders but is preliminary to its reception. In the ceremony, the bishop or his delegate cuts or snips small portions from the hair of the candidate, front, back, two sides, and crown, inviting the candidate to accept the Lord as "his portion." The candidate is then invested with the surplice. Tonsure may be given at any time. It is the practice in some religious orders to shave the top of the head in a circle, having but a "corona" of hair around the crown, as a permanent tonsure.

TOTIES QUOTIES. Literally, "so often as," this term is used in the granting of indulgences and declares that the indulgence may be gained as often as the action required and the necessary conditions are fulfilled. (*Cf.* PORTIUNCULA.)

TRACT. 1. A short penitential prayer which immediately follows the Gradual of the Mass and precedes the Gospel. It may be considered as a part of the Gradual with the Tract forming a Sequence or a second Gradual. When sung, it is chanted straight through without stop (*cf.* MASS). **2.** The name given to a short writing or treatise, usually in the form of a leaflet, written about a religious subject.

TRACTARIAN MOVEMENT. *See* OXFORD MOVEMENT.

TRADITION. In a special sense, there is but one source of revealed truth and this source is divine Tradition. By this is meant the body of revealed truth handed down from the apostles through the ages and contained in the doctrine, teaching, and practice of the Catholic Church. This is, as the Council of Trent defined (Sess. IV, EB 46), inclusive of both the written Scriptures and the unwritten traditions or oral tradition. It is the Church in her living magisterium, "the holders of Tradition," which gives life to Scripture. Tradition, as a distinct part of historic theology, is also inclusive of two main sources of teaching, namely, the writings of the fathers of the Church, and the archaeological, liturgical, and symbolical (tradition of the instruments) research which presents the historic proof of the practices of the Church as a continuing stream from its founding to the present (2 Tim. 2:1–2).

TRADITIONALISM. This philosophical system of the 18th and 19th centuries which erroneously held that human reason without aid could not arrive at truth, particularly in the moral and religious orders, was condemned by the Church and today is generally rejected because of its gratuitous assumptions.

TRADITORES. The Council of Arles (314) applied this term to those clerics who surrendered sacred vessels and writings into the hands of the persecuting authorities.

TRADUCIANISM, the erroneous teaching of the 5th century that the soul of offspring is originated and transmitted by the parents. It was condemned by St. Anastasius II (d. 498).

TRANSFIGURATION. The divinity of our Lord was made manifest to SS. Peter, James, and John by this event in the life of Christ (Mt. 17:1–8; Mk. 9:1–8; Lk. 8:28–36). As the Scripture scholar Lagrange states, "the transfiguration serves as a sure pledge of Christ's future glory." A tradition, dating back to the 4th century, identifies the mountain of transfiguration as that of Tabor in Galilee. St. Leo the Great gives as the purpose of this event the removal of the scandal of the cross from the hearts of the disciples. The transfiguration of Christ, together with the appearance of Moses and Elias, was a confirmation to the apostles of what Christ had taught them concerning Himself as the Son of God and His relation to the Old Law. In the Church calendar a feast commemorates the transfiguration on Aug. 6.

TRANSUBSTANTIATION. As defined by the Council of Trent, transubstantiation is "a singular and wondrous conversion of the total substance of bread into the body and of the total substance of wine into the blood of Christ, the external appearances only remaining unchanged." It is by this transubstantiation that the body and blood of Christ are present in the Holy Eucharist (Mk. 14:22–25).

TREE OF JESSE, a representation of the Blessed Mother of God. This symbol dates from the 11th century and is based upon the prophecy of Isaias 11:1–5. (*Cf.* JESSE WINDOW.)

TRENTAL. The Gregorian Masses are commonly so named in England.

TRENT, COUNCIL OF. The 19th ecumenical council of the Church, known as the Council of Trent, opened its first sessions in 1545, by action of Pope Paul III. This period closed in 1547. It was reconvened in 1551 by Pope Julius III and adjourned the following year. Its third period, opened in 1562 under Pope Pius IV, closed finally after 25 sessions in December 1563. It drew up a platform of practical reform, defined doctrines, authenticated the Vulgate, enacted legislation on marriage (Tametsi), and formulated a revision of the Roman Breviary. Its work was so scholarly and extensive that for more than 300 years no other council was held.

TRIBUNALS, ROMAN. These are the courts of the Holy See, namely, the Sacred Apostolic Penitentiary, the Apostolic Signature, and the Sacred Roman Rota. (See entries under individual titles.)

TRIDUUM, name of a three-day period of prayer. It is often held in preparation for a special feast.

THE MOST HOLY TRINITY—Some of the symbols used in Church art: (a) The Baptism of Christ from the Sarcophagus of Theodorus, 7th century; (b) The Three Fishes; (c) The Triangle; (d) The Trefoil; (e) Medieval diagram.

TRINITY, THE MOST HOLY. The most sublime mystery of the Christian faith is this: that "God is absolutely one in nature and essence, and relatively three in Persons (Father, Son, and Holy Ghost) who are really distinct from each other," but these Three are consubstantial, i.e., identical with the divine substance. Christians are and know themselves to be the children of the living God, for under the New Law they have been raised to the state of sonship (1 Jn. 3:1f). Christ the Son has revealed God the Father to those whom He has raised to sonship by the redemption, and has taught them to pray

"Our Father" (Mt. 6:9). At the same time, the Father reveals the Son: "This is My beloved Son, in whom I am well pleased" (Mt. 3:17). Thus, in the Son we see the Father and through Him we go to the Father (Jn. 1:18). And this mystery of the Father and the Son is confirmed by the Holy Spirit, the "Spirit of truth," whom the Son sends from the Father and the Father sends in the name of the Son (Jn. 15:26). Through this revelation we have the Trinity which for us is a to-and-fro relationship of our possession of God and God's possession of us: "The grace of our Lord Jesus Christ, and the charity of

TRIPTYCH—Florentine, 14th century.

God, and the fellowship of the Holy Spirit be with you all" (2 Cor. 13:13). And our life of sonship, our continuance in grace, through the Church, are functions of the Holy Spirit to whom is attributed: the inspiration of Scriptures; the sanctification of Christ's mystical body; the distribution of the charismata; and the sanctification of the faithful. And Christians who receive the revelation of this tremendous Trinity through baptism and who, by being confirmed and benefited by grace, become "partakers of the divine nature," advance with faith assured, hope secure, and responding in love (2 Pet. 1:3–5).

TRIPLE CANDLE, the threefold candle once used in the liturgy of Holy Saturday. It represents the Blessed Trinity.

TRIPTYCH, threefold tablets joined by hinges. (*Cf.* DYPTYCH.)

TRISAGION. This term is given to the triple repetition of the word "holy" (Is. 6:3). It indicates that God is superlatively holy.

TRIVIUM. *See* QUADRIVIUM.

TRUCE OF GOD. Accomplished by the Council of Elne (1027), the Truce of God prohibited armed hostilities from sundown on Saturday to Monday morning. Later it was extended from Wednesday night to the following Monday morning. The Synod of Clermont decreed the truce should be observed from Advent to the octave of Epiphany and from Septuagesima to the octave of Pentecost.

TRULLO, COUNCIL IN. The 6th ecumenical council, the Third of Constantinople, held in 680, is also referred to by this name.

TRUTH SOCIETY, CATHOLIC. *See* CATHOLIC TRUTH SOCIETY.

TUNIC. Also called tunicle, this vestment is worn by the subdeacon at high Mass and other functions. It is a garment with an opening for the neck, with sleeves, and it is open at the sides and under the arms. It is less ornate than either the chasuble or dalmatic. (*Cf.* DALMATIC.)

TUTIORISM, a moral system of interpretation of the law. As absolute tutiorism it claims one must choose what is certain in every difference of opinion; as mitigated tutiorism it claims one is free from an obligation if the opinion in favor of liberty is most probable.

TWELFTH DAY, another name, little used, for the feast of Epiphany, 12 days after Christmas.

TYPE. *See* ANTITYPE; MYSTICAL SENSE OF SCRIPTURE.

TYPOLOGICAL SENSE OF SCRIPTURE. *See* MYSTICAL SENSE OF SCRIPTURE.

U

UNAM SANCTAM. Published in 1302, the bull *Unam Sanctam* of Pope Boniface VIII declared the primacy of the Holy See.

UNBAPTIZED INFANTS. *See* LIMBO.

UNCTION. Used in connection with the administration of sacraments, the term refers to the anointing with holy oils.

UNIAT (UNIATE) CHURCHES. Christians of the East who have been converted from the Orthodox Eastern Church and other older heresies are called Uniates. The Code of Canon Law designates them as "Orientales" (c. 1099). (*Cf.* EASTERN CHURCHES.)

UNIGENITUS. Literally, "one begotten," this is the first word and title of the bull of Pope Clement XI in which he condemned the Jansenistic teachings. It was published in 1713.

UNION, MYSTICAL. Being the highest state of the spiritual progression toward perfection, which is the culmination of the unitive way after experiencing the purgative and the illuminative stages, this full union (some call it "simple" union) is declared by St. Teresa of Avila to consist in this: God lays hold of all the powers of the soul and renders them fully passive so that the soul has no distraction and does not need to make an effort to maintain union. It is consciousness of the effects of sanctifying grace on the soul.

UNITY OF THE CHURCH. *See* MARKS OF THE CHURCH.

URBAN COLLEGE. *See* ROMAN COLLEGES.

URBI ET ORBI. From the Latin, meaning "to the city and to the world," this is the title applied to the solemn blessing given by the Holy Father immediately after his election, at his coronation, and during jubilee years. The faithful who with sentiments of piety and devotion receive this blessing given by the Supreme Pontiff, even by means of radio, may gain a plenary indulgence on the usual conditions.

USURY, a sin against justice and requiring restitution. It is committed when a lender demands a higher rate of interest on a loan of money than is established by law or custom.

UTRAQUISM, title of the erroneous concept advanced by the Hussites in the 15th century. It declared that the giving of Holy Communion under both the form of wine and bread is necessary to salvation.

321

V

VAGI, canonical term for those who have no domicile or quasi-domicile in any place. Such persons are bound by the laws of the place where they happen to stay. The ordinary of that place must be consulted when such a person wishes to marry (c. 91).

VALENTINIANISM. This Gnostic heresy, formulated by Valentinus (d. 160), taught that mankind is divided into three classes: material men predestined to destruction; psychic men who may attain salvation through the redemption; and spiritual or perfect men who are destined to eternal life. The Valentinians, of course, considered themselves to be this latter class. The heresy was refuted by St. Irenaeus.

VALID. As referred to the distinction between illicit and invalid, in canon law the term is thus interpreted: when the law simply forbids an act, it is sinful and unlawful to violate it, but the act is valid in spite of the violation. However, when the law is worded so that nullity results from the violation, the act has no legal value and is called an invalid act (c. 11).

VALIDATION OF MARRIAGE. A marriage contract which is invalid because of one of these three essential conditions: presence of a diriment impediment, absence of true consent, the lack of proper form, may be vali-
dated by dispensation or another correcting act. The procedure for validation is provided by canon law (c's. 1133–1137).

VATICAN. 1. The residence of the Supreme Pontiff in Vatican State. **2.** The shortened term often applied to the state of Vatican City. **3.** Descriptive term for the official position of the Roman Catholic Church upon matters of religion, etc. **4.** Term sometimes applied, but not properly, to pronouncements of the Holy See on questions of doctrine or administration.

VATICAN COUNCIL. The council convened in 1869 upon publication of the bull of assembly issued by Pope Pius IX in 1868. Its chief action was the definition of the doctrine of infallibility. In the debate over this, there were 14 general sessions and 64 speeches were made. The dogma was promulgated in the council on July 18, 1870. On the 20th of September of that year, Pius IX suspended the council following the entry into Rome of the army of United Italy. It was the twentieth ecumenical council, and the last to date but, while suspended indefinitely, it could be reconvened if necessary.

VATICAN STATE, CITY OF. The capital city of the Vatican State which includes the principal territory of the surrounding city of Rome was recog-

Humeral veil

Tabernacle veil

Chalice veil

Lenten veils

Gremial

Vimpa

VEIL—The Liturgical Veils of the Roman rite.

nized as sovereign land of the Roman Catholic Church by the Lateran Treaty. It includes the Vatican palace, its gardens, etc., the basilica and piazza of St. Peter's, and other official buildings on a plot of land about one square mile in extent with approximately 1000 residents, all of whom are citizens. It is called properly the papal state and is governed by the pope as the sovereign ruler with executive, legislative, and judicial powers which authority he exercises through commissions or delegated groups. There are other properties fixed by the treaty not adjoining Vatican State yet under its sovereign dominion. These are the basilicas and buildings of St. John Lateran, St. Mary Major, St. Paul-outside-the-Walls, and the Holy Apostles, and the churches of Saint Andrea-della-Valle and San Carlo-ai-Catarini with their adjoining buildings, the palace of San Callisto and the papal summer residence, Castel Gandolfo. (*Cf.* PAPACY.)

VEIL. There are six liturgical veils used in the Roman rite: the humeral veil, a vestment; the tabernacle veil; the chalice veil; the lenten veil, which is the purple covering placed over all crosses, statues and pictures of our Lord and the saints from before Vespers of Passion Sunday until after the Gloria of the Mass on Holy Saturday; the gremial veil, a pontifical accessory; and the vimpa.

VENERABLE. 1. Title permitted by the Church to be prefixed to the name of a candidate for beatification. This does not authorize public veneration (*cf.* BLESSED). **2.** The title of address of some religious and superiors. **3.** The title "Venerable Brother" is usually used by the pope in addressing a brother bishop in communion with Rome.

VENERATION OF THE SAINTS. Special worship, called *dulia*, is due to the saints and angels because they, as friends of God, participate in His excellence. It is permitted to venerate the saints anywhere, but those classed as "blessed" may only be venerated in those places where the Holy See permits and in the manner approved (c. 1277). Absolute veneration is that accorded to the saints or angels themselves; relative veneration is that given to images, pictures, etc. Only genuine relics may be exposed publicly for veneration. (*Cf.* RELICS; LATRIA; HYPERDULIA.)

VENIAL SIN. *See* SIN.

VERSICLE, a short part of the responses in the Divine Office. It is usually part of a Scripture verse.

VERSIONS OF THE BIBLE. *See* BIBLE.

VESPERS. The sixth of the canonical hours of the Divine Office, the evening hour, is usually composed of: five Psalms, their antiphons, a short lesson, versicle and response, a hymn, the Magnificat and antiphon, and the prayer of the day. As the evening service of churches, monastic and others, it is sung between 3 and 6 p.m.

VESSELS, SACRED. *See* SACRED VESSELS.

VESTMENTS. Historically, these are the garments worn by priests and assistants in the celebration of Mass. They were not borrowed or adopted from those of pagan priests and priestesses, nor were they invented by the Church merely as decorative adjuncts. They were derived from the garments worn by priests and laymen during the early days of the Church, especially during the persecutions. They have been retained because of motives of reverence and as symbolic

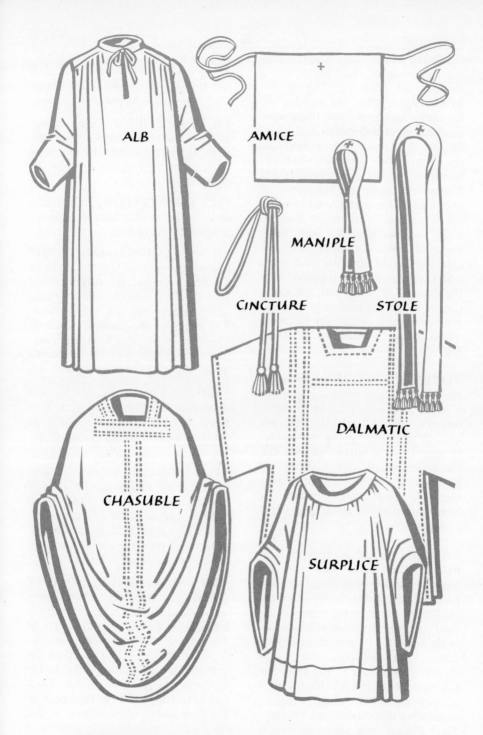

ALB

AMICE

MANIPLE

CINCTURE

STOLE

DALMATIC

CHASUBLE

SURPLICE

VESTMENTS—The principal vestments worn by priests of the Roman rite.

reminders of the early Church and the continuity of the Church down through the centuries. During the Middle Ages, after the number of vestments had been fixed, there were innovations of decoration and style, notably the Gothic, which modified their functional purposes, but retained the historic significance. In the Roman rite there are vestments of two kinds: The *outer* vestments of silk, the chasuble, dalmatic, tunicle, stole, and maniple; the *inner* vestments of linen, the amice, alb, and cincture. Canon and liturgical laws, and Church tradition together with the dictates of sacred art, prescribe the form and material of vestments. No new style or usage may be introduced without consulting the Holy See.

VIATICUM. This is the name of Holy Communion when it is given in a public or private manner to someone in danger of death, during an illness, or to soldiers going into battle. It may thus be given without the Communion fast and may be repeated during an illness as often as is required. When extreme unction is administered at the same time, viaticum precedes.

VICAR. In general, vicar is the prefixed title of a cleric who takes the place of another according to canon law and exercises authority in an ecclesiastical office in his name in accord with the limitations laid down in the law. There are several designations: Vicar-Apostolic, who serves directly subordinate to the Holy See (*cf.* PREFECT APOSTOLIC); Vicar Capitular, elected by the cathedral chapter to govern a diocese during a vacancy; Vicar Forane, one presiding over a deanery; Vicar General, who is appointed within a diocese and who exercises the habitual powers granted to the bishop by indult; Vicar Parochial, who takes the place of a pastor.

VICAR OF CHRIST. This title signifies the supreme authority of the pope as the representative of Christ on earth and the visible head of the mystical body.

VICE CHANCELLOR, an assistant to a chancellor of a diocese; also appointed by the bishop.

VIENNE, COUNCIL OF, the 15th ecumenical council. Opened by Pope Clement V in 1311, it instituted many laws of reform and corrected the idea of Franciscan poverty as practiced. The edicts of the council, however, are only known from contemporaneous writings since the original records of the council have disappeared.

VIGIL. In Church use, the term is applied to the day preceding a feast which is observed as a preparation for the feast by acts of penance or devotion.

VIGIL LIGHT, the widely used term for a small votive candle usually burned before a shrine. These small candles, burned in cup-like glass containers, are symbolical of the light of prayer but they are not blessed and are not required or liturgical.

VINCENT DE PAUL, SOCIETY OF ST. The members of this society are commonly referred to as Vincentians. It is an international society of Catholic laymen who serve as volunteers and have for their purpose the performance of works of charity for the poor. In particular, their objective is to relieve the physical need of the poor and to counsel them so that they may overcome their wants and satisfy their spiritual needs. The society is under the regulation of the general council in Paris, and is established with national, central, and diocesan councils, the branches of the latter being particular councils. The society was begun in the United States in 1845, with the first branch in St. Louis, Missouri.

VIRGIN BIRTH OF CHRIST. This dogma of the Church declares that Christ, the Son of God, was born by external generation of but one parent, the Blessed Virgin Mary, and that she being a virgin did not lose her virginity, either physical or spiritual. This doctrine is evident in the manner of expression, in the fact, and in the interpreted meaning of the Gospel record (Lk. 1:26–38). Mary was vowed to virginity; the angel in replying to Mary's question (Lk. 1:35) declares that God's design will not affect her vow, since the Child is to have no father but God, i.e., be conceived of the Holy Ghost. "Jesus is the Son of God not because of His temporal but because of His external generation."

VIRGIN MARY. Accusation has been made by many rationalists and others attacking the perpetual virginity of Mary because of reference in the Gospel to the "brethren" of our Lord. This reference solely denotes a group of cousins of different origin. It is clear from the Gospels that Mary kept her resolve and had no further children after the virginal birth of Christ. Christ is named as the "only" child (Lk. 2:41ff) and was known in Nazareth as "the son of Mary" (Mk. 6:3). Further indication is given that Christ, in dying on the cross, gave his Mother into the care of St. John (Jn. 19:26–27). The doctrine of Mary's virginity as a perpetual state is also attested in the Church by the writings of SS. Jerome, Ambrose, John Chrysostom, and Augustine..(*Cf.* VIRGIN BIRTH OF CHRIST; MOTHER OF GOD.)

VIRTUE, a habit which perfects the powers of the soul (intellect, will and memory) and inclines one to do good. Virtues according to their *source* are either *natural*, those acquired by human activity, or *supernatural*, those infused by God. Virtues according to their *object* are either *divine* (theological) or *moral;* the former having God as their object, the latter, something created by God as their object, e.g., one's fellow-man.

VIRTUES, one of the choirs of angels. (*Cf.* ANGELS.)

VISITATIO LIMINUM APOSTOLORUM. *See* AD LIMINA.

VISITATION, EPISCOPAL. The rule requires that bishops make a canonical visit throughout the whole of their dioceses once every five years.

VISITATION OF THE BLESSED VIRGIN MARY. The visit made by the Blessed Mother of Christ to her cousin, Elizabeth, while Mary was pregnant, is recorded in the Gospels (Lk. 1:39–45). The greeting given to Mary by Elizabeth, the mother of St. John the Baptist, namely, "Blessed art thou among women" is, in the Hebrew idiom: "More blessed art thou than all women." It was at this visit that the Blessed Virgin spoke her canticle, the Magnificat. (*Cf.* MAGNIFICAT.)

VISITOR, APOSTOLIC, a special legate of the Holy See. He is assigned the duty to visit and report on a diocese, an ecclesiastical territory or the province of a religious order.

VOCATION. In the ecclesiastical sense, vocation is the calling of one to a religious life, particularly the calling to the priesthood. There is an essential distinction: first, the vocation must be considered from the standpoint of the person. Thus, if a man has the moral and intellectual fitness and a sincere supernatural motive, he may be considered to possess the disposition, at least, for aspiring to the priesthood. Secondly, from the standpoint of the need of the Church: i.e., the direct call to serve given by the bishop after he has judged the candidate and invited him to accept holy orders. The fact of not receiving such a call or accepting it on the part of a seminarian does not mean that the failure has been an instance of fault in the personal aspects of the aspirant (first distinction). Both priests and laity should prudently encourage and instruct those who show an inclination to the priesthood (c. 1353).

VOCATIONUM, OPUS. This is the title of a pious association whose main objective is the development and fostering of vocations to the priesthood. It may be canonically established in a diocese in order that a sufficient supply of priests be available and to provide prayers, alms and sacrifices by priests and people upon which this supply often depends. Canonically established, this association is "The Sodality for the Development of Priestly Vocations," under the patronage of Mary Immaculate, Queen of the Clergy. (A.S.S. 1922, 449.)

VOTIVE MASS. The name is given to a Mass which is said according to the intention or desire of the celebrant rather than according to the feast of the calendar. A votive Mass may also be said because it is directed by authority or because of circumstance. (*Cf.* MASS.)

VOTIVE OFFERINGS. Such offerings are things, spiritual or material, vowed, promised, or dedicated to God or one of the saints.

VOTIVE OFFICE, an office other than that which is proper for the day. The only votive office permitted now is that of the Blessed Mother, said on Saturdays when no other special feast occurs.

VOW. A vow is a deliberate, voluntary promise made to God, binding under sin, by which one obliges oneself to do something that is pleasing to God and which does not hinder or prevent a higher good (c. 1307). A vow is public when it is made before a representative of the Church, e.g., before one's parish priest; it is private when made without the intervention of any official person. Vows may be simple or solemn.

VULGATE. *See* BIBLE.

W

WAR, MORALITY OF. According to Catholic teaching, both offensive and defensive war is lawful for a sufficiently just cause. This cause must be serious enough to justify the great evils which are associated with war. No one may take part in an evidently unjust war. In waging war it is not permitted to do any act or use any means forbidden by divine or international law. Whereas murder is forbidden by divine law, killing of the enemy is permissible in war on the ground of the lawfulness of one to defend himself against an unjust aggressor or to secure his rights if no one in higher authority will protect them.

WASHING OF FEET. *See* MAUNDY THURSDAY.

WATER, HOLY. *See* HOLY WATER.

WAY OF THE CROSS. *See* STATIONS OF THE CROSS.

WEEK, HOLY. *See* HOLY WEEK.

WHITSUNDAY. *See* PENTECOST.

WINE, LITURGICAL USE OF.
1. For the use in the Sacrifice of the Mass, the wine must be true, pure grape wine, i.e., to be good it must be properly fermented. It should not have less than 5% alcohol (with less it will spoil) and not more than 18%. **2.** The pope after a solemn Mass, and newly ordained priests immediately after Communion, receive a drink of unconsecrated wine. **3.** A cask of wine is offered by a priest when he receives consecration as a bishop. **4.** Wine is used in the ceremonial washing of an altar before consecration; also wine is used in the consecration of the *antimension*, or portable altar, of the Byzantine rite.

WISDOM, BOOK OF. The title of this book of the O.T. in the Greek versions is "The Wisdom of Solomon." It is acknowledged generally that this book was written in the Greek language, which rules out Solomon as its author. It was written in the first half of the 2nd century B.C. by an unknown author or authors. Its style is that of an imaginative meditation on sacred history. In content, it is broadly concerned with the rewards and punishments after death. It is a deuterocanonical book.

WORSHIP. *See* LITURGY; LATRIA.

WREATH—An Advent Wreath.

WREATH, ADVENT. It is a custom, though non-liturgical, to suspend a circlet of boughs of cedar or pine, the circle being quartered and a candle placed at each quarter, as a symbol of the "Light of Christ" being born into the world.

WYCLIFFITES. *See* LOLLARDS.

X

XEROPHAGY. The fasting practiced by the members of the Montanist heresy, was given this name.

 Y

YOUTH, IMPEDIMENT OF. This term is sometimes used for "impediment of age." (*Cf.* IMPEDIMENTS.)

YOUTH ORGANIZATION, CATHOLIC. Abbreviated C.Y.O., this is an organization founded in Chicago, Ill., by Bishop Bernard J. Sheil, in 1930, to promote leadership, worthwhile occupation, and development in all phases of its members' lives, social, cultural, educational, and athletic. The organization may be established as autonomous in any diocese and is directed as an agency of the diocese.

 Z

ZACHARIAS, BOOK OF. The prophetical book of the O.T., written by the Prophet Zacharias (the name in Hebrew means "God remembers") in the 5th century B.C., is one of the most difficult and enigmatical books of the Bible, but its central theme is Messianic, and in doctrine it refers to the eternal Jerusalem, heaven.

ZACHARY, CANTICLE OF. *See* BENEDICTUS.

ZEAL, the motive of love and the resulting action which prompts one to serve God. It may be disturbed by a scrupulous attitude.

ZIMARRA, the black house cassock, worn by bishops and other prelates. It has a cape, purple sash, and purple buttons and piping.

ZUCCHETTO, the small, close-fitting skull-cap worn by bishops, abbots and other prelates. It is usually made of a fine leather covered with silk. Also called *pileolus*.

ZWINGLIANISM. The name of this teaching is derived from its advocate, the Swiss Protestant leader, Huldreich Zwingli (d. 1531). It advocated abolition of the Mass and of the sacraments of penance and extreme unction.